商务
文体翻译

顾维勇　编著

Translation of
Business Stylistics

WUHAN UNIVERSITY PRESS
武汉大学出版社

图书在版编目(CIP)数据

商务文体翻译/顾维勇编著.—武汉:武汉大学出版社,2019.3(2020.9 重印)

ISBN 978-7-307-20754-7

Ⅰ.商… Ⅱ.顾… Ⅲ.商务—英语—翻译 Ⅳ.F7

中国版本图书馆 CIP 数据核字(2019)第 035155 号

责任编辑:谢群英　　　　责任校对:汪欣怡　　　　版式设计:马　佳

出版发行:**武汉大学出版社**　　(430072　武昌　珞珈山)

(电子邮箱:cbs22@whu.edu.cn 网址:www.wdp.com.cn)

印刷:湖北金海印务有限公司

开本:787×1092　1/16　印张:18　字数:435 千字　插页:2

版次:2019 年 3 月第 1 版　　**2020 年 9 月第 3 次印刷**

ISBN 978-7-307-20754-7　　定价:49.00 元

作者简介

　　顾维勇，教授，南京市语言学会副会长（2014年），中国教材教法研究中心商务英语教学示范基地负责人（2009年），《大学英语教学与研究》编委（2013年始），江苏省翻译协会常务理事（2014年），全国社科项目通讯评审专家（2017年），教育部考试中心国考命题专家（2017年），第四次商务英语翻译及外语教学研究国际论坛组委会副主席（2017年），《商务翻译》编委（2018年）。

　　从事商务英语翻译与教学研究30余年，共发表论文40余篇，其中在翻译类核心期刊《中国翻译》和《上海翻译》发表商务翻译研究论文各3篇。这6篇中对"十五"、"十一五"国家级规划教材《商务英语翻译》批判性研究成果2篇。共出版著作26部，其中主编ESP英语教材10部，编著商务英语类教材5部，参编著作5部，主审教材4部。承担完成了20多项研究课题，其中省部级以上商务英语课题8项。

前　言

近年来，全国商务英语专业的建设与发展取得了规模效益。教育部于 2007 年批准商务英语专业招生，2012 年开设商务英语专业的大学为 62 所，2017 年已增加到了 367 所（教育部 2018 年 3 月公布）。

新的市场呼唤新的教材，新的教材要有新的内容，不断吸收新的研究成果。基于这些考虑，又基于原书售罄不再加印，编著者完成了第三次修订。

本书在前两版的基础上，增加了编著者近年商务英语翻译的研究成果，特别是发表在《中国翻译》2014 年第 1 期对国家级规划教材《商务英语翻译》误译译例的批判性研究成果。全书可谓集编著者 30 余年商务英语翻译的研究成果之大成。

本书共分为九章：商务文体翻译概述、商务翻译的文体意识、商务文体词语翻译、广告文体翻译、商标文体翻译、旅游文体翻译、公示语翻译、商务文书文体翻译以及商务法律文体翻译。

本书的主要特色如下：

1. 提出了商务文体翻译的文体意识。在商务文体的翻译实践中，文体意识对于理解原文或选择语义方面有着十分重要的指导意义。这种意识是指译者的思维应当进入所读或所译源语的语境，时刻提醒自己正在翻译的是商务英语文体，所以特别当你对某些词语乃至句子无法用目的语准确表达的时候，更应警觉到这种意识，从文本的文体着手，根据语境找到源语的所指。

2. 创新翻译理念。本书提出了翻译（主要指笔译）是不断追求完美译文的过程。译文越是接近原文作者所要表达的意思，越是符合目的语的表达规范，就越加完美。无论是文学文体翻译还是其他文体的翻译都得经过这个过程。而且这个过程有的时间会短些，有的会长些。它不但受到译者个体的认知水平和群体的认知水平的约束，而且还受到社会认知需要的制约。

3. 从文体角度论述商务翻译。本书从文体的特点出发，分章节论述了商务活动中主要文体的翻译。

4. 专业性强。本书涉及的例句都是与以外贸为核心的商务活动相关，特别关注外贸活动中涉及的专业知识。专业知识中涉及大量的专业术语，而术语的最大特点是词义的单一性，所以，商务文本的翻译有别于文学文本的翻译，不可能是见仁见智的活动。

在编写本书的过程中，有借鉴传承，亦有批判创新。值此修订出版之际，感谢前人们的研究成果，主要参考书目已附书后。同时本人也提醒学习或从事商务文体翻译的同仁及后人，做商务文体翻译一定要掌握商务专门知识，提供的译文不能辜负读者的期望。

此书可作为商务英语等相关专业翻译课程的教材使用。建议在基本学完专业课程后开设，40 左右课时，具体可根据培养方案自行安排。

教学中注意"一核心两个点"，即以商务文体意识为核心，教授语言点和专业知识点，以便让学习者通过英语媒介掌握商务专业知识。

此次修订由于时间紧迫，所以文中涉及译例仅限于编者现阶段的认知水平，译例中的译文有待日趋完美。

参加此次修订工作或提出重要修订建议的老师还有：南京晓庄学院的汪璧辉、孙维林，南京理工大学紫金学院的戚佳鸣、刘玲、张烨，黄河科技学院的贾和平，吉林华桥外国语学院的王艳等，在此一并表示衷心的感谢。

武汉大学出版社外语分社谢群英社长为本书的出版倾注了大量的时间和精力，提出了建设性的修改建议，在此向她表示诚挚的谢意。

顾维勇

2018 年 11 月 29 日

于南京聚福园

目　　录

第一章　商务文体翻译概述 …………………………………………… 1
1.1　关于翻译 …………………………………………………………… 1
1.2　关于商务文体 …………………………………………………… 12
1.3　商务文体的翻译标准 …………………………………………… 13

第二章　商务翻译的文体意识 ……………………………………… 16
2.1　术语对等 ………………………………………………………… 16
2.2　复数 ………………………………………………………………… 30
2.3　专业知识 ………………………………………………………… 41
2.4　近/同义词叠用 …………………………………………………… 46
2.5　词语组合 ………………………………………………………… 47

第三章　商务文体词语翻译 ………………………………………… 49
3.1　商务文体词语翻译种种 ………………………………………… 49
3.2　常用或流行语译例 ……………………………………………… 61
3.3　各种"公司"的翻译 ……………………………………………… 65
3.4　揣摩语境，选取语义 …………………………………………… 76

第四章　广告文体翻译 ……………………………………………… 81
4.1　概述 ………………………………………………………………… 81
4.2　广告英语的词汇特点 …………………………………………… 82
4.3　广告词汇的翻译 ………………………………………………… 83
4.4　广告英语的句法特点 …………………………………………… 84
4.5　广告翻译的技巧 ………………………………………………… 84
4.6　广告语修辞手段的翻译 ………………………………………… 93

第五章　商标文体翻译 ……………………………………………… 102
5.1　概述 ……………………………………………………………… 102
5.2　商标的语言特点 ………………………………………………… 103
5.3　商标汉英翻译的用词应遵循的原则 …………………………… 105
5.4　商标汉英翻译的文化因素 ……………………………………… 106

5.5　商标翻译的技巧 ·· 107

5.6　汽车商标的翻译 ·· 111

第六章　旅游文体翻译 ·· 131

6.1　概述 ··· 131

6.2　旅游文本的文体特点 ·· 131

6.3　旅游资料翻译方法 ·· 132

6.4　敏感词的处理 ·· 137

6.5　美学风格的等化 ·· 138

6.6　楹联的翻译 ··· 140

6.7　中菜与主食的英译 ·· 141

第七章　公示语翻译 ·· 148

7.1　概述 ··· 148

7.2　公示语的语言特点 ·· 149

7.3　公示语的应用示意功能 ·· 152

7.4　商业公示语的特定应用功能 ······································ 154

7.5　警示性公示语的翻译 ·· 154

7.6　常用公示语译例 ·· 155

7.7　公示语集锦 ··· 160

第八章　商务文书文体翻译 ·· 163

8.1　电报的翻译 ··· 163

8.2　信用证的翻译 ·· 168

8.3　提单及租船合约的翻译 ·· 178

8.4　商务合同的翻译 ·· 185

第九章　商务法律文体翻译 ·· 214

9.1　法律英语的文体特点 ·· 214

9.2　英译技巧 ··· 220

9.3　近义词和同义词的翻译 ·· 225

9.4　文本翻译范例 ·· 234

练习参考答案 ··· 263

主要参考文献 ··· 278

第一章 商务文体翻译概述

1.1 关 于 翻 译

"翻译 translating/translation"（translate：to render in another language, from Latin：past participle of trānsferre）是多义词，用英文可区别出不同含义和不同用法，主要有以下五个方面：

（1）翻译过程（translating）

（2）翻译行为（translate/interpret）

（3）翻译者（translator/interpreter）

（4）译文或译语（translation/interpretation）

（5）翻译工作（事业）（translation）

按翻译过程，翻译可定义为：翻译是按社会认知需要，在具有不同规则的符号系统之间传递信息的语言文化活动。这一定义包含三层意思：第一，翻译的目的在于满足不同的"社会认知需要"；第二，翻译的媒介物存在于"具有不同规则的符号系统之间"；第三，翻译的性质是传递信息的语言文化活动。

语言是人类传递信息的最重要的符号系统。译者主要跟语言符号打交道，所以"不同规则的符号"主要指不同的语言符号系统（此外，还有计算机语言、工程图学语言等）。语言、文化与社会不可分割，所以这里的"传递信息"不是单纯的不同规则的转换，而是语言的具有社会意义和文化意义的转换与传递。语言深深地植根于民族的文化之中，生动地反映着民族的生活方式、风俗习惯、文化传统和心理特点。翻译必然涉及两种语言的不同文化。

翻译是传递信息的语言文化的活动。信息内容可包括语义的、文体风格的、文化的。传递方式可以是书面的、口头的、图像的、机器的或人机交互的。

冯庆华（2002：3）认为，"翻译是许多语言活动中的一种，它是将一种语言用另一种语言重新表达出来的语言实践活动"。前者为源语（source language），而后者为译语（target language）。

奈达主张翻译即译意。所谓翻译，是指从语义到文体在译语中用最贴近而又最自然的对等语再现源语的信息。

许钧教授在《翻译论》（2003：75）中将翻译定义为"翻译是以符号转换为手段，意义再生为任务的一项跨文化的交际活动"。这一定义高度概括了翻译的本质属性，既定义了翻译的跨语言性，又定义了翻译的跨文化性；既定义了翻译的符号和意义转换性，也定义了翻译的交际性。正是翻译这种活动使得世界各地使用不同语言的人们能够相互交流、相互了解，所以，翻译在人们的交往中起着不可或缺的联系作用。

翻译离不开社会认知的需要。自古以来，翻译总是按一定的社会集团利益来进行的。我国古代的佛经翻译、明清时期的西学东渐、"五四"时期的新思潮的引进，以及改革开放中的翻译，无不是为了适应社会的需要。翻译的认知需要，除了社会需要之外，也包括个人认知的需要。

翻译形式分为口译（interpretation）与笔译（translation）两种，口译是通过两种不同言语的转换来表达同一信息，笔译则是通过两种不同文字的转换来表达同一信息。无论是口译还是笔译，其目的都是要把别人的意思用译语尽可能准确无误地传达出来，而不是用译者自己的意思来代替别人的意思。翻译的这一性质，决定了一个称职的译者应担当起两种语言之间传递信息的作用，而不能随意表达源语所要表达的意思。因此，翻译的成败得失，取决于译语能否准确地再现源语的意思，这也是评判译文的基本标准。

冯庆华（2002：3）认为："如果把写作比成自由舞蹈，翻译就是戴着手铐脚镣在跳舞，而且还要跳得优美。因为原著的创作不受语言形式的限制，而翻译既要考虑到对原文的忠实，又要按照译文的语言规则来表达原文的思想。从这个意义上来讲，翻译并不比创作容易，有时甚至更难，难度越大，其艺术性也就越高。翻译是一门永无止境的艺术，它的艺术美已经远远超出了语言的范畴。"

李景端（2011）撰文指出："翻译作为一门学科，不是一种可以轻易复制的技术，而是需要不断变化出新的学术与艺术。为此，当然需要严谨、考查与耐心。人们常说脑力劳动快工难出细活，这话是有道理的。翻译是转换不同文字的智力劳动，要实现它的认知飞跃，需要经历理解、思考、选择、表达等一系列的思维过程。迄今为止，已有的机器翻译或电子翻译，尽管速度快了，但一直只能机械地处理文字对应的转换，无法体现翻译过程中人的思维逻辑。成熟的翻译家，正是不惜精力对译稿反复进行修改，才使自己的翻译思维逻辑得到充分体现，而做到这一点，当然需要时间和过程。"

就笔译而言，翻译是不断追求完美译文的过程。译文越是接近原文作者所要表达的意思，越是符合译语的表达规范，就越加完美。无论是文学文体翻译还是其他文体的翻译都得经过这个过程，而且这个过程有的时间会短些，有的会长些。它不但受到译者个体的认知水平和群体的认知水平的约束，而且还受到社会认知需要的制约。

我国大翻译家严复曾说过"一名之立，旬月踯躅"，译名之难，可见一斑。据说西文的 logic 一词，至清末时，在我国有 50 种译名。该词定名为"逻辑"并最终为国人接受已是 20 世纪下半叶。难怪有人要说："一词之立，费三百载"！一词一名就如此费时费力，更何况一个段落、一个篇章、一部巨著。

翻译活动一般包括三个阶段：理解原文、用目的语表达、校验修改译文。其中，理解是表达的基础或前提，表达是理解的结果，即认识与实践、分析与综合的过程，它们既是彼此衔接的同一过程，又是互有交叉、互臻完善的两个阶段，是同一问题不可分割的两个侧面。

理解（comprehension）指弄懂源语的种种含义，是译者认识事物之间联系的本质与规律的一种思维活动。理解分为直接理解和间接理解。直接理解是马上实现的，是过去已经理解的事物的重现。间接理解是逐步实现的，需要从不理解到理解的过渡过程，通常是在感知、表象与再造想象的基础上借助于思维过程实现。从语言是客观世界的能指这一角度来说，任何语句序列都是对客观世界的描述，它可能是具体的，也可能是抽象的。那么译者必须把语言的所指找出来，搞清楚原作者要表达的语用含义。理解的核心是找出源语的所指。对于翻译来说，理解是关键，只有正确的、深刻的理解，才有可能有完善的表达。

表达(expression)指译者把自己从原文中所理解的内容用译语说/写出来。在表达过程中，译者经常想着读者，考虑如何用他们能够自然接受的语言，传达原作的思想和风格。理解是表达的基础，表达是理解的结果。但理解正确并不意味着表达必然正确，在表达上译者有许多具体的方法和技巧需要解决。表达的关键是用规范的目的语把源语的意思呈现给读者。

下面即为理解不正确、表达不精当的译例：

● As a means of satisfying needs, exchange has much in its favor. People do not have to prey on others or depend on donations. Nor must they possess the skills to produce every necessity. They can concentrate on making things they are good at making and trade them for needed items made by others. Thus, exchange allows a society to produce much more than it would with any alternative system.

原译 1：作为满足<u>欲望和需求</u>的方式之一，交换具有诸多优点：人们不必<u>占他人便宜</u>或者依赖他人，也不必具有每种必需品的技术，因而他们可以专心生产所擅长的物品，然后用以换回由他人生产的自己所需要的物品。这样一来，交换就使整个社会能够生产出更多的东西。(刘延玫，2011：117)

原译 2：作为满足<u>各种需求</u>的方式，交换具备较多优点：人们不必<u>再占他人的便宜</u>或者依赖他人的<u>施舍</u>，也不必具备各种技术来生产每一种必需品。这样他们就可以专心生产自己最擅长生产的产品，然后用以换取他人生产的自己所需物品。可以说，交换就可以比运用其他任何方式更能使得整个社会生产出更多的产品。(李明，2011：13)

此译例中，译者对原文中有关国际贸易的意象世界认知不够，即理解不够，对"needs"这样的特定概念理解出现了偏差，甚至随意添加了原文之外的含义"欲望"。实际上，在国际贸易领域，交换源于剩余产品的产生，社会大分工的细化导致不同的人有不同的需求，最终演变为商务活动中的交易。"欲望"是人们在日常生活中谈论相关话题时的普通词语，原文译者将其引入国际贸易领域并不恰当。prey on 意为 plunder or pillage，即"抢劫""掠夺"；单数 donation 是集体名词，泛指"捐赠"，而复数 donations 则代表"捐赠物"。同时，"不必具有每种必需品的技术"的译法也表达不清。所以，原译文容易误导读者的认知过程，使他们无法正确把握国际贸易的特殊认知特点。

改译：交换作为一种满足人们<u>需求</u>的方式颇具优势。人们不必<u>掠夺</u>他人物品或依赖<u>别人赠予</u>的物品，也不必掌握生产每种必需品的技术。他们可以集中精力制造自己所擅长制造的物品，并以此交换自己所需的物品。如此一来，较之其他任何方式，交换都能使社会生产出更多的物品。

● We regret to inform <u>you</u> that there is short weight of 6 M/T <u>only</u>. Therefore, we lodge a claim against you for the <u>short weight</u> of 6 M/T as follows:

　　原译：我们遗憾地通知<u>你们</u>，货物<u>仅仅短缺</u>6公吨，因此我方就此<u>短缺</u>6公吨一事提出索赔如下：（韩宁，2010：111）

　　按照《新牛津英汉双解大辞典》（2007：1970）的解释，short weight 是指 weight that is less than that declared（短斤少两），在国际贸易实践中，它指的是实际交货的重量比合同或单证中标明的重量少了，而原译文中的"短缺"是指"缺乏，不足"，并非参照某一个具体标准而言相对较少，有时甚至表示"没有"。所以，short weight 不能译为"短缺"，其专业所指为"短交货"或"短重"，即交货时的实际数量与运输单证所述数量短少之差，按照国际贸易惯例，收货方对这些"短重"可提出索赔。另外，only 一词的所指可以是"仅仅"，但在此处的特定语境中，only 在数字后表示"整"的意思。you 在此特定的商务语境下应该理解为"贵方"，而不是"你们"。

　　改译：我方遗憾地通知<u>贵方</u>，货物<u>短重</u>6公吨<u>整</u>。因此，我们就此6公吨短重提出如下索赔：

　　• Should you find interest in any of the items in our catalogue，please <u>do not hesitate to send enquiries</u>.

　　原译：如对目录中的任何项目感兴趣，请<u>径直</u>寄来询盘。（金利明、李晓惠，2008：55）

　　在这个译例中，"项目"的所指未切中商务英语的认知关键点，尤其是对那些缺乏一定商务认知背景的读者而言，无法提供有效信息，满足其认知需求。译者还是应该遵循商务知识的认知规律，引导读者获取清晰明确的认知结果。另外，原文中的"not hesitate"是希望对方不要犹豫，即刻采取"询盘"的行动，而译文读者对"径直"的理解可能是不通过其他人直接询盘或希望对方不要含混其词，这样的理解和表达都无法使译文正确。

　　改译：如贵方对目录中的任何产品感兴趣，请<u>立刻</u>发来询盘。

　　• This is a special offer and is <u>not subject to our usual discounts</u>.

　　原译：这是特惠报盘，并非根据我方一贯的折扣政策而定的。（张丽，2010：126）

　　该译例中，译者非常清楚原文重在强调"特惠报盘"，且优惠力度与 usual discounts 不同，即折扣更大。商务文体中常习惯使用典型短语 not subject to，此处应理解为"不以……为条件"，即"不符合……条件"，但汉语表达一般不会出现"不以……折扣政策为条件"或"不根据……折扣政策而定"。实际上，"不享受……折扣"才是更自然专业的汉语搭配。同样，usual discounts 是固定搭配，指给予一般或普通客户的折扣，区别于给予特殊客户的特惠折扣，我们翻译时不能将 usual 和 discounts 的字面意思简单组合，而应考虑该词组内涵在汉语中对应的习惯搭配，即"普通折扣"。原译文没有考虑这些差异，表达复杂拖沓。

　　改译：这是特惠报盘，<u>不享受我方普通折扣</u>。

　　• The rate charged is less than <u>that</u> for almost any other type of loan available to consumers.

　　原译：支付的利息低于消费者可以得到的差不多任何其他<u>贷款</u>。（叶玉龙等，1998：77）

　　原译中"利息低于……贷款"无疑表达有误。

　　改译：本贷款支付的利息低于提供给消费者的其他各种贷款的<u>利息</u>。（或译：与提供给消费者的其他所有种类贷款的利息相比，本贷款支付的利息较低。)

● In the direct overseas trade, any change in import duties are considered to be the importer's risk.

原译：在这种直接的对外贸易中，进口税则的任何改变，其风险均由进口商承担。(叶玉龙等，1998：78)

改译：在这种直接的海外贸易中，因为进口税率变化而造成的风险由进口商承担。

● We reserve the right to claim compensation from you for the loss.

原译：我们保留对贵公司要求赔偿损失的权利。(叶玉龙等，1998：78)

原译严重欧化，术语表达不正确。claim 意为"索赔"。

改译：我们保留向贵方索赔(此项损失)的权利。

● Do the figures and words agree?

原译：大小金额是否一致？(陈仕彬，2002：43)

这里 figures 指"数字"，指金额的"小写"，而 words 为"文字"，指金额的"大写"，原译汉语表达有误。

改译：金额的小写与大写是否一致？

● WorldCom will have wireless, international, long-distance, and Internet businesses that, in many cases, meet or surpass those of the leader. (refer to AT & T)

原译：世界通讯公司将拥有数个无线、国际、长距离的互联网企业，在许多情况下都赶上或者超过老大的那些企业。(陈仕彬，2002：65-66)

原译中"超过老大的那些企业"怎么读都不符合汉语的表达习惯。如改为"超过那些居于老大地位的企业"则更通顺一些。另外对"长距离的互联网企业"，读者不禁要问：互联网有长距离和短距离之说吗？这里 long-distance 指"长途电话"(a long-distance telephone call)。WorldCom 为美国第二大长途电话公司，可译为"世界通信公司"，或仿拟中国的"联通"，译为"世通"。

改译：世(界)通(信)公司(WorldCom)将开办无线、国际、长途电话以及互联网等多项业务，这样它将在很多方面赶上或超过那些行业的龙头企业。(如美国电话电报公司)

下面几个译例理解与表达均含糊不清：

● Advertisers must realize that people usually are motivated by the goal of satisfying some combination of two or more needs, and the needs may be both conscious and unconscious.

原译：广告人必须明白，通常能够满足两个或者更多需要的综合目标才能促使人们购买，而且这些需要既可能是有意识的，又可能是无意识的。(张新红等，2003：77)

原译者评析：将 combination 一词"进行由'虚'向'实'的转化而具体地翻译成'综合目标'之后，译文就不仅通顺，而且意义明确"。实际上，这个译文既不通顺，意义也不明确。(1)"满足两个或者更多需要的综合目标"中"满足……目标"属汉语的动宾搭配不当；(2)"购买"太"实"了，广告的目的不一定要人们去"购买"，而是促使"消费"，只有商品广告才可能为了激励"购买"；(3)"有意识的""无意识的"表达不明确，用原译者的话来说不"实"。此例的原译同样不符合商务文体的语言规范与表达规范。

改译：广告商须知，人们在实现能满足两个以上综合需求的目标时才会激起消费欲，

5

这些消费需求既可以是有计划的，也可以是没有计划的。

● In a turnkey project, the seller plans, constructs, and places in operation a foreign facility that is then transferred to a local owner.

原译：在由承包商完全承包的工程中，卖主计划、建造并将一套国外设施投入运作，然后将其转让给地方雇主。（张新红等，2003：89）（李明，2011：95）

原译有下列几处不符合商务英语的表达规范：（1）a turnkey project 为"统包式工程/项目"，或"交钥匙工程/项目"；（2）places in operation 将上述设施"投入运行"，而非"运作"；（3）transfer 这里指"转交给"，统包工程的付款方式都有约定，工程完工了再作"转让"不符合一般的操作规范；（4）a local owner 原译为"地方雇主"有两点不妥："地方"通常相对于"中央"而言，而"雇主"则相对于"雇员"而言。这里的 owner 为"买方/主"，实际上是该设施的"所有者，物主"；（5）译句中有两个主语：承包商和卖主，他们的关系不明确。

改译：在统包式项目中，卖方负责规划、建造一套国外进口设施并使其投入运行后交付给当地的买主。

● A foreign business representative, neither overly sympathetic toward China nor overly disposed against it, would need to be convinced on a number of scores before he could responsibly commit his firm to taking an equity position in a Chinese enterprise.

原译1：一个对中国既无过度好感又无过度恶感的企业代表，在代表公司在华投资、与一定中国企业形成平等股权关系之前，必须考虑许多因素。（张新红等，2003：20）

原译2：一名外国企业代表，如果对中国既无过分好感，又无过分恶意的话，要动真格地实施向一家中国企业投资入股，就往往需要有一系列评估数据来帮助他作出最终决定。（李明，2011：30）

这个句子里有几点在理解和表达上值得商榷：（1）sympathetic toward，英语 sympathetic 一词常与 to/toward 连用，其意为 favorably inclined，即"赞同的"，与下文的 disposed against "反对的"形成对应，意为"既不过度支持中国，也不极力反对中国"，实际上，原文要表达的是：在对华的态度上，他是"采取中立态度的"；（2）foreign business representative，即"外资企业代表""外国商/业务代表"，根据下文 commit his firm to taking an equity position in a Chinese enterprise "代表其公司在中国的某企业取得股权地位"可推断其为"外企代表"；（3）equity 这里指"股权"，这个词的复数形式意为"普通股票"，原译的"平等股权关系"，把这个词既作"平等"解，又作"股权"解，欠妥。

改译：一个对华采取中立态度的（或译：既不十分支持中国，也不极力反对中国的）外国企业代表，需要考虑诸多因素方可代表其公司在中国的某企业获得股权地位。

● The retailers perform many functions. First, he may provide a convenient location. Also, he often guarantees and services the merchandise he sells. Third, the retailer aids in promoting the product, often through displays and advertising. Fourth, the retailer may finance the customer by extending credit. Further, the retailer performs storage function in his outlet, by having goods available.

原译：零售商还发挥许多功能。其一，可提供便利的场地；其二，对他所经销的商品提供担保和服务；其三，帮助促销产品，经常进行商品展示活动和发布广告；其四，为顾客提供信贷。另外，由于供货及时，零售商还可发挥其商店的仓储功能。（张新红等，2003：40-41）

原译中第三个功能似乎讲了并列的三件事，理解和表达均有误，第四个功能"为顾客提供信贷"显然是理解错误。finance 在这里用作动词，其意为"赊货给……"。如：We would like to finance the car for you. 我们愿意把车子赊销给你。extend credit 查词典有"提供贷款"的意思，但是零售商怎么可能有"提供贷款"这一银行的功能呢？这里应是"提供赊购/销"的意思。have goods available 是"使顾客能得到货物"，亦即"为顾客提供货源"，所以有其"商店的仓储功能"。

后半部分改译：其三，经常通过商品展销和做广告以帮助促销产品；其四，通过赊购方式资助顾客。此外，他能为顾客提供货源，所以，可发挥其商店的仓储功能。

- To avert the danger of major defaults and to restore security to the economic systems, Western bankers and governments will have to ensure that they are imposing reasonable repayment terms on developing countries, terms that will not provoke revolution or chaos.

原译：为了防止发生重大宣布无力偿还债务事件，并使经济体制恢复巩固，西方各国金融机构和政府必须确保对各发展中国家强制实行公平合理的还债条件，确保这些条件不至于引发革命或混乱。（张新红等，2003：42）

句中把原文 and to restore security to the economic systems 译成"并使经济体制恢复巩固"系理解错误造成表达错误。按原译的理解，似乎在实行公平的还债条件之前，经济体制已经崩溃。实际上，原文的字面意思是"把安全还给经济体系"，稍作调整，便可译为"为经济体制提供安全保障"。

- A more realistic approach toward international specialization is that of comparative advantage. This concept says that a nation has a comparative advantage in an item if it can produce it more efficiently than alternative products.

原译：参与国际分工的另一更为现实的做法是采取比较优势的做法。比较优势是指假如一个国家生产某种产品比生产其他产品的效率高，那么它就具有生产该产品的比较优势。（张新红等，2003：50）

international specialization 是指"国际专业化生产"，而 comparative advantage 是指"相对优势"，也有译为"相对利益"的。

改译：实现国际专业化生产的一个更为现实的途径是"相对优势"，这个理念是指某个国家生产某种产品比生产其他产品效率高，那么该国就具有生产此产品的相对优势。

- As each currency's value is stated in terms of other currencies, French francs, then, have a value in US dollars, which have a value in British pounds, which have a value in Japanese yen.

原译1：由于每一种货币的价值是用另外的货币表现出来的，那么法国法郎的价值可以用美元来体现，美元可以用英镑来体现，英镑可以用日元来体现。（张新红等，2003：52）

原译2：由于每一种货币的价值是用其他货币来体现的，那么，法郎的价值可用美元

来体现，美元的价值可用英镑来体现，英镑的价值可用日元来体现。(李明，2011：43)

"每一种货币的价值"怎么会"是用另外的货币表现出来的"呢？in terms of 意为"换算，折合，以……为单位"，be stated in terms of other currencies 是指"折换成其他币值来表示"的意思。

改译：由于每一种币值可以<u>折换成</u>其他各种币值，所以，法国法郎具有美元的币值，美元具有英镑的币值，英镑具有日元的币值。

• The bank of Japan intervened in market <u>shortly before 3 p. m.</u>, when the U. S. currency was on the verge of falling below ￥123.

原译：当美元兑换日元快要降至低于 123 日元时，日本央行就会在<u>下午三点钟不到的时候</u>干预市场。

上述句子的翻译有三点不妥：(1) 翻译时译者没有注意到时态；(2) "三点钟不到的时候"不精练；(3) "干预市场"概念不明确。

改译：当美元对日元的汇率即将跌至 123 日元时，日本央行在下午<u>临近三点时</u>干预了汇率市场。(on the verge of 在……的边缘，濒临……)

• <u>International trade</u> <u>occurs</u> when a country does not have enough of a particular item to meet its needs.

原译 1：当一个国家没有足够的某一特定商品来满足自身需求时，<u>就需要有国家贸易</u>。(张新红等，2003：64)

原译 2：当一个国家对于某一特定商品没有足够的量来满足其需要时，<u>就需要有国家贸易</u>。(李明，2011：64-65)

原译者分析：英语原文中，occur 之意为"发生"，相当于 take place。运用英语中的 takes place 替换本例中的 occurs 完全没有问题。但在将该句译成汉语时，若将该词直译成"发生"，译文就不符合汉语表达。故在译文中需要对其进行引申，以符合汉语表达。这里采用"需要有……"来翻译，符合汉语表达，同时又未偏离英语的原文原意。

原译与原句所表达的意思相去甚远，简直无法理解。原译 1 中"国家贸易"可能是"国际贸易"的笔误。

改译：当一个国家的某种产品没有足够的量来满足本国需求时，<u>国际贸易便应运而生了</u>。

• A firm's involvement in exporting products can <u>range from</u> a minimal commitment all the way <u>to</u> considering exports as necessary for the firm's survival and growth.

原译：公司在产品出口中<u>参与情况的程度不一</u>，从最低程度的参与一直到将出口视为公司生存和发展必要条件的参与都会存在。(张新红等，2003：75)

原译中的"参与情况的程度不一"不符合汉语的表达习惯。range from…to…意为"从……到……不等"，如：Prices ranged from 5 dollars to 10 dollars. 那时的价格自 5 美元至 10 美元不等。

改译：公司在出口产品中<u>参与程度迥异</u>，从最小的出口量直到视出口量为公司生存与发展的必要条件。

以下的译例表达过于口语化或表现出翻译腔：

- As to direct and indirect exporting, which approach is best depends on such factors as the company's size, its export volume, the number of foreign countries involved, the investment required to support the operation, the profit potential, the risk present, and the <u>desires</u> of the overseas buyers.

原译：至于直接出口业务和间接出口业务，哪一种方式最好取决于许多因素，比如公司的大小，出口数量的多少，公司业务所牵涉国家的多少，出口所需投资的多少，可赚利润的多少，存在风险的大小，以及海外买主的<u>要求</u>，等等。（张新红等，2003：35）

原译在表达方面显得过于口语化，如"大小""多少"的重复使用，这样整个句子不像书面翻译。

改译：就直接出口与间接出口哪种方式最好而言，下列诸多因素需要予以考虑：公司的规模，公司的出口量，出口所涉及国家的数量，支持出口所需投资额，利润空间，出口风险以及海外买主的<u>需求量</u>，等等。

- When mineral oil is refined into petrol, it is used to drive internal combustion engine. To it we owe the existence of the motor-car, which has replaced the private carriage drawn by the horse.

原译：当矿物油被提炼成汽油之后，就可以用来驱动内燃机。就是有了这种油，我们才能用上汽车，以代替私人马车。（张新红等，2003：41-42）

原译将英语的被动句译成了汉语的被动句，表达显得欧化或翻译腔，而且"就是有了这种油"指代不清是哪种油。

改译：矿物油精炼成汽油后可用来驱动内燃机。所以，正是有了汽油，我们才用上了汽车，取代了私家马车。

- Loading on board or shipment on <u>a named vessel</u> may be indicated by preprinted wording on the bill of lading that <u>the goods have been loaded on board a named vessel or shipped on a named vessel</u>, in which case the date of issuance of the bill of lading will be deemed to be the date of loading on board and the date of shipment.

译文：装船或装运于记名货船，可以这样表明，即要提单上预先印就这样的文字——货物已装载到记名货船或已装运于记名货船，在此情况下，提单的签发日期即视为装船日期和装运日期。（李明，2011：21）

改译：表达"货物装船或已装上指定的船舶"可以在提单上预先印上下列字样：货已装船（即：货已装上指定的船舶）。这时，提单签发日期即视为货物装船日期或装运日期。

- Britain could not have advanced her industrialization so rapidly, if, just when owners of facories needed it most, an abundant supply of cheap labor had not made itself available.

原译 1：英国工业化进展得如此之快，如果不是各厂家老板正当急需之时，在大量廉价劳动力可供使用，那是不可能的。

原译 2：如果当时正当工厂主最急需大量廉价劳动力之时，市场上却没有大量的廉价劳动力可以提供，那么，英国就不可能将自己的工业化进程以如此的速度往前推进。（李明，2011：122）

原译表达啰嗦、不简洁，尤其是经过反复推敲的译文 2。

改译：如果不是在工厂主急需时大量的廉价劳动力能够供应市场，英国的工业化进程不可能如此之速。

• In addition to visible trade, which involves the importing and exporting of tangible goods, there is also invisible trade, which involves the exchange of services between nations.

原译：除了这种进出口商品的有形贸易以外，还有一种国与国之间进行交换服务的无形贸易。（李明，2011：95）

改译：除了有形贸易，即（有形）货物进出口，还有无形贸易，即国家间进行服务交换。

• The voyage was a smooth one. The wind was favorable and the weather fair.

原译：一路上非常顺利，风是顺风，天气是晴好的天气。（张新红等，2003：60）

voyage 通常指"海上航程"，说的是海上运输的语境，不能译为"一路上"。原译者没有注意到把英语的"果因"结构转换成汉语的"因果"结构，且译文显得啰嗦、口语化，没有达到良好翻译的表达水准。

改译：天气晴好，风助船行，航程顺利。

• Although efforts to rein in (rein in v. 放慢，止住，控制) the money supply resumed in October, investment grew rapidly as local governments, heedless of central efforts to tame the economy, raced to boost local growth rates.

原译1：虽然对货币供应量的限制在十月重新启动，但地方政府不顾中央抑制经济过热的努力，继续争着提高经济增长，使得投资急速增加。

原译2：尽管在十月份又恢复了对货币供应量严格控制的努力，但由于地方政府不顾中央抑制经济过快增长的努力，竞相提高当地的经济增长率，因此，投资急速地增加了。（李明，2011：122-123）

句中 efforts 为"努力采取的行动"或"措施"。tame the economy 意为"调控经济"。

改译：尽管十月重新启动了控制货币供应的措施，但地方政府对中央调控经济的措施置若罔闻，竞相提高地方经济增长率，因此，投资迅速地增加了。

• As you raise your problem with thoughtful consideration of the situation of the opposite side, you are more likely to get what you want, because, not being put into embarrassment, the opposite side sill accept it more easily.

原译1：因为你提出问题时考虑到了对方的处境，不至于使对方难堪，这样对方更容易接受，所以你就越能达到你的目的。

原译2：由于你方提出问题时充分考虑了对方的境况，因此，你方更有希望得到所期望的东西，因为，你方没有让对方难堪，对方更容易接受你方的需要。（李明，2011：97）

改译：你提出问题时充分考虑对方的处境，没让对方难堪，因此，对方容易接受你的要求，你就更易如愿以偿。

下面的译例属于因理解不当导致翻译的错误：

• The documentary credit offers a unique and universally used method of achieving a commercially acceptable compromise by providing for payment to be made against documents that

10

represent the goods and makes possible the transfer of rights to those goods.

原译：跟单信用证提供一种独特而广为采用的方法，即凭借代表货物的单据来支付款项，这就使得这些货物的权利转移成为可能，它也实现了从商业角度看可以接受的折中方案的实施。（李明，2011：122）

句中有2处理解错误：（1）a commercially acceptable compromise 意为"商业经营中可以接受的折中解决方案"；（2）the transfer of rights to those goods 意为"所有权转移到该货物"。

改译：跟单信用证提供了一种普遍采用但又无与伦比的方法，即凭借代表货物的单据来支付款项，这就使得将所有权转移到货物成为可能。这种方法实现了商业经营中可以接受的折中解决方案。

• International business has emerged as a separate branch of management training, because the growing scale and complexity of business transactions across national boundaries gives rise to new and unique problems of management and governmental policy that have received inadequate attention in traditional areas of business and economics.

原译：国际商务作为管理训练的一个分支出现，是由于跨国界的商业交易日益增长的范围和复杂性产生了新的、特殊的管理问题和政府政策问题。这些问题没有在传统的商业和经济领域里受到足够的注意。（张新红等，2003：92）（李明，2011：96）

a separate branch of management training 意为"管理培训的一门独立课程"。

改译：国际商务已经作为管理培训的一个独立分科应运而生，是因为跨国商务交易规模的不断扩大并日益变得复杂化，而在管理以及政府政策等多方面产生了新奇独特的问题。在传统的商务和经济领域，这些问题并未受到足够的关注。

• Unemployment in America (as of mid-1990) was running near 5.25 percent. That is somewhat higher than used to be considered full employment, but it is not a serious figure in the aggregate.

原译：1990年年中美国的失业率近5.25%。按以往的标准，这个比例偏高，没有达到充分就业。但就整体来说问题并不严重。（张新红等，2003：108）（李明，2011：105）

改译：1990年年中，美国的失业率接近5.25%。与以往全民就业的标准相比，这个比例略微偏高。但总的来说这个比例并不严重。

以下译例属于没有正确理解语用意义而导致的误译：

• There is every possibility that some price cut will justify itself for an increase in business.

原译：一定程度的减价很有可能是通过增加销售量来平衡它。（李明，2011：58）

every possibility 意为"每一种可能"，即"完全可能"；some 这里指"少量，些许"；increase in business 意为"增加业务量"。

改译：小幅减价完全可以通过增加业务量得以抵消。

• The company and the six main banks are expected to reach a basic agreement in early November about the scope of the financial assistance and asset sales.

原译：该公司及那六家主要银行有望于11月初就资金援助和资产销售的范围达成基本的一致意见。（李明，2011：82）

（1）early November 在商务英语语境下通常指"11 月上旬"，early 意为"上旬"，middle 意为"中旬"，late 意为"下旬"；（2）银行给公司的 scope of the financial assistance 的字面意义为"资金援助的范围"，实际上是银行贷款给公司的额度，即"融资额度"；（3）asset sales 意为"资产的销售量"，这里复数 sales 表示"销量"。

改译：该公司有望于 <u>11 月上旬</u>与六大银行就<u>融资额度和资产销量</u>达成一个基本的协议。

● The new prosperity may <u>represent</u> a long, sustained plateau of brisk demand, plentiful jobs, and increased living standards.

原译：新的繁荣<u>可能是一段较长时间的、持续的平稳状态</u>，其中<u>有大量的需求、重组的</u>就业机会，生活水平也得到了提高。（李明，2011：116）

原文中的 represent 未理解并译出；brisk demand 意为"需求激增"；"重组的"应该译为"充足的"，打印错误。

改译：新兴的繁荣会<u>呈现长期持续稳定的状态</u>，<u>需求激增</u>，就业充足，生活改善。

从以上的误译译例中，我们可以归纳出原译的误译缘于理解错误，或者理解正确，但表达不对。所以正确理解是正确表达的前提，不正确的理解不可能有正确的表达，正确理解也不等于表达是正确的。

1.2　关于商务文体

语言是传递信息和交流感情的手段，是人们实现社会交际的工具。语言交际常常伴随着不同的交际环境、交际方式、交际对象和交际目的等种种因素，各交际方会选择具有不同功能的语言"变体"（Varieties）或相应的表现手段，这些变体或表现手段就是人们所说的"文体"或"语体"（Styles）。20 世纪 70 年代中期，人们将现代语言学及文学研究成果运用于各种文体或语体特征的探讨，便产生了"文体学"（Stylistics）这门新兴的学科。刘宓庆在其著作《文体与翻译》（1998：3-4）中说，"70 年代欧美翻译理论研究工作已进入到另一个重要的学科领域，即文体学"。

徐有志（2005：2）在其专著《英语文体学教程》中对"文体学"的定义是："简单地说，文体学就是研究运用语言方法的学科；它是研究使用中的语言文体的学科。"（Simply defined, STYLISTICS is a discipline that studies the ways in which language is used; it is a discipline that studies the styles of language in use.）

刘宓庆（1998）认为，"早在 60 年代就有人从文体学角度探讨文体与翻译理论的关系及翻译教学问题。功能文体学对'各类英语'（Varieties of English）的深入探讨始于 60 年代初。研究各类英语的特点对确定翻译工作和译文的社会功能具有重大的实践意义，并为翻译理论的探讨开辟了新的途径。翻译理论之所以能借助文体学研究，是因为这两个研究领域的目的性是并行不悖的，即：如何凭借有效的语言手段进行社会交流。二者都强调交流功能的社会标准；同时，二者也都不忽视文风的时代性及风格的个人性。翻译必须随文体之异、随原文风格之异而调整译文，必须保证译文对原文文体和风格的适应性（Adaptation）。文体学对语域（Register）的研究以及对句与句之间、段与段之间的逻辑发展关系的探讨，即所谓 Discourse Analysis（'篇章分析'，在口语中称为'话语分析'），对翻译理论的探讨与实践都具有不可忽视的意义"。

刘宓庆（1998）把文体分为以下六种类型：新闻报刊文体，论述文体，公文文体，描述及叙述文体，科技文体和应用文体（包括广告文体、公函文体、契约文体、教范文体）。

本书所讨论的商务文体主要是指在商务和外贸活动中使用的文体。这类文体涉及的领域颇广，语言特点的跨度较大，就其主要的文体形式而言，包括公文体（如信函）、广告体（如广告、商标）、契约体（如合同、协议等）、应用体（如招商通告、说明书、公示语等）、法律文体（如商法、合同法、运输法、公司法等）。就文本而言除了上述所列，还有旅游、各类商务文书、电报电传电子邮件、外贸运输文件、海外劳务、境外投资、技术引进、国际金融、涉外保险等方方面面。这类文体所用语言不同于一般的英语或文学语言，它们都有特殊的语言规律。因此，翻译的方法和技巧也不尽相同，如广告、商标、旅游文体强调使用对公众有吸引力的语言；而商务文书、外贸运输文件、商贸法律的文体又以其正式、严肃、庄重为特点，大多以术语的形式出现。一般文体中常用的翻译技巧如直译意译、增字减字等不一定合适，译者的任务是必须找到对应的表达，决不能自行发挥、生拼硬凑。

1.3　商务文体的翻译标准

商务文体的翻译因为文体的变化与迥异，标准也是多元化的，即根据不同的文体来确定相应的标准。

方梦之教授（2011：68）把翻译的标准定义为：翻译标准是"指翻译活动必须遵循的准绳，是衡量译文质量的尺度，是翻译工作者不断努力以期达到的目标"。

刘敬国、何刚强在《翻译通论》（2011：82-92）一书中，把翻译标准分类为：（1）以文本为中心的翻译标准，有严复的"信、达、雅"、傅雷的"神似"与钱锺书的"化境"、泰特勒的"翻译三原则"、等值翻译等；（2）以读者为中心的翻译标准；（3）以译者为中心的翻译标准。同时他们提出了翻译标准的多元化。

在 20 世纪 60 年代，美国的翻译理论家尤金·奈达大力提倡翻译的"动态对等"（Dynamic Equivalence）理论，这无论是在西方还是在中国都得到很多人的认同。奈达在《翻译科学探索》一书中首次提出了"动态对等"翻译观。所谓"动态对等"是指"译文接受者和译文信息之间的关系，应该与原文接受者和原文信息之间的关系基本上相同"（1964：159）。

在与塔伯（C. R. Taber）合著的《翻译理论与实践》一书中奈达进一步解释动态对等指"用接受语言复制出与源语信息最切近的自然对等，首先是意义对等，其次是文体对等"，"译文接受者对译文的反应应与原文接受者对原文的反应基本上相同"（1969：12；200）。

后来，奈达在与德瓦尔（de Waar）合著的《从一种语言到另一种语言：论〈圣经〉翻译中的功能对等》一书中把"动态对等"改为"功能对等"（Functional Equivalence）。功能对等意思更清楚，没有动态对等那么容易引起误会，"它可以突出翻译的交际功能"（1986：iii）。这一理论的贡献在于对译界长期争论的直译与意译提供了一个令人称好的答案。直译强调忠实，即语言形式的对等，忽略了效果；意译强调语言优美，忽略了对等。而动态对等把焦点放在了两种效果之间的对等上，较好地解决了这个问题。

如果把奈达教授的"对等"理论运用到商务文体翻译中，我们就要做到"使原文（source language）的语义信息与译文（target language）的语义信息对等（equivalence of semantic message of source language and target language）；原文的风格信息与译文的风格信息对等（equivalence of stylistic message of source language and target language）；原文的文化信息与译文的文化信息对等（equivalence of cultural message of source language and target language）；原文的读者反应与译文的读者反应对等（equivalence of response of source language readers and target language readers）"。（翁凤翔，2002：46-47）四对等的中心是第一项——语义信息对等。

一个胜任工作的译者，在翻译商务文体前首先应具备商贸业务知识，包括源语（source language）和译语（target language）知识，也就是说他必须是专业的译者。否则，碰到下面这样的句子他会无从下手，难以将其变成准确而又专业的译语：

本合同规定美元的价值由议付日中国银行公布的美元对德国马克、法国法郎的平均买卖汇率的比率来确定。

可译为：

The value of US Dollars under this contract is determined by the ratio of the mean buying and selling rates of US Dollars against Deutsche Marks and French Francs published by the Bank of China on the date of negotiation.

如果译者不具备合同付款方面的知识，他也许想不到用 under this contract 译"本合同规定"，也不会将"美元对德国马克"中的"对"字译为 against 而绝不是 to。这一翻译实例说明了商务英语翻译工作不仅要求译者具备相当高的英语水平，而且要求他们通晓国际商务。

所谓的翻译标准也只不过是译者应追求的理想。季羡林教授（2005）在谈到翻译标准时说："我没有深入研究过翻译理论，凭我自己的经验，不同门类的翻译有不同的要求。有的需要严格对应，有的无需或很难对应，能达意也行，所以翻译很难有统一的标准。即使是严复的'信达雅'，或者后人新提出的，那也不能算是翻译标准，只是对翻译的一种要求、一种期盼。"所以面对各种商务文体我们宜采用不同的翻译标准或原则。

刘法公曾提出了商务英语翻译应遵守如下原则：忠实理解源语、准确表达译语、统一术语名称（2002：45）。

彭萍曾指出一般的翻译标准如"忠实""等值"等都不能够指导商务文本的翻译。但她提出了商务文本的翻译标准应是"意思准确、术语规范和语气贴切"（2004），这一标准对于商务合同和商务广告的翻译又不完全适合。合同语体正式，具有法律效力，不能用语气贴切来衡量，而广告是通过带动读者的感情来达到宣传产品或服务的目的，意思准确也不是最重要或首先要考虑的问题。

商务文体的多样性决定了翻译标准的多元化。除了季羡林教授所说的"不同门类的翻译有不同的要求"以外，王佐良教授在20世纪80年代末亦提倡"根据文体定译法"。他说译者"似乎可按照不同文体，定不同译法""当然，体中有体，不能同样对待"（1989：4）。

对于多元化翻译标准的提法，英国翻译理论家纽马克亦有论述。纽马克(1982)将文本按照语言的功能分为表达型文本(expressive text)、信息型文本(informative text)和呼唤型文本(vocative text)，并指出译者应针对不同的文本类型采用不同的翻译方法：以表达功能为主的文本采用语义翻译法，以信息功能或呼唤功能为主的文本采用交际翻译法。语义翻译强调对原文和原作者的忠实，交际翻译则更重视原文内容的忠实再现是以读者可接受的方式来实现的(Newmark，1982：15)。他还明确指出，语言的主要功能表现为表达型(即主观型或"我"型)、描述或信息型("它"型)，以及呼唤、指示或诱劝型("你"型)，并且所有文本都具有上述三大主要功能的一些综合特点(The main functions of language are expressive (the subjective or "I" form), the descriptive or informative (the "it" form), and the vocative or directive or persuasive (the "you" form). All texts have aspects of the expressive, the informative and the vocative function.)。

同时，纽马克还按体裁将严肃文学作品、官方文告、自传文学、私人书信等归结于"表达型文本"；将自然科学、科学技术、工商经济等方面的文本、报告、文件、报刊文章、备忘录、会议记录等归入"信息型文本"；而通告、说明书、公共宣传品、通俗作品等体裁归为"呼唤型文本"。

刘宓庆(1998：5-7)根据功能文体学的基本设想，归纳了文体翻译四个基本原则：重理解，重对比，分文体，重神似。在"分文体"的原则中，他认为，"不论英语或汉语都有不同的文体类别，不同的类别具有不同的文体特点。译者必须熟悉英汉各种文体类别的语言特征，才能在英汉语言转换中顺应原文的需要，做到量体裁衣，使译文的文体与原文的文体相应，包括与原文作者的个人风格相适应"。

第二章　商务翻译的文体意识

在商务文体的翻译实践中，文体意识对于理解原文或选择语义方面有着十分重要的指导意义。这种意识是指译者的思维应当进入所读或所译源语的语境，时刻提醒自己正在翻译的是商务英语文体，所以特别当你对某些词语乃至句子无法用目的语准确表达的时候，更应警觉到这种意识，从文本的文体着手，根据语境选择正确的语义。

下例就是因为没有进入商务英语文体的语境，也没有文体意识而造成的误译：

• The word "document" comes from the Latin *documentum* meaning official paper. The word also carries meanings of "proof" and "evidence". Therefore, a document is <u>an official paper</u> that serves as <u>proof or evidence of something</u>. (Hinkelman，2009：1)

原译：（后半句）：所以，单据是用来<u>证明或证实某一事件</u>的<u>官方文件</u>。（李月菊，2009：ii）

根据原作者的解释，单证源自拉丁语 *documentum*，意为"正式文件"，而且还含有"证明"的意思。原译者翻译时脱离了商务语境和商务意识，把 official paper, proof or evidence of something 分别译成了"官方文件"和"证明或证实某一事件"，没有把原意译出。"官方"相对于"民间"而言，"证明或证实"根据英语 proof or evidence 译来，但同义词叠用乃商务英语常用的表达方式，以达到精准的目的，而"某一事件"对译 something，指代不清是什么事件，应该明确指"某项交易活动或商务活动"。

改译（后半句）：所以，单证是用作<u>证明某交易活动</u>的<u>正式文件</u>。

就文体而言，商务英语与普通英语是截然不同的，翻译商务文体英语文本时译者必须要有文体意识，这里我们主要从术语对等、复数、专业知识、近/同义词叠用以及词语组合等方面讨论这种意识在商务翻译中的体现。

2.1　术　语　对　等

商务英语词语翻译中的术语对等（terminology equivalence）是一条重要的原则。

商务英语文本涉及范围广泛，专业术语及行话普遍使用，译者须找到源语对应的专业术语及行话。有些词语虽不是专业术语或行话，但在商务英语文本中，根据语境，有其特定的意义，翻译时，译者应尽力找到其"所指"。

何为"术语"？《辞海》（2000：1508）"术语"条："各门学科中的专门用语。每一术语都有严格规定的意义。"商务英语中大部分的词语都有其在各门类中特殊的术语含义，如 trade mark，汉语术语为"商标"，用于指定公司产品的名称或标记，一经注册，受法律保护，不得冒用侵权。我们不能把它译作"交易标志"或其他说法。一般说来，术语具有单一释义的特点，即一个英语词语对应一个汉语名称，如：free trade，自由贸易，这是个关税术语，指不对进出口货物征收关税，不能译作"自由交易"，或者"自由买卖"等。

比术语再广义一点的我们可用"行话"（jargon/jargoon），即行业内约定俗成的说法。《辞海》（2000：959）对"行话"的定义是："各行业为适应自身需要而创造使用的词语。"其实，商务行话也就是我们平时所说的专业用语或业务用语，亦即"地道"表达法。叶玉龙等（1998：21）认为，"所谓地道，就是译文应体现出商务英语的特色，遣词造句说的是内行话，符合商界的习惯表达"。李朝（2003：163）认为"无论是源语还是译语，从结构用词及表达方式上均有各自语言的约定俗成的习惯格式。因此，由源语译成译语时，应先将源语所表达的内容进行透彻的、准确的理解，然后再去想如何将源语的内容用译语的方式和语言再现出来"。例如 knocking copy 为一广告学用语，指（对竞争者的产品进行的）攻击性的广告字眼，译成其他的表达就不地道，不是行话。又如 knock-out agreement，这是一个拍卖业内的行话，即"不竞价协议"。

金隄认为，"翻译就是用另一语言的种种形式表达相同的内容"（1998：36）。同时，"翻译涉及两种语言的转换，其复杂性当然是不言而喻的，但是就其必须适应两边的规范性这一点而言，仍然有科学的规律可循，尤其是现代信息科学可以帮助我们掌握语际交流的复杂规律，这些都是显而易见地表现了翻译学的科学性内容"（1998：6）。把金隄的这一理论应用到商务文体英语词语翻译中，就是词语的术语对等。尽管语言不同，但在谈到一个具体的词语时，特别是专业术语，一般都有一个对应的术语或行话，这也是商务文体翻译不同于文学翻译的一个方面。《牛津英汉双解商务英语词典》（512）stop loss "限损；避损"，如改为"止损"，不是更专业吗？（297）line and staff management "各级负责及行政管理"，这不就是"直线职能管理"体制吗？

金隄（1998：44）说："凡是狭义的翻译，不论是文学性还是非文学性的，都要争取可能范围内最接近原文的效果，这是一个基本的共同原则。"多么精当的概括啊！

商务英语因文本的不同而涉及各种专业的术语，在翻译过程中，对这些术语的理解和翻译都应当是专业行话。但在翻译实践中存在着大量术语不对等的情况。译者在没有理解源语意思的情况下，望文生义，一译便错。如：

- From the <u>Survey Report</u> issued by the Commodity Inspection Bureau here, you will see that there is a shortage of 868 kilos.

原译：由此处商品检验局出具的<u>检测报告</u>中可知短重 868 公斤。（叶玉龙等，1998：78）

句中的 Survey Report 为外贸运输交货时针对交货数量所用的一个术语，指"验货报告"，如果是对质量的检验，其术语可译为"检测报告"。这是因短交货而索赔的文本语境，you 可译为"贵方"，这是商务信函中必须遵循的礼貌原则。"短重"亦可说"短交货"。

改译：从本地商检局出具的<u>验货报告</u>中（贵方）可知短重 868 千克。

- Provided we receive your order by 30 October, we make <u>you</u> a <u>firm offer</u> for delivery by the middle of November at the prices quoted.

原译：现按所列价格，报供 11 月中旬交货的<u>确盘</u>，以 10 月 30 日前收到你方订单为准。（叶玉龙等，1998：102-103）

firm offer 这一术语通常译为"实盘",指不可撤销的发价,实盘有时限,在时限内不可撤销,其反义为 non-firm offer,即"虚盘"。

改译:现按所列价格报 11 月中旬交货的<u>实盘</u>,以 10 月 30 日前收到贵方订单为准。

- Stock prices of many major commercial banks <u>closed lower</u>, as they had in previous trading.

原译:正如先前的交易那样,许多大的商业银行的股票价格<u>收盘低开</u>。(李明,2011:29)

股市下午收盘怎么可能是低开呢?早上股市开盘时可能"高开高走""高开低走",或者"低开高走""低开低走"。下午收盘时可能是"收盘走高",或者"收盘走低"。

改译:一如先前的交易,许多大型商业银行的股价<u>收盘走低</u>。

- In order to protect vested interests and interfere with the entry of new businesses, <u>some public interest corporations</u> began setting their own standards and obliged private companies to undergo inspections and receive certifications.

原译:为了保护既得利益,干预新兴企业的加入,<u>一些公众利益公司</u>着手制定自己的标准,迫使众多私人企业接受各种审查,获取各种认证。(李明,2011:34)

public interest corporation 为行业术语,意为"公益法人"。公益法人是指以公益为目的的事业法人。公益法人不得以营利为目的,民法通则中规定的事业单位法人多属于公益法人,社会团体法人中的消费者协会、慈善基金会等也属于公益法人。

改译:为了保护既得利益并干预新企业的加入,<u>公益法人</u>着手制定自己的标准,迫使私企接受审查,取得认证。

- Yet money market funds have loans <u>outstanding</u> to French banks of around $200 billion, according to <u>J. P Morgan estimates</u>. That's about 12 percent of the assets under management, a proportion that hasn't changed much over the last year, according to a Fitch survey of the 10 largest prime money market funds, despite <u>Greece's financial woes</u>.

原译 1:然而据摩根大通的<u>估计</u>,货币市场基金已经给法国银行贷出了约 2000 亿美元的贷款。惠誉国际一份关于 10 大货币市场基金的调查显示,尽管<u>希腊财政状况令人担忧</u>,但这些贷款仍占了基金管理下资产的 12%,与去年接近。

原译 2:然而,根据<u>世界 500 强摩根大通公司</u>估计,货币市场基金向法国银行提供了约 2000 亿美元的贷款。这个数字,根据惠誉国际就 10 家最大的一流货币市场基金进行调查的结果显示,尽管<u>希腊在财政方面经历了困苦</u>,却占据了其所管理资产中的约 12%,这一比例在过去一年中均没有多大改观。(李明,2011:50-51)

原译者对句中两个术语的意思没有弄明白。outstanding 意为 publicly issued and sold,即"已公开发行/出售的";J. P. Morgan estimates 行业上专指"摩根大通的研究报告/评估报告",非"估计","估计"是难以表达其内容的科学性、可靠性的。financial woes 意为"财政灾难",即"金融危机"。

改译:<u>摩根大通的研究报告</u>显示,货币市场基金向法国<u>发放了</u> 2000 亿美元的贷款。根据惠誉国际对 10 大货币市场基金的调查结果,这个数据占了该基金管理资产的 12%,尽管<u>经历了希腊财政灾难</u>,该比例在过去的一年里未有太大变化。

- Exports and imports of goods between nations with different unit of money introduce a new economic <u>factor</u>, the foreign exchange rate, which gives the price of the foreigners' unit of money <u>in terms of</u> one's own.

原译：在使用不同货币单位的国家之间进行商品出口和进口会引出一个新<u>经济因素</u>，这便是外汇汇率。所谓外汇汇率，是指<u>以自己国家的货币来给外国货币标出</u>的价格。（李明，2011：65）

factor 这一术语指"率""系数"，如：debt factor 负债系数；in terms of 根据……折算。

改译：使用不同货币单位的国家之间进行货物进出口贸易就引发了一个新的<u>经济系数</u>——外汇汇率，即根据本国货币单位的价格折算出外国货币单位的价格。

- Should for certain reasons the Buyers not be able to inform the Seller of the foregoing <u>details</u> 10 days prior to the arrival of the the vessel at the port of loading or should the <u>carrying vessel</u> be advanced or delayed, the Buyers or their <u>chartering agent</u> shall advise the Sellers immediately and make necessary arrangement.

原译：若买方由于某种原因不能于<u>装运轮船</u>抵达装运港十天前将上述详细情况通知卖方，或<u>装运轮船</u>提前或推迟抵达，买方或其<u>运输代理人</u>须立即通知卖方并做出必要的安排。（李明，2011：93）

carrying vessel 这一术语专指"承运船"，而非"装运轮船"；chartering agent 这一术语专指"租船代理人"，而非"运输代理人"；details 意为"细节"。

改译：由于某些原因买方不能于<u>承运船</u>抵达装货港前 10 天将上述<u>细节</u>通知卖方，或者<u>承运船</u>提前或推迟，买方或其<u>租船代理</u>须立即通知卖方并做出必要的安排。

- The dollar buying increased Japan's foreign exchange reserves by 50 percent <u>on a year-on-year basis</u>.

原译：<u>与去年同期的数字相比</u>，美元的购入给日本增加了 50% 的外汇储备。（李明，2011：102）

on a year-on-year basis 或 year basis 专指"同比"。同比增长率：year on year growth/quarter-on-quarter growth；环比增长率：the annulus growth/quarterly growth（comparing to the previous quarter）

改译：购买美元使日本外汇储备量同比增长了 50%。

- As <u>a good corporate citizen</u>, the Company actively contributes to each community in which it conducts business.

原译：作为<u>一个好的市民企业</u>，该公司在其所经营业务的每一个社区都在做着积极的贡献。（李明，2011：102）

a good corporate citizen 专指"优秀的企业公民"。企业公民是国际上盛行的用来表达企业责任的新术语，始于 20 世纪 80 年代。其核心观点是，企业的成功与社会的健康发展密切相关。企业在获取经济利益的时候，要通过各种方式来回报社会。企业公民的要素构成，有社会责任和道德责任两大类。

改译：作为<u>一个优秀的企业公民</u>，该公司积极地为其业务所在的每个社区作出贡献。

- At the financial statement date of December 31, 2010, the Corporation signed an agreement to borrow up to ＄1,000,000 to refinance notes payble on a long-term basis.

原译：在 2010 年 12 月 31 日的财政决算日，该公司签订了一项高达 100 万美元的协议，以便长期对到期应付票据进行再融资。（李明，2011：102）

notes payble on a long-term basis 专指"应（支）付长期票据"，notes payble 指"应付票据"。

改译：公司于 2010 年 12 月 31 日财政决算日签署了一项高达 100 万美元的借款协议，为应付长期票据再融资。

- When there is a particular average loss，other interests in the voyage，such as the carrier and other cargo owners whose goods were not damaged，do not contribute to the partial recovery of the one who suffered the loss.

原译：在发生个别的海损时，海运中的各相关方，例如承运人及货物没有受损的船主，不必分担受损一方的那部分补偿费用。（李明，2011：117）

particular average 专指"单独海损"。单独海损（Particular Average）是指保险标的物在海上遭受承保范围内的风险所造成的部分灭失或损害，即指除共同海损以外的部分损失。这种损失只能由标的物所有人单独负担。other interests 意为"其他各方"，不是"各相关方"；in the voyage 意为"该航次中"；other cargo owners 意为"其他货主"；partial recovery 是"部分赔偿"。

改译：一旦发生单独海损赔偿，航次中的其他各方，如承运人以及其他货物未损的货主，不需承担受损方的部分赔偿。

在翻译实践中，我们经常会遇到一些十分普通的词语，但它们常常是专业术语，如果翻译时没有术语对等意识，难免译错。举例如下：

cap 术语为"上限"；对应的为"下限"（floor）；而"封顶"则用 ceiling。

call 术语为"赎回"，如：call-adjusted yield 赎回调整收益率；call feature 赎回特征；call price 赎回价格；call provision 赎回条款；call risk 赎回风险；callable option or warrant 可赎回期权或权证；callable swap 要赎回互换；called bond 已赎回债券，但 call protection 术语为"抗赎回保护"。

call 的另一术语为"买权/买进"，如：call swaption 买进型互换期权；call spread 买权利差；call or put（COP）买权或卖权；call premium 买权溢金；call option 买进型期权；call of more option 多选择买权。

2.1.1　译者对原文的理解错误造成误译

- 《朗文国际贸易词典》中，average 词条下（a）A particular average is an insurance loss that affects specific interests only.（b）A general average is an insurance loss that affects all cargo interests on board the vessel as well as the ship herself.

原译：（a）个别海损（particular average），指仅涉及某项具体财物的保险损失（b）综合海损（general average），指涉及船上的所有货物和船本身的保险损失。（下画线为笔者所加，系误译，下同。）

本词条是一个货运保险条款中的术语，有三处误译：（1）particular average 这一术语为

"单独海损"，即货物损失只涉及各货方和船方中的某特定的利益方（specific interest）；（2）specific interests 中的 interests 为该保险涉及的"利益方"；（3）general average 这一术语应为"共同海损"，损失由该保险涉及的各货方和船方分摊。

改译：（a）单独海损，即（货物的）保险损失仅涉及特定的利益方。（b）共同海损，即（货物的）保险损失涉及船上货物各方以及货船本身。

同样的误译出现在辞典 common average（315-316）中：A loss that affects all cargo interests on board a vessel as well as the ship herself.

原译：公共海损，共同海损：一种影响船上所有货物利益以及货船自身的损失。

- ballast（57）：Heavy material strategically placed on a ship to improve its trim or stability.

原译：压舱物：旨在改善船只平衡或稳定状态而置放于船内的重物。

ballast，trim，stability 均为术语，分别译为"压载"，"平衡首尾吃水"，"船舶稳性"。

改译："压载"：（在船舶轻载航行特别是空载航行时）为了平衡首尾吃水或提高船舶稳性而置于船内的重物。

- general cargo vessel（316）：A vessel designed to handle breakbulk cargo such as bags, cartons, cases, crates and drums, either individually or in unitized or palletized loads.

原译：普通货船：一种设计用来或单独或联合或平行地装载诸如包裹、纸板箱、箱子、板条箱和圆桶等散装货物的货船。

显然，这是译者对此项外贸运输业务不甚了解而造成的误译。此名称应为"杂货船"，原文列举的"袋子"（bags）、"纸箱"（cartons）、"箱子"（cases），"板/柳条箱"（crates），"桶"（drum）等都是"杂货"（breakbulk）的包装物，这些包装货可"单独"（individually）装载，也可"成组"（unitized）装载，或者"货盘（化）"（pattetized）装载。

- break-bulk cargo（76）：Cargo which is shipped as a unit but which is not containerized. Examples are any unitized cargo placed on pallets, or in boxed.

原译：散装杂货，杂（散）货：未装入集装箱的散装货物。例如用托盘或装盒运输的货物。

实际上，这里 break-bulk 指"杂货"，即"非集装箱装运的，如装于货盘上或包装内的成组货物"。所以，辞典（76）break-bulk vessel 也是"杂货船"，而非该辞典所译"散装船"。

"散装货船"的英语为 bulk carrier（79）：一种"专门用于运输散装货物的船舶。散装货船有两类：一种用于运输固体散装货，例如谷物和矿石；一种用于运输液体散装货，如石油"。

- production and distribution schedules（150）原译：生产和分配计划时间表

改译：生产和销售计划/安排

distribution 是一个非常普通的商务英语词语，意为"分销；销售"，又如：

- The company's main activities are manufacturing, marketing, and distribution.

该公司的主要业务是制造、营销和销售。

在辞典第 220 页上，该词同样被错译。

- entrepôt：An intermediary storage facility where goods are kept temporarily for distribution

21

within a country or for reexport.

原译：仓库，关税货栈：一种中间储存设施，货物临时在这里保存，以备<u>向国内分派</u>，或者再出口。

distribution within a country 应译为"供国内销售"。

Distribution 一词的又一误译在辞典第 612 页：

total cost of distribution 原译：<u>总分配费用</u>

改译：销售总成本(包括运输费、提取存货费、仓储费、包装费、保险费、在途或存储产品的报废和失窃费用。)

- loaded on board an ocean vessel 原译：<u>装上远洋货轮的甲板</u>（167）

改译：装上远洋船

on board 为一常用词语，意为：上船(或火车、公共汽车、飞机等)；在(船、火车、公共汽车、飞机等)上，可作状语、定语或表语等。如：

We went/got on board the ship. 我们登上轮船。

Everybody on board was worried and we were curious to find out what had happened.
飞机上的人都很着急，而且我们急于想了解出了什么事。

When everybody was on board, the ship sailed. 所有人都登船后，轮船起航了。

- to prevent damage or breakage by <u>preventing movement</u>

原译：以防<u>搬动过程中损害货物</u>（212）

这里译者对原文的理解显然不对，原文是要说明填舱物料的作用，即塞紧货物防止运输过程中的位移以达到防止货损或破包的目的。

改译：通过<u>防止位移</u>而<u>防止货损或破包</u>

- such as live animals, <u>human remains</u>, or automotive vehicles

原译：如鲜活动物、<u>人体器官</u>或汽车（240）

查词典 human remains 一词有两种解释：一为"人文遗迹"，二为"人的尸体"，根据语境，显然为第二种释义，相对于前者的"鲜活动物"而言，可将其译为"<u>死尸</u>"。

- hatch: The <u>opening</u> in the deck of a vessel which gives <u>access to the cargo hold</u>.

原译：舱口：<u>船只甲板上用于装载货物的门</u>。（342）

改译：舱口：<u>货船甲板上进入货舱的开口</u>。

- irritating material 刺激物（394）词条下有一描述：

may burn but do not ignite readily

原译：未点燃却自发燃烧

译者初看原文，不甚理解，便急着翻译，以致译错。

改译：会灼伤但不易点燃(这种材料因其刺激性而灼/烧伤人的皮肤，但不易点燃。)

- labels: labels attached to each piece of multiple lot shipment for identification purposes.

原译：<u>大宗标签</u>，识别标签：给多批货物每件贴上标签以便于识别。（427）

一见 lot 就出了"大宗"，望文生义。

英语 lot 一词在外贸运输中指"<u>票(货物)</u>"，即发给同一收货人的不同货物或发给不同收货人的相同货物均为一票货物，装船时要进行隔票(lot separation)，即把每一票货物分隔堆装，以便卸货。贴标签的目的则在于方便识别每一票货物。

改译：票签(货票标签)

· priority logistics management 原译：优先后勤管理(518)

查词典，logistics 意为"后勤(学)"。可是随着全球经济的发展，英语词语的语义也在不断地变化，旧词翻新义，这是一种常见的新词构成的方法，这里 logistics 已成为当代的"物流"新概念了。又如：

logistics enterprise 物流企业

logistics system analysis 物流系统分析

改译：优先物流管理（即及时运输理论的运用。）

· protest 原译：抗议(524)

商务英语中它是一个常见的术语——"拒付"。这是一个非常专业化的贸易术语，而且这个词条下的释义也非常清晰地描述了"拒付"的概念。所以，下一词条(525) protest system "抗议系统"应译为术语"拒付系统"。

胡壮麟、李战子(2004：121)认为："引起歧义的原因之一是句中有几个词有一个以上的词义。"这话也许能给上述的误译作出"合理的"注释吧。

再看下面的译例：

· mate's receipt：A declaration issued by an officer of a vessel in the name of the shipping company stating that certain goods have been received on board his vessel. A mate's receipt is not a title document. Used as an interim document until the bill of lading is issued.

原译：收货单，大副收据，卸货单：船上官员以船运公司的名义表示某种货物已在其货船甲板上收到的声明。收货单不是所有权文件，仅作为提单开具前的临时文件使用。(437)

mate's receipt 这一术语一般译作"大副收据"。officer 为船员职务名称，在甲板部有 chief officer/mate 大副，second officer/mate 二副，third officer/mate 三副。所以这里不能译为"官员"；on board his vessel 为"在他的船上"，即货物"已装船"；title document 一般写作 document of title，即"所有权/物权凭证"，所以这里 document 为"凭证，单据"，而非"文件"。

改译：大副收据：由船上大副以航运公司名义开具的表明货物已装船的声明，它不是物权凭证，只是作为临时凭证，以后换取提单。

· stowage：The arranging and packing of cargo in a vessel for shipment.

原译：装载，堆仓，理仓：为方便货运而在轮船上整理和包装货物。(587)

stowage 是一个外贸运输术语。

改译：船舶配载/船舶积载，指对船舶航次所承运的货载作出堆装位置的合理安排和正确堆装。

下文的 stowage plan 术语为"船舶配载图/船舶积载图"，而非"船上货物堆积图"，从"它是标明货物在船上具体位置的示意图"来看，应该是"船舶配载图"。

· survey：To examine the condition of a vessel for purposes of establishing seaworthiness and/or value.

原译：鉴定：检验船舶的适航性条件或者价值。（595）

改译：船检/验船，检验船况以确定船舶的适航性和/或船舶的价值。

2.1.2　译者对译入语术语驾驭不力引起的误译

- Balance of trade deficit is when a country imports more than it exports.

原译：当进口大于出口时表现为贸易赤字差额。（56）

初看似乎原译也没什么错，但读起来觉得不地道，表达不到位。

改译：进口大于出口为贸易逆差。

- Balance of trade surplus is when a country exports more than it imports.

原译：当出口大于进口时即为贸易盈余差额。

改译：出口大于进口为贸易顺差。

deficit, surplus 分别表示"亏损""盈余"，但当它们表示一个国家的贸易状况时，要注意其意义。如：

a surplus country 顺差国，a deficit country 逆差国

- perils of the sea 原译：海上风险（91）

改译：海难

- handle 原译：处理（143）

在商务英语语境下，应译为术语："作业"，指装卸货作业，相当于 load and discharge。

- less handling 原译：对货物的处理工作量较小（143）

改译：减少了货物装卸作业量

再看第 653 页 unitization 词条下

- for easier handling 原译：为了更便于处置

改译：为了更方便/便利的装卸作业

- a unitized load on a carrier-owned pallet

原译：用承运人的托盘装载成单元的货物（143）

改译：用承运人的托盘一体化装载

- limits of liability

原译：责任的界限（148）

改译：责任范围

- loss of or damage to the goods

原译：货物损失或损害（154、177、182）

这似乎不是错译，但表达很不专业。

改译：货物的灭失或损坏，通常也译为行话：货失或货损，即：货失货损。

- credit balance

原译：信用平衡（189）

balance 商务语境中常指"余/差额"。下文说这种余额随时可兑换成纸币或硬币。

改译：信用余额

- sophisticated technology

原译：复杂技术（192）

译者的译语驾驭不力，此语通常译为：尖端技术。

- This（document）includes bills of lading, dock receipts, export declarations, manifests, etc.

原译：包括：提单、码头收据、出口报关单、证明信等。（202）

这里 manifests 术语应为舱单/载货单，表明船舶所载货或旅客的清单。

同样，辞典 Entry Manifest（222）原译：入关货物清单，应改译为术语：进口舱单。

- port, airport, or terminal

原译：港口、机场或终点站（226）

terminal 术语为：码头或装卸区（尤指油码头或集装箱运输码头），而非终点站。

- associations 原译：联合会（249）

通常译为术语：协会，如：

African Railway Association 非洲铁路协会；

American Arbitration Association〈律〉美国商务仲裁协会；

American Banker's Association 美国银行协会；

Equipment Interchange Association 运输设备交换协会；

Exporters' Association 出口商协会；

International Air Transport Association 国际航空运输协会；

National Association of Export Management Companies 全国出口管理公司协会［美国］

Protection and Indemnity Association 保护与赔偿保险协会，简称"保赔协会"。

- inhaled 原译：呼吸（270）

改译：被吸入

- amount of charges 原译：费用数量（306）

改译：运费

- export clearance 原译：出口报关（307）

改译：结关

"报关"英语单词是 declaration，与"结关"为两个不同的术语和概念。

- gang 原译：班组，合伙行动，组（309）

改译：工班，指码头装卸货作业组。

- general cargo rate 原译：杂货运费率，一般货物运费率，普通货物运费率。（316）

这里应保留第一个译名，删除后两个。

- hull 原译：船壳，船身（347）

改译：船体

- in bond shipment：An import or export shipment which has not been cleared by U. S. Customs officials.

原译：保税货物：尚未被美国海关官员结清的进口或出口货物。（355）

改译：保税货物：未经美国海关官员结关的进出口货物。

这里"结关"为专业术语。

- forwarder 原译：发送商（370）

改译：货运代理/承揽行

商务英语中，forwarder = forwarding agent = freight forwarder 货运代理行，它不仅承运货物，也办理货运单证、海关手续、订载位以及保险等事务并收取服务费。有些货运代理行还负责港口间的收货、运货和送货。

- terms and conditions 原译：项目和条件（372）

改译：条款

略具商务英语知识的人都明白这个术语。这是一个十分常用的术语，其构词运用商务法律英语中常见的词语叠用现象，即同义词或近义词往往由 or 或 and 连接并列使用，这种词汇并列、同义重现的现象表明法律语言对词义正确、语义确凿的追求，从而形成了法律语言的复杂性和保守性。

这类短语的作用通常是使包括的内容更全面，也更具有弹性。

- intermodal transport 原译：协调联运，中间型运输（374）

改译：协调运输，多式联运

- offshore exploration industries 原译：离岸勘探（383）

改译：近海勘探

- key currency

原译：枢要货币，关键通货，主要通货，关键货币，主要货币，基本货币，基准通货（403）

本词语通常译为：主/枢要货币，等于 international currency，指在清偿债务时被多数国家承认和接受的货币，如下文提到的美元、英镑、德国马克、瑞士法郎、法国法郎、荷兰盾、日元和加拿大元。

- Lloyd's Registry 原译：英国劳氏船舶登记簿（424）

改译：劳氏船级社，劳埃德船级社，英语亦写作 Lloyd's Register，它是英国一家世界一流的船级社。

- poisonous material 词条下 highly toxic，moderately toxic，least toxic

原译：高度有毒、中等毒性、很少毒性。（509）

改译：高度毒性（剧毒）、中度毒性、轻度毒性（微毒）。

- Public Limited Company（PLC）：（United Kingdom）Designation for a public corporation with limited liability to shareholders.

原译：公开有限公司，公共有限责任公司：对股东承担有限责任的公共公司的名称。（527）

改译：（股份公开）上市公司。这种公司根据英国公司法注册，核定股本（authorized share capital）不少于 50000 英镑，股份在证交所买卖。如：

Public limited companies must use the initials "plc" in their names.

上市公司的名称需使用首字母缩写"plc"字样。

Britain now uses "plc" for a public limited company whose shares are offered to the public at large.

英国现在用"plc"代表向公众发行股票的股份公司。

注意，public corporation 为"公营公司"或"国有公司"，即属于国家所有的，负责为全国提供服务或经营国有化产业。如：

The British Coal Corporation and the British Broadcasting Corporation are public corporations.

英国煤炭公司和英国广播公司都是国有公司。

- salvage 原译：抢救费(551)

改译：救助费

- joint and several liability 原译：联合的和多种的责任(571)

改译：连带并个别责任，共同并个别负债

- tramp steamer：A steamship which does not operate under any regular schedule from one port to another, but calls at any port where cargo may be obtained(625)中的 regular schedule 译成"常规计划"，显然是错的，正确的翻译为：定期时间表。

该词条译文：不定期班轮：不按照定期时间表运行于港口间的班轮，一旦有货装运可停靠任何港口。

- tying arrangement 原译：附有条件的安排，搭销安排(635)

这里的 arrangement 不是"安排"，而是"协定/议"。

金隄(1998：114)说，"准确也好，通顺也好，都不能脱离读者。翻译是沟通两种语言的信息传递，所谓准确的翻译，就是把原文变成译文之后，译文给读者的信息与原文给读者的信息基本上相同"。商务文体中英语词语的翻译也要遵循这一翻译原则，把等效等值等同的术语提供给译语读者，这是我们商务文体翻译工作者的责任。

2.1.3 汉译英术语名称统一的途径

翻译过程中，译者保持术语名称统一的途径有以下三条：(刘法公，2002)

2.1.3.1 具有中国特色的词语

翻译具有中国特色的词语时，我们可参照《中国日报》(*China Daily*)、《中国建设》(*China Construction*)、《北京周报》(*Beijing Review*)等英文报刊上的译名，或《中国翻译》封底上提供的译名。

下面这些汉语词英译名就来自上述刊物：

出口配额 export quota

超前分配 deficit distribution

化解金融风险 defuse financial risks

世界经济格局大变革、大调整 major changes in the global economic landscape

人工智能 artificial intelligence（AI）

包容的全球化　inclusive globalization

贸易保护主义 protectionism

区域一体化 regional integration

一带一路倡议 the Belt and Road Initiative

可持续发展 sustainable development

自由贸易区 free trade zone

社会术语和经济用语层出不穷，任何部门都无法全面规定什么术语和用语该以何种英语译名出现。术语和用语的英语译名必须经过人们较长时间的使用，基本约定俗成之后才能统一。商务文体翻译最困难的任务是将新生的词语恰当地译成英语。唯一的解决办法是译者加强学习，不断阅读相关报刊，及时掌握新生词语的翻译动向。

2.1.3.2　商贸英语文献

翻译商贸领域通用术语时，译者应参阅国际商贸英语文献，保持商贸通用术语汉英译名的稳定性和统一性，商贸领域通用汉语术语几乎都有固定的英语表达，译者的任务就是把双语同一概念相对应的译名加以匹配，做到始终如一，例如：

- 绝对优势理论——absolute advantage theory（商贸通用英语术语），而不是 overwhelming superiority theory（自编英语术语）

- 相对优势理论——comparative advantage theory（商贸通用英语术语），而不是 relative advantage theory（自编英语术语）

- 贸易盈余——trade surplus（商贸通用英语术语），而不是 trade profit（自编英语术语）

- 原产地——place of origin（商贸通用英语术语），而不是 original producing place（自编英语术语）

- 可兑换货币——convertible currency（商贸通用英语术语），而不是 changeable currency（自编英语术语）

译者能作出正确选择的关键是，他既要通晓商贸源语，更要熟悉商贸译语，还要了解商贸业务。遗憾的是，我国的商务文体翻译中，乱译术语的现象还比较普遍。不使用国际统一的英语术语，译者无法使其译文被读者读懂，最终译者也就不能完成传递语言信息的任务。下列翻译就出现了类似的问题：

原文：

同时，我国政府已同瑞典、罗马尼亚、德国、丹麦、荷兰签订了相互促进和保护投资协定，同加拿大、美国、法国、比利时-卢森堡经济联盟、芬兰、挪威、泰国、意大利、奥地利签订了投资保护协定，还同日本、美国、法国、德国、英国、比利时等国签订了避免双重征税协定。我国还参加了《保护工业产权(包括技术转让)巴黎公约》。

原译文：

The Chinese Government in the meantime, has signed agreements of investment promotion and protection with Sweden, Romania, Germany, Denmark, the Netherlands; agreements on investment protection with Canada, U.S.A., France, Belgium-Luxembourg Economic Alliance, Finland, Norway, Thailand, Italy and Austria; agreements of double tax prevention with Japan, U.S.A., France, Germany, Britain, Belgium and other countries. China is a member of the *Paris Convention on Industrial Property Protection* (including assignment of technology). (某市经济技术开发区中英文简介)

上述原文涉及的许多商贸术语在英语中已有固定译名，若任意译出则难以让英语读者对描述的内容产生共识。译文中的这些自编译名有的与通用译名相似，有的差别很大，足以让商贸专业的英语读者莫名其妙，请看比较：

- 相互促进和保护投资协定：译者自译 agreements of investment promotion and protection，国际通用译名：agreements on mutual promotion and protection of investment
- 比利时-卢森堡经济联盟：译者自译 Belgium-Luxembourg Economic Alliance，国际通用译名：Belgium-Luxembourg Economic Union（BLEU）
- 投资保护协定：译者自译 agreements on investment protection，国际通用译名：agreement on protection of investment
- 避免双重征税协定：译者自译 agreements of double tax prevention，国际通用译名：double taxation relief treaty
- 《保护工业产权巴黎公约》：译者自译 *Paris Convention on Industrial Property Protection*，国际通用译名：*Paris Convention for the Protection of Industrial Property*
- 技术转让：译者自译 assignment of technology，国际通用译名：technology transfer

从上段译文中找到的这 6 例翻译可以充分说明，不统一的译名必然造成误解，使读者对译文不知所云。这样的翻译源于译者的知识水平，但更应归咎于译者对翻译的敷衍态度。译者即便缺少专业知识，只要细心查一下专业词典便可得到上述国际通用译名。

2.1.3.3 专业词典

翻译中国特有的商品品名时，译者应主要参考专业汉英词典。俗话说，工欲善其事，必先利其器。从事商贸汉英翻译离不开商贸专业词典。如果我们要英译中国特有的商品名称，就应参阅《汉英对外经贸词典》《汉英英汉实用外经外贸辞典》《实用外贸英汉词典》或《汉英中国商品品名词典》之类的专业词典，普通汉英词典上的译文往往是靠不住的。作为出口的许多中国商品，经过商贸专业人员多年的共同努力，基本上都有了固定的英语译名。这些英语译名在国际上流通已久，译者若随便翻译，必然导致物名分家。

笔者在长期的翻译实践中发现下列专业词典比较可靠，读者可根据自己的使用情况选购，不限于下面所列：

杨佑方. 外贸经济英语用法词典[Z]. 成都：四川人民出版社，2002.

中华征信所企业股份有限公司. 国际贸易金融大词典[Z]. 上海：世界图书出版公司，2002.

廖美珍，等. 汉英国际贸易和金融词典[Z]. 北京：外语教学与研究出版社，2000.

格雷厄姆·班诺克等著，郑风田等译. 商务词典（英汉）[Z]. 北京：人民邮电出版社，2007.

John Pallister 等编，童珊等译. 牛津英汉双解商务词典[Z]. 上海：上海外语教育出版社，2007.

Allene Tuck 等著，俞利军等译. 牛津英汉双解商务英语词典[Z]. 北京：华夏出版社，2000.

加里·加斯蒂尼等著，谌季强等译. 金融风险管理词典[Z]. 北京：华夏出版社，2007.

黄斌元编，陈敏强译. 英汉路透金融词典［Z］. 北京：中国金融出版社，2005.

2.2　复　　数

"商务英语文本中的复数是一个非常独特的现象，其意思一般是要表达'量'，'款额'等，翻译实践中，译者必须高度重视，误译概率极高。"（顾维勇，2014）

在商务英语文本的翻译中，我们经常碰到一些复数形式的名词所表达的意思与单数形式的名词不完全相同甚至完全不同。值得一提的是，目前市面上见到的出版物中，商务英语复数形式的理解和翻译绝大部分是错的，而且错得很离谱。

有的语法学家或学者也已注意到了这一事实。如《商务英语翻译》（2003，高等教育出版社）的作者张新红等就指出："英语中名词单、复数歧义是个独特的语法现象，如不加注意，往往会造成误译。"（2003：154）但是在翻译实践中，译者又经常忽略了这些特殊的复数形式的名词，在没有考虑到原文作者实际想要表达意思的情况下，信手译来，难免犯错，这样的译文也就无法准确地再现原文的意思，所以，大量的误译与此有关，请看下面的译例：

- In the event the Buyer does not furnish the seller with shipping instructions on or before August 17, 1987, the Seller may at his option cancel this contract and demand the Buyer to pay any damages he has sustained on account of such failure of the Buyer to give such instructions.

原译：如买方在 1987 年 8 月 17 日或在此之前未向卖方发出装运通知，则卖方可自行决定取消本合同，并要求买方赔偿因未发出装运通知而使其蒙受的一切损失。（张新红等，2003：196）

这里 damages 指"经济损失（额）"，也就是要求买方支付"因损失而引起的赔偿费"。

在《国际贸易实务》（孙湘生等，2005）一书中，作者将 damages 误译为"损失"，原文是：

damages 损失

Where the action can be founded on breach of contract, **damages** for physical loss, i. e. for death, personal injury or damage to property, as well as for economic loss, i. e. loss of profit or other financial loss, can be recovered to the extent that the loss is not too remote. （孙湘生等，2005：44）

在商务英语中，短语 recover the damages 意为"得到赔偿"；"damage to"或"loss of"常搭配使用，表示"对……的损坏"或"……的损失"，如：damage to or loss of cargo 意为"货失货损"。原文中 damages for physical loss... as well as for economic loss...指"对于有形损失以及经济损失的赔偿"。在法律英语中，remote damages 指"间接损害赔偿金"。

改译：（损失）赔偿费

全句译文：一旦发现违反合同的行为，有形的损失（即死亡、人员的受伤或财产的损坏）以及经济损失（即利润损失或其他经济损失），只要该损失不是太间接，均可以获得一定的赔偿费。

再如：liquidated damages 原译：核定损失额，清偿损失额，预定违约金，规定的赔偿金，确定损失额，议定补偿损失额。

根据其英语释义：A sum of money that a contracting party agrees to pay to the other party for breaching an agreement，particularly important in a contract in which damages for breach may be difficult to assess. 我们可将其译为："清偿违约金"。

- When a negotiating bank makes payment to an exporter，it is really extending an advance against foreign collections. The bank is thus entitled to charge interest until it receives reimbursement from the opening bank.

原译：议付行向出口商支付货款，实际上是拓展其对外托收预付业务，这样就可以从中收取利息，直到开证行还款为止。（叶玉龙等，1998：198）

句中的 foreign collections 是指"国外托收额"，extend 意为"提供"，这里可理解为"支付"。

改译：议付行向出口商支付货款，实际上它根据国外托收额支付一笔预付款。这样，该银行有资格在收到开证行的还款之前对这笔款项收取利息。

国内外的语法专家们对复数词语这一语法现象也有论及，其中也列举到了某些商务英语中的用法。如：

章振邦在他的《新编英语语法》（1981）中阐述了复数形式意义不同或增加新义的名词，"有些名词的复数形式在意义上不同于它的单数形式，而有的则在原有的意义之外，增加了新意义"。（1981：59）在举例中他也引用了单数 damage 意为"损害"，而复数 damages 意为"损害赔偿金"。

张道真在他的《实用英语语法》（1995）一书中说"有些名词经常以复数形式出现"，这些名词"有的是以 ing 收尾的词"，（1995：39）如：belongings 所有物，savings 储蓄，earnings 挣的钱。同时他又指出："另外还有些名词，其复数形式有时可以表示特别的意思"（1995：40），例如：goods 货物；customs 关税，海关；damages 赔偿费；imports 进口货物。

L. G. 亚历山大在《朗文英语语法》一书中提及了"单数和复数意义不同的名词"（1991：91），列举的词中有下列几个与商务文体英语有关：customs 海关；damages 赔偿金；funds 现款；manners 礼貌；minutes 会议记录；savings 储金。他指出："有时这些词的意义相差很远（如 air/airs），有时又相当接近（如 fund/funds）。"

语法学家们虽然已意识到了这一特殊的英语语法现象，但对于这种现象在商务文体英语里使用的各种情形未给予足够的阐述，我们将进行归纳与研究，旨在让译者在遇到这类词语时能按商务英语的规范进行翻译。

在商务文体英语的语境下，复数词语所表达的概念与单数词语所表达的概念有时迥然不同。通过对商务文体中多例复数词所表达的意思进行分析，我们发现，作为一种特殊的语法现象的这些复数词语在商务语境里一般用来表达"量"或"数"的概念，译者须对此高度重视。从意义上讲，复数形式的词语可表示数量与款项，表示数量时有两种情况，一是单复数表示相同的概念，二是单复数表示的概念不同；表示款项时一般表示金额、债券或股票。从形式上说，大部分复数词语均为名词复数，也有从形容词转化而来的复数；大部分为单个词的复数，也有少数复数词叠用的。

2.2.1　从意义上讲，单数用来表达一个名称概念，而复数表示该概念或名称的数量

2.2.1.1　复数表示的量与单数名词所表示的名称概念相同或相近

常见的词有：

import 进口→imports 进口量，进口的货物；

export 出口→exports 出口量，出口的货物；

stock 库存(货)→stocks 库存量；

flow 流→flows 流(通)量(inflows 流入量，outflows 流出量)；

reserve 储存→reserves 储藏量，储备额/量，如：international reserves 国际储备(的量或种类)，黄金、特别提款权，外汇及会员国在 IMF 的储备净额；

holding 持有(不可数)→holdings 持有量，储备；

shipment 装船→shipments 装船货(的量)；

sale 销售→sales 销量，销售额；

supply 供应→supplies 供应量。

注意下面的例句中复数形式名词的意义及翻译：

• The balance must be matched by flows of international reserves that is, of gold — into Britain, The gold inflows into Britain automatically reduce foreign money supplies and increase Britain's money supply, driving foreign prices downward and British prices upward. (顾维勇，2015：3)

必须通过国际黄金储备的大量输入英国来达到收支平衡。黄金大量流入英国自动地减少了外币的供应量，增加了英国货币的供应，结果造成外国物价下跌，而英国物价上涨。

注意上例中多个名词的复数形式表示"量"的概念，flows 流通量；reserves 黄金的储备量；inflows 输入量；supplies 供应量。

• Eventually, reserve movements stop and both countries reach balance of payments equilibrium. (顾维勇，2015：3)

本句中的 reserve movements 指"黄金储备的运输活动"，即为了完成国际收支而进行的黄金输出与输入活动，其原意为"(货物的)运输"，而非指其他"运动"或"运转"。此句译为：

最后，黄金储备的运输活动停止了，两个国家都达到了国际收支平衡。

• However, the response of central banks to gold flows across their borders furnished another potential mechanism to help restore balance of payments equilibrium. Central banks experiencing persistent gold outflows were motivated to contract their domestic asset holdings for the fear of becoming unable to meet their obligation to redeem currency notes. (顾维勇，2015：3)

然而，各国央行对跨国界黄金流通所作的反应提供了另一个潜在的机制以帮助恢复国际收支平衡。经历了持续黄金输出的那些央行不得不减缩其国内资产的持有量，因为它们担心无力履行兑现的职责。

句中，flows 指"流通量"；outflows 指"输出量"；holdings 指"持有量"。

● Government interference with private gold exports also undermined the system.（顾维勇，2015：3）

政府对私自的黄金出口采取干预措施也破坏了这一体系。

复数 exports 指"出口量"。

● Starting in the early 1960s, member nations started to negotiate stand-by arrangements, referring to advance permission for future borrowings by the nation in IMF.（顾维勇，2015：18）

从 20 世纪 60 年代开始各成员国着手磋商安排备用信贷款，它是指事先许可国际货币基金组织某成员国未来的借款额。

这里 arrangements 指与国际货币基金组织（IMF）"安排总借款"（General Arrangements to Borrow）有关的一个概念。复数 arrangements 实际上是指"安排备用信贷额"；stand-by arrangements 为 IMF 给予成员国安排的备用信贷款。根据规定，成员国需要其他国家货币时，可用本国货币从 IMF 购买，数额为每年不得超过本国份额的 25%。如需要更多外币时，成员国须向 IMF 申请，由 IMF 给予一定数额的备用信贷。而复数 borrowings 指"借款额"。

下例的原译者没有弄懂复数形式的词义而望文生义，导致错译：

● Lucasfilm, for example, receives a percentage of the sales made by companies marketing Star-wars, thus Lucasfilm's revenues increase with each additional toy that Parker Kenner sells in the United Kingdom.

原译：举例来说，卢卡斯制片公司承担了影片《星球大战》的部分销售任务，因此，该公司在英国的代理帕克肯勒公司每销售出一部拷贝，就能使该公司的收益增加。

英语原句中的 sales 显然是复数，表示"量"或"额"，即"销售额"。

改译：比如，卢卡斯制片公司从推销玩具"星球大战"公司的销售额中收取一定比例的提成，所以，帕克肯勒公司在英国每销售出一件玩具，卢卡斯公司的收益都会有所增加。

2.2.1.2　复数名词表示由单数名词引申出的数量或款项，与单数名词表示的概念不同

例如：

damage 损坏→damages 损坏而引起的赔款，损失赔偿额（如：ordinary/general damages 普通损害赔偿费/额；substantial damages 实质性损害赔偿费/额；loss and damages 损失及赔偿费）；

earning 所得→earnings 挣得的财物，工薪；

effect 效果，作用→effects 财物，动产（如：no effects 无存款）；

liability 责任，义务→liabilities 债务，负债；

engagement 从事→engagements 债务；

proceed 前进，但复数 proceeds（从事某种活动或变卖财物的）收入，收益，在商务语境下通常指"汇款""货款"（如：net proceeds 净售得款）；

receipt 收到→receipts 收入，收益；

return 返回→returns 收益，收入；

risk 风险→risks 风险损失赔偿额；

gain 收获→gains 利润，收益；

yield 产量(不可数)→yields 收益，利润，利息率；

collection 托收→collections(应)收款额；

price 价格→prices 价格上涨而获得的钱。

下面以 proceeds 一词为例，请注意这些例句中该词的理解及翻译：

- Corporations may purchase "key executive" insurance covering certain corporate officers. The proceeds from this insurance help offset the loss of the services of these key people if they die or become incapacitated.

公司会购买承保某些公司要员的"关键管理者"保险，由此类保险得到的资金可以弥补这些要员死亡或能力丧失而无法供职的损失费用。

- He sold his house and lives on the proceeds.

他卖掉房子，以房款收入为生。

- The estate agent required 2% commission on the proceeds from the sale of the house.

房地产经纪人要求收取出售房子实得款项的2%作为佣金。

- One-sixth of the gold paid into the IMF in quotas was to be returned to members, one-sixth to be auctioned by the IMF to private buyers with the proceeds being used to benefit the developing countries. (顾维勇，2015：39)

按配额付给国际货币基金组织黄金的六分之一返还给成员国，另六分之一由国际货币基金组织拍卖给私人买主，此拍卖所得款项用于援助发展中国家。

再看下面例句中复数名词的含义及翻译：

- Collections are money collected or received. 收取款指收到的钱。

单数名词 collection 一般指"托收"。如：

- We are sending our draft through the Bank of China on (for) documentary collection.

我们把汇票交由中国银行跟单托收。

复数名词 collections 则为"收取款项"，即"收款额"。如：

- The total collections today amounts to $78,990. 今天收款总额为78990美元。

再如：

- He was awarded $500 damages for the injury he had suffered in the accident.

他因事故受伤得到了500美元的损害赔偿(费)。

- They claim £700 damages for the loss sustained. (or: They claim damages of £700 for the loss sustained.)

对所受损失，他们索赔700英镑的损害赔偿费。(杨佑方，2002：381)

- They found difficulty in meeting the engagements. 他们发现还债(指：债款)有困难。

- All expenses and risks thereinafter shall be born by your side.

此后发生的一切开支费用及风险损失费均由贵方承担。

- No salary shall be paid and charged against the operating expenses, provided that the commission or brokerage of the Second Party shall be paid and charged as a part of the operating expenses.

若应将支付第二方的佣金或回扣作为<u>营业费</u>的一部分，则不应在<u>营业费</u>中支付和计算薪金。

下面例句中原译者忽视了复数形式而造成了误译：

● Another factor behind the increase in merger activity is the record performance of stock markets, which has enabled companies to finance major acquisitions on the strength of their inflated share <u>prices</u>.

原译：导致合并不断增加的另一个因素是股票市场的空前繁荣。股票市场的空前繁荣使得各家公司可以依赖其上涨的<u>股票价格</u>去资助各种大规模的购进。（张新红等，2003：39）

译文 2：企业并购现象不断增加，这背后的另一个原因是，股票市场达到了空前繁荣。这种空前繁荣，使得各家公司能够依靠其<u>因股票上涨而获得大量资金</u>这一实力，为各种大规模并购项目提供资金保障。（李明，2011：69）

这里译者显然没有考虑到商务文体英语里的这种独特的语法现象。公司依赖其"上涨的股票价格"怎么能资助"各种大规模的购进"呢？这里复数形式 prices 表示"量"，是一个由 price 引申出来的"量"，指"股价上涨而获得的资金"。

改译：导致公司购并增长的另一个原因是股票市场的空前繁荣。许多上市公司可以用<u>股价上涨获得的资金</u>为大的购并项目提供金融保障。

● Cargo insurance is to protect the trader from <u>losses</u> that many dangers may cause.

原译：货物保险会使贸易商免受许多风险所可能造成的<u>种种损失</u>。（张新红等，2003：39）

此例中的 losses 为 loss 的复数形式，表示"<u>经济损失额</u>"，然而原译者却认为，这里的复数形式 losses 在译文是"通过重叠量词'种'来体现其复数的"，这就忽视了这种特殊语法现象。

改译：货物保险可以保护商人免遭各种危险可能造成的<u>经济损失</u>。

但注意下句中的 losses 不是指"经济损失"：

● Governments effectively suspended the gold standard during World War I and financed part of their massive military <u>expenditures</u> by printing money. Moreover, labor forces and productive capacity had been reduced sharply through war <u>losses</u>.（顾维勇，2010：12）

第一次世界大战期间，这些政府有效地暂停了金本位制，以印钞的方法支付了大量的<u>军费开支</u>中的部分款项。而且，由于战争<u>伤亡</u>，劳动力和生产力急剧下降。

句中的 expenditures 为复数形式，指"军费开支额"，但后一个 losses 并非商务英语中常用的"经济损失"，而是指"（战争中人员的）伤亡"。

● Subject to the above stipulations, the <u>profits</u>, <u>losses</u> and <u>risks</u> of the Joint Venture Company shall be borne by the Parties in proportion to their respective <u>contributions</u> to the registered capital of the Joint Venture Company.

原译：在上述规定范围内，各方按各自对合资企业的注册资本出资比例分享合资企业的<u>利润</u>，并承担合资企业遭受的<u>亏损</u>和<u>风险</u>。

35

这里 profits，losses，risks，contributions 分别指利润额、亏损额、风险赔偿额、出资额。

改译：在上述规定范围内，各方按各自对合资企业的注册资本出资比例分享合资企业的利润额，并分担合资企业的亏损额和风险赔偿额。

• International business activities also include an extensive range of optional methods available to firms for doing business internationally that involve different degrees of foreign direct investment commitments.

原译：国际商务活动也包括一系列可供公司作选择的进行国际贸易的方法。这些方法包括外国直接投资的不同程度的承诺。（李明，2011：96）

复数词 commitments 专业所指为"投资款；承付款项，佣金"，这里指"投资额"。

改译：国际商务活动也包括大量可供公司从事国际贸易选择性的方法，涉及外国直接投资的不同额度。

• International countertrade is a practice whereby a supplier commits contractually — as a condition of sale — to reciprocate and undertake certain specified commercial initiatives that compensate and benefit the buyer.

原译：国际对等贸易作为一种销售条件，是指供应方以合同方式，承诺对某些特别的、给购买方以补偿和利益的商务提案予以回报和承办的一种做法。（李明，2011：118）

原作者说明：对照原文的语序和汉语译文的语序便可发现，变序翻译的意义就在于译文根据地道、通顺的汉语来行文，从而让译文读者一看便明白原文所传达的意义所在。

实际上，作者对源语的所指不明白，特别是 undertake certain specified commercial initiatives 确保约定的商业盈利/利润，复数 initiatives 的所指是本句理解的关键所在。

改译：国际对销贸易的一般做法是，供应商以合同的形式承诺，作为销售条件，互惠交换货物，确保约定的商业利润以补偿买方。

2.2.2 复数表示款项或有价证券

2.2.2.1 表示费用、金额等

在商务文体语境中，复数词语常用来表示款项或费用，尤其是一些与支付有关的词语大量地见于商务文体中。常见的词语如下：

advance 进展，（数量、价格等的）增长→advances 垫付预支款（bank advances 银行放款）；

cost 成本→costs 费用；

charges 泛指费用，单复数均可（landing charges 上岸费，卸货费；bank charges 银行费用，也说 ledger fees）；surcharges 附加费；

amend 修改→amends 赔款；

deposit 存款→deposits 存款额；

benefit 利益，好处（不可数）→benefits 救济金，补助金；

credit 信用，信誉→credits 信贷额；

debt 债务→debts 债款；

arrears 应付欠款，（如：inter-enterprise arrears 三角债）；

drawing 提款→drawings 用汇票支取的金额；

dues 应缴款，码头的各种费用(light dues 灯塔费)；

expenses 开支，经费(如：operating expenses 营业费用，traveling expenses 差旅费)；

tax 税→taxes 税额；

fund 基金，专款→funds 资金，存款(如：no funds 没存款)；

loan 贷款→loans 贷款额；savings 存款；

outstandings 未偿付贷款，未清算账目，股东持有的股票；

payment 支付(不可数)→payments 付款额，支付的款项(可数)，与此词同根的有 prepayments 预付款；

wage 工资(不可数)→wages 报酬；

profit 利润→profits 利润额；

borrow 借→borrows 借款额。

注意下列例句中上述相关复数词的意义及翻译：

• Thus, the much looser Marshall Plan — the European Recovery Program — was set up to provide U. S. finance to rebuild Europe largely through grants rather than loans.

所以，相当宽松的马歇尔援助计划——欧洲复兴计划——被提出，在很大程度上通过拨专款而非贷款为美国提供资金用于欧洲的重建。

• From 1948 to 1954 the United States gave 16 Western European countries $17 billion in grants.

从 1948 年至 1954 年美国给 16 个西欧国家总计 170 亿美元的专用拨款。

以上二例中的 grants 意为：a giving of funds for a specific purpose "专用拨款"。

• The fiscal discipline imposed by Bretton Woods made the U. S. the only nation that could afford large-scale foreign deployments within the Western alliance.

布雷顿森林体系推行的财政纪律使美国成了西方同盟国唯一能支付大规模对外军费的国家。

deployments 本义为"军队的部署，调度"，这里指"军费开支"，相当于 military expenses。

• While the IBRD raises most of its funds on the world's financial markets, IDA is funded largely by contributions from the governments of its richer member countries. Additional funds come from IBRD's income and from borrowers' repayments of earlier IDA credits. (顾维勇，2010：85)

当国际复兴开发银行(IBRD)在世界金融市场筹措其大部分资金时，国际开发协会(IDA)则得到了其较富有成员国政府的捐资。另有资金来自于国际复兴开发银行的收入，以及早期国际开发协会贷款借款国的还款。

这个句子中有多个复数词语：funds 资金，contributions 出资额，repayments 还款，credits 贷款。

- Its founders saw IDA as a way for the "haves" of the world to help the "have-nots". (顾维勇，2010：86)

其缔造者们设想国际开发协会(IDA)会成为世界上"富国"帮助"穷国"的一个途径。

这里 haves 指"富国"，have-nots 指"穷国"。

- ADB raises funds through bond issues on the world's capital markets, while also utilizing its members' contributions and earnings from lending. These sources account for almost three quarters of its lending operations. (顾维勇，2010：89)

亚洲开发银行通过向世界资本市场发放债券来筹集资金，同时也利用其成员国的出资以及发放贷款所得收益。这些资本资源几乎占了其贷款业务的四分之三。

句中复数词 funds，contributions，earnings 均含有"款额"的意思。

- Real estate loans were spread throughout the financial system in the form of CDOs and other complex derivatives in order to disperse risk; however, when home values failed to rise and home owners failed to keep up with their payments, banks were forced to acknowledge huge write downs and write offs on these products. These write downs found several institutions at the brink of insolvency with many being forced to raise capital or go bankrupt. (顾维勇，2010：240)

整个金融系统全面开展房贷业务，其形式包括担保债务凭证和其他复杂的衍生品以分散风险。然而，当房价停涨而且房主无法还贷时，银行被迫承认这些房产巨大的减记额和销账款。这些减记款导致少数机构濒临破产，还有许多机构被迫集资或宣布破产。

句中 loans 表示"贷款额"，payments 表示"付(还)款额"，write downs 和 write offs 分别表示"减记额"和"销账款"。

- Alternative policies were adopted but resulted in very limited success. They included the increase of short-term interest rates to discourage short-term capital outflows, the decrease of the long-term interest rates to stimulate domestic production, interventions in foreign exchange markets, and a number of direct controls over capital outflows. (顾维勇，2015：19)

尽管采取了多种政策但收效极其有限。这些政策包括提高短期利率以阻止短期资金外流，降低长期利率以刺激国内生产，干预外汇市场，以及一系列直接控制资金外流的措施。

句中 outflows 为"流出额"，即：流向国外的资本。

- Your letter of credit is to allow 2% more or less in drawings.

贵方信用证支取款允许2%的上下浮动。

- After the Second World War some countries in Europe agreed to make their currencies freely convertible into gold for international payments only, thus forming a gold standard that was entirely external.

"二战"后，有些欧洲国家同意其货币可以自由兑换黄金，但只限于国际支付款。这样就形成了完全对外的金本位。

名词 payment 作"支付""付款"解时，为不可数，如：

- Payment will be made upon receipt of the goods with a discount of 5% for cash payment.

收货付款，现金支付九五折。

38

而复数形式 payments 表示"支付的款项"，如：

- You agree to repay this loan by 10 weekly <u>payments</u> of £10.

你同意每周<u>支付</u> 10 英镑，十周还清此贷款。

- In this case, foreigners' net imports from Britain are not being financed entirely by British <u>loans</u>. （顾维勇，2015：3）

既然这样，外国人从英国的净进口就不可能全部用英国的<u>贷款</u>来支付。

- Buyer must be responsible for all <u>movements</u> of the goods from inland point of loading, and pay all transportation <u>costs</u>.

买方应负责将货物从内陆装货地开始的所有<u>运输活动</u>，并支付一切运输<u>费用</u>。

名词复数 costs 指"费用"。

- One way that the banks themselves make money is by lending their <u>funds</u> at a higher rate of interest than they pay.

银行自己挣钱的一种手段是以高于其支付（给储户）的利息贷出其存款资金。

再讨论几个更高层面的复数翻译问题。

2016 年 9 月 30 日新华社报道：10 月 1 日，人民币将正式进入特别提款权（SDR）货币篮子中，比重为 10.92%，成为继美元、欧元、日元和英镑之后的第五种"入篮"货币。"入篮"SDR 是人民币成为国际储备货币的重要标志，有了国际货币基金组织（IMF）的认定，未来人民币国际化进程会明显加快，人民币的国际地位也会显著提高。国际货币基金组织（International Monetary Fund，IMF）的 SDRs 被译为"特别提款权"。根据本小节所述内容，这里的 rights 为有权提取的款项，而不是提款权。

- In 1962, the IMF negotiated <u>the General Arrangements to Borrow</u> up to $6 billion from the so-called "Group of Ten" most important industrial nations (the U.S., the United Kingdom, West Germany, Japan, France, Italy, Canada, the Netherlands, Belgium, and Sweden). （顾维勇，2015：17）

- Starting in the early 1960s, member nations started to negotiate <u>stand-by arrangements</u>, referring to advance permission for future borrowings by the nation in IMF. Nations negotiated these arrangements for defense against anticipated destabilizing hot money flows. National central banks also began to negotiate so-called <u>swap arrangements</u> to exchange each other's currency to be used to intervene in foreign exchange markets to combat hot money flows. （顾维勇，2015：18）

上面两例中，出现了几个概念：the General Arrangements to Borrow，stand-by arrangements，swap arrangements，它们的核心词是一个复数 arrangements，官方媒体均定名为"安排"，分别为"借款总安排""准备安排""交换安排（协定）"，值得深思。

2.2.2.2　复数表示债券或股票

在商务文体英语中，有些名词的复数形式表示债券或股票，翻译时值得注意。如：
bonds 意为"不记名债券（不可数）"，其单数 bond "债券"则为可数；bunds 指"由政府或公司发行的债券"，而 debenture 通常指"公司债券"，即：由国家或政府的公司或机构发行的无担保的债券，以发行者的信誉作保障（an unsecured bond issued by a civil or governmental corporation or agency and backed only by the credit standing of the issuer）。

securities 为"有价证券"的统称；

shares（Br. E）和 stocks（Am. E）都表示"股票的量""股份额"；

ways-and-means advances（英格兰银行的）短期贷款；

yearlings 一年期定期债券；

gains 涨价的股票；

interests 利益，股份；

floaters 政府不记名债券；

Kaffirs（英伦敦证券交易所的）南非金矿股票（不可数）；

funds（英国）指只付利息的长期公债，当作公共有价证券使用，常与 the 连用。

这类词语中也有少数由形容词转换而得的名词复数，如：industrials 工业股票或债券；irredeemables 不赎回债券，无偿还债券。

2.2.3　从形式上看，有两个或两个以上名词均用复数

terms and conditions 条款：前者指总括性纲领性条款，后者指细则性条款；

fixtures and fittings 固定装置及设备，房屋固定附属物；

ways and means（达到某种目的的）方法，资金；

goods and chattels 个人动产；

receipts and payments account 收付账；

haves and have-nots 富人与穷人，富国与穷国。

2.2.4　有少数由形容词转换来的名词形式表示数量

值得一提的是，这类词的复数形式也常用来表示量或款项，如：

movable 活动的，变动的→movables 动产；

overhead 在头上的，高架的→overheads 企业管理费用，相当于 overhead costs/expenses；

invisible 无形的→invisibles = invisible imports and exports 无形出口商品与无形进口商品。同样地，visibles = visible imports and visible exports 有形进出口商品；

receivable 可接受的→receivables 应收账款；

outstanding 未付清的，已发行的→outstandings 未偿付的贷款，未清算的账目，股东持有的股票；

valuable 有价值的，贵重的→valuables 贵重物品。如：

- receivables turnover 应收账款周转率
- cash and receivables 现金及应收账款
- Banks originated as places in which people took their valuables for safe-keeping, but today the great banks of the world have many functions in addition to acting as guardians of valuable private possessions. 银行在其起源时曾是为人们安全保管贵重物品的地方，但如今，除了担当贵重私有财产卫士的角色以外，世界大银行还有很多的功能。

2.2.5 其他复数形式

这些复数词中，名词所表达的概念与单数的概念完全不同，但不表示量或款项。如：

custom 习惯→customs 海关；

document 文件→documents 单证；

ends 生产经济目标；

majors = major oil companies 大石油公司；

specification 具体规定→specifications 规格；

hand 手→　hands 办理；

going 进展→goings 行为举止；

minority interests/shareholders 少数股东；

majority shareholders 多数股东。

在翻译实践中，我们必须重视这些复数形式的词语，弄清这类复数词语的意义，也就是源语的"所指"，否则会因错译而贻笑大方。

2.3　专　业　知　识

翁凤翔（2002：35）在谈到国际商务英语的特点时说，"国际商务英语实用性的特点使得国际商务英语的翻译者明白，为了提高翻译质量，他必须对众多的国际商务业务有所了解，并且精通其中一门专业"。从事商务文体翻译的译者须具备两个基本的条件，即扎实的英语语言功底和一定的专业知识，这两者缺一不可。光有扎实的语言功底，对源语的理解似乎完全正确，如果没有较好的专业知识，译文不可能符合商务文体的表达要求。其实在缺乏专业知识的情况下，译者无法找到或译出相关专门的表达，尤其是"术语""行话"的表达不可能做到地道、对应。所以，在某种意义上说，增加专业知识的意识是做好商务文体翻译的核心意识。

● The largest single issue in the preparation, presentation, and verification of documentation by sellers, buyers, and banks is consistency among documents. （Hinkelman，2009：13）

原译：在准备、提交和审查单据时，最大的问题是单据的一致性。（李月菊，2009：ii）

原句中的三个表达：preparation, presentation, and verification of documentation 分别指"制单、交单和验单"，而非"准备、提交和审查单据"。preparation of documentation 指单证的缮制，presentation of documentation 指提交单证，而 verification of documentation 指单证的验审，是单证办理的三个阶段，业内通常表达为"制单、交单、验单/审单"，尤其是 preparation of documentation 不可译为"准备单据"，"准备"在这里不是专业表达。

改译：卖方、买方及银行在制单、交单和验单过程中最大的问题在于单证的一致性。

● STOWAGE INSTRUCTIONS These are specific instructions given by the consignor in a letter or on a shipping line or freight forwarder's pre-printed form regarding how or where a shipment should be stowed during transport. For example, a shipper may require that the shipment be placed below deck and amidships for greater protection from the elements and movement of the ship. (Hinkelman, 2009: 39)原译：装载或理舱须知，理舱须知(李月菊，2009: iii)

英语 STOWAGE INSTRUCTIONS 是一个外贸运输中的专业概念，原作者在解释中说得非常清晰：

这些是发货人以信件或以货运公司或货代打印格式给出的专门指令，说明运输途中货物应如何或在何处装载。如：发货人可要求其货物舱内(甲板下)装载或船舯装载以获得更好的保护免遭来自船舶及其航行造成的影响。

根据原文的语境，英语 STOWAGE INSTRUCTIONS 应译成对应的专业表达："配/积载指令"。英语 STOWAGE 可以指"配载"，亦可指"积载"，有双重释义。"配载"是将货物分配到各个船舱或舱面，回答货物 where to be stowed 的问题，而"积载"指货物堆装，回答货物 how to be stowed 的问题，指不同阶段的两项不同的活动。

● Many small service firms fail to analyze their services' total cost, and therefore fail to price them profitably.

原译：许多小型劳务公司不去分析劳务总成本，因此也无法为服务项目定出有利可图的价格。(叶玉龙等，1998: 69)

此译例中，译者对商务英语语境下 service 的概念理解有误。service 在商务英语中常常理解为"服务(业)"。在国际贸易中，根据贸易的内容分为商品贸易(commodity trade)、服务贸易(service trade)和技术贸易(technology trade)。商品贸易为有形贸易(visible trade)，而服务贸易和技术贸易均为无形贸易(invisible trade)。我们常说的"劳务"或"劳务输出"是指劳动力作为类似于商品的输出，应属有形贸易。

改译：很多小型服务公司因为没有分析其项目的总成本而无法为其服务项目制定可赢利的价格。

除了语言功底和商务知识以外，译者在翻译过程中必须有强烈的商务语境意识，注意商务文体中的语用信息的正确理解与翻译。这种意识体现在译者阅读原文时就应警觉到商务英语的语境，进而从商务的视角去理解原文所要表达的意思。

● The credit which evidences shipment of 2,000 tons of steels may be used against presentation of the shipping documents.

原译1：该信用证证明装两千吨钢材凭提交装船单据使用。

原译2：该信用证证明装运两千吨钢材，可凭提交装船单据加以议付。(叶玉龙等，1998: 23)

这里译者在改译中已经注意到了商务的语境，将 use 理解并翻译为"议付"，但是作为商务语境下的表达仍需改进。根据本句的语境，shipping documents 应理解并译成"装运单证"。

改译：本信用证证明两千吨钢材已装船，凭装运单证议付。

● Buyers or their chartering agent shall advise the Seller by fax 10 days prior to the arrival of the carrying vessel at the port of shipment of the contract number, name of the carrying vessel, approximate loading capacity, lay days and port of loading.

原译：买方或其租船代理人须于载货轮抵达装运港 10 天前以传真方式通知卖方合同号、船名、<u>大约受载重量</u>、<u>预计抵达日期</u>及装运港名。（张新红等，2003：96）

此译例有以下几方面值得商榷：（1）在商务语境下 chartering agent 一般称作"船代"，全称为"租船代理人/商，租船代理行"，与其对应的词语为 freight agent "货代"，全称为"货物代理人/商，货物代理行"；（2）lay days 是指规定的船舶在港装卸货天数/时间，如果超过了这个时间就要付"滞期费"demurrage，也称"搁港费"；（3）carrying vessel 术语为"承运船"而非"载货轮"；（4）approximate loading capacity 意为船舶的"近似载重量"；（5）原译句式欧化，不符合商务文本的表达规范。

改译：在承运船抵达装货港 10 天前，买方或其船代须将合同号、承运船名、<u>船舶的近似载重量</u>、<u>船舶在港时间</u>和装货港以传真的方式告知卖方。

● International business as a field of management training <u>deals with</u> the special features of business activities that across national boundaries.

原译 1：作为管理训练一个领域的国际商务<u>具有</u>跨国家边界商务活动的专门特征。（张新红等，2003：66）

原译 2：作为管理训练领域中的国际商务，<u>具有</u>跨疆界的各种商务活动的独特性。（李明，2011：65）

原译 2 的译者解释：英语原文中"deal with"的基本意思是"安排""处理""涉及""做生意"，选择这些表达中的任何一个均无法同后面的"独特性"搭配起来，因此需要对"deal with"这一短语进行引申而翻译成"具有"才能通顺地表达原文之意。

此例是典型的缺乏商务知识而导致对"国际商务"这个概念的定义错译的例句。其中：（1）management training 为"管理培训"，非"管理训练"。"培训"（training）相对于"教育"（education）而言，前者是让"受培训者"（trainee）接受一个专项的或专门的培养训练，而后者是让"受教育者"（educatee）接受全面系统的正规教育；（2）deal with 这里是"研究，讨论"的意思，而非"具有"；（3）field 这里意为 a topic, a subject, or an area of academic interest or specialization "主题，课题"，亦指学术兴趣或专业课程。

改译：作为管理培训的一门课程，国际商务<u>研究（讨论）</u>跨国界商务活动的特征。

● Frequently parties to a contract are unaware of the different <u>trading practices</u> in their respective countries.

原译：合同当事人对于他们各自国家之间不同的<u>贸易习惯</u>，往往不甚了解。（叶玉龙等，1998：95）

practice 在商务英语文体中通常理解为"惯例"，即常规的做法，与"习惯"的含义不同。

改译：合同各方常常没有意识到（或译：常常忽视）各国间不同的<u>贸易惯例</u>。

商务英语文体中词语的语用信息必须结合商务英语语境来理解，即词语所指的是与商务相关的内容，而非普通英语语境下的含义。只有当这些语用信息被完全准确地理解后，译者才可将正确的译文呈现给读者。否则，一味地望文生义，译出的作品令人啼笑皆非。

● There is a tendency for an organization of this type to be rather <u>romantic</u>; <u>this place</u> isn't romantic — it actually makes money. He is impressed equally by the open information policy, which circulates details of all meetings to employees, and the rapid growth.

原译 1：这样的公司常常是很浪漫的，但这个<u>地方</u>并不浪漫，实际上它是赚钱的。公司的信息公开政策同样给他以很深的印象，所有公司的会议的细节及迅速发展状况都传达给雇员。（张新红等，2003：109）

原译 2：这种类型的机构往往有着相当浪漫的气息。但这个<u>地方</u>并不<u>浪漫</u>——它实际上是个赚钱的<u>地方</u>。他印象同样深刻的是，公司采取了信息公开制度，根据该制度，所有会议的细节以及公司快速发展的细节都要一一传给员工。（李明，2011：117）

原译 2 的译者分析：对比原文和译文不难发现，译文基本上按照原文的语序行文，但原文中各个句子的主语同译文中各个句子的主语不完全一样。原文第一句话中第一个分句的主语是"tendency"，第二句话中的主语是"he"，主句之后的非限定性定语从句由关系代词"which"引导，"which"指代前面的先行词"the open information policy"，整个汉语译文基本上是按照英语原文的语序行文，但汉语译文对其中很多表述上的细节作了更改，使得汉语译文充分突出了所描述公司的所作所为及其理念。

此例句中译者因缺乏商务专业知识而对几个关键词语的语用意义理解错误造成误译。

（1）romantic 一词应当如何理解、如何翻译？根据句中对某种公司（organization）的描述，并与下文联系起来审读我们不难发现此词可理解为"虚构的；夸大的；不真实的"imaginative but impractical；not based on fact，imaginary（*The American Heritage Dictionary*，1982：1070）。如：a romantic scheme"不现实的计划"；a romantic report "失实的报道"。所以，原译"浪漫的"显然是对此词语用信息的误译；（2）place 一词译为"地方"，很明显是讲不通的，而且所指不明确。根据此句的商务语境，其语用意义应为 a business establishment or office，即"商务公司"或"办事处"，与上文的"公司"（organization）在意义的表达上方可一致；（3）除了两个词语的语用意义误读外，译者对原句结构理解也有错误。

改译：这种类型的公司常有浮夸的倾向，而这家公司并非如此——实际上，它是盈利的。公司的信息公开政策以及迅速成长的态势在相同程度上给他以深刻的印象，信息公开政策是指所有会议的具体内容都传达到全体员工。

- All services in business — such as gift wrapping, delivery, and credit — have some amount of costs associated with them, and these costs must be <u>covered</u> by higher prices.

原译 1：商业中所有的服务——诸如礼品包装、送货以及赊账——都有相应的成本，而这些成本要靠较高的价格来<u>弥补</u>。（张新红等：2003：64）

原译 2：商业中的一切服务——如礼品包装、送货及赊账——都有相应的成本，而这些成本要靠较高的价格来<u>弥补</u>。（李明，2011：64）

原译 1 的译者其译文下的分析中说明："cover 一词在英语中的意思是'包括，包含，覆盖'，这里选取任何一个意义来翻译本例句中 cover 一词都无法充分再现原文的意义。将该词引申为'弥补'才符合地道的汉语表达"。

从这个说明中我们可以看出作者已经注意到了商务文体的语境，但对此语境下 cover 一词的语用信息因缺乏商务英语专业知识而造成理解错误。

查阅《美国传统词典》，cover 词条下有 to compensate or make up for "赔偿，弥补"的释

义，也有 to be sufficient to defray，meet，or offset the cost or charge of，(AHD，1982：334)"足以支付，足以补偿，足够支付"的意思。

在商务英语文体中，cover 是一个常用的词汇，通常表示"支付"。在保险业中，它指"承保"的险别(the security provided by insurance or assurance against a specified risk (*Oxford Dictionary of Business*，2000：135-136))。如：It is our usual practice to arrange credit to cover the shipment at least one month ahead. 我们的惯例是至少提前一个月开具支付货款的信用证。(杨佑方，2002：358) You have to cover TPND (Theft，Pilferage and Non-Delivery) insurance for our order. 你必须给我们的订货保盗窃提货不着险。(杨佑方，2002：358)

改译：商务活动中的所有服务，诸如礼品包装、送货和赊购等都有其相应的成本，而这些成本必须通过提高价格得到补偿。

● The higher IMF estimates may be better yardsticks of economic progress.

原译：国际货币基金组织的较高的<u>估计</u>可能是衡量经济进步的比较科学的标准。(叶玉龙等，1998：79)

读者一看便知，此译有误。IMF"较高的估计"怎么可能是"比较科学的标准"呢？显然 estimates 的商务专业语用信息被误读误译了。英语中 the Estimates(注意复数形式)指"(英国财政大臣每年提交议会的)国家支出预算"，这里指国际货币基金组织(International Monetary Fund)所作的"预算"，它可以用来判断或衡量世界经济的发展。这里两个比较级的形容词 higher 和 better 的语用意义也要作一些分析。前者一般理解为"高级的"或"高等的"，IMF 所作的"预算"应该是"权威的"，笔者认为可省去不译；而后者可理解为"更合适的""更合理的"。

改译：国际货币基金组织的<u>预算</u>可以作为衡量(判断)世界经济发展更为合适的标准。

● A given currency could，therefore，never rise above nor fall bellow <u>fixed points</u> which are called intervention points.

原译：因此，一种货币上升时既不得高于<u>固定点</u>，下降时也不能低于它。这个固定点就被称为"干预点"。(叶玉龙等，1998：85)

译者同样因为缺乏商务英语专业知识而没有读懂原文里 fixed points 以及 intervention points 的语用信息，信手译来，必定犯错。细心的读者会发现这里 points 用的都是复数，而且讲了两种情形——"升值"与"贬值"，而不是原译的"上升"和"下降"，翻译时译者如能考虑到这点的话也不至于译错。intervention points 是指"价格波动的上下限"，同样含有"升值"与"贬值"两种情形，不能合二为一。

改译：因此，某种货币升值时不得高于<u>上限定点</u>，贬值时亦不得低于<u>下限定点</u>。这两个定点就称作为干预点——币值波动的上下限。

● Banks assume no liability or responsibility for the consequences arising out of delay and/or <u>loss</u> in transit of any <u>messages</u>，letters or <u>documents</u>.

原译：任何通知、函件或<u>单据</u>因投递迟误或在邮寄途中<u>遗失</u>，银行概不承担责任或义务。(陈仕彬，2002：27)

(1)messages 在商务语境中通常指电报报文或无线电电文，通常可译为"信文"，这里可理解为"(简短的)信息(或消息)"，包括"通知"。商务英语中"通知"大多用 "notice"

一词；（2）letters 这里指"信件"；（3）documents 指"单证"；（4）transit 指"（跨国）运送/输"。习语 in transit 意为"在运输中"；（5）and/or 广泛应用于法律或商务文件中，表示"其中之一项或两项都"，通常译为"和/或"；（6）liability or responsibility 为近义词语叠用，因此，这里 assume no liability or responsibility for…指"对……概不负责"。在商务英语中，"责任和义务"通常用 duties and obligations 来表示。

改译：对于寄发中的通知、信件或单证的延迟和/或灭失所引起的一切后果银行概不负责。

- 3/3 original clean on board bills of lading plus non negotiable copies made out or endorsed to the order of Israel discount bank fright prepaid and due to danger of confiscation warranted vessel is not to call at ports and not to enter the territorial waters of Syria, Lebanon, Jordan, Iraq, Saudi Arabia, Yemen, Sudan, Libya or other Arab countries prior to unloading in Israel unless in distress or subject to Force Majeure.

原译：受益人须提交 3 正 3 副已装船清洁海运提单，抬头做成凭以色列贴现银行指示或记名背书给该行并注明运费预付。鉴于货物存在被有关国家没收的危险，货物在运抵至以色列之前相关载货船舶不得在叙利亚、黎巴嫩、约旦、伊拉克、沙特阿拉伯、也门、苏丹、利比亚或阿拉伯国家的港口停靠或进入以上国家的领海，除非船舶在运输途中遭受海难事故或不可抗力。（梁雪松、陈黎峰：2007）

上述条款一般在中东国家的信用证上都有注明。译文中有几处缺乏国际贸易运输专门知识而误译：（1）warranted vessel 指"（授权许可的/正当的）承运船"，而"相关载货船舶"表达不专业；（2）in distress 指船舶"遇险"，而非"遭受海难事故"。

商务英语文体与普通英语文体有别，因此翻译规范亦完全不一样。商务文体包括多种文体，所以根据这种体中有体的特点，译者需要研究各种文体的语言特点和翻译要求，遵循商务文体的翻译规范。译者须明确，我们面对的文本所涉及的内容大多为商务类活动，其语言有着强烈的商务特色，而这类文本大量地涉及商务方面的专业知识以及行业独特的表达方式和专业术语，译者不但需要掌握翻译的技能还要具备相当的专业知识，才能胜任此项工作。同时，商务英语翻译专著的作者们在撰写著作时也须有商务专业知识，避免理论上讲得比较翔实，让读者感到是那么一回事，可一看译例又觉得不是那么一回事。这样，读者就会误入歧途。

而且，翻译商务英语的诸类文体时，译者必须考虑不同的文体特征，充分运用商务知识，采用不同的翻译方法与手段，将准确的译文呈现给读者。准确译文的内涵主要应包括：商务术语（行话）的对应表达、商务语言的正确运用、源语的正确理解以及译语的行文规范。

2.4　近/同义词叠用

近/同义词叠用是商务英语中频繁出现的一种表达方式，通常在合同等法律文书或法律文件等正式文体中使用。这种叠用确保了所用词语的意思不被曲解，并使原文意思高度完整、准确，更好地体现文本的严肃性，同时它使得表达更趋合理，内容更全面，也更具有弹性。这种词语叠用通常用 and 或 or 连接，如：loss or damage"灭失或损坏"，arising or resulting from"引起"，agent or representative"代表"，terms and conditions"条款"，alter and change"改变"，before and on（date）"在（某日期含该日）前"，void and null"无效"等，译者常因不了解这一专门知识而误译。

- Marketing occurs when people decide to satisfy needs and wants through exchange.

原译：当人们开始通过交换来满足欲望和需求的时候就出现了营销。（张新红等，2003：14）

原句中的 needs and wants 是指人们的各种"需求"，显然这是同义词叠用。

- Business is a combination of all these activities：production，distribution and sale，through which profit or economic surplus will be created.

原译：商务是指生产、配送、销售等一切活动的组合，通过这些活动，创造利润和经济盈余。（张新红等，2003：88）（李明，2011：94）

此句中，词语 profit or economic surplus，后者是对前者的解释说明，并非两个概念，可以看作同义词叠用。a combination of all these activities 译成"一切活动的组合"，不符合商务文献的表达规范。

改译：商务是指生产、配送、销售并创造利润的所有关联活动。

- Traditionally，business simply meant exchange or trade for things people wanted or needed，but today it has a more technical definition，which is the production，distribution，and sale of goods and service for a profit.

原译：传统上，商务仅指人们所需要的物品的交换或贸易。但是，今天商务有更为科学的定义，它是指为了利润而进行货物和劳务的生产、配送和销售的一种活动。（张新红等，2003：91）

在商务语境下，原译在以下几方面有误：（1）exchange or trade，wanted or needed 均为近义词叠用；（2）exchange or trade for things people wanted or needed 译为"人们所需要的物品的交换或贸易"不符合原意；（3）service 指"服务业务"而不是"劳务"，如：We provide a number of financial services. 我们提供多种金融服务。另外，这种有偿的或有利可图的"服务业务"恐怕不能"生产、配送和销售"。

改译：传统意义上的商务是指为了获得人们需求的物品而进行的交易活动。但是现在商务有了更为科学的定义：商务是为了获取利润而进行的商品的生产、配送和销售活动以及提供服务业务。

2.5 词语组合

在商务英语文本中我们会看到一些词语在不同的组合或搭配中表达完全不同的意思，在翻译的时候须充分考虑这个因素，如果顾名思义不加分析进行翻译同样会译错。

如 call loan 意为"短期同业拆借"；call market 意为"成批执行市场，把买卖订单归批处理的各类市场"，亦称 *Walrasian Market* "沃尔拉斯市场"。

broken space 如译成"打破了的空间"则无法理解。在国际贸易运输的语境下表示"亏舱",指货物装船时的一种情形,即舱未装满;broken amount 意为"零头股",指不规则股数,如 67 股;broken date 则指"非标准交易日期",亦称 odd date,反义为 even date"规则交易日期";broken cross rate 意为"有差距的套汇汇率",如:

- They seldom permit a broken cross rate in excess of 1 percent which suggests that when the break in cross rates crosses a threshold of between 1and 2 percent, it triggers on exchange rate change.

他们很少让有差距的套汇汇率的差距超过 1%,这表明当套汇汇率的差距超过 1% ~ 2% 的界限时会引发汇率的变化。(杨佑方,2002)

再看下面的例句中词语组合带来意义的改变:

- The rapid drop in value of securitized assets also forced margin calls as some hedge funds, for example, did not have sufficient additional collateral to protect against the margin call. (顾维勇,2010:243)

证券化资产的急剧跌价也迫使追加保证金,比如有些套利基金没有足够的追加担保品作为备款以支付追加保证金。

句中的 margin calls 为"追加保证金";hedge funds 为"套利基金"。

- In the event credit does not become more available in the near future, as owners' debt obligations come to maturity (especially in high leverage interest only deals), many will default due to their inability to make the balloon payment. (顾维勇,2010:251-252)

结果,在不久的将来不可能得到更多的贷款,当房主的债务到期还款时(尤其是高杠杆仅付息型贷款),其中很多房主会违约不还款,因为他们无力偿还大数额尾款。

这里的 balloon payment 指分期付款中最后一笔特大数额的付款。

在商务文体翻译实践中,文体意识涉及多个方面,这里主要讨论了五个方面,其中最基本的最重要的是要有提升专业知识的意识。同时,在商务文体翻译的教学中,这种文体意识涉及教材的文体意识和教学的文体意识,光有教材的文体意识,没有教学的文体意识不行。首先,教材的作者必须具备正常的文体意识进行教材的编著,符合商务英语及对应汉语的专业化表达;其次,商务英语的教师必须有文体意识,这些教师应当具有相当的专业经验或知识再加上强烈的文体意识才可以正确地理解文本、解读文本,在此前提下,方可给出正确的译文。

同时,从众多的错误译例中,我们也应意识到,商务文体翻译或者商务英语翻译的研究尚处于初始阶段,如何使翻译理论与翻译实践结合起来是亟待研究和解决的课题。那种理论上讲得头头是道,实践起来错误百出的翻译理论只能是空中楼阁;翻译理论研究必须联系翻译实际,并能指导翻译实践,不能应用于并且指导翻译实践的理论只能是纸上谈兵,没有实际意义;商务文体英语的翻译宜考虑不同的文体特点,采用不同翻译方法和技巧,取得良好的翻译效果。

第三章　商务文体词语翻译

由于商务文体种类不同，各种文体中的词语亦有不同的释义，所以在翻译时，我们要根据不同的文体和语境，选择不同语义。词语是构成句子的基本单位，词语的理解影响到整个句子的理解。因此，本章将讨论商务文体词语的翻译。

3.1　商务文体词语翻译种种

在商务文体的词语中，很多是一看便知其对应的词义，汉语说"顾名思义"，但由于商务文体的特点决定有大量的词语为专业术语或专门的名称，在翻译这类词语时往往需要译者的高度重视，否则，就不可避免地出现误译错译而贻笑大方，下面分别举例说明。

3.1.1　字面上能看出对应词义的词语

3.1.1.1　字面意义对等，所指亦明确的词语

- **face value**（货币及其他金融票据的）面值。
- **for the attention of** 由某人亲启；致某人：指明具体的收件人。此语常用缩略语为 attn，如：

for the attention of Mr. Brown 布朗先生亲启。

Attn Ms. Howard 本信由霍华德女士亲自处理。

- **horizontal integration** 横向合并：把生产同类商品或从事同一生产程序的公司合并。如：

The aim of horizontal integration is to eliminate competition.

横向合并是为了消除竞争。

- **multiple pricing** 多种定价：给同一产品在不同市场上定不同的价格。

Multiple pricing means that a lot can be saved on an item if you shop around.

多种定价意味着多转几家商店可节省不少钱。（货比三家不吃亏。）

- **price-earnings ratio** 价格收益比，（股票）市盈率。
- **purchasing power** 购买力。

注意此词语作"购买力"解时有两层意思，一是指"个人、组织、国家的购买力"（the amount of money that a person, an organization or a country has to buy goods and services），如：

Increased incomes have led to increased purchasing power in the community.

收入的增加导致了该社区购买力的提高。

该词语亦指"货币在某时期的购买力"（the value of a currency at a particular time），如：

an increase in the purchasing power of RMB 人民币购买力的上升

- **sale as seen** 凭现样销售：买方已查看货物，卖方对质量不作任何保证。
- **seasonal rate** 季节性收费/价格。如：

The seasonal rate is too high for us to advertise in the color supplement.

在彩色增版上做广告的时价对我们来说太高了。

- **secondary data** 第二手材料；间接资料。
- **third party insurance** 第三方保险：就投保人对第三方造成的人身伤害或财产损失提供赔偿。如：

You need to produce a third party insurance certificate.

你需要出示第三方保险凭证。

- **chamber of commerce** 商会。
- **commission** 佣金，回扣。
- **implied term** 暗含条款，默认条款。如：

It was an implied term that the bulk of the goods would correspond to the sample.

实际货品应与样品一致是暗含的条款。

- **intellectual property** 知识产权。如：

If you copy this design you will be infringing (i. e. encroaching) on intellectual property rights. 你若抄袭这项设计，就侵犯知识产权。

3.1.1.2　字面意义对等，但具有专门含义的词语

- **black economy** 黑市经济，专指涉及偷税、出售非法进口货物等的经济活动。

类似的用法还有：

- **black market** 黑市，指非法经营商品、买卖货币或劳务；
- **blacklist** 黑名单，包括不值得信任的个人或组织；
- **grey market** 灰市，指合法买卖供应短缺的商品；
- **heavy market** 在英国，此语意为"呆滞市场"，指价格下跌且买方不活跃，而在美国却意为"交易活跃市场"，指买卖量大且价格稳定。
- **black knight** 黑骑士，指试图收购(take over) 不愿意出售的公司。如：

A black knight has made an unwanted takeover bid.

黑骑士出价收购不愿意出售的公司。

类似的用法还有：

- **grey knight** 灰甲骑士，指企图收购某家公司，但不公布发展计划。
- **white knight** 白骑士，指把公司从不利的收购建议(takeover bid)中挽救过来的个人或机构。如：

A white knight stepped in and made a better offer.

一白骑士介入并提出更好的要约。

- **confidentiality agreement** 保密协议，指由雇员签署，声明不向竞争对手泄露公司秘密的协议。如：

All new employees must sign a confidentiality agreement.

全体新雇员必须签订保密协议。

· **dawn raid** 黎明突袭，指在股票市场开市头几分钟内乘证券经纪不备，突袭式大批买进一家公司的股票。

· **dead cat bounce** 死猫弹跳，指股价在大跌后短暂的回升。如：

Analysts in the City noted a slight recovery in share prices today, but some referred to it as a dead cat bounce.

伦敦城里的分析人士注意到今天股价稍有回升，但有些则称之为死猫弹跳。

· **inertia selling** 惰性销售，把货物发送给没有订货的人，对方若不购买就需把货物退还。

· **intervention price** 干预价格，指欧共体根据其共同农业政策（common agricultural policy）向无法售出产品的农场主收购农产品所支付的价格。如：

The Council of the European Community determined the intervention price on wheat.

欧共体委员会决定小麦的干预价格。

· **invisible exports/imports** 无形出口/进口，前者指一国向另一国提供的银行、保险和旅游等服务，后者指别国提供的银行、保险和旅游等服务。

· **kite mark** 风筝标记，指合格标记，它是形似风筝的标记，表明产品获得英国标准协会认可。如：

Always look for the kite mark when purchasing expensive goods.

购买贵重物品时，务必看清合格标记。

· **law of one price** 单一价格定律，它是一种获得普遍接受的观点，认为在没有贸易限制和运费的情况下，同样的商品在所有国家会以相同的价格出售。

The law of one price is linked to the belief in free trade.

单一价格与自由贸易的信念相关联。

· **letter of credit** 信用证，由一家银行发给另一家银行，表明客户等的第三方可获取款项。

I have arranged for any branch to send a letter of credit to the branch nearest to the hotel.

我已安排让本分行给离旅馆最近的分行发出信用证。

下面这些与信用证有关的词语字面意义似乎对等，但都有其所指，如：

· **circular letter of credit** 流通信用证，指由开证行发给其所有分行、往来银行和代理行。

The issuing branch sent out a circular letter of credit. 开证的分行发出了流通信用证。

· **confirmed letter of credit** 保兑信用证，须由支付银行担保。

The confirmed letter of credit forced the paying bank to honour the transaction.

保兑信用证迫使付款行承担这笔交易。

· **direct letter of credit** 直接信用证，由开证银行向特定的分行开出的信用证。

With a direct letter of credit money can be obtained at only one particular source.

使用直接信用证只能从唯一指定的来源提取款项。

· **documentary letter of credit** 跟单信用证，出口商须同时交出提货单、保险证等其他单证，才能向银行收取款项。

Money could not be obtained as the documentary letter of credit did not have an insurance certificate with it.

跟单信用证未附保险凭证，因此无法获得承兑。

* **irrevocable letter of credit** 不可撤销信用证，指除非信用人同意，信用证不得撤销。

He insisted on an irrevocable letter of credit. 他坚持只接受不可撤销信用证。

* **limited letter of credit** 有限信用证，只能在某些地方使用的流通信用证。

* **traveler's letter of credit** 旅游信用证，旅游者凭证可在签发银行在国外的任何代理行预支某限额的款项。

When the traveler's letter of credit is used up it should be sent back to the issuing bank.

旅游信用证的款额用完后，该证应寄回开证银行。

* **unconfirmed letter of credit** 不/非保兑信用证，指开证行不保证兑付所开立的汇票。

This company will not accept unconfirmed letters of credit.

这家公司不接受未保兑的信用证。

* **marketing mix** 营销组合，指公司能够控制的影响销售的四个要素，包括产品(Product)、定价(Pricing)、促销(Promotion)、地点(Place)，一般称为四个"P"。

We have worked hard to get the right marketing mix for the launch of the new range.

我们努力找出新产品系列的合适营销组合。

3.1.1.3 机构等专有名称

* **the Advisory Conciliatory and Arbitration Service** [英]咨询调解仲裁局。

* **the Advertising Association** [英]广告协会，旨在维持广告的水平，保护广告客户及代理商的利益。

* **the Advertising Standards Authority** [英]广告标准管理局，旨在保护公众不受广告误导。

* **the Bank for International Settlement** 常用略语 BIS，国际清/结算银行。

* **Federal Reserve Bank/Board/System** 分别指美国"联邦储备银行/委员会/系统"。它们的功能为：联邦储备委员会总部设在华盛顿，负责管理美国的中央银行系统，即联邦储备系统；联邦储备系统向政府和其他银行提供融资，并发行纸币和硬币；而联邦储备银行属于联邦储备系统，负责向各州立及国家银行提供融资。

* **International Monetary Fund** 国际货币基金组织，这是联合国的一个机构，负责向贫穷国家贷款以促进贸易和经济发展。

3.1.1.4 缩略词语

* **MRP**：manufacturer's recommended price 制造商/厂家建议零售价

* **pr**：public relation 公共关系

* **ppi**：producer price index 生产者价格指数；生产物价指数

* **vat**：value added tax 增值税

- **afmd**：aforementioned 前面提到的，上述的。这种用法仅用于书面语。如：

Please note afmd name. 请注意上述名称。

- **c/o** 1. care of 由……转交。如：

Mr. Brown, c/o Mr. and Mrs. Philips 由菲利普斯夫妇转交布朗先生

2. certificate of origin 原产地证明书

- **EEC**：European Economic Community 欧(洲经济)共(同)体
- **EFTA**：European Free Trade Association 欧洲自由贸易联盟

3.1.2 字面上看不出对应词义的词语

这类词语主要是一些专业术语或是行话，有其约定俗成的表达，不得随意改变或杜撰其对应语义。下面从几个方面举例说明。

3.1.2.1 字面意义不等，但所指语义明确的词语

- **accommodation bill**（由票据融通人 accommodation party 签署作为担保人的）融通汇票
- **accommodation paper** 融通票据(附有融通背书)
- **account terms** 确认付账

invoice marked "account terms" 标明"确认付账"字样的发票

- **act of God** 不可抗力；天灾。另有一些同义词语，如：irresistible force, ［French］force majeure, ［Latin］vis major, 等。
- **adoption of contract** 承认可撤销的契约
- **back order** 未交清订货；待发货订单
- **back out** 不履行协议
- **block release** 短期脱产进修(一星期至数星期)。如：

We're short-staffed at the moment as two of our team are on block release.

我们目前人员不足，因为队里有两人脱产进修。

- **blue chip** 蓝筹股，指公司经营稳健，风险较小的股票。如：

She put her money into blue chips. 她将资金投资在蓝筹股上。

- **carriage forward** 常缩略为：**carr. fwd.** 或 **CF**，外贸运输术语，意为"运费到付；运费由收货人支付"。
- **the Civil Service** 常缩略为 **CS**，意为"文职/行政部门(除军队以外的政府部门)"。如：

The government has announced pay rises for members of the Civil Service.

政府已宣布文职公务员的加薪幅度。

- **Clean bill of health** 健康证明书，也指外贸运输中(港务局签发的)无疫证明书。如：

Owing to an epidemic in the port locality, the ship left without a clean bill of health.

由于港口地区有流行病，船舶离港没有获得无疫证明书。

- **clear** 一词是个常用词，但在商务文体中下列几个释义值得注意。(1)商贸中的"抛

售"；（2）银行业务中的"票据交换；结算"；（3）进出口贸易中的"清/结关"。

● **consumer durables** 耐用消费品，如汽车、家具、冰箱、电视机等。与此词语相反的是 **consumer non-durables** 非耐用消费品，如食品、饮料、报纸等。

● **del credere agent** 保付代理人，受货主委托代收货款，并承担买方拒付的风险。类似的词语还有：**del credere commission** 保证收取货款佣金。

● **declosed factoring** 显名应收账款承购，指应收账款承购商 the FACTOR 以公开身份购入出口商的应收账款债权，反义语为：**undisclosed factoring** 隐名应收账款承购，或隐名代理融通，指应收账款承购商让购制造商的贸易债务，但身份不为债权人所知。如：

We used undisclosed factoring to improve our cash-flow without upsetting our customers.

我们以隐名代理融通来改善现金流动，而不搅扰顾客。

● **part-exchange** 折价贴换；贴旧换新

● **job lot** 搭配销售的物件；拼组出售的货物。如：

The house furniture was sold as a job lot. 这些住房家具成套出售。

● **loss leader** （为招徕顾客而）亏本出售的商品

to sell a particular brand of coffee cheap as a loss leader

廉价出售某种牌子的咖啡以招揽生意

Shops use loss leader to attract customers.

商店用亏本出售某些商品的办法来吸引顾客。

● **lot money** 拍卖佣金；拍卖费，即拍卖商（auctioneer）对每个拍卖出的项目收取的费用。这个词语中的 lot 是指"拍卖的一个项目或一组物品；一拍货"。如：

The figure quoted does not include the auctioneer's lot money.

所报价格不包括拍卖人的佣金。

● **petty cash**：a small amount of money kept in an office to pay small expenses 零用现金；小额备用金。与此类似的词语：**petty average** （航行期间由船长支付的）小额酬金。

3.1.2.2　字面意义不等，有其专门所指语义的词语

● **abandonment clause** 指外贸货运保险中的"委付条款"，不能译为"放弃条款"。这是海损保单的一个内容，其实际所指意义为"允许船东放弃受损船舶，尤其当修理费高于船货总值时，以换取保险赔偿金"。

● **absorption costing** 会计术语指"归纳成本法"，指"将生产有关的所有成本计算在售价中"，不能译为"吸收成本"。如：

Absorption costing usually prevents underpricing.

归纳成本法通常可避免定价过低。

● **alpha stocks** 热门股票，专指在伦敦国际证券交易所自动报价系统中成交最活跃的大公司股票。

● **at a premium** 意为：rare or difficult to obtain and therefore expensive 因罕有或难得而昂贵。

Building land in cities is at a premium. 城市建筑用地昂贵。

● **bill of lading**，常用缩略语 **b/l；B/L**，外贸运输术语"提单"，列明托运货物

（consignment）详情，由承运人（carrier）给托运人（consignor）作收据，收货人（consignee）提货亦以此作为凭证。视货物提交时的状态，又分为清洁提单（clean bill of lading）和不洁提单（dirty/foul bill of lading），前者指托运货物完整无损，而后者指所托货物已受损。

- **escalation clause** 价格自动调整条款，滑动条款。这是个商贸合同术语，指容许因制造成本变动等因素而更改价格。

- **escape clause** 例外条款。商贸合同术语，指容许合同中的一方在特殊情况下可不履行合同条款。

- **extended facility** 中期贷款，连续贷款

- **joint and several liability** 连带并个别责任；共同并个别负债。用于一组人共同建立的商业活动，小组所有人作为共同的整体以及单独的个人均对清偿债项等负责。

- **general average** 共同海损。为解除船舶或货物受威胁而采取措施造成的损失，可以要求保险赔偿，损失由船主和货主分摊。与此词对应的一词是 **particular average**（单独海损），指在船舶本身的安全未受到威胁的情况下，被保险货物一部分遭受全部灭失，或全部或一部分遭受的损害。这种损失是否应由各有关货主自行承担，应视保障单之约定为准。

与上述两词语类似的另两个词语为：

general lien 和 **particular lien**，前者意为"统/总括留置权"，指扣押某人的货物、钱财或单证作为他们全部未清偿债务的担保。而后者意为"特定留置权"或"个别留置权"，指扣押某人的货物、钱财或单证作为指定债项的担保。

- **kite-flying** 开空头票据，指用无效的票据向银行贴现。如：

Banks must always beware of kite-flying. 银行必须随时注意空头票据。

- **knocking copy** （对竞争者产品进行的）攻击性广告字眼

- **knock-out agreement** 不竞价协议。指交易商之间商定在拍卖中出价时，彼此不相互竞价的协议。如：

An illegal knock-out agreement accounted for the unusually low prices at the auction.

非法的不竞价协议导致拍卖价格低得出奇。

Even the best auctioneers however, find it difficult to stop a "knock-out", whereby dealers illegally arrange beforehand not to bid against each other, but nominate one of themselves as the only bidder, in the hope of buying goods at extremely low prices. If such a "knock-out" comes off, the real auction sale takes place privately afterwards among the dealers.

然而，即使是拍卖高手也发现难以阻止不竞拍的行为，竞拍者事先非法地安排好不相互竞拍，而是指定其中一人作为唯一的出价人，指望以最低的价格购得货物。一旦此事如愿以偿，事后由他们私下再进行真正的拍卖。

- **know-how** 专门知识；技术诀窍（尤指筹划新事物所必备的）

It is essential to get someone with the right know-how before we start this project.

在启动这个项目之前首先要找到掌握这门技术诀窍的人。

- **landing charge** 卸货费；起岸费。指货物抵达目的港时必须支付的费用。

All landing charges must be paid before unloading. 卸货前必须支付全部起岸费。

- **landing order** 卸货单；起货令。由关税与消费税务局发出，允许进口商从仓库运走货物。

No goods will be moved without a landing order. 没有起货令不得运走任何货物。

- **land waiter** 海关货检员，其职责是在港口查验应税货物，以确保关税和其他税款已缴清。

The cargo is about to be examined by a land waiter. 货物将由海关货检员查验。

- **lead time** 此词语有两个语义：（1）备运时间，指从订货至交货所需时间。如：

The lead time on this item is two months. 这项货的备运时间为两个月。

（2）购物酝酿期，指消费者为作决定购买某物所需的时间。如：

Threatening to take something off the market decreases a consumer's lead time.

消费者面对市场上将要停止销售某物的威胁会加速做出购买的决定。

- **less-than-container load**（运送的货物与他人的货物）共用一集装箱；不足整柜

Take care in unloading because this is a less-than-container load.

卸货时小心，这是拼箱货。

- **material fact**（1）（法律规定申请加入保险者必须声明的）重要事实。如：

All material facts must be supplied before the underwriter will accept the risk.

申请人必须提出全部重要事实，保险商才愿意承担风险。

（2）（证人在案件审判过程中提供的足以影响法院判决的）重要事实。如：

The witness produced a new material fact. 证人提供了新的实质性证明。

- **Memorandum of Association** 公司章程。依据法律表明公司存在，载有公司的名称和地址、核定股本 authorized share capital 及其构成、说明债务清偿办法的有限责任声明、公司的宗旨及经营范围。如：

All essential information is contained in the Memorandum of Association.

公司章程中载有全部基本信息。

- **Memorandum of Satisfaction** 还债备忘录，说明某项抵押贷款已偿还。如：

The Registrar of Companies has received the Memorandum of Satisfaction for the company property. 公司注册员已收到公司的财产完债备忘录。

- **off-the-shelf** 非专门设计或定制的；现成的。如：

to buy something off-the-shelf 购买现成货

- **open position** 未结清期货合同，未平仓交易（交易商已购进商品、证券或货币而未售出）。如：

An open position is vulnerable until the position can be closed.

未平仓交易必须予以平仓才能降低风险。

类似的词语还有：

- **bear/short position** 卖空；空仓；超卖（卖出的比持有的多）
- **bull position** 多头，指投资者因期望价格上升而持有证券或期货。
- **outstanding o/s** 意为：unpaid; owed 未偿付的，拖欠的。如：

There is still an amount outstanding on your account.

你的账户上仍有一笔欠款。

to pay off an outstanding debt 付清一笔到期的债务

• **penalty clause** 意为：a condition in a contract that states the amount of money to be paid by the person who breaks the contract 违约条款。如：

The contract contained a penalty clause to ensure that the work was finished on time.

该合同包含一项违约条款以保证工作按时完成。

• **price-fixing** 意为：an agreement between traders not to sell goods below a certain price 价格垄断；物价操纵。如：

Price-fixing keeps prices artificially high. 价格垄断造成物价人为地居高不下。

• **price ring** 意为：a group of sellers in the same industry who have agreed to fix a minimum price for a product 价格同盟。如：

It is illegal to form a price ring. 结成价格同盟属非法。

• **qualified acceptance** 附条件承兑；有条件承兑：只有在符合日期、地点等条件限制下承兑汇票。如：

The holder refused to take qualified acceptance. 持票人拒绝接受附条件承兑。

• **real estate** 房地产；房地产交易。如：

He owns a lot of real estate in Florida. 他在佛罗里达拥有大量的房地产。

She works in real estate in Chicago. 她在芝加哥从事房地产业。

• **real terms** 按实值计算的数目；实额（扣除通货膨胀后的实际购买力）。如：

In real terms, houses are cheaper than they were three years ago because of the housing slump. 由于房地产市场不景气，住房实际上比三年前便宜了。

• **red tape** 繁文缛节；烦琐手续。如：

The project will start as soon as we get through the red tape.

办完烦琐的手续后，这个项目马上启动。

• **round figures** 整数。如：

Give me the sales estimates in round figures.

请告诉我估计销量的整数。

• **second** 意为：to support an idea put forward by somebody else at a meeting 附议。如：

Will anybody second this motion? 本提案有人附议吗？

• **self-employed** 个体经营的。如：

She used to work for a design agency, but now she is self-employed.

她过去在一家设计行工作，但现在干个体了。

• **sharp practice** 不择手段的行为；诡诈行为。如：

We suspect there has been some sharp practice, but cannot prove it.

我们怀疑其中有诈，但还不能证实。

• **short list** 初选名单（供最后筛选）。如：

I was on the short list, but I didn't get the job. 我初选入围，但未能得到那份工作。

• **terminal market** 期货市场

- **umbrella fund** 境外基金
- **unique selling proposition** 意为：a feature of a product that makes it different from other products and therefore attractive to consumers 可推荐的产品特色。如：

The durability of this car is its unique selling proposition.

这辆车以其耐用性独树一帜。

A unique selling proposition gives a product added interest.

产品的特色有助于提高人们的兴趣。

- **With Average**（缩 W. A.）〈保〉水渍险。

3.1.2.3　缩略语

- **AOB**：any other business 任何其他议题。常用在会议议程结束时。

Any AOB? 有其他议题吗？

- **CAD**：cash against document 凭单付现，付现交单
- **MD**：managing director 总裁；董事总经理；常务董事
- **o. n. o.**：or nearest offer 可还价或略低于此价

Car for sale：£2,000 o. n. o.

此车出售：开价 2000 英镑，面议。

- **pp**：per procurationem：on behalf of or with the authority of someone 由……代表/办/行
- **P. N.** promissory note = bank-note，note of hand 本/期票，指出票人签发的保证见票后或在规定日期内无条件地付给受票人一定金额的票据。
- **KPI**：key performance indicators 关键业绩指标。是企业的目标式量化管理指标，很多大型企业都采用这种绩效考核制度。所以有的招聘广告中会出现这个术语。
- **MOU**：memorandum of understanding 合作备忘录。指企业与企业签订正式合同书之前，记录协商内容的协议书，一般来说 MOU 不具备法律约束力。

3.1.2.4　外来语

- **à compte** 源自法语，通常使用缩略语 à. c.，仅用于书面语，意为：in part 部分。如：

The sum was paid à. c. 部分金额已支付。

- **bona fide** 源自拉丁语的形容词，有两个释义：（1）genuine 真正的；名副其实的。如：

This is a bona fide reduction in price. 这是名副其实的降价。

The deal is all quite bona fide. 这笔交易名副其实。

（2）honest or having an honest intention 善意；真实。如：

The bona fide purchaser did not know that the seller was not the legal owner of the goods.

这位善意的买主不知道卖方为非法的货主。

- **per procurationem** 源自拉丁语，实际使用时通常用缩略语形式 pp，意为：on behalf of or with the authority of someone 由……代表/办；代行。

The letter was signed J. Smith and Sons Ltd., pp.

该信件签名是 J. 史密斯父子有限公司的代表。

- **force majeure** 合同/保险/法律用语，来自法语，意为：不可抗力。
- **vis major** 意为：An overwhelming force of nature having unavoidable consequences that under certain circumstances can exempt one from the obligations of a contract. 不可抗力。这是一个源自拉丁语的词语。
- **ad valorem** 这是一个税务词语，意为：(按商品价值百分比计算税款的) 从价征税的。如：

VAT is an ad valorem tax. 增值税是一种从价税。

- **curriculum vitae** 常缩略为 **cv**，来自拉丁语，意为：简/履历，指求职者列出其资格、爱好、工作经历等，美国英语常用 **résumé**，源自古法语，注意区别英语的 resume。
- **entropôt** 源自法语，意为：货物集散地，指在机场或港口存放待转运的货物；亦为：转运港口。
- **entropôt trade** 意为：转口贸易。如：

Rotterdam and Singapore are centers for entrepôt trade.

鹿特丹和新加坡是转口贸易中心。

- **ex officio** 源自拉丁语，意为：按照职务的(地)，可作形容词或副词。源自拉丁语的 ex 主要用作介词，其本身的词义为："在……交货，在……外，无，无权获得，未"，因此，商务文体中还有些用 ex 搭配的词语，如：
  - **ex bond**(进口港)关栈/关税仓库(外)交货(价)；
  - **ex quay/wharf/dock** 目的港码头交货(价)；
  - **ex ship** 目的港船上交货(价)；
  - **ex point of origin** 现场交货(价)，当地交货(价)，如下列这些均属于现场交货贸易条件：ex plane (出口地)机上交货(价)；ex plantation 农场交货(价)；ex godown (启运港)仓库交货(价)；ex stock 现货/库存交货(价)；ex store 店铺交货(价)；ex warehouse 仓库交货(价)；ex mine 矿场交货(价)；ex works/factory 工厂交货(价)，等。

在股票业中又有：

- **ex-claim/new** 无权要求新股，指供销售的股票不附参与有购股权证券发行(rights issue) 及红股发行(scrip issue)的权利，与"ex-rights 除权"同义；
- **ex div/dividend** 不附股息；
- **ex growth** 指股份或公司过去大幅升值但短期内应不太可能"显著增长"，等。

其他用法还有：

- **ex bonus** (**x. b.**)/**scrip** 不附(本期)红利；
- **ex interest** (**ex int.**) 无(下期)利息；
- **ex commission** 无佣金；
- **ex distribution** (x. d. /ex dist.) 不包括(下期)股息；
- **ex coupon** (ex cp. /x cp)无息票，等。
- **loro account** 第三方账户，他账(户)，由一家银行在另一家通常为海外银行开立的账户。loro 为意大利语，即英语的 their，如：

credit the loro account of the bank to which funds are being transported

把数额记入接到资金的银行第三方账户

与此词语类似的还有：

- **nostro account** 我方账户，往账。nostro 为意大利语，相当于 our，如：

The money is held in a nostro account. 钱存在我方账户上。

- **vostro account** 你账，来账。意大利语 vostro 意为 your。

- **Mala fide** 不诚实；不守信义；欺诈。该语源自拉丁语。

The deal was conducted mala fide. 这笔交易有诈。

- **per annum**　p. a. ［拉丁］每年。

The position offers a salary of £25,000 per annum.

该职位年薪 25000 英镑。

- **prima facie** 是一个源于拉丁语的词语，可以作形容词或副词。（1）at first sight；before closer inspection 初看时；据初次印象。如：

They had, prima facie, a legitimate complaint. 他们拥有一个初看起来很合法的控告。

prima facie case【律】表面上证据确凿的案件

prima facie evidence【律】表面上确凿的证据，初步证据

（2）true, authentic, or adequate at first sight；ostensible 初看时真实的、可靠的或合适的。如：

prima facie credibility 初看时的可信度

（3）Evident without proof or reasoning；obvious：自明的，无争论余地的。如：

a prima facie violation of the treaty 明显违反合约的

a prima facie right 无争论余地的权利

3.1.2.5　由其他专业词义派生的新词义，这类词语在翻译时最易含混不清或造成错译。

- **acid test** 是一个化工词语，意为"酸性测试/定"，但在商务文体英语中，其意为：a test proving the true value of something/someone 证明真正价值的考验。如：

The acid test is whether or not somebody will actually buy the product.

决定性的考验在于是否确有人会买这种产品。

- **acid test ratio** 这个词语更不能从上述词语来推断其词义，这是常用于国际金融/会计专业的术语，意为：a measure of a company's liquidity by comparing its LIQUID ASSETS to its CURRENT LIABILITIES 流动资产与流动负债比率；速动比率。如：

The acid test ratio shows that the company is unable to pay its debts on time.

流动资产与流动负债比率显示该公司不能按时偿还债务。

- **catch a cold** 初看，会想到"感冒"释义，但这是个商贸术语，意为"蚀/亏本"。如：

The price of shares has fallen heavily today and many recent investors are likely to catch a cold. 今天股票价格大跌，很多新近的投资者可能要亏本了。

- **ceiling** 不要总译为"天花板"，此为商贸用语，意为：the upper limit 上限。如：

The OPEC members tried to put a ceiling on oil production.

欧佩克(石油输出国组织)成员国力图规定石油生产的上限。

2.1.2.6 常用动词搭配

• **make good** 赔偿；替换；修理

make good a loss 赔偿损失

All cracks in the ceiling will be made good. 天花板上的裂缝都能修好的。

• **make out** 填写；开具

To whom do I make out the cheque? 支票抬头应写什么名称?

Invoices should be made out in triplicate. 开具发票应一式三份。

• **make up** 使合起来；完成

The accounts have been made up to the end of the month.

截至月底的账目已整理好。

to make up an order 完成一次订货

• **mark up** 提高标价；加成，指成本或批发价上增加一定百分比，以定出零售价或销售价。如:

We marked all the goods up in order to increase profit.

我们将所有的货物加成以增加利润。

Prices have been marked up by 10%. 价格已提高百分之十。

3.2 常用或流行语译例

本土化 local adaptation（localize/localization 为误译，意为：使局部化，使具有地方性）

餐饮经理/人员 catering manager/staff

餐饮业 the catering business/industry/trade

厂家建议零售价 manufacturer's recommended price

产品发布 launching the product

策划 mastermind

成功的上流人士，上流公司 white shoe

传销 pyramid selling/scheme

大包装 economy size

大型的商贸活动需要雇请饮食供应商提供餐饮服务，这种供应商为 caterer。

懂电脑 computerate（computer + literate e. g. Applicants for the position must be computerate. 这一职位的申请者必须懂电脑。）

独树一帜的产品特色 unique selling proposition（USP）

对环境无害 environmentally-friendly

（个人、企业等的）业绩 track record

工作午餐 business lunch/luncheon

管理人员 management 或 management staff（通常译为 managerial staff，但英语更常用现译，如：高/中/基层管理人员 senior/middle/junior management）

顾客对品牌的信赖感 brand loyalty

基本生活费 living wage

集体讨论会/群策会 brainstorming session（不译为 group discussion）

交易会 trade fair

杰出人才 whizz-kid

经济优惠（包）装 economy pack

可行性研究 a feasibility study

礼品券 gift voucher［美］优惠购货券 token

寄出一定数量的商品标签、赠券等而获得的赠品为 free offer。

免费样品 free sample

名牌 brand name

品牌形象 brand image

企业标识 corporate identity（建立/采用/突出/推广企业标识 establish/introduce/project/promote a corporate identity）

容易使用 user-friendly（例如：傻瓜相机 a user-friendly camera）

上门推销 door-to-door salesman；salesperson；saleswoman；commercial traveler；traveling salesman

生产或使用绿色产品 go green

生产基地 production facilities（通常译为：production base，而这里 facility 意为：buildings for a particular activity）

猎头 headhunt

跳槽 job-hopping

找工作 job-hunting（a job-hunter）/job seeking（a job seeker）

职介所 employment agencies

拓展业务 branch out

外籍经理 expatriate manager（不译：foreign manager）

现代化建设 modernization drive（过去译为 modernization construction。drive 指大家参与、为实现某种目标共同努力的大规模运动。）

行政秘书 office administrator/assistant（不可照字面译为 administrative secretary）

以旧换新 trade in

饮食一条街 food court

优惠券 cash voucher(a cash voucher for 2 *yuan* off a hamburger 买一个汉堡可减 2 元钱的优惠券)

赠品（随所购商品赠送的物品）free gift

招待费/交际费 entertainment allowance/expenses

总公司 head office

专卖店 boutique（专售女装）　outlet（某产品的分销店）

专业资格 professional qualifications

资格证明（书）；资历 credentials

咨询所 consulting firms

纵向联合 vertical integration（横向联合/合并 horizontal integration）

做市场研究 research the market potential

熟女 cougar

恶搞 spoof

大片 blockbuster

镇馆之宝 key highlights of a/the collection

黑客 hacker（白客：tracker/online security guard 而不宜译成 white clan）

秒杀 seckill(ing)

闪存 Flash Memory

等离子体 Plasma（as in plasma TV），该词在医学术语里指"血浆"。

IPOD：苹果公司推出的 MP3 播放器和平板电脑。

Megapixel：百万像素，用于表达数码相机的解析度。"像素"(Pixel)是 Picture(图像)和 Element(元素)的拼合词，是用来计算数码影像的单位。

炒作 hype

紧急财政援助（以应对金融危机）bailout

愤青 the Angry Young

海归 the Returnee

封口费（指目睹或知晓某人不可告人的秘密，所以当事人给知情人一定费用，则知情人不予声张）hush money

动图 GIF；2012 年的牛津年度热词。

自拍 selfie；2013 年的牛津年度热词。

电子烟 vape；2014 年的牛津年度热词。vape 是个新生词汇。它最初只是作为 vapour 或者 vaporize 的缩写，有蒸汽或汽化的意思。2014 年 8 月，牛津在线词典将其收录。根据牛津词典部主席 Casper Grathwohl 的说法，年度热词的评选不仅仅基于使用频率，它必须蕴涵复杂而丰富的社会现象。而 vape 作为 2014 年的牛津年度热词，也在一定程度上反映了人们对健康领域的关注。

想成为中国好男友，学会称呼自己的女朋友 bae 是第一步。"Hey, bae!"——现在潮人们就时兴这么说。其实 bae 就是"baby"的简称，但也有人说 bae 是"before anyone else"(排在所有人之前)的缩写。不管怎样，用来称呼女生最受用了。

表情，表达"喜极而泣(Face with Tears of Joy)"Emoji；2015 年牛津年度热词。这个词却并非由字母组成，而是一个表情：

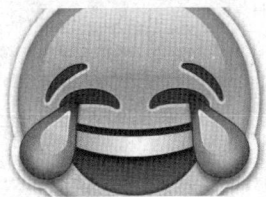

post-truth 后真相；2016 年牛津年度热词。

post-truth 指的是个人情感或信念较客观事实容易引起大众共鸣的现象。"后真相"一词并非如字面上解释为"发现真相后"，相反地，则是在表达"真相沦为其次"的趋势。例如特朗普虽然于大选辩论中多次出现失控且不实的言论，但最后仍赢得大批选民支持而顺利当选总统。

alt-right 另类右派。由 alternative 与 right 合成，是美国右派思想中较为保守一派，其核心理念是反对政治正确、外来移民及多元文化，部分支持者更表达白人优越主义及种族主义的思想。

Brexiteer 英国脱欧支持者。2016 年 6 月底闹得最沸沸扬扬的国际事件就属英国脱欧了。Brexit(英国脱欧)这个词由 British 及 exit 组合而成，反义词则是 British 及 remain 合在一起形成的 Bremain(英国留欧)。-eer 这个词根是"人"的意思，因此将 Brexit 加上 -eer 则变成英国脱欧支持者。

年轻人的行为对政治、社会或文化变迁造成重大的影响 Youthquake；2017 年牛津年度热词。The noun, youthquake, is defined as "a significant cultural, political, or social change arising from the actions or influence of young people".

独角兽 Unicorn；2017 年牛津年度热词。Unicorn denoting something, especially an item of food or drink, that is dyed in rainbow colours, decorated with glitter, etc.

男性说教 Mansplain；2018 年牛津年度热词。A man explaining something needlessly, overbearingly, or condescendingly, especially to a woman, in a manner thought to reveal a patronising or chauvinistic attitude. 男性在解释一些事情时，表现出一种不屑的、傲慢的、屈尊的态度，特别是对于女性，完全用一种高高在上的大男子主义的嘴脸。

另一个和它意思相近的新造词 manologue(man + monologue，用来指"男性滔滔不绝独霸一场谈话的行为")，反映的也是同一种文化社会现象。根据哈佛大学的一项研究，男人的确更喜欢滔滔不绝，而且越是人多的时候，就越是如此。

私人专属时间 Me time；2018 年牛津年度热词。An individual devotes time to doing what they want in order to relax. 个人专门找时间做某事来放松。

顶层设计 Top-level design

脑残 brainless, brain-dead, brain-impaired, have a dysfunctional brain 网络用语中用于形容愚蠢，言语和行为举止逻辑不通而让人无法理解和不可接受，以及被认为大脑不正常的人。

Do not talk with him again, he is virtually brainless!

别再跟他说了，他简直就是个脑残！

脑洞大开 greatly enrich one's mind (brain), greatly open up one's eyes, greatly widen one's horizon，就是脑补的意思，指的是给大脑补充了新的知识，含有让人知识大涨、眼界大开等意思。

This article greatly enriched my mind. 这篇文章让我脑洞大开。

狗不理 Go Believe

闻着臭 吃着香 Smell smelly, taste tasty

棒棒哒 for the win（FTW）

Found a frozen yogurt place a block away, and this one's rat-free. FTW！

我在一条街以外的地方又找到了一家冻酸奶店，这家没有老鼠。棒棒哒！

什么鬼？ what the f＊＊＊？（WTF）

WTF, why does Justin Bieber keep wearing leather harem pants?！

什么鬼？贾斯汀·比伯为啥老穿吊裆哈伦皮裤啊?！

一个叫本·齐默的专家在网络新闻讨论组上一篇名为《闲扯淡》的文章里找到了最早使用 WTF 的证据。网名叫 Jay Fields 的网友写道："Upon booting I received a message saying 'PLEASE INSERT WORD MASTER'. I asked myself, 'W. T. F.'?"（"我启动程序的时候收到一条消息，上面写着'请插入单词大师'。我当时问自己'这是什么鬼'?"）

对于这类词语，我们可以经常关注权威网站的发布，以跟踪最新的信息。

3.3 各种"公司"的翻译

3.3.1 company & corporation

在"公司"一词的翻译中，我们用得较多的英语单词为 company 和 corporation，它们之间有什么区别吗？请看下面一段英语描述：

Now, there is a functional equivalent in Chinese with "公司". And the Chinese term "公司" implies that the entity is "法人"or literally, a "legal person". However, there is a substantial difference between "company" and "corporation" in terms of the legal person status.

In the common law, the term for an entity with legal person status is corporation. The word company can refer to a partnership or association of people that is not incorporated. In common usage, however, the word company almost always refers to an incorporated company — i. e. a corporation. Therefore, under Chinese law, the nearest functional Chinese equivalent to corporation might be "公司".

company 的缩略形式为：co. /Co 其意为：（1）A business enterprise; a firm 公司；商行（2）A partner or partners not specifically named in a firm's title 合伙人：没有专门用商行命名的一个合股人或多个合股人。如：

Lee Rogers and Company　李·罗杰斯与其合伙人

而 **corporation** 在《牛津商务英语辞典》（*Oxford Business English*）中的释义为：

1.（UK）an organization that has legal recognition and is made up of people whose rights and responsibilities within the corporation are separate from their rights as individuals; a large group of companies 法人团体（依法成立，成员在法人团体内的权利和责任与他们作为个人的权利是分开的）；法人，公司。如：

the British Broadcasting Corporation 英国广播公司

a banking corporation 银行集团

The city corporation is responsible for parks and gardens within its boundaries.

市政公司负责管理界内的公园及游乐场所。

2.（US）a limited company 股份有限公司；企业。如：

General Motor Corporation 通用汽车公司；

corporation farm［美］规模巨大的农场；

corporation law［美］公司法；

corporation lawyer（attorney）美公司法律顾问；

corporation police［美］（公司等的）自备警察。

《朗文国际贸易辞典》（*Longman Dictionary of International Trade*）对 corporation 的释义为：

（law）An association or entity created by persons under the authority of the laws of a particular jurisdiction. A corporation is treated as distinct from the persons（referred to as shareholders）who created it，and therefore the shareholders enjoy limited liability and the corporation has the right to own property，enter contracts，and bring suit，similar to those given to individuals. 公司：〈法律〉个人或法人按照某个特殊管辖范围的法律创建的组织或实体。公司与创立公司的股东不能同等看待，股东享有有限责任，而公司拥有一定的法律权利，譬如占有财产的权利，签订合同和提出诉讼的权利，即同赋予个人的权利类似。

而：

Ltd. *abbr*. limited 有限公司

limited company：A company whose members are only responsible for its debts up to a limited amount，usually the amount of unpaid shares 有限责任公司/股份有限公司：公司成员对清偿债务的责任有限，一般只包括未缴股本。

limited partnership：A partnership in which at least one partner has general liability and at least one of the other partner has limited liability. 两合公司，有限合伙公司，有限合伙商：一种合伙企业，其中至少有一个合伙人负全部责任，在其余的合伙人中也应至少有一名负有限责任。

3.3.2　有限责任公司与股份有限公司的英译

在我国，有限责任公司（简称有限公司）是指由两个或两个以上的股东共同出资，每个股东以其所认缴的出资额对公司承担责任，公司以其全部资产对其债务承担责任的企业法人。

股份有限公司是指注册资本由等额股份构成并通过发行股票筹集资本，股东以其所认购的股份对公司承担有限责任，公司以其全部资产对公司债务承担责任的企业法人。

对于我国公司法确认的有限责任公司，可译为"…Co.，Ltd"或"…Ltd"。目前国内有不少公司英译为"…Co. Ltd."，Co.，与 Ltd. 之间无逗号隔开，此译法不妥。在此，Ltd. 是用以界定 Co. 的性质，即该公司为有限责任，而不是无限责任、两合或其他，它具有补充说明的作用，与 Co. 分属不同层次，须用逗号相隔。如单独使用 Ltd. 表示有限责任时，也需在 Ltd. 之前加逗号与公司名称的其他内容隔开。

陈浩然（2005：40）认为，"欧美的企业、公司是有限公司（company limited 缩写为

Co., Ltd.)，在美国叫 corporation 或 incorporation，用法律语言说，叫做'法人'或'公法人'，缩写为 Corp. 或 Inc."。

3.3.3 与 company 有关的"公司"

export trading company：a corporation or other business unit organized and operated principally for the purpose of exporting goods and services, or of providing export related services to other companies. An ETC can be owned by foreigners and can import, barter, and arrange sales between third countries, as well as export. 出口贸易公司：出口货物和服务或为其他公司出口提供相关服务，而组建和经营的公司及其他商业机构。一个出口贸易公司可以归外国人所有，可以从事进口、以货易货和在第三国组织销售以及出口等项活动。

mutual insurance company：a type of life insurance company in which there are no shareholders and apart from the money used for running expenses, all profits are distributed to policyholders 互助保险公司：这类人寿保险公司没有股东，除日常开支外全部利润分配给保险单持有人。如：

He has a policy with a mutual insurance company. 他持有互助保险公司的保单。

private limited company：a company that may not offer its shares for sale to the public 私人有限公司；私人股份有限公司：不得向公众出售其股份

A private limitd company has the word limited or the initials Ltd after its name.

私人有限公司名称之后有 limited 或 Ltd 字样。

registered company：(UK) a public limited company or a private company registered under the Companies Act 注册公司：按照公司法注册的公开股份有限公司或私营公司

statutory company (UK)：a company that provides a public service, e. g. one that provides gas or water, formed by special Act of Parliament 法定公司：由国会通过特别法案成立的提供公共服务的公司，例如天然气/自来水公司。

British Telecom and British Gas were formed as statutory companies.

英国电信公司和英国天然气公司是通过特定法律成立的。

subsidiary company：a company of which at least half the share capital is owned by another company, called a parent of holding company 附属公司；子公司。

Each subsidiary company trades under its own name.

每家子公司以各自的名义经营。

3.3.4 PLC *abbr.* Public Limited Company

此词有下列释义：(1)(United Kingdom) designation for a public corporation with limited liability to shareholders 只对股东承担有限责任的上市公司　(2) A company registered under the Companies Act, that must have an AUTHORIZED SHARE CAPITAL of at least ＄50,000 and whose shares can be bought on the Stock Exchange 股票上市公司(根据公司法注册，核定股本不少于50000美元，股票在证券交易所买卖)亦称 public company(意大利语"股份公司"的缩写为 **S. P. A**，法语为 **S. A.** "公司中的股份"，西班牙语为 **accion**，法语为 **action**，

意大利语为 **azione**)。

上市公司还可说为：

- **listed company**：a company whose shares are recorded on the main market of a stock exchange 上市公司；交易所挂牌公司。如：

The shares are only in listed company. 这些仅仅是上市公司股份。

而"上市/挂牌证券"的英语表达就用 listed securities。如：

Members of the Stock Exchange only deal in listed securities.

证券交易所成员只买卖上市证券。

- **close corporation**：不公开上市公司，股份不公开公司，股票不公开发行公司，闭式公司

- **closely held corporation**：a corporation with a small number of shareholders, who usually directly operate the corporation and have limited liability. A maximum number of shareholders is usually fixed by law. The minimum capitalization for a closely held corporation is less than that for a public corporation, and fewer formalities are required for managing it. The requirements for closely held corporations vary among jurisdictions. 股东人数有限的公司：由少数通常直接参加管理并承担有限责任的股东组成的公司。该种公司股东人数上限通常由法律固定，其投资资本总额的下限通常低于公营公司，而且开办公司的手续也较为简单。对这种公司的要求因法律而异。

相关的公司还有：

holding company = parent company：the leading company of a group that holds all or more than half of the shares of the other companies 控股公司(持有一半以上的股权)，也用 **holdings**，如：

British Motor Holdings (BMH) 英国汽车控股公司

joint-stock company：合股公司

We have pooled our assets and formed a joint-stock company.

我们把资产集合起来，成立了一家合股公司。

immediate holding company：a company that has control over a subsidiary company because of the number of shares that it owns, but is itself under the control of a holding company 直接控股公司(对子公司有控制权而本身又受控于另一公司)。

但是，**public corporation** 是指 an organization owned by the state and set up to provide a national service or run a nationalized industry 公营公司；国有公司：属于国家所有，负责为全国提供服务或经营国有化产业。

The British Coal Corporation and the British Broadcasting Corporation are public corporations. 英国煤炭公司和英国广播公司都是国有公司。

3.3.5 其他种类的"公司"

agency：代理公司，中介公司。如：

a market research agency 市场调查代理公司

an advertising agency 广告代理公司

a recruitment/employment agency 职业介绍所

a commercial property agency 房地产中介公司（real estate agent 房地产经纪人；real estate company 房地产公司；real estate investment trust 房地产投资信托公司）

place：a business establishment or office 办事处，公司

concern：财团，公司，商行。如：joint stock concern 股份公司；paying concern 有收益的企业。

incorporated：此词有下列释义：（1）formed into or organized and maintained as a legal corporation 组成公司的；作为合法公司而建立或组织并保持的；（根据法律）组成公司的，成为法人组织的。

an incorporated company 股份有限公司

（2）（United States）designation for a corporation with limited liability to shareholders 股份有限公司，美国一种公司的名称，股东承担有限的责任。

该词的缩略语为 **inc**. *Also* **Inc**. 此词用于商店名称之后，表示其为公司组织。

注意另一个词 incorporator，有人将其译为"公司组织者"其意似乎不错，但查一下公司法的有关内容，将其译为"发起人"则更为贴切。

operator 运营公司。如：

This is an operator offering corporate hospitality services.

这是一家提供企业社交/公关服务的专业公司。

service 商业性服务公司。如：

an office design service 办公场所设计公司

a travel service 旅行社

a translation service 翻译公司，等。

firm：two or more people in business to make a profit by selling goods or services：商号/行

group：a HOLDING COMPANY together with any subsidiary companies in which it owns more than half of the share capital 集团：控股公司（HOLDING COMPANY）连同占一半以上股权的附属公司

line：a passenger or cargo system of public or private transportation，as by ship，aircraft，or bus，usually over a definite route（固定路线的）运输系统：通常有固定路线的公有或私有货运或客运系统，如船运、空运或汽运；A company owning or managing such a system（固定路线的）运输公司：拥有或经营这种运输系统的公司。如：

Shipping lines，airlines，trucking companies and railroad companies are all carriers.

海运公司、航空公司、卡车公司和铁路公司均为承运人。

syndicate：a group of people or companies who work together on a project to make money 辛迪加；企业联合组织；财团。如：

An international syndicate will be responsible for building the dam.

该大坝将由某国际财团负责建造。

trust：a combination of firms or corporations for the purpose of reducing competition and

69

controlling prices throughout a business or an industry. 企业联合：为在一商业或工业内部减少竞争及价格垄断而形成的商行或公司联合；托拉斯；操纵某种行业的组合。如：

holding trust 控股托拉斯

motor manufactory trust 汽车工厂托拉斯

conglomerate：a number of companies, sometimes involved with different products, joined together and run as one large company 联合企业；集团企业；跨行业公司

multinational/transnational：a very large organization that owns companies in more than one country in order to obtain cheap raw materials and make efficient use of a local workforce 跨国集团/公司：在不止一个国家拥有公司，以便获得廉价原料和充分利用当地劳动力等。

business a person or group of people making, distributing, buying or selling goods or providing services；a firm or company 公司，工商企业。如：

a furniture, an insurance, a dry-cleaning **business** 家具商/保险公司/干洗店

a small/family/one-man/one-woman **business** 小规模企业/家庭企业/个体企业

In a **business** the workers take orders from the entrepreneur. He is the leader, and the employees follow his direction.

公司/企业里，工人们听从企业家的指令。因为后者是领导者，而员工须听他指挥。

A proprietor is a person who owns or owns and manages a **business** or other such establishment. 所有人是拥有或拥有而且经营一家公司或其他企业机构的人。（女性为：**proprietress**）

There are three main types of **business** ownership in the United States：（1）single proprietorships，（2）partnerships，and（3）corporations.

美国有三种主要的公司所有制类型：（1）独资，（2）合股，以及（3）有限公司。

Single proprietorships are **businesses** owned and operated by one person.

独资企业指个人拥有并经营的公司。

Partnerships consist of two or more owners who share the responsibilities and profits of a **business**. 合资企业由两个或更多的业主构成，他们共担职责，分享利润。

However, nearly all partnerships are small **businesses**.

然而，几乎所有的合股公司均为小公司。

The approval of a majority of the stockholders may be required for certain major decisions that affect **business** operations. 对某些影响公司运作的重大决定需要征得大部分股东的同意。

Most corporations are larger than **businesses** owned by individuals or partners.

大多数有限公司的规模大于独资或合股公司。

Proprietors can start a business with a small amount of capital and few legal formalities. Most of these **businesses** close down if the owner dies or runs out of capital. 经营者具备一小笔资金和合法的手续即可开办公司。如果公司的所有者死亡或资金短缺，大部分这样的公司就关门歇业。

Partnerships consist of two or more owners who share the responsibilities and profits of a **business**. In most cases, each partner is liable for all business debts. 合伙人由两人或以上的所有者组成，他们分担公司职责，分享公司利润。在大部分情况下，每个合伙人都承担公司

的债务。

The productive resources of a **business** are also known as inputs.

公司的生产性资源也称作投入。

For example, such service **businesses** as hotels and telephone companies need the work of many employees. 例如，旅馆、电话公司之类的服务性机构需要大量员工的工作。

The goal of nearly all business firms is to earn a maximum profit. Most **business** policies are based on this profit motive. 几乎所有商号的目标是赚取最大的利润。大部分的经营方针亦基于这种利润动机。

Certain types of **businesses** have few or no competitors. Most of these **businesses** provide essential services to the public. For example, many public utility **companies** have a legal monopoly（法定专利）in their fields. In providing such services as electricity and water, one company may be able to operate more efficiently than several competing **firms**. Other enterprises, such as airports and railroads, are too expensive for several **companies** to operate in the same area. In these types of **businesses**, government regulation replaces competition in setting prices and establishing standards of quality.

某些公司少有或者没有竞争者。大部分这样的公司为公众提供必需的服务项目。譬如，很多公用事业公司在其领域有法定专利。在提供诸如水电服务项目时，比起多家竞争公司来说，一家公司也许运作更有效率。其他企业，如空港、铁路，多家公司在同一地区运作成本很高。就这些公司而言，政府的规定取代了确定价格和制定质量标准中的竞争。

Trademarks are proper terms that identify the products and services of a **business** and distinguish them from products and services of others. 商标是识别一家公司产品和服务的专用名称，并且可以将它们与其他公司的产品和服务区别开来。

establishment：a place of residence or business with its possessions and staff 公司；企业；设立的机构。如：

Gas/Service/Filling station is a retail **establishment** at which motor vehicles are refueled, serviced, and sometimes repaired 汽车加油站是为机动车提供加油、服务和修理的零售公司。

Beauty parlor is an **establishment** providing women with services that include hair treatment, manicures, and facials. 美容院是向妇女提供包括美发、修指甲和脸部按摩服务的机构。

house：（1）a commercial firm 商业机构。如：

a brokerage **house** 经纪人事务所

（2）a publishing company 出版公司。如：

a **house** that specializes in cookbooks 专门出版食谱的出版公司

又如：

issuing house：a financial institution, usually a merchant bank, that sells the shares of a new company to the public 证券承销/发行公司：向公众出售新成立公司股票的金融机构，通常为商人/证券银行。如：

The new issue of shares was marketed through an **issuing house**.

这次新股发行由一家发行公司承销。

acceptance house 承付所；票据承兑行

accepting house 承兑公司，承付所

brokerage house 经纪行

business house 商行，商店

commercial house 商号，商行

commercial paper house 证券交易所，商业票据商号

commission house 代办行；证券经纪公司

confirming house 保付行，保付公司

discount houses 折扣商店，贴现公司，贴现银行

xport house 出口公司，出口管理局

finance house 金融公司(商行)

first-rate house 头等商号

odd lot house 专营零股的经纪行

organization：(1) a group of people, departments or institutions that work together 组织，机构，系统；(2) a structure through which individuals cooperate systematically to conduct business 公司。如：

work for a large manufacturing **organization** 替一家大制造企业工作

The International Chamber of Commerce is the leading world business **organization**.
国际商会是最主要的世界性商业机构。

Smaller firms may have a single department, while very small **organizations** may have a single person responsible for all human resources activities. 小一点的商号可能只有一个部门，非常小的公司只有一个人负责人力资源方面的所有工作。

A new type of managerial position that is appearing in many **organizations** is that of information manager. 信息/情报经理是许多公司中出现的一种新的管理职位。

association：a group of people, departments or institutions joined together for a common purpose; an organization 协会，社团，组织

federation：a group of companies, societies or trade unions with a common interest and controlled by a central organization (由有共同利益的若干公司、团体、工会等组成的并由一中央组织控制的)联合会；联盟

上述这些形形色色的"公司"中，明确指代"公司"意义的有：

firm 指"行/商号"；

company (limited company, private limited company, registered company, public limited company), corporation, corporated, incorporated 等指"公司"(含"有限公司")；

而 holdings 为"控股公司"；

service 指"商业性服务公司"；

operator 指"运营公司"；

agency 指"代理公司"或"中介公司"；

group, conglomerate 指"集团/控股公司"，后者指"大型联合企业或跨行业的公司"；

multinational/transnational 指"跨国公司"。

其他的词语在指代"公司"的意义时是模糊的，翻译时可根据上下文的语境来确定词义。

business 多指"企业公司"；

establishment 多指"服务性的公司"或"设立的机构"；

house 多指"商业公司/金融机构"；

organization，甚或用 enterprise 常指广义上"公司"，且由语境决定此释义；

association，federation，institution 指代"公司"的意义较弱。

place：a business establishment or office 办事处，公司

3.3.6 一些非英语国家使用并已收入英语词典的公司

Aksjeselskap（A/S）：［Norway］designation for a joint stock company with limited personal liability to shareholders ［挪威］有限责任股份公司

Aktiebolag：（AB）（Finland，Sweden）designation for a joint stock company with limited personal liability to shareholders ［芬兰、瑞典］有限责任股份公司

Aktiengesellschaft（AG）：［Austria，Germany，Switzerland，Liechtenstein］designation for a joint stock company with limited personal liability to shareholders ［奥地利、瑞士、列支敦士敦］有限责任股份公司

Aktieselskab（A/S）：［Denmark］designation for a joint stock company with limited personal liability to shareholders ［丹麦］有限责任股份公司

Besloten Vennootschap met Beperkte Aansprakelijkheid（B.V.B.A.）：［Belgium/Netherlands］designation for a private limited liability corporation with limited liability to shareholders ［比利时/荷兰］私人有限责任股份公司

Chaebol：［South Korea］Korean conglomerates which are characterized by strong family control，authoritarian management，and centralized decision making. Chaebol dominate the Korean economy，growing out of the takeover of the Japanese monopoly of the Korean economy following World War II. Korean government tax breaks and financial incentives emphasizing industrial reconstruction and exports provided continuing support to the growth of Charbols during the 1970s and 1980s. In 1988，the output of the 30 largest chaebol represented almost 95% of Korea's gross national product. ［韩国］柴坡尔，大型联合企业：带有强烈家族控制、独裁管理和集中决策特征的韩国大型联合企业。这些在第二次世界大战之后，韩国经济摆脱日本垄断财团控制中发展起来的大型联合企业支配着韩国经济。20世纪70年代和80年代，韩国政府通过减免税赋和金融优惠政策推进工业改组和出口，继续扶持了这些大企业的发展。1988年，30家大型联合企业的产值几乎占当年韩国国民生产总值的95%。

Commanditaire Vennoot-schap（C.V.）：［Netherlands］designation for a limited partnership in which at least one of the partners has general personal liability and at least one of the other partners has limited liability ［荷兰］有限责任合营公司在这种公司中，至少有一名合伙人承担一般个人责任，同时在其他合伙人中至少有一名合伙人承担有限责任。

Compagnie(Cie)：［France/Luxembourg］general designation for a business organization［法国/卢森堡］公司：对企业的一般称呼。

Interessantelskab（I/S）：［Denmark，Norway］designation for a general partnership，in which all partners have joint and several liability［丹麦、挪威］合伙制：一般合伙制的名称，所有合伙人共同承担连带和个别责任。

Kabushiki Kaisha（KK）：［Japan］designation for a joint stock company with limited personal liability to shareholders［日本］株式会社，股份有限公司

Kommanditgesellschaft（KG）：［Austria，Germany，Switzerland］designation for a limited partnership in which at least one of the partners has general liability and at least one of the other partners has limited liability［奥地利、德国、瑞士］（无限、有限股份）两合公司：在有限合伙人中，至少其中一个合伙人承担全部责任，而合伙人中至少有一位承担有限责任的公司的名称。

Kommanditselskab（K/S）：［丹麦］（无限、有限股份）两合公司

Limitada（Ltda.）：［Brazil，Portugal］designation for a private limited liability corporation with limited liability to shareholders［巴西、葡萄牙］私人有限责任股份公司：对股东承担有限责任的私人有限公司的名称。葡萄牙亦称 Sociedad por Quota。

Limitée：（Ltée）［Canada］designation for a public corporation with limited liability to shareholders［加拿大］有限公司：一种对股东只负有限责任的公营公司的名称。

Maatschappij（Mij.）：［Netherlands］designation for a combination of two or more persons who enter into a joint arrangement to conduct certain business activities［荷兰］合作公司：两个或两个以上的个人，签订合作协定以进行商务活动的联合体名称。

Naamloze Vennotschap（N.V.）：designation for a joint stock company with limited personal liability to shareholders［比利时、荷兰］有限责任股份公司

Offene Handelsgesellschaft（OHG）：［Austria］designation for a general partnership，in which all partners have joint and several liability.［奥地利］合伙公司：一般合伙制企业的名称，所有的合伙人承担连带和个别责任。

Osakeyhtiot（Oy）：［Finland］designation for a joint stock company with limited personal liability to shareholders［芬兰］私人有限责任公司：股东承担有限责任的股份公司的名称。

Private Limited（Pte. Ltd.）：［India，Rhodesia，Singapore］designation for a private limited liability corporation with limited liability to shareholders［印度、罗得西亚、新加坡］私人有限责任公司：对股东承担有限责任的私人有限责任公司的名称。

Proprietary Limited（Pty. Ltd.）：［Australia，South Africa］designation for a private limited liability corporation with limited liability to shareholders［澳大利亚、南非］私人有限责任公司，（有限责任的）股份有限公司：对股东承担有限责任的私人有限责任公司的名称。

Sociedad Anónima（S.A.）：［Latin America，Mexico，Spain］designation for a joint stock company with limited personal liability to shareholders［拉丁美洲、墨西哥、西班牙］有限责任股份公司：对股东承担有限责任的联合股份公司的名称。

Sociedad a Responsabilidad Limitada（S.R.L.）：［Latin America，Mexico，Spain］

designation for a private limited liability corporation with limited liability to shareholders [拉丁美洲、墨西哥、西班牙]有限责任股份公司

Sociedad por Quota (S. Q.)：[Portugal] designation for a private limited liability corporation with limited liability to shareholders [葡萄牙]私人有限责任股份公司：对股东承担有限责任的私人有限责任公司的名称。

Società a Garanzia Limitata (S. G. L.)：[Switzerland] designation for a private limited liability corporation with limited liability to shareholders [瑞士]私人有限责任股份公司：对股东承担有限责任的私人有限责任公司的名称。

Società Cooperative a Responsabilità (SCaRL)：[Italy, Switzerland] designation for an incorporated association with limited liability for its members, unless its articles provide otherwise [意大利、瑞士]有限责任公司

Società in Accomandita Semplice (S. A. S.)：[Italy] designation for a limited partnership in which at least one of the partner has general liability and at least one of the other partners has limited liability [意大利]有限合营公司：一种有限合营公司的名称，其中至少有一个合伙人承担无限责任且在其他合伙人中至少有一名合伙人承担有限责任。

Società per Azioni (S. p. A.)：[Italy] designation for a joint stock company with limited personal liability to shareholders [意大利]有限责任股份公司：对股东承担有限个人责任的联合股份有限公司的名称。

Société (Sté)：[France, Luxembourg, Switzerland] general designation for a corporation, partnership, or association [法国、卢森堡、瑞士](通用名称)公司，合营公司

Société Anonyme (S. A.)：[Belgium, France, Luxembourg, Switzerland] designation for a joint stock company with limited personal liability to shareholders [比利时、法国、卢森堡、瑞士]股份有限公司，有限责任股份公司

Société à Responsabilité Limitée (S. R. L.)：[France, Luxembourg, Switzerland] designation for a private limited liability corporation with limited liability to shareholders [法国、卢森堡、瑞士]私人有限责任股份公司

Société en Commandité par Actions (S. C.)：[France, Luxembourg] designation for a limited partnership in which the partners have limited liability [法国、卢森堡]有限合营公司：合伙人承担有限责任的有限合营公司的名称。

Société en Commandité Simple (S. C. S.)：[France, Luxembourg] designation for a limited partnership in which at least one of the partners has general personal liability and at least one of the other partners has limited liability [法国、卢森堡]有限合营公司：一种有限合营公司的名称。其中至少有一个合伙人承担无限责任且在其他合伙人中至少有一名合伙人承担有限责任。

Société Cooperative (Sté Cve.)：[Belgium, Switzerland] designation for an incorporated association with limited liability for its members, unless its articles provide otherwise [比利时、瑞士]有限责任公司：对其成员承担有限责任(除非其章程另有规定)的公司的名称。

Société de Personnes à Responsabilité Limitée (S. P. R. L.)：[Belgium] designation for a private limited liability company with limited liability to shareholders［比利时］私人有限责任股份公司：对股东承担有限责任的私人有限责任公司的名称。

Société en Nom Collectif（S. N. C.）：［France，Luxembourg］designation for a general partnership，in which all partners have joint and several liability［法国、卢森堡］普遍合伙公司：一种普遍合伙公司的名称，其中所有的合伙人承担连带和个别责任。

Vennootschap Onder Firma［Netherlands］designation for a general partnership，in which all partners have joint and several liability［荷兰］无限责任公司：在这种合营公司中，所有合伙人都负有连带和个别责任。

3.4　揣摩语境，选取语义

美国语言学家、翻译家和翻译理论家尤金·奈达在其专著 *Language and Culture——Contexts in Translating*（2001）中从不同的侧面分析了语言与文化的密切关系，进而从语境角度论述怎样处理翻译中的种种关系和问题。他认为词语及词义的选择"主要取决于其所处语境的多个方面"（p. 138），而且，在决定词义时"语境的作用最大"，"与所分析的术语相比，特定的语境事实上提供了更为独特的语义"（JOOS 1972）。而英国著名的翻译理论家彼得·纽马克教授在其《翻译问题探讨》（2001）一书中对语境在翻译中的重要作用也有独到的论述，他认为："语境在所有翻译中都是最重要的因素。其重要性大于任何法规、任何理论、任何基本词义。"

刘敬国、何刚强（2011：128）在论述"翻译与语境"时指出，"'语境（context）'一词本来的含义是特定句子之前或之后的词或句子"，"翻译从来不是在真空状态下发生的，它必然发生在一定的社会文化语境之中，依托特定的历史潮流，受制于特定的社会意识形态，服务于特定的社会阶层。因此，翻译必然会受到特定时代或特定社会文化语境的影响，从而体现出特定的时代特征和群体特征"。

所以，在翻译实践中，译者须明白英语词语的意义通常由其所处的语境来决定。这一点尤其表现在不同的学科之间，同样一个词，用在不同的学科，其意相去甚远，甚或毫不相干。当我们遇到冷僻难解的词语时我们不妨查一下词典，大多情况下不会出错。然而，一些非常普通熟悉的词语往往因其"容易"而麻痹了译者，特别是当它们出现在不同学科的语境中时，我们常因"似曾相识"或"忽略不计"而造成误译。如：bridge，普通英语中指"桥"，也转喻"起沟通作用的东西，纽带"，但在舰船上指"驾驶台，桥楼"，天文学上指"（跨越太阳黑子的本影的）亮桥"，而化学及摔跤运动中的"桥"又各有其不同的含义。再如 spring 一词，陆谷孙教授主编的《英汉大词典》（1993 年版）就其不及物动词列有 20 种释义，及物动词列有 12 种释义，而名词列有 13 种释义，还未包括航海学中"倒缆""船首迎风现象"，气象学中的"大潮"等释义。所以在翻译中特别是从事商务文体或科技文体的翻译时我们必须揣摩语境，选取语义，以免误译。

3.4.1　常用的词语在不同的语境中有其特定的语义

有些常用的词语，乍一看便知其含义，但在不同的语境中有其特定的语义，翻译时一不小心，就会造成误译。英语中有很多词或词语在不同的语境中出现就有新的释义。所以翻译之前译者必须确定理解了上下文的含义。下面所举误译正应了奈达(2001，184)教授之言："通常这就意味着在没有考虑邻近段落甚至整个原文的情况下要理解一个句子是不可能的。"

● "Everything comes to an end," he said finally. "You need to know when to let go. She's given us 40 wonderful years. Now it's time to move on."

原译："凡事总有尽头，"最后他说，"你们需要知道何时让她离去。她已经给了我们40年的美好时光。现在是继续前进的时候了。"(宗奕扬，1996，113)

在同一篇文章的下文中，作者再次使用了 move on：

● He had been right to sell her, I realized now, because he knew the aging *Phyllis* couldn't be kept just for its memories——any more than we can continue reliving any other experience over and over beyond its time. We have to move on.

原译：我现在认识到父亲将她卖掉是正确的，因为他懂得陈旧的"菲莉斯"不能只因纪念它而保留——就像我们不能在超过一定时间以后继续重温任何别的经历一样。我们必须要向前走。(宗奕扬，1996，116)

这两个句中的 move on 有"继续前进""向前走"的意思，也指"(交通警察用语)走开，不要逗留"，如：

"Come on, sir, move on", said the policeman. 警察说："快点！先生，继续向前走。"

The man seemed to be annoying people, so the policeman moved him on.

那个男人好像在打扰别人，所以警察要他走开。

但在本文的语境中，作者讲述的是爸爸要卖掉家中的"菲莉斯"号旧船，理由是这船跟随他40年了，已破旧不堪，所以现在是"更换主人"的时候了，我们不得不"换掉她"，购置一条新船。根据这一上下文，move on 应是"更换……"的意思。又如：

I think we've talked enough about that subject, let's move on.

关于那个问题我认为我们已经谈得够多了，让我们改谈别的吧。

Some people believed in the dogma for a time and then moved on.

有些人一度相信过这种教条，后来改信别的了。

● Mr. Bixby handled the engine bells, and in due time the boat's nose came to the land, (and the next moment we were standing up the river again, all serene.)

原译：比克斯比先生操纵着蒸汽机车钟，船头在适当的时候接触到陆地。(接着，我们又继续站着，往河的上游驶去，一切正常。)(王善武，1996，41)

英语中 stand 是一个使用频率极高的词，人们最能想到的词义是"站立"，而在外贸运输业中，该词指船舶"取特定的航向"，这里后接 up the river 表示航向是"朝上游驶去"。故原译宜改译为：

接着，我们又继续往河的上游驶去，一切正常。

● Now and again we came to a rapid, of no great consequence when compared with the turbulent rapids of the Yangtze, but sufficiently swift to call for trackers to pull the junks that were going up stream; and we, going down, passed through them with many shouts, shot the foaming breakers, and presently reached water as smooth as any lake.

原译：我们也不时遇上急流，当然和扬子江上的汹涌急流相比，那简直不值一提，不过那水流也相当急湍，必须雇几个拉纤夫才能把船拖往上游去。我们走下船去，和他们比肩而过时总要喊上一阵，给如雪的浪花拍了几张照片，然后一瞬间又到了如平湖一样的水面。（于岚，1995，53）

这里 going down 是相对于上文的 going up stream（驶往上游）而言的，即"驶往下游"，而 shot the foaming breakers 与其前的"passed through…"及其后的"reached…"三个动作并列作谓语。

shot 为 shoot 的过去式，诚然 shoot 有"拍摄……"的意思，但根据语境，作者的船从他们（驶往上游的船只）中间经过，穿过（shot）激浪，转而来到平湖般的水面这一连串的动作，译者取 shoot 的"拍摄"词义不妥，这里是"在……迅速穿过""使（船等）飞速行进"的意思。又如：

shoot a rapid 迅速通过急流

shoot a bridge 从桥下迅速地穿过

上文的后一分句应改译为：

我们正驶向下游，大喊大叫着从他们中间驶过，迅速地穿过了飞沫激浪，瞬间又到了平湖般的水面。

3.4.2　同一个词语在不同的专业中有其特定的语义

其实在本节的开头部分已提到这一问题。请看例句：

• The sailors slept in bare wooden bunks with straw mattresses. Conditions for the officers were better, but still very bad by modern standards.

原译：水手们睡在光秃秃的木板铺位上，上面只铺着草垫子。官员们的条件要好些，但用现在的标准衡量仍然很差。（赵琏，1986，85）

这段文字中的 officers 并非指一般的"官员们"，而是相对于 sailor（水手），motorman（机工）等"普通船员"而言的舰只或船舶上的"高级船员"，如果在甲板部是指"驾驶员"，他们又分为大副（the chief officer）、二副（the second officer）、三副（the third officer）三个等级，officers in charge, officers on duty 通常译为"值班驾驶员"，而不译为"值班官员"；在机舱部则指大管轮（second engineer）、二管轮（third engineer）、三管轮（fourth engineer）；此外，当然还包括船长（captain）和轮机长（chief engineer）等。

改译：水手们睡在铺着草垫子的木板铺位上，而高级船员们的条件更好些，但用现在的标准衡量仍然很差。

• When it was half its present distance from the earth, it's power over the ocean tides was eight times as great as now, and the tidal range may even then have been severed hundred feet on certain shores. But when the earth was only a few million years old… The range of the surf was enormously extended by the reach of the tides, so that the waves would batter the crests of high cliffs and sweep inland to erode the continents.

原译：当其位置还在与地球的现有距离的一半的时候，它施加于海潮的力量是现在的八倍，而那时候潮水席卷之范围在某些海岸可达百尺以上。可是当地球只有几百万年的时候……潮汐汹涌，拍岸浪波及的范围大大扩展，波浪冲击悬崖峭壁的顶峰，席卷内地，侵蚀大陆。(《英语》教参编写组，1989，346)

原文中的 tidal range 等于 range of tide，意为"潮差"或"潮高"。下文的 the range of surf 为"激浪(拍岸浪)的浪差"或"激浪的高度"。这里 range 是一个专业术语，意为"distance between limits"，即汉语的"差距，较差"，而不是通常的"范围"之意。又如：

the annual range of temperature 每年的温差

改译：当它(月球)离地球的距离只有现在的一半时，它作用于海潮的力量是现在的八倍之大。就在那时，在某些海岸潮差可达上百英尺。然而，当地球只有几百万年的时候……潮水到达时，激浪的高度大大增加。大浪冲击高高悬崖的顶峰，席卷内地，侵蚀大陆。

3.4.3 历史文化背景决定语义

有些词语因其所指的事物有着特定的历史文化内涵，所以词义须根据其所指而定。奈达(2001，5)认为："有些人以为翻译中的最大难题是在目的语中找到正确的词语和结构。相反地，对译者而言最难的事是要完全正确地理解被译原文的所指意义及关联意义(designative and associative meaning)。"

下面这个例句中的 province 一词所表达的"行政区划"可以说明这个问题：

• Before he reached the age of thirty he was made governor of the Chinese Province of Yan gui.

原译：不到三十岁他就被任命为中国扬州城的总管。(赵琰，1982，33)

译者在译注中，将画线部分又译成"被任命为扬州省的总管"。

究竟是"扬州城"还是"扬州省"呢？两者均不对。这里译者显然是在没有搞清 province 在本文中所指意义的前提下进行的翻译。

英语 province 一词，相当于我国现在的"省"，但根据本文的语境，作者叙述的是马可•波罗在我国的元朝忽必烈时代发生的事，这就有必要考证一下 province 所表示的我国特定历史时期的"行政区划"了。实际上，这里的 province 指历史上的"路"，这是我国古代宋、金、元的地方区划名。宋初为加强中央集权，仿唐代道制分境内为二十一路，其后分合不一，至道二年(公元996年)始定为十五路，真宗时增为十八路，神宗时又分为二十三路。北宋分路以转运司为主，前所称十五路、十八路、二十三路等，皆指转运司路而言；南宋分路则以安抚司为主。金仿宋制，分境内为十九路。元朝时降为第二等地方行政区划，置总管府，隶属于省。明朝时废除。查《辞海》"扬州"条下第3项载："州、路、府名。隋开皇九年改吴州为扬州，治江都(今扬州市)。唐辖今江苏扬州、泰州、江都、高邮、兴化、六合、泰兴、海安、如皋、姜堰和安徽天长等市县地。元改路，明改府。"(《辞海》编辑委员会，1999，808)所以有时"对于译者来说，百科全书通常比词典有用得多"(奈达，2001，159)，当你在词典查不到合适的释义时，你最好考虑去翻阅其他相关的书籍，也许不失为一个有效的选择。

正确的译文应是："……被任命为中国(元朝)扬州路的总管"。

在这种情况下为了能使你的译文得到正确的理解，对明朝的这一行政区划还可进一步加注说明。

包惠南等认为，英语中还"存在着在特定语境中词语的指称意义与语用意义不一致的情况"，如：

John can be relied on. He eats no fish and plays the game.

原译：约翰为人可靠。他不吃鱼，还玩游戏。

从字面上看，译句与原文形式对应，词义贴切，似乎无可挑剔，但由于译者缺乏文化背景知识，仅译出了句子的表层意思。原来在英国历史上新旧宗教派别之间斗争十分激烈，旧教规定在斋戒日只许吃鱼，新教推翻了旧教后，新教徒拒绝在斋日吃鱼，以表示皈依新教，忠于新教，所以 to eat no fish 表示"忠诚"之义；to play the game 原是游戏、比赛术语，表示"按规则进行比赛"，转义为"光明正大""为人正直"。

改译：约翰为人可靠。他既忠诚又正直。

另外，不同行业中也有一些行业文化的语言表现形式。例如：

The boy had just eaten his dinner and been called to the bar.

原译：这个男孩刚刚吃完饭就被叫到酒吧去了。

这样的翻译似乎表达没错，但如果是用在英国法律界，那就不可以这样翻译，因为 bar 这里指的是"律师席"，应译为"这个年轻人刚刚取得律师资格，新近当上了律师"。在英国律师界有个习惯，大学法律系的学生每学期必须到律师公会参加若干次聚餐，才有资格当律师。句中 dinners 就是指律师公会所举办的聚餐会。

综上所述，语境对词语的选择至关重要，词语出现在不同的上下文有其不同的含义。虽然有时词语并不难，但要正确地理解并用恰如其分的汉语表达出来并非易事。"译事难"，不同学科的翻译更是如此。奈达（2001）在谈到胜任的译者时说："人们总是认为译者至少能通两国语言（bilingual），但事实上这是不够的。完全胜任的译者还需要了解两种文化（bicultural），以便能'读出字里行间的意义'。"的确，英语和汉语之间不但语言上差异很大，而且两种文化也绝不相同，所以语言—文化—翻译三者互相联系，密不可分，在翻译过程中更要反复揣摩原文的语境，把读懂语境作为选择语义的先决条件。只有"通过多个不同的语境来决定某些特定词语的释义或多个释义，其结果可能获得对全文的正确理解而无须查阅所有可疑的或陌生的词语"（奈达，p. 176）。在翻译商务英语专业性内容时，译者更要注意对该专业的术语有所掌握或了解，否则，译文无法通畅达意，有时还会贻笑大方。

第四章 广告文体翻译

4.1 概　述

冯庆华(1998：419)在论述应用文体的范畴时认为，"应用英语不是一种统一的文体类别，它的体式最为驳杂"。广告与其他多种文体一样，属应用文之列。"广告英语在英语语体中是一种独特的语类，文体学上一般将它分为两种体式：书面广告语体和口语广告语体"(冯庆华，1998：419)，本书着重讨论书面广告语体。

贾文波(2005：157)认为，广告类文本"按纽马克的划分，应归属于'呼唤型'文本"，其目的是使人认识、理解某种商品或服务，以说服消费者产生购买欲望和购买行为，其功利性强。广告语言风格独特，富于感召力，译文也应有助于达到这一目的，做到简洁、精练、生动、形象，富于感情色彩和感染力，符合译文读者的期待。

广告语是一种非常特殊的语言表达，遣词造句十分讲究，总让读者感到幽默中见智慧，平淡中显新奇。如"海尔"产品在中国家喻户晓，它有一则英语广告语：

Haier and Higher.

它巧妙地用海尔的汉语拼音 Haier 与英语 Higher 相似的发音，在美国市场上一炮打响，而此广告语译成中文为"海尔，越来越高"，不久后在电视上我们又见到了"海尔，永创新高"的译语，显然后者比前者更符合汉语的表达习惯，而且更体现了广告语的宣传和带动功效。

再如 2002 年世界艾滋病日的主题语为：

Live and Let Live.

直译为：活着，也让人活着。或者译为：自己活，也让他人活。

上述翻译不能将这一主题鲜明地再现出来，而译成"相互关爱，共享生命"则富于感情色彩，并起到了富有感召力的宣传效果。

从语言文化角度考虑，汉英两种语言广告的表现形式大相径庭，通用文体规范(general style conventions — Nord，2001：52)不太一样，读者的期待和关注点亦不尽相同，具体表现在：英语表达客观具体，突出信息功能，而汉语讲究以言感人，偏重呼唤功能；英语强调用户至上，消费者利益高于一切，突出 YOU-ATTITUDE，因而形式上多用 YOU-FORM，而汉语突出企业至上，以我为中心，但惯用第三人称进行表达，以树立其形象，博得用户的信赖；英语行文简洁通俗，便于记忆，而汉语表达夸张，充满评述性的话语。这些都与两种文化的差异、思维方式和阅读习惯的不同不无关系。译者进行这类文体翻译时，切忌照搬照译，注意正确地传递信息并感染读者。所以广告文体既具有"信息型"的特征，又具有"呼唤型"的特点。译者可运用 Nord 的观点从内容到形式进行适当的调整，即：（1）文化知识的差异要求对文本明示的信息以及暗含的信息进行调整（the difference in cultural knowledge may require an adjustment of the relationship between explicit and implicit information in the text）；（2）对特有文化类型的不同期待要求对译语文本形式按目的语的文化语境和文体规范进行改写（the difference in culture-specific genre expectation may require an adaptation of the text's form to target culture textual and stylistic conventions）（Nord，2001：63），以将合格的译文提供给读者。根据体裁、风格、写法，广告可分为直述式、叙述式、描写式等，翻译时译者要根据广告的具体文本形式进行表达。

4.2　广告英语的词汇特点

广告英语用词与普通英语有着较大的区别。广告英语的创作遵循 AIDA 原则，即 Attention 引起注意→Interest 激发兴趣→Desire 刺激需求→Action 采取行动。要说服对方，首先要引起对方的注意（Attention），令他产生兴趣（Interest）。假如对方对这一主张产生兴趣而加以审读，成交的希望就很大。因此，要让对方觉得"这个好""这个有需要""买这个看看"，以对他有益和有效的说辞，来刺激他的需求欲（Desire）。当然要做到这一点必须采取行动（Action），举出实际的方法与步骤，使对方的需求欲立即受到鼓励。所以，作为一种特殊的文体，广告英语自然在用词方面有其独到之处。

4.2.1　创新造字，引起注意

在英语广告中，创作人员故意把一些大家熟悉的字词拼错或加上前缀、后缀，以达到生动有趣、引人注意的目的，有效地传播商品信息。如下面这则造字（Coinage）广告：

The Orangemostest Drink in the world.

显而易见，这是一则饮料广告，orange + most +est。most，-est 都是英语形容词的最高级，在这里与 orange 连用，使读者联想到这种橙汁饮料的"高纯度、高营养"。

再如"天美时"牌手表 Timex，用 time + excellent，充分强调了手表超高的精准度。所以在英语广告中，用 super-，ex- 构成的词频频出现，其目的就是强调产品或服务的优异性。如：supercalendered, supercolossal, superexcellent, superfine, supernatural, superlight, Rolex, Playtex, Kleenex 等。

再看一则错拼（misspelling）广告：

Drinka

Pinta

Milka

Day

这是一则牛奶广告，连起来读的效果相当于 Drink a pint of milk a day。但 of 这个词常被弱读，而其后的 milk 一词又以辅音开头，因此/əv/便弱化为/ə/，与字母 a 的发音相同，a 便成了它们的后缀，不但可引起人们的注意和兴趣，而且音律优美，朗朗上口。

4.2.2　多语并用，增强效果

英美国家中，许多产品从国外进口，或本国生产却富于国外风味。所以广告中经常出现多种语言(最为常见的有法语和西班牙语)并用的现象，表示产品的异国风味或优质，以吸引消费者的注意。

Order it in bottles or in cannes.

Perrier…with added *je ne sais quoi*.

je ne sais quoi 为法语，意为 I don't know what。这样既增加了读者对饮料的好奇，又表明了它是正宗的法国风味，无疑增加了产品的吸引力。

另有一则旅游广告，画面上左边是伦敦标志性建筑大本钟(Big Ben)，右边是巴黎标志性建筑埃菲尔铁塔(the Eiffel Tower)，从两建筑物的上部连起了一行字：

START IN DOWNTOWN LONDON AND IN 3 HOURS，ARRIVEZ AU CENTRE DE PARIS.

这则广告意为"从伦敦闹市起程 3 小时抵达巴黎市中心"。有趣的是前半句"从伦敦出发"用的是英语，而"抵达巴黎市中心"则是法语。一方面表示直达，另一方面表示需要改变的只是语言，体现了创作者的别出心裁，达到了妙趣横生的效果。

同样，汉语广告在用词方面也十分讲究，但最明显的特点是四字结构，其中有的是约定俗成，有的是随意组合，通过并列、重叠、排比的方式结合起来，以加强语义，增加语势、强化广告的艺术感染力。无论是汉译英还是英译汉，都要注意到不同语言的措辞特点。

4.3　广告词汇的翻译

4.3.1　常见的动词译法

have，get，give，buy，keep 表示消费者取得和拥有某种商品；take，use，have 表示消费者使用某种商品的动作和过程；而 like，love，need 表示消费者对其喜爱程度。

4.3.2　广告中常见的形容词变化

为了达到形象、生动的目的，用来修饰、描绘名词，自由充当主语补语和宾语补语的形容词使用极多。good，new，great，fine 使用率最高。翻译时可搭配使用变化中的很多表达法。

4.3.3　复合词的灵活运用

广告中有许多随意组合的复合词，用法特殊新颖，给人印象至深。如 fresh-tasting milk，easy-to-dress clothes，look at the oh-so-comfortable size…这些词如译得好，可使语言更加口语化，令人感到亲切。

4.4　广告英语的句法特点

4.4.1　多用并列句，少用主从结构

侯维瑞(1988)在《英语语体》(*Varieties of English*)一书中指出，"广告英语为求得简洁，常倾向于更多地使用并列结构，而相对较少使用复合结构。"这句话高度概括了广告英语在句法结构方面的一个重要特点，相对于复合结构而言，并列结构读起来更亲切自然，易于为人们所接受。例：

- Polaroid instant movies.　　宝丽得/拍立得速成电影
  Easy to make.　　　　　　　制作简单
  Easy to show.　　　　　　　放映便捷
  Hard to believe.　　　　　　难以置信

Polaroid 是物理学名词，意为"人造偏光板"，或"(用于太阳镜、车窗的)偏振片"，又指"拍立得照相机"，为美国拍立得公司于1947年制成，照相曝光60秒即可取得相片 (= Polaroid camera 商标名称)。

4.4.2　频繁使用疑问句和祈使句

据统计，每30句广告语中就有一句疑问句，这是因为疑问句要求读者对问题作出回答，易激起共鸣。如：

- Are you going grey too early?
  You will buy this special gift to your darling, don't you?

祈使句具有明显的劝购导向作用，如：

- Our sandalwood soap not only possesses all the merits sandalwood soap may have, but also does no harm whatever to your skin. Just try it, and you will see our sincere recommendation is rather convincing. 我厂生产的檀香皂不仅具有檀香皂的独特优点，而且对皮肤无害。君请试之，方知言而有信。

4.4.3　使用省略句

省略主语、谓语或其他成分，如：

- Fresh up with seven-up. 饮七喜，提精神。

4.5　广告翻译的技巧

丁衡祁(2004)认为，广告口号(slogans)、广告语句(catch phrases)等是一种非常特殊的语言。它们通常都有一些共同点，如语言上引人入胜、说服力强，修辞手段的运用别具一格，如语意双关、文字游戏等，幽默中见智慧，平淡中显新奇。广告语言在形式上也极具特色，或行文工整、对仗押韵，或节奏感强、朗朗上口，或一鸣惊人、耳目一新，有耐

人寻味、经久不忘的效果。广告语言的特点可以归纳为以下四个方面，即吸引力（attractive — catch the reader's attention）、创造力（creative — project an image）、说服力（persuasive — urge the reader to act）和影响力（impressive — produce an impact）。广告通过图案和语言树立各自的独特形象，用标新立异的手法来体现其个性特点，其技巧的运用在常人的想象之外，却又在情理之中。一则好的广告图文并茂、双管齐下，用有针对性的感情化的图画和语言来吸引人和打动人。

本小节将引用对外经济贸易大学丁衡祁先生 2004 年所撰"翻译广告文字的立体思维"中的主要内容对广告汉—英、英—汉翻译的技巧作一介绍。

在翻译英语广告文字时，无论是英译汉还是汉译英，绝不能满足于字面上的翻译，做"表面文章"，必须使译文既准确又地道，尤其是要把原文中的"潜台词"（message）或言外之意传达出来。此外，还要利用一些常用的技巧和手段，把广告词语的个性（personality）表现出来，这样，广告的"呼唤型"功能才能凸显得淋漓尽致。

要想达到上述效果，必须树立端正的工作态度。首先要创造必要的前提条件，那就是具备扎实的语言基本功，需拓宽知识面、培养创新的思维模式以及提高研究和写作的能力。要把翻译的过程当作研究和创作的过程，投入大量的心血和劳动，反复琢磨、数易其稿，做到左右逢源、千锤百炼。只有这样，才能在充分消化原文意思、吃透原文精神以及掌握原文特点的基础上，翻译出具有欣赏价值和市场效益的广告语言。

4.5.1 汉译英

有一则《理财》杂志的广告很简单，但非常有意思，只有四个字在那里颠来倒去，像绕口令一样：

● 你不理财，财不理你。

其意为：如果你想生财，就必须学会理财，而想学会理财，就应看我《理财》杂志。

把这则广告译成英语，既传达原文的意思，又表现其形式上的特点，切入点在哪里呢？有人想到了 leave sb. alone 这个表达法，抓住了关键，于是产生了 If you leave money alone, money will leave you alone. 这个雏形。下一步就是翻译"理财"。"理财"的正式英语表达是 corporate finance 和 personal finance，但为了形式上的需要，我们选择了 manage money 的说法。这样一来，就得到了如下译文，既传达了原文的意思，又基本上表现了原文的形式：

译文：You leave *Managing Money* alone, Money will manage to leave you alone.

广告语"你不理财，财不理你"所使用的手法，实际上是一种常见的玩弄文字游戏（play on words）手法，类似绕口令。这种手法在英语广告中屡见不鲜。下面的三个例子都属这一类，分别在"美"字、"优"字、"包"字上做文章。这类翻译的切入点就是要突破关键词。

● "美的"牌家用电器的广告语："美的"家电，美的全面，美的彻底。

"美的"一共出现三次。但由于"美的"牌的英译是 Midea，没有"美"的含义，所以翻译时就难以做到音意双全，一箭双雕。三个"美的"可以用三个 beautiful 来代替，但必须"拐个弯儿"：Midea home appliances are beautiful — beautiful from head to toe, beautiful inside out.

- "三优"牌家具的广告语：优良的质量，优惠的价格，优质的服务。

"三优"牌家具的标识是三个英文字母 U，在翻译成英语时，必须考虑到把其与汉语中的"优"字相对应，做到意音形三者兼顾：

Unrivalled quality.

Unbeatable prices.

Unreserved service.

- "三包"承诺：我们实行"三包"：包修、包退、包换。

翻译时，译者除了要考虑到"三包"的缩略特点之外，还应尽量符合市场营销的表达习惯，例如：We give our customers satisfaction guarantee.

译文：We offer 3-R guarantee, namely guaranteed repair, replacement and refund.

翻译广告语句有时候需要左右逢源，运用多种翻译技巧，从不同的角度进行多层次的处理，这样才能有达意、传神和表形的翻译效果。例如：

- 茅台酒的广告语：茅台一开，满室生香；国酒茅台，源远流长。

茅台酒源远流长，是指在公元前 135 年，茅台镇就酿出了使汉武帝"甘美之"的酒，盛名于世。1915 年，茅台酒荣获在美国旧金山举行的巴拿马—太平洋万国博览会的金奖，并先后十四次荣获国际金奖，同 Scotch Whiskey 和 French Cognac 一起成为世界三大名酒。在翻译这条广告语的时候，要做一点变通，采取意译。原文中"茅台"出现两次，在译文中应该避免。关于"开酒瓶"，如果是香槟酒，可以生动形象地翻译成 pop open，但对茅台酒就不合适了。"国酒"如果翻译成 a liquor of national status 或 a liquor for state banquets 都太长，它可以用 national favor（全国宴会用酒首选）来代替。而 VIP treatment 则是"款待贵宾"的意思。"源远流长"如果翻译成 has/with a long history 就显得太平淡，不如将它具体化，指出它早在 1915 年就已经得过大奖，同时在括号中注明它源自公元前 135 年。在形式上，把"茅台酒——陈年佳酿"作为标题，主体部分还是分作两行，大体上对称，而且让芳香 aroma 和证书 diploma 两个词互相押韵。

译文：Moutai — a vintage liquor

A VIP treat which diffuses the finest aroma

A national favor that won a 1915 diploma (Originated in 135 B. C.)

广告语汉译英时要有很强的"翻译意识"，即脑子里要为外国读者着想。所以对含有汉语拼音的词要认真处理。下面例子中的 LongCard 就不能写成 long card：

- 建设银行的龙卡广告语：衣食住行，有龙则灵。

翻译"龙卡"时，要模仿 MasterCard 的联写法，同时把"龙"变成斜体 *Long*，以便与英语中的 long 相区别。

译文：Your everyday life is very busy,

Our *Long*Card can make it easy.

包通法（2005）认为，从商业角度来看，上述译文仍显得冗繁拖沓，拘泥于汉语的对仗形式。改译为：

*Long*Card makes your busy life easy.

86

基于同样的道理，对于外国读者可能感到模糊或产生误解的词要尽量交代清楚，看下例：

- 集邮杂志的广告语：方寸之间，深情无限。

翻译这条广告时，要说明"方寸"指的是什么，"深情"是指的何种感情。即使是中国人，如果不是集邮爱好者，也不清楚这里说的是什么。对外国读者就更加有必要交代清楚了。下面的译文基本做到了整齐押韵。对于 frank 一词的用法做了一些变通，把它的意思做了延伸：其原来的意思是，在信封上盖邮资已付的戳，这里借用来表示把集邮爱好者之间的友谊凝固到邮票上。

译文：On these tiny postage stamps

       Philatelists' friendship "franks".

- 《全球杂志》的广告语：一册在手，纵览全球。

有一种译文是：With a single copy of *The Globe* in hand,

       you can enjoy a wide view of the world.

这里有几点值得考虑：1. 用 single 一词来表示强调有点多余；2. "纵览"(look far and wide, scan) 一词的气势似乎没有表现出来；3. enjoy a wide view 有可能理解成欣赏景观；4. hand 与 world 不能算作押韵；5. 此译文只是字面上的翻译，是一句平铺直叙的话而不大像广告语言。这个例子和下面的几个例子的原译文都是字面上的翻译。

译文：With a copy of *The Globe* in your hand, the world unfolds before you so grand.

更简洁的译文：*GLOBE* widens your view of the world. (包通法：2005)

- 某皮鞋厂的广告语：皮张之厚无以复加，利润之薄无以复减。

原译：The leather shoes made here are thick enough;

       the profit that's obtained is slight enough.

此译文与原文的意思有出入：原文说的是皮张厚，而译文说的是鞋子厚(有可能误解为"松糕鞋")。另外，made here, that's obtained, slight 等都属于意思表达不清或词语搭配不当。这里翻译的关键是要把"加"与"减"的对比表现出来。

译文：The leather we use is quite thick;

       the profit we make is fairly thin.

改译：Thick leather shoes profit you thick. (包通法：2005)

改译虽没有对仗，但显然简洁明了。

- 某皮鞋油的广告语：第一流产品，为足下增光。

原译：This first-rate shoe polish adds luster to your shoes and honor to you, our friends.

adds luster to your shoes and honor to you 只是字面上的翻译，并且 our friends 似乎有点"画蛇添足"；另外，此译文更像是一句平铺直叙的话而不大像广告语言。还有一个关键"为足下增光"这个双关语没有表现出来。"足下"有"阁下"和"脚下"的双重意思，翻译时可以"一分为二"，分开表达：

译文：Our shoe polish is surely of the first rate;

       It shines your shoes and you look great.

对此译包通法教授(2005)评论"既无神韵又不符合广告口号求洁的要求，读起来亦拗口，缺乏号召力"，改译：Fine shoe polish polishes your shoes fine.

- "青岛"啤酒的广告语：不同的肤色，共同的选择。

原译：The same choice for different colors. 其意思是"大家都选不同的颜色"，与原意相去甚远，令人感到莫名其妙，也就谈不上原文中"不同"和"共同"的对照形式了。这样一个优质的产品和知名的品牌被宣传成了"四不像"，实在可惜。

译文：People's skin colors are different — far and near,

　　　　but their choice can be the same — for *Qingdao* Beer.

- 脚踏双星鞋，潇洒走世界。Double-Star Shines Your Way.（包通法：2005）
- 仁者近山，智者近水。（房产销售广告）

原译 1：The good are close to the mountain, the wise are close to the water. 该译文虽然"达"，结构也较为严谨，但直译明显，读起来不够朗朗上口。

原译 2：Gentle men prefer the mountain, wise men the fountain. 该译文虽然"达"，结构也较为严谨，但 gentlemen 尤指君子，相对于小人；同时 prefer 略显不足；另外，fountain 给人产生一种人造水源之感，脱离了本意，尽管对仗押韵。

这则广告模仿"仁者乐山，智者乐水"（The wise man delights in water, the good man delights in mountains.（by Arthur Waley））。参照 Arthur Waley 的译文，根据修辞结构平衡或趋向平衡的原则，把后半句放到句首，利用对偶省略的形式(尽管音步有所不同)，古英语不带连词 and 的特点，连同房产营销的目的给出下面的译文：

Wise men prefer to live near water, good men near mountains.

4.5.2　英译汉

分析几则专做体育用品公司的广告语。

- 耐克的广告语：Nothing is impossible.

它的另一广告语是：Just do it. 放胆做。Just do it 类似于 go for it.

耐克这句广告语是广告中的经典，既简单清楚又很口语化，而且从不同人的角度去看都会有不同的意思。从消费者的角度，意思是：我只选择它；就用这个。从商人的角度是：来试试。而将这句话用在日常的生活中就有了更丰富的含义，根据语境可以理解为：想做就做；坚持不懈，等。

just do it，突出年轻人的自我意识，强调运动本身。

just 的意思是"仅仅……"，可以引申为"不要考虑太多"。

"just do it" 也是耐克公司体育理念。

Nike 在 1988 年提出了这个广告语，当时 Nike 委托波特兰广告公司(Portland ad firm)的丹·威登(Dan Wieden)创造了这句广告语。

威登认为 do it 是唤起运动员向伟大竞技者转变的连接装置("connective device")，之后加了个 just 去强调。

还有一种说法，在一次会议上，威登因为很欣赏 Nike 说做就做的精神，对 Nike 员工说："You Nike guys, just do it!"

他个人在解释这个创意时说，just do it 不仅能应用到竞技运动的层面上，也能应用到普通人健身的层面之上。

- Impossible is nothing. 没有不可能。

广告创意的功效是吸引注意力。这里双重否定表示肯定，意为 everything is possible。它否定了"不可能"的存在，什么事情都是可能的。Nothing is impossible 意为"没有什么事情会不可能，无论多么困难总有成功的可能"。

而 Impossible is nothing 字面理解为"不可能的事是没有的事"，其语用意义是"他人认为不可能的事是没有价值的"，即使他人认为注定不可能的事也不惧怕。广告语的汉译为：没有不可能。

Impossible is nothing 比 Nothing is impossible 更有力，可以说掷地有声。Adidas 的广告策划者把 nothing 和 impossible 的位置前后对调，旨在通过这个广告语向读者充分传达公司的理念——创新超越。只有读者或消费者认同产品后才会接受产品，产生购买欲。此广告语透出了公司不畏艰难勇往直前的精神，必会获得读者认可。广告策划者特邀了拳王阿里等参与推广活动，阿里说："我的一生中超越了无数人们所认为的极限，我完全相信'Impossible is nothing'！"所以，Impossible is nothing 广告语传达出一种勇于挑战极限的精神。

阿迪达斯的广告让患帕金森综合征的拳王阿里重回拳台，"Impossible is Nothing"。只有不断面对挑战，超越极限，才能从不可能中激发潜能、创造奇迹。

Impossible is nothing. Adidas. 没有不可能。它所传达的理念和意境深深吸引着人们，在带来视觉上的新奇效果的同时，还给人们带来强烈的心灵震撼。它的作用已经超越一句广告语，成为鼓舞人们积极进取、勇敢面对挫折与困境的哲理短语。

- You were born to run. And we were born to help you do it better. You'll find us anywhere smart sports people buy their shoes. Adidas, the all sports people. 奔跑是你的天性。让你跑得更快是我们的天职。在优秀运动员买鞋的任何地方，你都能看到我们。阿迪达斯，运动者的代名词。

- Anything is impossible. 李宁，新推出"90 后李宁"栏目：make the change 让改变发生。"90 后李宁"有两层意思，一层是李宁要重新改革自己，吸引 90 后的消费群体；另一层是李宁创始于 1990 年，属于 90 后企业，希望让大家看到一个 90 后企业的风采。"20 岁的李宁希望通过一种方式告诉消费者：我们还是李宁，但是，是新李宁。"

把英文广告翻译成中文看起来很简单，其实不然。如果没有对英文原文进行深入准确的理解（包括字里行间的意思，语言的风格特点和所采用的技巧），没有灵活的思维方法和娴熟的中文表达能力，很难取得好的翻译效果。

- Petal-Drops

For the girl who wants a petal-soft skin

With Petal-Drops Moisturizing Bath-Essence you can give your skin a petal-fresh softness and fragrance that will last and last the whole day through.

All sorts of oils, delicately perfumed herbal essences and the gentlest of toning agents—all combined with our loving care to give that oh-so-good-to-be-alive feeling.

Relax. Petal-Drops your way to a smooth, silky skin.

Choose from two exciting fragrances：New Petal-Drops Coriander — with its faintly spiced hint of seductiveness，or the classic Petal-Drops Lavender.

润肤花露精

献给想让肌肤嫩如花露的少女

沐浴润肤花露精，将使你的肌肤柔软细嫩，昼夜芬芳。

各种油脂之上品、自然芳草之精华、毫无副作用的增益剂——与我们的精心爱心完美结合，才造就出这种美好生活的全新感受。

放心吧！有花露精精心呵护，你的皮肤会光滑，光润，光洁如丝。

有两种美妙的香型供你选用：新近研制的芫荽香型暗藏幽香，会使你平添魅力；你也可选择传统的香草香型——花露精。

- Deliciously simple，simply delicious. 美味地道，地道美味。

把英语的 simple 翻译成"地道"确实是一种地道的处理手法。

- Good to the last drop. 滴滴香浓，意犹未尽。

- The days of wine and roses. 美酒玫瑰醉人心。（情人节广告语）

- Interflora 花店的广告语：Flowers by Interflora speaks from the heart. "茵特"之花，表达肺腑之言。

Interflora 是一家花店的招牌。广告语中用了拟人的手法，突出鲜花代表的甜蜜和温馨，这种感情必须在译文中体现出来。有些花商的广告中用 heart specialist（把"心脏病专家"转意为"善解女人之心的人"）也是为了达到同样的目的。

- 摩尔香烟的广告语：Ask for More.

原译：摩尔香烟，我更满意。或：再来一支，还吸摩尔。

这两种翻译意思上都对，但文字效果上显得不足。Ask for More 是一语双关：More 既是香烟的品牌（摩尔牌），买香烟的时候指明要这个品牌；同时它又有"还要更多"的意思。在翻译的过程中，这种一语双关的效果只有通过"一分为二"的办法来实现：摩尔香烟，多而不厌。

- 某贸易公司的广告语：A deal with us means a good deal to you.

原译：和我们做买卖意味着您做了一笔好买卖。

这个译文把原文的意思基本传达出来了，但它没有表现出 a good deal 的双重意思即"一笔好买卖"和"许多"的好处。这里也可以用"一分为二"来对付"合二为一"。

改译：同我们做买卖，都是回报丰厚的好买卖。

- Only your time is more precious than this watch. 表贵，您的时间更宝贵。

众所周知，时间比什么都宝贵，把手表和时间相提并论，既突出说明了时间也显现了表的宝贵。

- Drive @ earth. 驰骋地球，关爱地球。（三菱汽车）

@ 原是重量单位和容积单位，后来成了工程用语，然后成了 DOS 命令，如常用语句"@ echo off"；再后一开始纯粹表示英文单词 at，但这种用法逐渐少了，又多了两种高频用法：用@代替邮箱用户名与域名间的间隔符"at"；表示单价，如 sell @ 1 pound 表示以 1 英镑单价出售。后来网络用语中@又增加了三种用法：1. @时代，即网络时代；2. @ 是一个很酷的表情，表示开心、高兴等；3. @族，即 14-29 岁的人。

广告的设计者巧妙地运用了@，表示车行驶的地点在地球上，喻意该品牌的汽车会风靡全球。而译者又将@的发音与"爱"音相谐，提示开车不忘爱护地球。

- Live with Focus. (Ford Focus 汽车) 福克斯相伴——活得精彩。

原文意思：与福克斯车一起生活。喻意驾驶福克斯车生活精彩无限。有人将上述广告翻译成：

自由天地，我有福克斯。

精彩生活，尽在福克斯。

拥有福克斯，尽享生活新情趣。

把原文一个十分简洁明了的广告翻译得如此冗长，不符合广告翻译的原则。

- A Diamond is Forever. 钻石恒久远，一颗永流传。(De Beers)

这句广告词可能真的会像钻石一样永久流传。1947 年，N. W. Ayer & Son 公司为戴比尔斯公司打造了这则广告，并被奉为经典。事实证明，经典的广告语总是丰富的内涵和优美的语句的结合体，戴比尔斯钻石的这句广告语，不仅道出了钻石的真正价值，更赋予爱情以钻石的品质，妙不可言。

- Don't dream it. Drive it. 告别梦想，尽情驰骋。

"告别梦想，尽情驰骋"，召唤人们对自己梦想的座驾发起行动。捷豹（Jaguar）的这句广告语巧用押头韵，dream 和 drive 读起来富有韵律感，单词的选择和组合传递出了完整的含义，令人过目不忘。

- Good to the last drop. 滴滴香浓，意犹未尽。(Maxwell House)

麦氏咖啡的广告语，简单而经典，读出来韵律也极美，像极了咖啡醇厚的味道，令人口齿生香。

- Because you're worth it. 你值得拥有。(L'Oreal)

美妆品牌多如满天繁星，萦绕耳际的却总是"巴黎欧莱雅，你值得拥有"。这句广告语让女人们感觉值得让自己拥有美丽，享受美好，而此生没有欧莱雅将是一大憾事，这就是欧莱雅的目的。

- Maybe she's born with it, maybe it's Maybelline. 或许因为天生丽质，或许因为美宝莲。(Maybelline)

化妆品牌的广告语多半令人印象深刻，美宝莲也一样。这句广告语推崇的是自然美，而使用它们的产品，天生丽质的女人将更完美。Maybe、born、maybe、Maybelline 这几个词中重复出现的几个音节，极富韵律。

- Melts in your mouth, not in your hands. 只溶在口，不溶在手。(M&M's)

这是著名广告大师罗瑟·瑞夫斯的灵感之作，堪称经典，流传至今。它既反映了 M&M 巧克力糖衣包装的独特，又暗示 M&M 巧克力口味好，以至于我们不愿意使巧克力在手上停留片刻。

- Every Little Helps. 点滴都有用。(Tesco)

连锁超市乐购以低廉的价格和物资的丰富而著名，"Every Little Helps"这句广告语完美体现了这两个特点。多年来，这句三个词的标语(tagline)已深深印入人们的脑海中。

- Quality never goes out of style. 质量与风格共存。(Levis)

牛仔裤品牌李维斯这句广告语品质与时尚兼顾，率性而自信，令人激赏。

- 某品牌香烟的广告语：All is well that ends well.

原译：烟蒂好，烟就好。

All is well that ends well 出自莎士比亚喜剧的剧名《皆大欢喜》。其含义是，结局好就一切都好。

香烟的质量在于烟丝、配料和加工，至于"烟蒂"（cigarette end/butt/stub）是指抽剩下的烟头，怎么能说"烟蒂好，烟就好"呢？这则香烟广告语的意思可能是说：这香烟是越抽到后来越有劲儿，就像"这茶喝到这会儿才喝出味儿来"一样。

改译：越抽越有味儿。或：抽到最后，烟味十足。

- 《泰晤士报》的广告语：We take no pride in prejudice.

这则英文广告词巧妙地援引了英国作家简·奥斯汀的《傲慢与偏见》（*Pride and Prejudice*）这部在英语文化国家中家喻户晓的文学名著，体现了《泰晤士报》秉承公平、公正的办报原则，收到了很好的广告效果。但译成中文时，两种文化间的差异使译者很难把原广告的效果传达出来。有一种翻译是"对于您的偏见，我们没有傲慢。"译者试图体现这则广告语的引用，把《傲慢与偏见》书名中的两个关键词强加到译文中，但对这样的措辞，读者都会有一种"师出无名"的困惑，读了之后感到莫名其妙。

原文 We take no pride in prejudice 是报社为了说明自己的报道是客观公正的。它的字面意思是：我们并不为偏见而感到骄傲。换句话说：我们并不喜欢做带有偏见的报道。所以，有人将它改译为："对于有失偏颇的报道，我们并不引以为自豪"。

其实，改译虽然勉强表达出了公平、公正的意思，但给人的感觉却是《泰晤士报》并不总是报道真实的新闻。更何况有失偏颇的报道本来就不应该见诸报端，也谈不上引以为豪，如果真的这样，这种世界大报的风采也就荡然无存了。

在既难以保留原文的意思，又难以达到广告宣传目的的情况下，译者可以采取另译的方法。比如，译成"舆论的导向，公正的保障"，比译成"正义的力量，舆论的导向"更为贴切，前者既表达了《泰晤士报》对舆论的导向作用，又把其公正的报道态度展现了出来。而且尾韵应了原文的头韵，读起来朗朗上口，掷地有声。

- 万宝路香烟的广告语：

  Come to where the flavor is.

  Come to Marlboro Country. — Marlboro

原译：光临风韵之境！万宝路世界。

这里必须指出几点：1. "风韵"与 flavor 的意思并不完全一致，"光临风韵之境"好像有点旅游广告的味道；2. "万宝路世界"似乎与 Marlboro Country 也不能等同；3. 这条广告语的潜台词（message）和个性（personality）未能体现出来。

这里的 flavor 有双层意思，一是指这种香烟的独特品位，二是指抽这种烟的人特有的装扮和风度；Marlboro Country 是指抽这种烟的人所驰骋的天地。这就是 Marlboro Man 所代表的一个世纪以来最成功、最有影响的品牌形象：他身着牛仔服装，骑着高头大马，嘴里叼着香烟，背景是一片荒原和蓝天。这一切象征着潇洒、豪放、自由、"酷"味儿十足，是许多青年男性所追求的。广告词的内容同广告插图的形象应该是统一协调的，同样也能使人联想起那令人神往的美国西部荒原和那吸引眼球的西部牛仔形象。这则广告的"潜台词"就是，抽万宝路香烟的人与众不同，有着西部牛仔的独特风度。为了更好地把 Come to where the flavor is. Come to Marlboro Country 中所暗含的上述内容展现给中国读者，在翻译时应该搬开文化屏障，把"西部"和"牛仔"直接展现出来。

译文：万宝路香烟：追寻牛仔风度——西部潇洒走一回。

- Butlin's 旅游公司的广告语：

Butlin's — the right choice. Don't labour the point, or be conservative in your choice, or liberal with your money. Come to Butlin's for the real party. Great Party Ahead.

原译：布特林旅游公司——您的正确选择。不要讲个没完，不要保守，也别犹豫，不要放任自由地乱花钱。到布特林旅游公司，参加实实在在的聚会吧。盛大的聚会正等着你！

很明显，译文中的"实实在在的聚会"和"盛大的聚会"偏离了原文的意思。此广告中的 labour，conservative 和 liberal 是工党、保守党、自由党三个政党的名字，在这里都是语意双关；labour（工党）即劳工党，the point 特指你要找旅游公司的意图或愿望，labour the point 意思是在找旅游公司的意图上劳心费神；Party 也是一个双关词，既指"政党"，又指"旅行团"，传译其双关意思也很困难。准确翻译这种文化差异太大的语言难度很大。

改译：布特林旅行社——你明智的选择。想旅行不必费神似劳工党；选旅团不必谨慎如保守党；花旅费不会放任像自由党。来吧，加入"布特林"，大团去旅行。

（布特林旅行社——你明智的选择。宣传不用太劳工费神，选择不必太保守谨慎，花钱不要太自由放任。我们的工作不是结党而是组团——快来参加我们充满欢乐的旅行团吧。）

- 雀巢咖啡广告语：We make the very best. 味道好极了。

4.6　广告语修辞手段的翻译

在激烈的商品市场竞争中广告词的创作者总是深思熟虑，用新颖独特的词汇、精练的语句以及巧妙的修辞手法，赢得消费者对其产品或服务的认可和青睐。通常地，汉语广告用词十分讲究，以四字结构多见，辅之以修饰语来加强语气，但英语广告则通过各种修辞手段及幽默风趣的语句给读者以强烈的感官刺激，留下深刻的印象。下面分别讨论英语广告语的几种修辞手段及其翻译。

4.6.1　谐音双关（Homophonic pun）

- More sun and air for your son and heir. 这里有充足的阳光，清新的空气，一切为了您的子孙后代。（海滨浴场）

- Trust us. Over 5,000 ears of experience. 相信我们吧。历经 5000 多只耳朵的检验，有着 5000 多年的经验。（助听器）

- Forget hot taste.

Only Kool, with pure menthol has the taste of extra coolness.

Come up to Kool.

忘掉辛辣的感觉。

只有"酷"牌，纯正的薄荷口味带给你特别清凉的酷爽感受。

想"酷"你就来！

这是一则 KOOL 牌香烟广告，Kool 与 cool 谐音，所以一语双关，既是烟的牌子，又是凉爽的感觉，这种 cool 的感觉与首句 hot taste 形成强烈的对比，自然吸引消费者来购买此烟。

- Not fairly white — fairy white. 不只是显白——炫白！

Fairy white 为一洗衣粉的牌子。fairly 和 fairy 谐音，突出此洗衣粉的增白功能，以吸引消费者购买。

4.6.2　语义双关（Homographic pun）

- The label of achievements. Black Label commands more respects.

酒是功成名就的标志。黑色标志使您更显尊贵。

本例广告中的 Label 既有"标签，标志"的意思，又是酒的品牌 BLACK LABEL 中的关键词，广告设计者巧妙地运用同形异义的双关手法，将酒的品牌与"事业成功的标志"和谐地连到一起，可谓天衣无缝，不仅让消费者一下就记住了品牌，而且引发凌云壮志，渴望功成名就，不妨去品尝一下该酒的消费欲望。

- OIC：Oh, I see.（glasses）

- Asking for More. No cigarette gives me More taste.

再来一支摩尔烟吧，它品位独特，令我难舍。

- 某油漆的广告语：

Start with the finish. 你完工，我开始。

finish：完成；末道漆

- 旅游公司的广告语：

After you get married, kiss your wife in places where she's never been kissed before.

婚后，带你的妻子去她从未去过的风景胜地吻她从未被吻过的迷人部位。

places 一词既指"身体的部位"parts of the body，又指"风景胜地"scenic spots，翻译时可将其"一分为二"。

- A lawyer and a wagon wheel must be greased. 车轮需润滑，律师需贿赂。（律师和车辆都需要加润滑油。grease 兼有"润滑油"和"贿赂"二义）

- Pick an Ace from Toshiba. 东芝品牌，卓越超群。

Ace 是最大的牌，想表达东芝是最好的品牌。

4.6.3　对比（Contrast）

在句中或叙述中，用两个词义相互对立的词说明同一个事物，以形成鲜明的对比或对照的修辞方法称为对比。这种修辞手法通过差异的对比更鲜明地提示事物复杂矛盾的性质，给读者以深刻的印象。在广告中，作者通过词义决然对立的反差，突出某一商品的特性或建议、忠告等深刻含义。

- Cancer is often curable. The fear of cancer is often fatal. 癌症常可治，惧癌会致命。

这则广告通过 curable "可治的" 和 fatal "致命的" 两个形容词词义的对比，告诉人们癌症并非都是不治之症，而对癌症的恐惧却是最为可怕的，从而鼓励所有癌症病人鼓起勇气，坚定信心，乐观地与病魔顽强抗争，达到治愈的目的。

4.6.4 夸张(Hyperbole)

用主观的眼光去渲染、铺饰客观事物，故意"言过其实"的表现手法叫做夸张。修辞上的夸张不同于说假话，夸张只是为了语言生动，达到强调的目的。广告中的夸张更是为了迎合消费者的心理，让消费者对其商品有一个完美形象而故意"夸大其词"甚至"言过其实"，以增强广告的宣传效果。

- 美国花旗银行(Citibank)现时广告标题为：

A word to wealthy. 一言致富。

在美国，特别在大城市，各类专业银行等金融机构繁多，为了尽可能多地吸引储户，银行间竞争激烈，加强广告宣传为有效的手段之一。花旗银行的上述广告明确告诉读者该行的导储员会根据你款额的多少及存期的长短在名类繁多的储种中为你选择或推荐一种最为合适的储种，让你获得最佳的利息收入。读者看到这样一则既合乎情理又明显夸张的广告，极有可能把去该行存款作为首选。

- 某香水的广告语：

Her smile could heat up a nation. Her fragrance captured a country.

迷魂牵魄笑貌，倾国倾城芳香。

4.6.5 拟人(Personification)

拟人的修辞手法是把没有生命的事物比作有生命的事物，赋予它们以人的思想、情感和性格。广告英语中采用此种修辞方法将商品和服务人格化，让消费者对它们产生一种真实感、亲切感。

- 某花店的广告语：

Flowers by Interflora speak from heart. "茵特"之花，表达肺腑之言。

买花相赠适于很多场合，如探视病人、拜望尊长、走亲访友、喜庆婚宴、生日祝寿等，通过不同的花卉表达不同的感情。这家花店的广告将花拟人化，能表达肺腑之言，诸如"祝您早日康复""祝君生日快乐""恭祝健康长寿"这一类。即便你公务繁忙不能亲临登门，只要在花束上附上卡片一张，也能将你要表达的感情传递给受花人。

4.6.6 重复(Repetition)

重复是一个词语或词组反复出现在连续的几个句子中的语言现象，它能有效地增强语势和语言感染力。广告英语中的重复更能增强商品和服务的宣传力度和宣传效果，让消费者过目不忘，产生一种认可欲买的心理倾向。

- 立顿(Lipton)牌茶叶的广告标题:

When you're sipping Lipton, you're sipping something special. 啜饮立顿茶, 品尝独特味。

句中, sipping 重复两次使用, 其目的是强调饮茶的方法——啜饮, 品茶的结果——醇香独特, 回味无穷。

- 某航空运输公司的广告:

First in airfreight with airfreight first. 第一货运, 运货第一。

4.6.7 明喻(Simile)

为了鲜明形象地刻画某一事物, 人们常常将具有共同特征的两种不同事物加以对比, 用另一种事物比仿所要说明的事物, 在修辞学上, 这种对比叫做明喻。明喻中本体与喻体之间常用 as, like 等介词联结, 使人产生一种清晰具体的联想。

广告的设计者正是利用这种修辞手段, 以便消费者更加具体形象地了解商品和服务, 熟悉品牌, 进而赢得他们的认同和喜爱。

- 服装广告标题:

Light as a breeze, soft as a cloud. 轻如微风, 柔若浮云。

这则广告用来形容服装的用料轻如拂面之微风, 软若天空之浮云, 消费者自然联想到穿上这种衣服的轻松舒适感, 产生购买的欲望。

- 某洗发液的广告语:

It gives my hair super shine, super body, and leaves it smelling fresh as a meadow.

它令我秀发柔顺光滑, 熠熠生辉, 幽香飘逸, 犹如绿茵草坪, 清新芬芳。

此广告用喻体 meadow "草坪" 来比喻清洗后的秀发清新芬芳, 生机盎然, 这种洗发液能给你美的享受, 使你充满青春活力, 成功地达到了劝购导购的目的。

- Breakfast without orange juice is like a day without sunshine.

没有橘子汁的早餐就像没有阳光的日子。

4.6.8 暗喻(Metaphor)

暗喻是根据两个事物间的某种共同特征或某种内在联系, 把一个事物的名称用在另一个事物的名称上, 说话者不直接点明, 而要靠读者自己去领悟的比喻。广告英语中暗喻的含蓄比较, 可更加激发读者丰富的想象力。

- 旅游保险公司的广告语:

You're better off under the Umbrella.

"安伞"(Umbrella)旅(行)保(险)公司让你无忧无虑尽情享受旅程乐趣。

外出旅游安全为要。抓住游客的这一心理, 广告用 Umbrella(保护伞)这一喻体, 形象地使游客感到购买"安伞"旅保公司的保险犹如置己于安全保护伞下, 可自由自在地享受旅程的快乐(better off: 较自在, 较幸福)。

- Blessed by year round good weather, Spain is a magnet for sun worshippers and holiday makers. 蒙上帝保佑, 西班牙一年四季天气晴朗, 宛如一块磁铁, 吸引着酷爱阳光、喜好度假的人们。

这则广告语中"西班牙"被比作了"磁铁"magnet，说明那里是人们度假休闲的绝好去处。

4.6.9　换喻(Metonymy)

换喻，亦称转喻，是利用一个事物的名称替代与它有密切联系的另一个事物名称的修辞方法。如"白宫"(White House)指代美国政府，"唐宁街"(Downing Street)指代英国政府，"鸽子"(Dove)象征和平。

- 日本东芝公司为其生产的计算机所做的广告为：

Pick an Ace from Toshiba. 东芝品牌，卓越超群。

在扑克牌中 A 是最大的牌，此广告借 A 牌喻指其产品卓越超群的性能和质量，读者可放心购买，满意使用。

4.6.10　头韵 (Alliteration)

头韵是由相邻的起首字母(元音或辅音)发音相同而产生渲染对比的效果，加深印象、宣泄感情，经常在广告中使用。如：

- It's flavor wins favor. 以我茗香，赢君品尝。(以香取胜。)(茶)
- Safety, Security and Simplicity. 安全，安心，实用。(手机)

该款手机设置了 911 报警一触键(one-touch 911 button)，是给你自己、给亲友的一个安全的礼物(the gift of safety)；手机的设计者考虑了你的安全保障(security)，当任何时候需要求助、需要亲友时，一键即通，操作简易实用(simplicity)，使用安心放心。

- Great time, great taste, McDonald's. 美好时光，美味共享。——麦当劳

4.6.11　尾韵 (End-rhyme)

- Pepsi-cola hits the spot,

Twelve full ounces, that's a lot,

Twice as much for a nickel, too,

Pepsi-cola is the drink for you.

百事可乐味道好，足足 12 盎量不少，

五元钞票买 24 盎，百事可乐供您享。

这则广告使用 AABB 押韵，文笔优美，抑扬顿挫，读来朗朗上口。

有的广告头韵尾韵并用，更是妙趣横生，如：

- My goodness! My Guinness! 太棒了! 吉尼斯啤酒!

Guinness 为爱尔兰生产的强性黑啤酒之商标名，与 goodness 既押头韵也押尾韵，真是妙不可言。

- Workout without wearout.

这是一则运动鞋的广告，通过 workout，wearout 两个词的列举，强调了该产品对脚部的良好保护性能，更妙的是三个词既押头韵，也押尾韵，读来语调铿锵，经久难忘。

4.6.12 仿拟(Parody)

仿拟修辞是借某种固定形式,如词句、语篇等,而造出的异于原形式的表达手段。上文中《泰晤士报》的广告语:

- We take no pride in prejudice.

就是仿拟奥斯汀的名著 *Pride and Prejudice*,再如:

- Where there is a way, there is a Toyota. 丰田汽车,风行天下。

广告语言的汉英互译是一项非常困难的任务,尤其是汉译英。有些玩弄文字游戏或者文化内涵浓重的广告语甚至是无法互译的。要想翻译得好,译者必须反复实践,经过长期艰苦的努力,做到左右逢源、千锤百炼。光做"表面文章"是不行的,切忌望文生义、对号入座式的字面上的肤浅翻译。

翻译练习

一、翻译下列广告语,说出所用的修辞手法。

1. Looks like a pump, feels like a sneaker.

2. NEWS WEEK — Tomorrow's High Tech Office.

3. Come sit with me a while.

4. I'm More satisfied!

5. The unique spirit of Canada:We bottle it.

6. Extra Taste. Not Extra Calories.

7. Childhood isn't childhood without it.

8. Give a Timex to all, and to all a good time.

9. Deliciously simple. Simple delicious.

10. Not all mobile phones are created.

11. Practice really does make perfect.

12. Do more. Work less.

13. Once an imperial palace, Now a luxury hotel.

14. Enjoy your glass to the full.

15. Choose your glasses carefully.

16. A business in million, a profit in pennies.

17. A world of visiting cards, a universe of duplication.

18. We've hidden a garden full of vegetables where you'd never expect. In a pie.

19. Little wonder they don't build cars like they used to. Building a pen is difficult enough.

20. If people keep telling you to quit smoking cigarettes, don't listen…They are probably trying to trick you into living.

二、将下列英语广告语译成中文。

1. Adidas Sports Shoes

Over twenty-eight years ago, adidas gave birth to a new idea in sports shoes. And the people who wear our shoes have been running and winning ever since. In fact, adidas has helped them set over 400 world records in track and field alone.

Maybe that's why more and more football, soccer, basketball, baseball and tennis players are turning to adidas. They know that, whatever their game, they can rely on adidas workmanship and quality in every product we make.

So whether you're pounding the roads on a marathon, or just jogging around the block, adidas should be on your feet.

2. 胸针(Pin)广告语

Swan Symbol of a Life-Long Romance

In swan lore, when two young swans pair, they swim to a secluded spot, touch forming a heart and become mated for life. Gliding dreamily across their imaginary pond, reflected light glitters in water droplets at wing tips represented by 14 tiny diamonds.

As a symbol of life long romance, the Cross Swan Pin is a deeply moving gift conveying the essence of that foul-felt bond of love between two people. With genuine ruby eyes, 14K yellow gold combination pin-pendant comes beautifully gift-wrapped with the sentiments expressed by this piece on a small card tucked inside the velvet box.

3. 香烟(Cigarette)广告语

Designed with taste.

Today's Slims at a very slim price.

4. 威士忌(Whisky)广告语

"King George IV was up here, back in 1822. He would drink nothing but the Glenlivet."

His Majesty was gracing Scotland with a state visit at the time. He brought with him a powerful thirst for the Glenlivet single malt Scotch.

As his host's daughter, Elizabeth Grant, recorded in her memoirs: "Lord Coryingham, the Chamberlain, was looking everywhere for the pure Glenlivet whisky: the King drank nothing else."

Bottle was swiftly brought up from the cellar and pressed into the king's hands. "What is not recorded," says our own Sandy Milne, "is whether His Majesty gave anyone else a sniff of the stuff."

The Glenlivet. The father of all Scotch.

5. 太阳镜(Sunglasses)广告语

Shades of Summer Prescription,

sunglasses from £59.99 complete.

Get set for summer with a pair of fashionable prescription shades from our exclusive collection. Prices start from just £59.99 and include reading or distance lenses plus a special coating to protect your eyes from the sun's ultra violet rays.

And, of course, all prescription sunglasses are covered by our unique Gold Seal Guarantee. For more details and to view the full range, simply call in at your local branch today.

6. 可口可乐广告语

America

If you'll stop and think for just a moment，you'll find we have more of the good things in this country than anywhere else in the world.

Think of this land. From the surf at Big Sur to a Florida sunrise. And all the places in between.

The Grand Canyon...the wheat fields of Kansas...Autumn in New Hampshire...

You could go on forever. But America is more than a place of much beauty. It's a place for good times.

It's the Saturday night.

It's a trip down a dirt road in a beat up old jalopy.

It's your team winning.

It's a late night movie you could enjoy a thousand times.

And，yes，when you're thirsty，it's the taste of ice-cold Coca-Cola. It's a real thing.

In fact，all of the good things in this country are real. They're all around you，plainly visible. We point to many of them in our advertising. But you can discover many，many more without ever seeing a single commercial for Coke.

So have a bottle of Coke...and start looking up.

The Coca-Cola Company

7. Come to New York and see the world. If you are looking for the place that has everything, there's only one place to visit，and that's New York. It's a whole world in a city.

8. Money doesn't grow on the trees. But it blossoms at our branches. （英国劳埃德银行 Lloyd Bank）

9. Feel the Power of the World's First Turbo Copier

Introducing the new Toshiba 2230 Turbo. The first turbocharged copier in history.

Beneath its sleek exterior is a copying system. So remarkable it's actually patented.

With it，you can produce 22 copies a minute. Or hit the turbo button and turn out 30 copies a minute. So now you have the power to work 40% more efficiently while using 33% less toner. And what's even more revolutionary，we've managed to do it all without turbo charging the price.

To arrange for a free demonstration，just call 1-800-Go Toshiba.

10. Bask in the Warmth of the Philippines

Bask... indulge... luxuriate... in beautiful white-sand beaches... Breathtaking scenic wonders... world-class facilities and efficient service.

But，best of all，bask in the special warmth and comfort that is uniquely，wonderfully Filipino.

三、将下列汉语广告语译成英语。

1. 电视广告语

享誉国内外的电视湘军倾尽全力承办了第一、二届中国金鹰电视艺术节，其大手笔、大投入、高规格操作的一系列精彩活动，为中国电视界营造了一个惊世骇俗、波澜壮阔的艺术天空，为中国广大电视观众精心调制了一系列精美的艺术大餐，并因其独特的传播方式、旺盛的人气积聚而成为收视热点，为中国所有的品牌营运商打造了一个超级传播焦点平台。

2. AA 特区工业发展总公司作为 BB 集团的下属公司及 BB 集团的对外窗口，背靠工业，立足国内，拓展海外，既建立了全国范围的销售网络，同时在美国、欧洲、菲律宾、巴西，以及中国香港、中国澳门等建立了分支机构，积极参与国际市场竞争，促进集团国际化。

3. CC 铁路车辆(集团)有限责任公司，正在奋力实现"再现国家队雄风、再造新世纪辉煌、再为社会主义增光"宏伟意愿，朝着"发展规模集团化、产品品种系列化、市场营销国际化、经营格局多元化、企业规模现代化"的目标迈进。公司将一如既往地坚持"信誉第一、用户至上"的宗旨，不仅以更多的高质量、高品位、高档次的新产品满足市场，而且以良好的作风，为广大用户提供一流的全过程的服务。

4. "雪山"牌羊绒衫色泽鲜艳，手感柔滑，穿着舒适，轻软保暖。其品质优良，做工细致，花型、款式新颖，尺码齐全，深受国内外消费者青睐。

5. 全兴特曲酒为中国名酒，产于中国四川省成都市锦江河畔。历史悠久，始产于满清道光四年。选用优质高粱、上等小麦为原料，采用传统工艺、陈年老窖发酵精心酿制。酒质最佳，具有窖香浓郁、醇和协调、绵甜甘洌、落口净爽的独特风格。

6. 西凤酒是久负盛名的名酒之一，远在唐代就被列为珍品。北宋末年，苏东坡任职凤翔，酷爱此酒，随之盛名益彰。1910 年西凤酒参加南洋赛酒会获奖，遂膺世界声誉。

西凤酒清澈透明，香气浓郁，淳厚圆绵，回味悠长，别具一格。饮后令人神志清爽，有通胃祛劳之功，历为广大群众所喜爱。

第五章　商标文体翻译

5.1　概　　述

经济的迅速增长已使中国成为当今世界最有潜力的商品市场，世界各国的产品纷纷跻身于中国市场，给中国的消费者留下了深刻印象，如西铁城（Citizen）手表、雪碧（Sprite）饮料、福特（Ford）汽车等。同样，某些中国本土商品以质优价廉的优势很快打开国际销路，享誉海内外，成为中外驰名商标，如海尔（Haier）、海信（Hisense）、方正（Founder）等。

在这些成功的产品营销活动中，商标的作用不容忽略。根据美国经济学家理查德·海斯（Richard T. Hise）的观点，商标（A brand, i. e. trademark）被定义为"a name, term, sign, symbol, design or a combination of them that tells who makes it or who sells it, distinguishing that product from those made or sold by others. A brand name is that part of brand that can be vocalized"。也就是说，商标是用以区别商品或服务来源的可视性标志，包括文字、图形、字母、数字、三维标志和颜色组合等元素。常见的商标主体一般是文字或文字与图形的组合。

目前，大部分企业的商标以文字设计为主，商标语言是商标设计中的重要内容。作为一种具有显著特征的标志，商标自然就带有广告的性质和功能。从这个意义上说，商标语言就是广告语言，属呼唤型功能文本，可以发挥宣传作用。好的商标名寓意深刻，引人注目，易给消费者留下深刻印象。在消费者的心目中，驰名商标代表优质的产品和良好的服务。

商标文字是一种特殊的语言形式。它用途专一，既区别于商品或服务，又为商品或服务专享，并由此建立生产厂家与消费者的沟通，宣传产品的功能、质量，树立产品的形象，进而促进消费。商标是商品的一部分，也是产品生产商的无形资产。商标的驰名与否固然在于商品和配套服务质量的高低，但商标名给人的感性魅力也起着很大作用，它涉及出口商品的形象及其商业机会。因此，商标译文有可能决定着此商标商品的国际命运。鉴于买卖双方所处文化语境的差异，商标语言的翻译便成为一个不容忽视的环节，应该引起商家的重视，更需要我们深入研究。

以中国产品的外销为例，虽然中国厂商十分重视产品的汉语商标名，甚至登报出重金为产品征集最佳商标名，但他们对产品的英语译名却少有关心。从商标英译的现状来看，缺乏对语言文化因素的考量很可能导致译名质量不尽如人意。

我们如果不注意译名的国际性，就会造成商标汉英翻译不佳。例如，上海生产的"白象"牌电池，在国内市场上以质量上乘著称，但其英语商标名"White Elephant"在欧美文化中具有负面含义。A white elephant 一词来源于印度，印度人对大象尤其是白象视若神灵。印度规定，白象不可以被宰杀，不能用来干活，拥有白象的人家要好好地养着它，不可以虐待它。后来，人们将白象视为一种累赘，表示"[喻]无用而累赘的东西；沉重的包袱；成为负担或招致亏损的财产"。欧美消费者应该不会喜欢这种代表无用甚至麻烦的商标。

中国人喜欢用"龙""红"这样的字眼，但西方人眼中的龙却是一种凶恶的动物，"红色"则代表着"极端"与"危险"。所以，我们要考虑外国人的接受度，注意东西方文化差异，避免产生歧义甚至误解。有时候，我们需要对这种民族性较强的文化意象进行淡化或泛化处理，增添国际化特色，提高在国外市场的接受度。例如：

- 海信(家电)→Hisense
- 金利来（领带）→Goldlion
- 小护士(防晒霜)→Mininurse，等。

英语商标的汉译也有许多可以借鉴的优秀译例。如：

- Seven-up（饮料）→七喜
- Coca Cola→可口可乐
- Pepsi Cola→百事可乐
- Buler（钟表）→宝来
- Crest（牙膏）→佳洁士
- Colgate（牙膏）→高露洁
- Aiwa（音响）→爱华
- Rejoice（洗发水）→飘柔
- Clean-clear（护肤品）→可伶可俐，等。

上述译名无不透着吉祥和美意，为人们所喜闻乐见。

所以，我们在翻译商标时应当研究商标语言、文化、风格及特色等问题，以便在译文中还商标的原貌。具体而言，我们需要从语用学、社会语言学、民俗学、文化语言学、营销学和消费心理学等角度来考虑，坚持基本翻译原则，即发音响亮、简短易记、措辞讲究、标新立异、国际性强、接受度高。

5.2 商标的语言特点

商标语是以词、字组成的语言符号，由个别人或个别企业精心挑选或创造而成，别具特色，用于区别其他企业商品或服务。这种专用符号所承载的意义和功能具有明显的特征，突出表现为显著性、专用性、联想性以及识别功能、质量保证功能、法律保护功能和广告宣传功能。

就语言风格而言，商标语主要具有以下几大特点：

5.2.1 描述

某些商标语暗示产品的质量，说明其特点和性能，如：slim 表明香烟形状细长，

playwell 玩具说明产品功能。

5.2.2　联想

有的商标会留给消费者一定的想象空间，让他们觉得用上这种产品后会产生某种特殊的效果。如：

- Clean Clear("可伶可俐")可能会让爱美的女性觉得，使用这种护肤品后皮肤光洁细嫩，似乎人也变得聪明伶俐起来了。
- "7 匹狼"是福州一家服饰厂的商标名，译成 Septwolves，让人联想到男子汉气概。

有些专有名词用于商标命名，使人联想到一些名人或历史事件或神话传说乃至神灵名称以及文学类或影视作品中人物的名称等。如：

- Ford 福特汽车，用的是创始人的名字。
- Wolsey 沃尔西针织品，取自英国历史上一位有名的红衣主教 Thomas Wolsey (1475—1530)托马斯·沃尔西。
- Lincoln 林肯轿车，使人想起林肯总统，显得华贵与显赫。

5.2.3　新奇

商标有一个很常用的设计理念即标新立异，让读者一看便能记住，因为它与众不同。于是设计者便想方设法去创造新颖奇特的词语(coinage)来吸引读者。如国内一畅销咖啡品牌"雀巢"译成 Nescafe，显然这个词是杜撰的，由 nestle 和 café 两个词合成。

再如世界闻名的石油产品商标 Exxon 的设计。起初在选用这个商标时，设计者动用电脑把英语中 4~5 个字母组成的词都搜索进来几经筛选后用了其中 8 个作为候选词，但还是不尽如人意。一位职员受候选词的启发，用元音和辅音字母组成了 Exxon，受到老板和专家们的拍手称绝，便定下作为商标名，即现在的"埃克森"品牌。

新造词商标分为两种情况，一是有词为理据的新造词，本身具有一定含义，暗示或间接说明商品的质量、效能以及用途等，如：

- Earex→药名，去耳疾。ear + excellent
- Ex-Lax→缓泻药，excellent + laxative
- Quick→洗涤剂
- Timex→天美时(手表)，time + excellent
- Kleenex→洁净(纸巾)，kleen 与英语 clean 谐音，加上 excellent 构成
- Windex→窗洁(门窗玻璃清洁剂)window + excellent

造词商标虽本身毫无意义，但一般醒目对称，易于读记，同样起到很好的广告宣传作用。如：

- Kodak→柯达(胶卷)。它是公司创始人 Goerge Eastman 创造的商标。K 是他偏爱的字母，用于开头和结尾，配上字母-oda-产生按动快门的拟音效果，真是神来之笔，生动形象，妙不可言。
- Adidas→阿迪达斯运动鞋

5.2.4　外来语

A. L. 克鲁伯曾说，每一种文化都会接纳新的东西，不论是外来的，还是产自本土的，都要依照自己的文化模式，将这些新的东西加以重新塑造。这意味着外来语进入异族文化的商标需要经过同化（assimilation）、吸收（absorption）、改造（transformation）的过程，所以源自外来语的商标词，乃不同文化交融的产物。

英国有种药皂商标为

● Valderma，它由 Value（有益）+ derma（希腊语：皮肤）组合而成，此商标显然可译为"益肤"。

● Shampoo 源自印度语，意为"按摩、推拿"，洗发时需要用手轻轻搓揉，对头皮进行按摩，18 世纪英国殖民者入侵印度后，该词英语写成 Shampoo，译为"香波"，芳香飘逸的秀发出自此洗发剂。

● LUX，"力士"香皂，乃英国 Unilevier(联合利华)公司生产，它取自拉丁文，有"阳光"之意，使用者不禁由阳光联想到健康的肌肤，其字形和发音又可使人联想到 Luck，Luxury 等词语。

5.2.5　缩略词

这类商标大多由企业名称、产品名称、产品成分或制造工艺等词语的首字母缩略词（Initials）构成。如：

● NEC→日电(电器)，它是 Nippon Electric Company，Ltd.（日本电气株式会社）的首字母缩写。

● JVC→胜利(电器)，它是 Victor Company of Japan，Limited（日本胜利株式会社）的首字母缩写。

● IBM→美国的 IBM 公司是由 International Business Machines 美国国际商用机器公司的缩略，现在它的原名倒已不怎么被人注意了，而 IBM 却成了家喻户晓的计算机商标。

5.3　商标汉英翻译的用词应遵循的原则

5.3.1　对应词

如果商标原文取自物名，尽量保持商标原文的特定内涵，选英语中的对应词译出，如：

● "椰树"牌椰子汁→Coconut Tree® Coconut Juice
● "猎豹"牌皮衣→Hunting Leopard® Leather Coats

5.3.2　译核心词

如果商标原文取自优雅吉祥的实义词，我们应当选用能表现原文核心意义的词译出，如：

    ● 中华多宝珍珠口服液：CHINA TREASURE Pearl Oral Liquid，而不用现在的译名：Zhonghua Duobao Pearl Oral Liquid；

    ● 康佳彩电 KAREWELL Color TV，该译名取自 carewell 的谐音，保存了部分寓意，比原来的 KONKA 要好一些。

5.3.3　修剪或拼接后再翻译

    如果商标原文太长或词语可能在译文中引起误会，我们需要做一定的修剪或拼接再选词翻译。如：

    ● 金嗓子喉宝 KINGVOICE Sore-throat Relieving Tablets，比原译名 JINSANGZI 活泼了许多。

    ● 青春宝®抗衰老片的英译名 Qing Chun Bao 并未传达"青春宝"在汉语中的文化内涵，可改译为"COYOUTH® Anti-aging tablets"，其中，前缀"CO-"意为"一起；共同；相伴"，"youth"则表示"青春"。

5.4　商标汉英翻译的文化因素

    汉语的商标名具有丰富的文化内涵。有些商标寓意，对汉语读者来说，文雅尊贵，情深意浓，如黑妹牙膏，满庭芳肥皂，丽人牌雨伞。有的商标取名于名山、名城、名舍，使人一见商标便联想到其产地，如天一阁牌椅子(宁波)，泰山牌拖拉机(山东)，黄鹤楼牌电吹风(武汉)。汉语商标中的这些丰富文化内涵要通过翻译完整地反映于译文中十分困难，因为汉语读者的文化背景与英语读者的文化背景差异很大，必然会导致文化因素的传递障碍。然而，汉英双语所涉及的文化差异并不能阻止我们运用灵活的翻译手段作适当调整，将汉语的文化寓意通过变通手段反映到英语译文中。问题的关键是，译者是否具备英语文化知识。译者掌握好英语的文化知识以及英语民族的风俗习惯，至少可以避免违背英语民族文化传统的译文出现。许多译者缺少英语文化知识，导致商标译文出现适得其反的文化效果。这方面的实例已有不少，请看：

    ● "孔雀"牌彩色电视机

    原译："Peacock" Color TV

    在中国，孔雀让人联想到美丽、优雅和鲜艳的色彩。用"孔雀"作为电视机的商标自然是暗指电视机的色彩逼真、质量上乘。但是，英语民族通常视"孔雀"为污秽、猥亵之鸟，常给人带来厄运。孔雀开屏被认为是自满、自傲的表现，因此，英语中就有下列一类说法：

    as proud as a peacock 非常高傲；

    play the peacock 炫耀自己。

    英语中用 peacock 作商标会损害商标的形象。如果把"孔雀"译作 peafowl（母孔雀），就能避免贬义，或者干脆用"孔雀"的内涵，译作 Kingbird。

    也许有人会说，译成 Kingbird，孔雀的意思还如何表达呢？这倒不必担心，因为商标的翻译并不注重等值，而在于符号形象的传递，只要译出的商标能大致反映原文的形象效果，译名就是可以接受的。

- "金利来"商标译成 Goldlion，就是一个优秀的样板。

商标作为一种标志语言给翻译提供了更大的自由度，但该自由度应当限定在文字形象优美、音韵和谐、寓意基本保持原文的内涵这个范围之内。这一点我们从一些产品的英语商标译成汉语的情况就能得到很大的启示，如：

- Rejoice→飘柔(洗发水)
- Crest→佳洁士(牙膏)
- Space→舒背思(床垫)
- Colgate→高露洁(牙膏)

所以，我们翻译汉语商标时思路可以更开阔些，把注意力转向商标在汉英两个不同民族心目中的形象效果的等效传递上，所以，"孔雀"商标译成 Kingbird，也就顺理成章了。

- "蝴蝶"牌电子灶

原译文：Butterfly Electric Cooker

中国人通常用"蝴蝶"象征友谊和爱情，而英美国家的人则把"蝴蝶"当作轻浮之物，比如英语中有下列一说：

social butterfly 交际花

所以，如果用 butterfly 来译此商标，英语国家的消费者会产生什么样的联想呢？他们或许会对该产品的耐用性产生怀疑。再说西方国家的人并不喜欢以鸟或虫类作商标名的电子产品，鸟虫用作商标往往给人以质量低劣的印象。

国外许多著名的产品商标都有较大的气势，或用物名，或用人名，象征着无限的力量和勃勃的生机。如：

- Apollo 阿波罗，取自希腊神话中的太阳神。
- Boom 丰年，喻意着一派繁荣昌盛的景象。
- Cosmos 宇宙，世界著名钟表的商标。
- Chrysler 克莱斯勒(汽车)，American automobile manufacturer who founded the Chrysler Corporation (1925). 沃尔特·珀西·克莱斯勒(1875 — 1940)，美国汽车制造商，建立了克莱斯勒公司(1925 年)。
- Lincoln 林肯(汽车)，林肯牌大轿车为福特汽车厂生产的名牌豪华汽车。
- Volvo 沃尔沃/富豪，是世界著名的瑞典产汽车的商标。

在翻译日用产品的汉语商标时，译者可以参考汉语原文的形、音、义来选取合适的英文词。例如：

- "花为媒"牌床垫，可译为 Howell Mattress，也可译为 Coflower Mattress, Comforter Mattress 等。这样的商标译文形象如原文一样引人注目。

5.5 商标翻译的技巧

5.5.1 音译

音译是商标翻译中较常见的方法。译者在具体的翻译实践中也要注意合宜性，并非每个商标都适宜音译。一般而言，当原商标构不成完整的意义，属新奇型或专有独用的，可采用音译。中国人喜用福、万、发、寿、康等吉祥的词语命名商品，翻译时也要注意这一民族的审美倾向，把辅音/b/、f/、l/分别译成宝、富、力；而把/si/、le/等音节译成"喜、乐"。如：

- Casio→卡西欧(电子琴)
- Dunhill→登喜路(服装)
- Marlboro→万宝路(香烟)
- Lincoln→林肯(轿车)
- Pierre Cardin→皮尔卡丹(服饰)
- Siemens→西门子(电器)
- Parker→派克(笔)
- Santana→桑塔纳(轿车)。这个德国产的汽车商标原来是以美国加利福尼亚州一座山谷名称命名的，此山谷经常刮起一股强劲的旋风，当地人称之为 Santana，而且该地还以盛产名贵葡萄酒闻名遐迩。所以此商标的设计者希望他们的轿车像这个山谷的旋风和葡萄酒一样风靡全球。
- Champagne 是法国的香槟酒产地，故译成"香槟"。

豪华的饭店 Shangri-la 音译为"香格里拉"，它取自英国著名作家詹姆斯·希尔顿的文学作品《失去的地平线》中虚构的地名，原址在我国云南省境内。那里四季如春，景色优美，成了世人向往的世外桃源，这也成了"香格里拉"遍布全球的魅力所在。

5.5.2　意译

与音译一样，并非每个商标都宜用意译。但意译作为商标翻译的一个重要手段，能较好地体现原商标设计者的初衷与希冀，而且与商标图案在意蕴上实现和谐一致。例如：

- Lion→狮(文具)
- Skinice→肤美灵(化妆品)：skin + nice
- Elegance→雅致(羊绒衫)
- Transformer→变形金刚(玩具)。英语 transform 为"变形"之意，表示该玩具能通过不同的方式组合成各种形状及型号的汽车、坦克、飞机、舰艇等。将-er 译为"金刚"是因为我国佛教文化中称侍卫为"金刚"，象征力大无穷、武艺高超、敢斗妖魔、百战百胜，成为儿童心目中的偶像而畅销市场。
- Nike→耐克(运动服/鞋)。这个商标词可追溯到 20 世纪 50 年代，美国曾将此词用于一种导弹的名称，从而赋予 Nike 速度与力量。
- 玉兔→Moon Rabbit，玉兔是我国神话中在月宫桂花树下陪伴吴刚的兔子，于是成了月亮的代表。此译体现了我国传统文化的风采。
- 熊猫(电子产品)→Panda

5.5.3　音义双关

音义双关，即音义兼译，属补偿式翻译手法(complementary translation)，是把与原文相近的谐音变成有意义的译名，用译语的多义信息来补偿翻译过程中的语义损失，激发读

108

者作出有益联想，收到理想的翻译效果。

- Benz→奔驰(汽车)。起初的译法为"本茨"，没有喻义。而现译"奔驰"二字使人联想到驾着此车风驰电掣般的速度，宣传效果决然不同。

- Goodyear→固特异。此为美国著名的轮胎商标，它以公司的创始人，也是硫化橡胶发明人 Charles Goodyear 的姓氏命名，但作为商标，意味着此轮胎经久耐用，所以汉译名为"固特异"，可谓音义结合，十分贴切。

- 美国超音速飞机 Boeing 是纪念该飞机公司创始人 William Edward Boeing，以其姓氏命名的，译成汉语"波音"，形象贴切，音义结合。

- 英国的威士忌 Whisky 和法国的白兰地 Brandy 均为世界名酒，但两者在香港市场上的销售量却大相径庭，后者较前者高出近 20 倍。问题就出在中文译名上。人们一看到商标便做出联想：威士忌，威(风凛凛的人/男)士(都)忌(喝)，何况我凡夫俗子，结果只有避而不买；而白兰地，白兰(盛开之)地，诗情画意，跃然纸上，购买欲望油然而生。

有人将这种音意兼顾的译法称为"音意合璧"(郭尚兴，1995)，"美乐"(牌电视机)译为 Melody 即是一例。越来越多的人认识到此法的优越性，因此，叫好称绝的译名层出不穷。如：

- Crest→佳洁士(牙膏)
- Flora→芙露(化妆品)
- Theragran Junior→小施尔康(小儿保健药)
- Pentium→奔腾(芯片)
- Budweiser→百威(啤酒)
- Canon→佳能(相机，复/打印机)。

- Coca Cola→可口可乐(饮料)。这个中译名是 20 世纪 30 年代英籍华人蒋彝先生颇具匠心的高明设计，既保留了 Coca Cola 的英语谐音，又以中文的"可口可乐"暗示了该饮料的美味，符合中国消费者的心理，切音切意。可口可乐能在中国市场销售成功，这一声意俱佳的绝妙译名功不可没。

- Safeguard→舒肤佳(香皂)。其功能是保护皮肤，使其舒适滑爽，效果极佳。译名音意俱上，诱发消费者的购买欲望，为商品销售平添优势。

- 美加净(化妆品/牙膏)→Maxam
- 飘柔(洗发液)→Rejoice. 一头飘逸的秀发，能不叫人欣喜吗?
- 西泠(电器)→Serene. 宁静无噪音的电器，人见人爱。
- 雅戈尔(服装)→Younger. 穿上此服，年轻潇洒。
- 回力(鞋)→Warrior. 具有回天之力的"勇士"，运动健将。
- 西尔灵(旅行小闹钟)→Sailing Travel Clock.

但值得一提的是，根据商标注册的有关规定，所选汉字的褒扬之意不能对商品构成直接的描述或过分夸大其词，否则，原商标词的法律保护功能丧失。如 Citizen 手表，原译"稀奇准"可谓音意合璧，但申请注册时被否定，后译为"西铁城"方获注册。

在音义合译时我们还需要考虑以下几个方面：

1)译音相近但不相同。即译语与源语词的读音不可能完全吻合，大多译例只能做到模糊相似。如：

- Johnson→强生(爽身粉)，而不是人名翻译"约翰逊"。
- Gillette→吉列(剃须刀)，而不是"吉乐特"。
- Head & Shoulders→海飞丝(洗发液)，原译"海伦仙度丝"更接近源语的发音，而现译只取了源语的首尾音素。
- Procter & Gamble，P & G→宝洁，注重了首音节和首字母的翻译。

2) 提倡简而不繁。译音不但音不完全相同，在字数上也尽可能删繁就简，易读利记。上述海飞丝就是一例。又如：

- Hewlett-Packare→惠普(电器)，亦有译成：惠尔浦，而不译成"休利特·帕克勒"。
- Mc Donald's→麦当劳(快餐)，而不译：麦克·唐纳。
- Kodak→柯达(摄影器材)，不译：柯达克。

3) 选词利于表达产品信息，读者见到商标名便知其性能功效等。如：

- Contac→康泰克(药名)。由英语 Continuous action 两词的第一个音节拼缀而成，暗示其药效持久。
- Decis→敌杀死([法]农药)。它是法国福克斯公司的一个农药商标。汉语译名将它的杀虫性能表现得淋漓尽致。
- Polarold→拍立得(照相机)。这个美国的一次成像照相机商标名也堪称妙译，是汉译的成功典范。下面两例也有异曲同工之妙。
- Coldrex→可立治(药名)
- Legalon→利肝灵(药名)

4) 能唤起消费激情，让消费者行动购买。首先要引起消费者对商标的关注，要从众多的商标中脱颖而出，展现商标的风姿，从而让消费者对此商品有好感。如：

- Xerox→施乐(复印机)，广施好乐。
- Holsten→好顺(啤酒)，饮用此啤酒，诸事好顺利。
- Pepsi Cola→百事可乐(饮料)，事事顺遂。Pepsi 是术语 pepsin"胃蛋白酶"的变体词，暗示这种饮料有"助消化"之功能。
- Avon→雅芳(化妆品)，优雅芬芳。
- Arche→雅倩 (化妆品)，优雅倩影。
- Ardoe→雅黛 (化妆品)，雅丽粉黛。
- Imari→绮曼丽(化妆品)，纤细身材，绮丽多姿。

- Lancôme→兰蔻，这是法国一化妆品商标 LANCÔME。蔻，本义"豆蔻"，植物名，比喻处女，因称女子十三四岁为"豆蔻年华"。小豆蔻 [cardamom]。东印度一种草本植物的芳香蒴果，用作调味品和用作芳香剂和健胃剂。这个翻译符合中国女性的审美要求，因此受到广大女性的认可。

- Chanel→香奈尔。法国香水 CHANEL "香奈尔"也是家喻户晓的品牌，1922 年推出著名的 Chanel No. 5 香水。其香水瓶是一个甚具艺术性的方形玻璃瓶。Chanel No. 5 是史上第一瓶以设计师命名的香水。

- Estée Lauder→雅诗兰黛。原产美国的化妆品商标 Estée Lauder 译成"雅诗兰黛"，很有诗意，亦深受国内女性的青睐。

为了把美丽带给每一位女性，雅诗兰黛夫人于 1946 年成立了以她名字命名的公司，同时推出了她的第一款产品：由她当化学家的叔叔研发的一瓶护肤霜。而在这面霜被最终贴上"雅诗兰黛"商标之前，它已经赢得了一群忠实拥护者。1953 年，具有革命性意义的 Youth-Dew 香水被推出之时，雅诗兰黛公司已经赢得了不断创新、精于研发、品质优良的美誉。

- Clarins→娇韵诗。CLARINS娇韵诗。Clarins 是产自法国的世界著名品牌，其产品销售欧洲，以及美国、日本等全世界许多国家。
- Amphora Aromatics→安芙兰
- Artistry→雅姿。世界著名美容化妆品品牌；是隶属于美国安达高集团安利公司旗下的五大类产品品牌之一。
- Avene→雅漾
- Biotherm→碧欧泉。BIOTHERM 在法国南部山区，有一种矿物温泉，它对人体，特别是对肌肤有着特殊功效。那里空气清新、绿意盎然，Biotherm 碧欧泉就于 1950 年在此诞生。现在，Biotherm 碧欧泉已经成为欧洲三大护肤品牌之一，它针对肌肤类型、护肤和生活习惯的不同以及不同的需要，为不同肤质适用的产品设计了不同的色彩，让每一位消费者都得到纯净健康的保护。译名也迎合了护肤者的消费心理。

除了上述译法以外，商标翻译中也常用造新词的译法，如：联合利华生产的男士去屑洗发露，商标的英语名是 Clear，中文译成"清扬"。这个译名把该产品"活力运动型——持久洁净清爽"的功能充分展现给消费者。

5.6 汽车商标的翻译

汽车商标词语言形式简单，往往由一个词或者几个词组成，但是要把这些商标词从一种语言翻译为另外一种语言，又能保留原词的音韵和内涵，并非易事。

汽车商标是用来传递信息的一种符号，是一种特殊的语言，具有特定的标志意义，还有丰富深刻的象征性。其发展变化与这一地区、国家或民族的文化息息相关，包含并传递着文化信息。与其他商标一样，汽车商标的命名也体现了命名者所在国度的文化底蕴。翻译汽车商标，译者不仅需要跨越语言的障碍，更需要避免文化冲突，才能使译名符合目标消费者的审美情趣和消费心理。

5.6.1 汽车商标的来源

专有名词是汽车商标的重要来源之一。

- 出自人名——突出个体主义价值取向

西方文化看重个体，重视个人价值，坚持个体本位，突出个体是西方哲学的一个重要方面。欧洲有很多大的汽车公司都把公司的创始人、产品发明人或者要纪念的某一位人物的名字作为商标词。一方面可以达到纪念的目的，另一方面也可以宣传企业的文化，提升公司的信誉，体现公司的个性，激发人们的信任感，促进公司产品的销售。

Mercedes-Benz

奔驰(Benz)是以汽车发明者 Karl Frederick Benz 的姓氏作为商标，以纪念奔驰汽车的第一位发明人和创始人。现在的奔驰汽车一般是以 Mercedes-Benz 为商标词。1873 年，担任 Benz 发动机厂技术部主任的哥特里布·戴姆勒，在给妻子寄去的明信片上，信手画上了一颗三叉星以代表他当时的住处，并特别声明：总有一天，这颗吉祥之星将会照耀我毕生的工作。1890 年，这颗吉祥星开始用于新成立的戴姆勒公司的产品上。1899 年 3 月，艾米·耶里耐克(当时担任奥地利驻匈牙利总领事和戴姆勒汽车公司管理委员会的委员)驾驶以女儿梅赛德斯("温文尔雅"之意)命名的汽车，在"尼斯之旅"汽车大赛上一举夺魁后，他建议戴姆勒公司生产的汽车都用梅赛德斯来命名，戴姆勒欣然同意。1901 年，由威廉·迈巴赫设计 Simplex 牌汽车首次采用戴姆勒·梅赛德斯作为商标。1909 年，戴姆勒公司将一颗大三叉星和四颗小三叉星及梅赛德斯置于圆环之中；1923 年，又将三叉星置于发动机散热器之上。从此，这颗吉祥的三叉星迎风傲立，气度高雅，甚是夺目。

RENAULT

法国雷诺汽车以公司的创始人路易斯·雷诺(Louis Renault)的姓氏命名。图形商标是四个菱形拼成的图案，象征雷诺三兄弟与汽车工业融为一体，表示雷诺能在无限的(四维)空间中竞争、生存、发展。1898 年，路易斯·雷诺三兄弟在比扬古创建雷诺公司。它是世界上历史最悠久的汽车公司之一。目前，雷诺公司是法国第二大汽车公司，车的质量及可靠性也被认为是一流的。

OPEL

德国汽车欧宝(Opel)，曾译为奥贝尔，取自创始人阿德姆·奥贝尔(Adam Opel)的姓氏。商标是由图案和文字两部分组成。图案代表公司的技术进步和发展，像闪电一样划破长空，震撼世界，又喻示汽车如风驰电掣，同时也代表它在空气动力学方面的研究成就；文字 OPEL 是创始人的姓氏。1862 年，阿德姆·奥贝尔在吕塞尔海姆创建了欧宝公司，公司最初生产缝纫机、自行车，1897 年开始生产汽车，1924 年，公司建成德国第一条生

112

产汽车的流水线，使汽车产量猛增，在德国廉价车领域独占鳌头。另外，奥贝尔家族可能对当时的德国政府存在顾虑，于 1929 年将公司 80%的股份卖给美国通用汽车公司，从此，欧宝汽车公司成为美国通用汽车公司在德国的子公司。

1900 年，安德烈·雪铁龙(A. Citroen)发明了人字形齿轮。1912 年，他用人字形齿轮作为雪铁龙公司产品的商标。后来，雪铁龙组织了横穿非洲大陆和横越亚洲大陆的两次旅行，使雪铁龙汽车名声大振。法国人生性开朗，喜欢新颖和漂亮，雪铁龙轿车就表现了法兰西这种性格，每时每刻都在散发着法国的浪漫气息。作为标准的法国车型，雪铁龙代表着一个国家的文化，它在骨子里体现着典型的法国浪漫、优雅、精致和新潮，就像它的标志——"两个'人'字重叠在一起"，一种真正的人本精神。而安德烈·雪铁龙，不仅创造了这个车，创造了这个名字，也奠定了这种车型的文化内涵。

英国汽车劳斯莱斯(Rolls Royce)公司的创始人，当初也想不到一列火车把两人联系在一起，并成了今天世界汽车工业最有名的高级轿车公司之一。经销法国汽车的商人查尔斯·劳斯(Charles Rolls)与制造起重机和汽车的工程师亨利·莱斯在同乘一列火车时邂逅，并一见如故，他们便一同北上去了曼彻斯特。当天，在午餐时两人畅谈人生和事业，下午又一同驾驶汽车游览曼彻斯特，从而更加深了友谊。1906 年 3 月 15 日，劳斯与莱斯达成协议成立了公司，由莱斯负责生产汽车，劳斯负责营销，并给予莱斯制造的汽车在市场上的独家优惠。同时，他们给汽车起名为 Rolls-Royce，曾译为"罗尔斯-罗伊斯"，后又译为"劳斯莱斯"。

劳斯莱斯的平面车标是以两个重叠的"R"为中心，上面写有公司创始人劳斯(Rolls)的名字，下方是另一位创始人莱斯(Royce)的名字，两个"R"叠合在一起说明两人紧密合作相互支持，寓意你中有我我中有你的团结奋进、精诚合作、共同创业的精神。两位创始人先后去世后，公司的继承人将双"R"车标由红色改为黑色以示纪念。

意大利兰博基尼(Lamborghini)公司创建于 1962 年，以创建人兰博基尼命名，因生产 V12 发动机而成名。

113

兰博基尼公司的标志是一头浑身充满了力气，正准备向对手发动猛烈的攻击的公牛。据说兰博基尼本人就是这种不甘示弱的牛脾气，也体现了兰博基尼公司产品的特点，因为公司生产的汽车都是大功率、高速的运动型轿车。车头和车尾上的商标省去了公司名，只剩下一头犟牛。

保时捷（Porsche），曾译名波尔舍，采用的是德国保时捷公司创始人费迪南特·波尔舍（Dr. Ferdinand Porsche）的姓氏。保时捷汽车的商标选用了公司所在斯图加特市的盾形市徽，"PORSCHE"字样在商标的最上方表明该商标为保时捷设计公司所拥有；商标中的"STUTTCART"字样在马的上方说明公司总部在斯图加特市；商标中间是一匹骏马表示斯图加特这个地方盛产一种名贵种马。商标的左上方和右下方是鹿角的图案表示斯图加特曾是狩猎的好地方。商标右上方和左下方的黄色条纹代表成熟麦子的颜色，喻指五谷丰登。商标中的黑色代表肥沃土地，红色象征人们的智慧和对大自然的钟爱。由此组成一幅精湛意深、秀气美丽的田园风景画，展现了保时捷公司辉煌的过去，并预示了保时捷公司美好的未来。

同属法国的汽车公司标致（Peugeot）也是以公司创始人阿尔芒·标致的姓氏为商标词。

法拉利（Ferrari）是一家意大利汽车生产商，1929 年由恩佐·法拉利（Enzo Ferrari）创办，主要制造一级方程式赛车、赛车及高性能跑车。法拉利是世界上最闻名的赛车和运动跑车的生产厂家，早期的法拉利赞助赛车手及生产赛车，1947 年独立生产汽车，其后变成今日的规模。菲亚特（FIAT）公司拥有该公司 90% 股权，但该公司却能独立于菲亚特公司运营。法拉利汽车大部分采用手工制造，因而产量很低，年产量只有 4,000 辆左右。公司总部在意大利的摩德纳（Modena）。特别值得一提的是，伴随着线条动人、马力惊人、颜色引人的法拉利赛车转战各地的"跃马"车徽，也有一段感人的故事。一位在第一次世界大战中捐躯的意大利空军英雄 Francesco Baracca 的双亲，看见法拉利赛车所向无敌的神采，正是爱子英灵依托的堡垒，于是恳请法拉利将其爱子座机上的"跃马"标志，镶嵌在法拉利车系上，以尽爱子巡曳地平线的壮志。法拉利欣然接受了这个建议，并在"跃马"的顶端，加上意大利的国徽为"天"，再以"法拉利"横写字体串连成"地"，最后以自己故乡蒙达那市的代表颜色——黄色，渲染全幅而组合成"天地之间，任我驰骋"的豪迈图腾。

另外"跃马"车徽还有另外一种说法。在世界大战中意大利有一位表现出色的飞行员，他的飞机上就印有一匹会给他带来好运的跃马。在法拉利最初的比赛获胜后，飞行员的父母亲，一对伯爵夫妇建议，法拉利也应在车上印上这匹带来好运气的跃马。后来飞行员死了，马就变成了黑颜色。而标志底色为公司所在地摩德纳的金丝雀的颜色。

1903 年，亨利·福特创建福特汽车公司，公司名称取自创始人亨利·福特的姓氏。福特生前十分喜爱动物，他经常忙里偷闲访问动物专家，读有关动物的书籍和报纸，他在这个领域也有较深的造诣。1911 年，商标设计者为了迎合亨利·福特的嗜好，就将英文Ford 设计成为形似奔跑的白兔形象，以博得福特的欢心。福特汽车公司的商标是蓝底白字的英文 Ford 字样，被艺术化了的 Ford 形似活泼可爱、充满活力、美观大方的小白兔。Ford 犹如温馨大自然中的一只可爱温顺的小白兔，正在向前飞奔，象征福特汽车奔驰在世界各地，令人爱不释手。1908 年，福特 T 型车诞生，为装在汽车轮上的美国立下了不朽功勋。因此，福特汽车公司名扬天下，福特本人也成为世纪名人。

Chevrolet(雪佛兰）是瑞士的赛车手、工程师路易斯·雪佛兰的姓氏。雪佛莱(Chevrolet)属于通用汽车公司的一个分部。该部除生产大众化车型之外，还生产各种运动型跑车。

商标图案是抽象化了的蝴蝶领结，象征雪佛莱轿车的大方、气派和风度。

凯迪拉克(Cadillac)是以北美法国总督、底特律汽车城的创立者命名的。

汽车公司成立时选用"凯迪拉克"之名是为了向法国的皇家贵族、探险家安东尼·门斯·凯迪拉克（le Sieur Antoine de la Nothe Cadillac）表示敬意，因为他在 1701 年建立了底特律城。当时底特律汽车公司重组并更名为凯迪拉克汽车公司，凯迪拉克公司的成立为世界交通运输工业的发展翻开了崭新的篇章。凯迪拉克公司创始人亨利·利兰德(Henry Leland)是英格兰的一名制造商，他非常重视加工精度、制造质量和零件的互换性，并且认为这是迅速发展汽车的关键。在这种思想指导下，1906 年凯迪拉克在底特律的工厂已成为当时世界上最大、最完善和装备最好的汽车厂。1909 年凯迪拉克公司加入通用汽车公司，从此凯迪拉克在设计汽车时，更加重视汽车的豪华性和舒适性。至今，凯迪拉克汽车仍保持这一传统，以豪华轿车而闻名世界。

林肯（Lincoln）轿车是以美国第 16 任总统的名字亚伯拉罕·林肯（Abraham Lincoln）命名的汽车，借助林肯总统的名字来树立公司的形象，显示该公司生产的是顶级轿车。林肯轿车是专门为总统和国家元首生产的高档轿车。由于杰出的性能、高雅的造型和无与伦比的舒适，自 1939 年美国的富兰克林·罗斯福总统以来，一直被白宫选为总统专车。其商标是一个矩形中含有一颗闪闪放光的星辰，表示林肯总统是美国联邦统一和废除奴隶制的启明星，也喻示福特·林肯牌轿车光辉灿烂。

1933 年，丰田喜一郎（Kiichiro Toyoda）在日本爱知县丰田市创建丰田自动织机制作所，1937 年 8 月成立丰田汽车公司，并用自己的姓氏作为公司的名称和商标。早期的日本丰田牌汽车商标，是将 TOYOTA 拼音的第一个大写字母 T 标在发动机散热器格栅上，而将公司名称的拼音形式 TOYOTA 标在车头或车尾上。20 世纪 90 年代，丰田开始使用新商标，新商标是将三个外形近似的椭圆形环巧妙地组合在一起，每个椭圆都是以两点为圆心绘制的曲线组成，它象征用户的心与汽车厂家的心是连在一起的，具有相互信赖感。而且使图案具有空间感，并将拼音 TOYOTA 字母寓于图形商标之中。大椭圆中的两个椭圆垂直交叉恰好组合成一个 T 字，T 代表丰田汽车公司；大椭圆表示地球，中间的 T 字与外面的椭圆重叠，使 T 字最大限度地占据了椭圆空间，使 T 更加突出，喻示丰田汽车走向世界。

- 源于神话人物——崇尚自由乐观性格

希腊、罗马文化是西方文化的摇篮。希腊罗马神话在西方历史，甚至整个人类历史上都有着重要的地位。古希腊罗马神话具有爱智慧的特点，崇拜知识，探求自然和人性的奥秘，其特点之一就是，每个神不仅法力无边，而且都像人一样，有丰满的性格，有丰富的思想，有七情六欲，充满人情美、人性美。而且担任各种职司的诸神，就是多种多样的文化创造者。古希腊罗马神话的姿态质朴、风韵自然，极富艺术感染力，对现代西方文学、宗教、艺术等方面有着深远的影响，也反映了西方人崇尚自由的乐观性格。

很多汽车公司也利用希腊神话中的人名作为汽车的商标名，凸显汽车的个性，强调汽车的性能，引起顾客美好的遐想。

Phaeton 辉腾，是大众汽车公司出产的最高档最豪华型轿车，Phaeton 一词来源于古希腊神话中太阳神儿子的名字，据说他擅长驾太阳车驰骋，辉照大地。18、19 世纪盛行于英国、美国的一种四轮无车门敞篷马车，就是以这个名字命名的，为当时绅士钟爱。此商标名暗示这款车敏捷潇洒而又风度翩翩。

又如 Dyane(狄安娜)，罗马神话中月亮和狩猎女神的法文名字，具有"上等""漂亮"的意思。Mazda 是波斯神话中的光明之神和善良之神，Aurora 是罗马神话中的黎明女神。

- 源于地名——彰显地方特色

在汽车商标词中也有不少是地名，例如企业的所在地或者产品的生产地，风景如画的旅游胜地，历史名城，或者是文学作品中的虚拟的地名。比如有的汽车商标词采用地名，如 Dodge，西部堪萨斯州的一个小镇，在美国历史上具有特殊的含义。在美国拓疆运动中，Dodge 处于东西交汇的地方，文明与野蛮冲突严重，警察、牛仔、匪徒以及拓荒者经常在那里发生激战，社会秩序混乱。因此，一提起这个小镇的名字，立刻让人联想起西进运动中美国式的野性、勇敢和暴力。用它作商标词，暗示其汽车强劲的动力和硬朗的风格。

又如 Shelby 阿肯色著名的牛仔之乡；Bonneville 美国西部以赛马闻名的地方；Grand Canyon 美国著名的大峡谷；Pontiac 取自美国密歇根州的一个地名；Subaru 富士，来源于世界闻名的富士山。

普通词汇是汽车商标的另一来源。

美国的拓疆运动不仅大大扩充了美国的领土，对美国的历史和文化以及美国的人文精神也都产生了巨大的影响。后来的美国汽车商标词中有相当多的一部分正是反映美国拓疆文化。有不少汽车商标名称是这些表达无畏的拓荒者行为的词，暗示汽车粗犷、豪迈的特性，如：Grand Voyager, Escort, Pathfinder, Conquers, Blazer, Trailblazer, Wrangler 等。

切诺基·吉普 Cherokee Jeep 是克莱斯勒公司生产的越野车，"切诺基"取自美洲印第安部族切诺基土人，他们世代居住在山区，由于生活和狩猎的需要，擅长在山地攀行，以此命名表示切诺基汽车能攀过岩石、涉过泥沙、征服任何艰难险阻，到达胜利的彼岸。

拓疆者在前进过程中，新大陆各种各样前所未见的飞禽走兽让他们着迷。后来的很多汽车商标词都采用了这些动物名称，通过这些动物的特征，暗示汽车的性能或者外形。比如 Mustang 野马，这种野马奔腾在北美的草原上，无拘无束，充满了动感和力量之美。用它作商标词，令人立刻对车的速度和性能有了美妙的联想。又如 Viper 蝰蛇，是道奇旗下的一款跑车，外形凶悍霸气，速度惊人，用毒蛇 Viper 作商标名称再合适不过。再如 Branco 烈马，Congar 美洲狮，Thunderbird 雷鸟，Falcon 猎鹰等。

欧美人喜欢户外运动，喜欢冒险，勇于挑战极限，因此很多车的商标词为体现车的实用性，拉近用户和车的距离，使用一些代表人的名词，使车拟人化，这些商标词都带着一种爱好自由的原始风情。例如 Explorer 探险者，Ranger 漫游者，Voyager 旅行者，Cavalier 骑士，Freelander 自由人，Prowler 神行者，Cruiser 漫步者，Tracker 追踪者等。

Beetle 甲壳虫。说到甲壳虫，德国人自然会想到他们喜爱的，又是这里常见的、被视为吉祥物的七星瓢虫，再加上与其短小的车身、流线瓢虫型的车顶相符合，于是"甲壳虫"的绰号由此叫响，甲虫车也成了德国人民地地道道的宠物车。

Golf 高尔夫一词，在德语里既是拥有广大草坪的高尔夫球运动，又有海湾之意。它正迎合了战后为恢复生产和经济腾飞奋战了近 30 年的德国人的心理。它象征着休息、娱乐，对生活在阴冷气候中的德国人而言，这个名字本身便是碧草、蓝天和灿烂阳光的象征。正如当初设计人员期望的那样，高尔夫车问世以来，很快受到世界各地各个阶层人士的喜爱。

Polo 波罗一词原意为马球运动，即骑马人要将草地上的木球击入球门的一项运动。可想而知，新款大众波罗也要为驾驶员带来舒适、安全而又能灵活机动的"坐骑"。

其他来源于普通名词的商标词如 Vantage，Lotus，Esprit，Venture，Intrigue，Skyline，Prairie Liberty，Presage，Evision，Multispace，Crown，Sonata。

- 源于外来词汇——推崇异国情调

有些汽车以生动形象的外来语命名。

Lupo 路波，此词为意大利语"狼"，取其肆野、灵活、狂猛之意。这种小型车经济、安全、质量优上。

Pajero 帕杰罗，为南美洲阿根廷一种行动敏捷的小野猫，寓意为粗犷与美的结合，作为三菱旗下一款 SUV 的商标词，恰如其分地突出了汽车的性能与外观的和谐统一。

Neu Kaefer 新甲虫，1998 年在底特律美洲国际车展上亮相时，便引起公众和传媒的一片惊叹。无疑它是老甲虫的再生，它独具风采的外形以及无与伦比的行驶风格会令人一见倾心。

Bora 宝来，为地中海地区的一种风名——布拉风。其车形一如车名，外观强劲而充满活力，曲线平滑，富有动感和个性。

Passat 帕萨特，是赤道区域由东北方向和东南方向刮来的风，因它的两个风向持久恒定，在汉语里被译为"信风"。信风也是这个区域帆船航行时必要的动力风。这个只有十几岁的新型汽车，是大众汽车公司的设计师与工程师们献给世界的新信风，伴君一路。

又如：Capri（源出希腊语 capricon 山羊星座），Matador（源出西班牙语，斗牛士），Nova（源出拉丁语，新星），Vega（源出拉丁语，落鹰）。

- 源于缩略词——简洁大方

一些汽车商标词直接使用生产厂商名称的首字母缩略词，如：BMW 宝马（Bayerishe Motoren Werke）；Saab 绅宝（Svenska Aeroplan Aktiebolaet）；菲亚特（FIAT）（Fabbrica Itliana Auto-mobi Ledi Torino 意大利都灵汽车制造厂），等。

5.6.2　汽车商标的翻译

商品本身就是一种文化载体，商品通过文化而增值，文化通过商品传播。当商标随着商品进入国际市场时其文化属性便使它进入了跨文化传通领域，商标的发出和接受实质上是一种文化的传通和信息的传递。因此，当我们把汽车商标词从一种语言翻译为另一种语言的时候，也要充分考虑到目标语国家与源语国家之间文化的差异，既要尽量保留原文的精华，又要使其译名符合消费者的心理。在翻译的过程中可通过音译与意译相结合的方法，注意选择音色与意义都与原意较为贴近的字词以达到满意的效果。

翻译前请注意有关汽车类型的几个小常识：

SUV 的全称是 Sport Utility Vehicle，中文意思是运动型多用途汽车。主要是指那些设计前卫、造型新颖的四轮驱动越野车。SUV 一般前悬架是轿车型的独立悬架，后悬架是非独立悬架，离地间隙较大，在一定程度上既有轿车的舒适性又有越野车的越野性能。由于带有 MPV 式的座椅多组合功能，使车辆既可载人又可载货，适用范围广。

MPV 是指多用途汽车（Multi-Purpose Vehicles），从源头上讲，MPV 是从旅行轿车逐渐演变而来的，它集旅行车宽大乘员空间、轿车的舒适性、和厢式货车的功能于一身，一般为两厢式结构，即多用途车。通俗地说，就是可以坐 7~8 人的小客车。从严格意义上说，MPV 是主要针对家庭用户的车型，那些从商用厢型车改制成的、针对团体顾客的乘用车还不能算作真正的 MPV。MPV 的空间要比同排量的轿车相对大些，也存在着尺寸规格之分，但不像轿车那么细。

FUV，英语全称 Fashionable Utility Vehicle，即时尚多功能车辆。FUV 兼具 MPV、三厢轿车，以及城市型 SUV 各自的箱体优势，一台 FUV 就能满足家庭多方面的用车需求。广州丰田汽车公司于 2010 年底发布了首款 E'Z（逸致）FUV 汽车。

5.6.2.1 音译

音译即利用源语商标词发音，用相应的译语词写出来。这种方法可以保留源语商标词的音韵美，体现商品原汁原味的异国情调。

Fiat 菲亚特，以及下列款车的商标：Perla 派朗，Palio 派力奥，Siena 西耶那（意大利中部城市），Wunuo 乌诺，Linea 领雅，Barchetta 巴切塔，Croma 科罗马。

美国 Dodge 道奇，有一款车商标为 Dakota 达科塔。

德国的 Volkswagen 大众汽车下列几款车的商标为音译：Gol 高尔，Polo 波罗，Golf 高尔夫，Santana 桑塔纳，Passat 帕萨特，Sharan 夏朗。

韩国 Daewoo 按韩语读音译为"大宇"，其下几款车商标均为音译：Evanda 艾万达，Kalos 卡罗斯，Lanos 拉诺斯，Lacetti 拉赛帝，Matiz 马蒂兹。

日本的 Daihatsu 商标按日语发音译为"大发"，该车创始于 1907 年，其下 2 款商标亦用音译：Terios 特锐，Bego 贝戈。

日本本田汽车有一款 Odyssey，译为"奥德赛"。

美国 Ford 福特汽车下列商标音译：Mondeo 蒙迪欧，S-Max 麦柯斯，Focus 福克斯。

罗马尼亚的汽车商标 Dacia 音译为"达西亚"，其下一款商标亦用音译法，Logan 罗甘。

英国宾利汽车有一款商标 Brooklands 布鲁克兰。

美国 Buick 商标音译为"别克"。其下几款商标亦是：Enclave 昂科雷，Rainier 雷尼尔，Lucerne 路赛恩，Terraza 泰拉莎。

英国汽车 Aston Martin 译为"阿斯顿马丁"，其下一款商标 Vantage 没有译成字面意义"优势"，而音译为"方塔奇"。

德国汽车 Audi 音译为"奥迪"。

美国汽车 Cadillac 音译为"凯迪拉克"。

美国汽车商标 Chrysler 音译为"克莱斯勒"。

日本雷诺-日产联盟 Infiniti 英菲尼迪。

日本丰田汽车公司 Scion 赛恩。

意大利生产的 Alfa Romeo 译为"阿尔法罗密欧"。"Alfa"是"Anonima Lombarda Fabbrica Automobili"汽车公司的缩写。阿尔法-罗密欧的车徽标志也是引人注目的：它沿用中世纪时米兰的领主维斯康泰公爵的家徽，左边的十字部分来源于十字军从米兰向外远征的故事，右边刻绘了一条正在吞食撒拉逊的蛇，象征着领主维斯康泰的祖先击退使城市人民遭受苦难的"巨蛇"的传说，这个标志也是意大利米兰市的市徽。Alfa(阿尔法)公司创建于 1910 年，但是它的前身却是由 Alessandro Darracq 于 1907 年在米兰创建的另一个小公司。在 Cavalier Ugo Stella 先生的领导下，阿尔法生产了一系列的具有很高操控性的产品，因而闻名当地，开始成为当时汽车市场上比较出名的品牌。

日本丰田下列几款车的商标为音译：Prius 普锐斯，Celica 赛利卡，Previa 普瑞维亚，Tacoma 塔科马(美国华盛顿州西部港市)，Alphard 埃尔法(希腊字母的第一个字母，喻意第一)，Hiace 海狮(商用车)，Fj Cruiser 酷路泽(Suv)，Avensis 爱文奇斯。

美国克莱斯勒有限责任公司 Jeep 商标音译为"吉普"，其下一款商标 Cherokee 切诺基。

意大利汽车 Lancia 蓝旗亚 Phedra 音译为"菲德拉"，而 Musa 现译为"缪斯"，与希腊神话中的 Muse 缪斯女神相混，建议改译为"缪萨"。

英国 Rolls-Royce 劳斯莱斯 Ghost 古斯特，Ghost 字面本意为"鬼，幽灵"，显然不适于作为汽车商标。

日本丰田公司 Lexus 雷克萨斯。

法国 Renault 雷诺, Megane 梅甘娜, Laguna 拉古那, Vel Satis 威赛帝, Koleos 科雷傲, Kangoo 甘果, Clio 克丽欧。

日本雷诺-日产联盟 Nissan 按日语发音译为"日产", 创建于 1933 年。其下列商标: Paladin 帕拉丁, Cube 库贝, Altima 阿蒂玛, Navara 纳瓦拉(皮卡), Xterra 克斯特拉 (SUV), Cima 西玛(豪华), Micra 米克拉, Serena 赛瑞纳(MPV), Lafesta 拉费斯塔 (MPV), Sentra 森塔, Murano 玛拉诺, Terrano 丹拉诺(SUV)。

日本 Suzuki 按日语发音译为"铃木"。其下列商标采用音译法: Alto 奥拓, Jimny 吉姆尼, Landy 浪迪, Liana 利亚纳, Kizashi 凯泽西。

英国 Morgan 商标译为"摩根"。

德国 Opel 译为"欧宝", Signum 译为"西格努姆", Antara 译为"安德拉"。

西班牙汽车商标 Seat 译为"西亚特"。

韩国现代汽车公司 Hyundai 现代下列商标: Elantra 伊兰特, Sonata 索纳塔, Rohens 劳恩斯, Getz 盖茨, Veracrus 维拉克斯, Atos 阿托斯。

美国通用汽车公司 Chevrolet 雪佛兰下列商标: Cruze 科鲁兹, Captiva 科帕奇(Suv), Camaro 科迈罗, Colorado 科罗拉多(皮卡), Monte Carlo 蒙特卡罗, Orlando 奥兰多(Mpv)。

法国 Psa 标致雪铁龙集团 Citroën 雪铁龙下列商标: Xsara 赛纳(具有法国特征), Berlingo 贝凌格(Mpv)。

中国的夏利 Xiali, 悦达起亚 Yueda Kia, 云雀 Yunque, 红旗 Hongqi。

5. 6. 2. 2 字面意直译

根据源语商标词的含义直接将字面意思译出, 保留源语商标词的蕴意。

丰田的几款车: Corolla Ex 花冠, Crown 皇冠, Matrix 矩阵, Sequoia 红杉(SUV), Tundra 苔原(皮卡)。

意大利菲亚特车的商标：Weekend 周末风，Panda 熊猫，Idea 理想。

美国道奇车的商标：Viper 蝰蛇，Ram 公羊（皮卡车），Stratus 层云，Charger 战马（军马，袭击者），Intrepid 无畏（本意：勇猛的），Challenger 挑战者。

德国的 Volkswagen 商标译为"大众"。大众汽车公司的德文 Volkswagen，意为"大众使用的汽车"（香港地区根据 Volkswagen 的译音称大众汽车为"福士伟根"）。大众汽车的商标是德文单词 Volkswagen 中的两个字母（V）olks（大众）（W）agen（汽车）的叠合，镶嵌在一个大圆圈内，然后整个商标又镶嵌在发动机散热器前面格栅的中间。图形商标形似三个"V"字，像是用中指和食指做出的 V 形，表示大众公司及其产品"必胜-必胜-必胜"。文字商标则标在车尾的行李箱盖上，以注明该车的名称。大众商标简捷、鲜明、引人入胜，令人过目不忘。

大众汽车有两款商标为字面义直译：Beetle 甲壳虫，Fox 狐狸。

英国 Bentley 宾利商标下有一款 Continental 译为"欧陆"。

美国 Buick 别克汽车有两款车商标直译其字面意义：Park Avenue 林荫大道，Century 世纪。

日本丰田汽车有一款商标 4Runner（SUV）译为"四信使"。Runner 有"信使""跑步者"的意思。

美国 Ford 汽车大部分商标用字面意直译：Fiesta 嘉年华（〈西〉节日（特指在西班牙和拉丁美洲以游行和舞蹈来庆祝的节日），祭典，圣日，假日），Edge（SUV）刀锋（另 Edge 爱虎，锐界），Cougar 美洲狮，Explorer 探索者，Expedition 远征，Scorpio 天蝎座，Mustang 野马（墨西哥和北美平原的）（跑车），Ranger 漫游者（皮卡），Freestar 自由星，Freestyle 自由式（SUV），Falcon 猎鹰。

英国的 Jaguar 商标，字面意为"美洲虎"，而商标名译为"捷豹"，象征一头敏捷高速奔跑的豹子。

美国凯迪拉克汽车一款商标 Eldorado 黄金国，原文的字面意为：理想中的黄金国，富庶之乡。

法国 Psa 标致雪铁龙集团 Citroën 雪铁龙下列商标直译：Elysée 爱丽舍，C-Triomphe 凯旋，（Xsara）Picasso 萨拉毕加索。

吉普牌汽车的下列商标采用字面意直译：Compasser 指南者，Commander 指挥官（SUV）Liberty 自由，Patriot 爱国者，Wrangler 牧马人。

美国汽车 Chrysler 克莱斯勒两款商标：Aspen 大齿杨，Pt Cruiser　Pt 漫步者。

兰博基尼一款 Murcielago，意为"蝙蝠"，是中世纪一头连战数场而不死的斗牛的名字。兰博基尼的董事会主席翻遍了关于西班牙斗牛的 11 本厚厚的书籍，发现了 Murcielago 的故事，用这个名字来命名新车，显然含有深意。兰博基尼另一款 Diablo 译为"鬼怪"，原意为"黑暗破坏神"。

英国 Rolls-Royce 劳斯莱斯两款：Phantom 幻影，Silver Seraph 银天使。

法国 Renault 雷诺两款：Scenic 风景，Latitude 纬度。

马来西亚宝腾集团汽车商标 Lotus 字面意直译为"莲花"。

美国 Lincoln 林肯三款：Navigator 领航员，Town Car 城镇(豪华车)，Aviator 飞行家。

日本 Nissan 日产下列商标字面意直译：Sunny 阳光，Frontier 边境，Armada 舰队，Titan 巨人(皮卡)，Skyline 天际线，Bluebird 蓝鸟。Bluebird 典出比利时作家 Maurice Materlinek 1911 年的童话剧 *Bluebird*。剧中 Bluebird 象征"未来幸福"，用作轿车的商标，转译为"幸福之源"。唐朝李商隐有诗云："蓬山此去多无路，青鸟殷勤为探看。""青鸟"乃蓬山仙境的使者，且汉语的"青"与"蓝"均可等同于英语的 Blue，"蓝鸟"二字不仅读起来朗朗上口，文化内涵也几尽相似。

德国戴姆勒股份公司的 Maybach 迈巴赫其下一款商标 Zeppelin 齐柏林。

韩国现代汽车集团的 Kia 起亚的几款商标：Cerato 赛拉图，Opirus 欧菲莱斯，Sorento 索兰托。

韩国 Ssangyong 双龙 Chairman 译为"主席"(豪华)。

美国 Mercury 水星 Mountaineer 登山家(SUV)，Milan 米兰，都按字面意直译。

日本丰田汽车公司的 Subaru 斯巴鲁 Forester 森林人(SUV)。

英国汽车 Aston Martin 阿斯顿马丁 Vanquish 征服。

美国通用汽车公司 Saturn 土星。

美国通用汽车公司 Chevrolet 雪佛兰下列商标：Equinox 春分（昼夜平分点，春分或秋分），Express 急速（MPV），Suburban 郊区/巨无霸（SUV），Impala 羚羊（黑斑羚，产于非洲中南部），建议改音意结合译法：羚跑。Avalanche 雪崩（皮卡），建议改译：雅兰捷，比原译更适于汽车的商标。Uplander 优普兰，建议改字面直译：高地，更能反映 SUV 车在高地驰骋的性能。

英国 Land Rover 路虎下列商标：Discovery 发现，Defender 卫士。

又如 Vanquish 征服，Continental 大陆，Azure 蓝天，Sunfire 太阳火，Landbruiser 陆地巡洋舰等。

5.6.2.3 音意结合

利用汉字表音又表意的特点，根据源语商标词的读音和意义，精心选择词汇，使其译名尽量保留源语商标词的音韵美，同时依托汉字所蕴含的多义文化信息，在传递汽车特性的同时，体现中国特色，补充在翻译过程中所出现的语义信息损耗，引导消费者进行有益的联想。这也是汽车商标词翻译中最常用的一种翻译方法。

瑞典汽车 Volvo 商标译成"沃尔沃"，听起来朗朗上口，联想车轮滚滚，永不休止。港台用译名"富豪"，的确身价不菲。据说是目前世界上安全性能最高的汽车。

Bora 宝来，似有财富收获之意。这是大众旗下的一款家庭型车，商标词原义为亚得里亚海的海风，一汽大众在引进这款车后为其取了一个具有中国特色的名字——宝来。一方面保留了发音的相似性，另一方面也符合中国人传统的招财进宝的观念，体现了吉祥如意的含义。尤其是作为一款家庭型轿车，其商标词更能吸引目标人群的注意力，引起美好的联想，为其开拓市场起到了推动的作用。

Porshe 保时捷。这是世界顶级跑车生产商，以其卓越的性能和惊人的速度闻名。其跑车在香港曾被音译为"波尔舍"，而大陆译为"保时捷"，既贴近原词的发音，又在意义上暗示了时速惊人，行动敏捷。现在一提起"保时捷"，人们的第一反应是它是一款风驰电掣、威风八面的跑车。

Benz 奔驰，这是音意相结合的一个典范，听到这个名字，能立刻联想起汽车马力强劲，一路畅通向前行驶的形象。其下有几款商标，Viano 唯雅诺，Vito 威霆，Sprinter 凌特，音意璧合，而没有按字面译成"赛跑选手"。

韩国现代汽车公司 Hyundai 现代下列商标：Tucson 途胜，Verna 瑞纳，Accent 雅绅（特），Veloster 飞思，Moinca 名驭，Matrix 美佳，Coupe 酷派，Genesis Coupe 劳恩斯-酷派，H-1 辉翼，Santa Fe 圣达菲（另一译名"胜达"，从音意结合的角度来看，此译名优于

"圣达菲"），Terracan 特拉卡（Suv），Equus 雅科仕。

Trajet 特拉杰，建议改译：雅捷，更能体现车子的外观优美，速度快捷。

Entourage 商标未有译名，宜采用意义结合的方法，试译为：安途瑞。

丰田下列几款商标：Vios 威驰，Yaris 雅力士，Camry 凯美瑞，Reiz 锐志，Verso 逸致，Dario Terios 特锐，Lexus 凌志，也译作"雷克萨斯"，但没有"凌志"的译名好。

菲亚特 Fiat 的几款车名：Bravo 博悦，Stilo 短剑，Doblo 多宝，Multipla 多能，Seicento 赛神托，Ulysse 优力赛，Grande Punto 朋多。

美国 Dodge 道奇车的商标：Caliber 酷搏，Avenger 锋哲（本义：复仇者），Caravan 凯领（Caravan 本义：（商队、游客经过沙漠时为安全起见而结队同行的）沙漠旅行队，大篷车），Neon 霓虹，Nitro 耐奇（Suv），Journey 酷威（Suv），Durango 拓远者。

大众汽车有下列款商标采用音意结合的译法：Jetta 捷达，Bora 宝来，Sagitar 速腾，Lavida 朗逸，Magotan 迈腾，Touran 途安，Touareg 途锐，Phaeton 辉腾（Phaeton 本义：一种轻快的四轮马车），Tiguan 途观，Caddy 开迪。

英国的 Bentley 商标译为"宾利"，其下有两款商标亦用音意结合译法：Arnage 雅致，Mulsanne 慕尚。

日本本田车有一款 Legend 译为"里程"，没有按字面本义译为"传说"。

Ford 汽车商标译为"福特"，也可以说是音意结合的，其下几款商标亦是：Transit 全顺（商用车），Fusion 福星，没有按字面义直译为"熔化，熔合"。

美国凯迪拉克汽车一款商标 Deville 帝威，音意结合，十分传神。

美国汽车 Chrysler 克莱斯勒一款商标：Borui 铂锐。

日本 Nissan 日产下列商标音意结合翻译：March 玛驰，Livana 骊威，Tiida 骐达，（又译：颐达），Teana 天籁，Primera 派美。

日本 Suzuki 铃木 Grand Vitara 超级维特拉。

日本 Mazda 马自达及两款车商标 Family 福美来，Premacy 普力马。

英国 Mclaren 汽车商标译成"迈凯轮"，喻意：豪迈凯旋的车轮。

英国 Mini 商标译为"迷你"，让消费者对该车着迷，跃跃欲试。

德国 Opel 音意皆备译"欧宝"，联想"来自欧洲的宝车"。其下列商标：Astra 雅特，Vectra 威达，Zafira 赛飞利，Meriva 美瑞拉，Corsa 可赛。

韩国现代汽车集团的 Kia 译为"起亚"，其下列商标亦为音意结合：Rio 锐欧，Soul 秀尔，Shuma 速迈，Forte 福瑞迪，Sportage 狮跑(猛狮一样奔跑)，Borrego 霸锐。

中国汽车商标 Roewe 译成"荣威"，取其"荣耀威武"之涵义。

美国通用汽车公司 Chevrolet 雪佛兰下列商标：Lova 乐风，Sail 赛欧，Cobalt 科宝，Astra 雅特，Corvette 考维特(跑车)，Malibu 美宜堡，Venture 万程。

2009 年中国奇瑞汽车公司生产 Riich 汽车，汉译成"瑞麒"，含有"吉祥"之意。

日本三菱集团 Mitsubishi 三菱旗下的商标大多用音意结合的译法：Lancer 蓝瑟，Lancer Ex 蓝瑟翼神，Lancer Evolution 蓝瑟翼豪陆神，Galant 戈蓝，Zinger 君阁 (SUV)，Grandis 格蓝迪(MPV)，Outlander 欧蓝德 (SUV)，Pajero 帕杰罗 (SUV)，Montero 蒙特罗 (SUV)。

荷兰汽车商标 Spyker 译为"世爵"。

韩国 Ssangyong 双龙 Actyon 爱腾(SUV)，Rodius 路帝(MPV)，Rexton 雷斯特 (SUV)。

日本丰田汽车公司的 Subaru 斯巴鲁，Legacy 力狮，Outback 傲虎(SUV)。

中国云南江淮汽车瑞风，译为：REFINE。

5.6.2.4　创新译法

这种翻译方法最灵活，可以抛开源语商标词的形式或读音限制，最大限度地发挥想象力和创造性，根据产品的性质特点，创新一个响亮醒目，完全符合目的语国家文化环境和审美心理的新名字。

BMW 宝马，原商标词是由 Bayerishe Motoren Werke 首字母缩写而成，代表生产厂商的名字，只是商品信息，无太多文化含义。在将其翻译成中文时，巧妙地利用 B 和 M 两个字母，译为"宝马"。马是中华民族喜欢的动物，象征着锐意进取，朝气勃勃，奋发向上。一提起宝马，立刻让人联想起"骁腾有如此，万里可横行"的气魄。

英国 MG 商标名为 2 个字母，按字母发音翻译成"名爵"，与 BMW 手法类似，显示了车主的名贵显赫的身份与地位。但民间有说法把"名爵"与另二字谐音联想：命绝，所以虽然车的性价比不错，但问津者较少。

德国品牌 Brabus(博速)有一款商标为 Smart 创新译为"精灵"，而没有按照字面意思译为"潇洒"或"时髦"。

瑞典通用汽车公司 1937 年始产 SAAB 汽车，其商标译成了"坤宝"，也见音译成"萨博"的，但前者远胜过后者。

大众汽车有一款车商标 Scirocco 译为"尚酷"。

美国 Buick 汽车下列几款商标采用创新译法，收到意想不到的效果，深为用户喜爱和

接受。Excelle 凯越，Regal 君威（字面本为"帝王的"），Lacrosse 君越（字面意思为"长曲棍球"），Rendezvous 朗迪（字面意思"集合点"），Royaum 荣御，Lesabre 名使。而 Excelle XT 译为"英朗"（别克品牌旗下继新君威、新君越以及昂科雷之后，第四款基于通用最新全球平台生产的车型，别克英朗源自欧宝新雅特，出自通用全球 Delta Ⅱ 平台。在国内，别克英朗的主要竞争对手将是刚上市不久的一汽大众高尔夫 6 车型。"英朗"不仅完美诠释了这款五门轿跑车与生俱来的英姿焕发的气质及飒爽硬朗的线条和驾驭感受，同时也辉映出新一代奋斗青年的"才能和智慧"以及"敢想敢为、利落干脆的处事作风"。"英朗"的命名为别克品牌精神注入了新的时代内涵。）

日本产汽车 Honda 按日语发音译为"本田"，而其下几款商标采用了创新译法：Civic 思域，Fit 飞度，Accord 雅阁（字面义为"调和，一致"），Crosstour 歌诗图，City 思迪（字面义"城市"），Spirior 思铂睿，无疑都是成功翻译的典范。

日本丰田汽车下的商标 Avalon 亚洲龙（*n.* 原义：阿瓦隆，凯尔特族传说中的西方乐土岛，据说亚瑟王及其部下死后尸体被移往该岛）。

福特一款商标 Maverick（SUV）翼虎，跟原词音义无关，喻意"如虎添翼"，其字面意思为"没打烙印的动物"。

美国凯迪拉克汽车一款商标 Escalade 译为"凯雷德"。

美国汽车 Chrysler 克莱斯勒一款商标 Grand Voager 译为"大捷龙"。

意大利汽车 Lancia 蓝旗亚 Thesis 商标译为"强音"。

日本 Nissan 日产下列商标创造性翻译，不乏优美之译：Sylphy 轩逸，Geniss 骏逸，X-Trail 奇骏，Patrol 途乐，Qashqai 逍客，Cefiro 风度，Quest 贵士（原义为：寻求），Fuga 风雅，Pathfinder 小旋风（SUV），Pathfinder 字面义为"探险者，开创者"。

日本 Suzuki 铃木的一款商标 Swift 译为"雨燕"，让人联想车像一只凌空的雨燕驰骋于自然之间。

德国 Opel 欧宝 Agila，译为"灵敏"。

日本 Acura 译为"讴歌"。

韩国现代汽车集团 Kia 起亚的下列商标为创新译法：Optima 远舰（原义：印刷中的光体字体），Cadenza 凯尊（原义为音乐的装饰乐段，华彩乐段），Carens 佳乐，VQ 威客。

日本 Nissan 日产 Maxima 译为"千里马"，maxima 为 maximum 的复数，"最大，极限"。

日本三菱集团 Mitsubishi 三菱 Space Wagon 菱绅（MPV），ASX 劲炫（SUV）均采用创新译法。

韩国 Ssangyong 双龙 Kyron 享御。

日本丰田汽车公司的 Subaru 斯巴鲁下列商标：Impreza 翼豹，Tribeca 驰鹏(SUV)。

日本丰田汽车第七代凯美瑞以 "New Era Sedan（新时代轿车）"为开发目标，将"Emotional"（感性）和"Rational"（理性）完美融合于一体，于 2011 年 11 月 8 日在上海盛装亮相，开创性推出旗舰、运动和混合动力三大车系，其英语名为 Camry，Camry SE，Camry HEV，分别命名为"凯美瑞"，"凯美瑞·骏瑞"和"凯美瑞·尊瑞"，后两个名称的翻译正是采用了创新性的译法。

所属大众汽车集团原产捷克 Skoda 斯柯达 Fabia 晶锐，Octavia 明锐，Superb 昊锐，均为颇具创意的好译。

韩国现代汽车公司 Hyundai 现代下列商标：Sonata Nf 索纳塔御翔，Sonata Nfc 索纳塔领翔，Azera 雅尊。

美国通用汽车公司 Chevrolet 雪佛兰下列商标：Spark 乐驰(另有一音译：斯帕可，效果远不如乐驰)，Aveo 乐骋，Epica 景程，Tahoe 豪放(SUV)，Trailblazer 全能先锋(SUV)(Trailblazer 开路的人，先驱者，开拓者)。

法国雪铁龙集团 Citroën 雪铁龙 C-Quatre 世嘉。

英国 Land Rover 译为"路虎"。其下商标：Range Rover 览胜，又译"陆虎览胜"。Freelander 神行者。

Ford 福特 Escape 译为"爱仕"，原词义为"逃跑"，显然，"爱仕"更适合汽车商标。

法国 Peugeot 译为"标致"。

Caravan 捷龙，Escort 雅仕，Evision 遨游

汽车商标的翻译涉及的知识面较广，尤其是中西方文化内涵有异，价值取向不一，翻译时译者应考虑到诸多因素，给每个商标一个恰如其分的译名，以获得消费者的认可，并利于汽车的销售。

（汽车商标的内容主要参考以下网页：

http://auto.sina.com.cn/j_kandian.d.html? docid＝fypnyqi3155120&subch＝iauto

https://baijiahao.baidu.com/s? id＝1552528326171800&wfr＝spider&for＝pc

http://baijiahao.baidu.com/s? id＝1555068411621243&wfr＝spider&for＝pc）

第六章　旅游文体翻译

6.1　概　　述

如前所述，旅游文本属"呼唤型"文本。所以，旅游文体的翻译，不但要传达源语信息，而且要注意它自身的特殊性。旅游资料的功能是通过对景点的介绍、宣传，扩展人们的知识，激发人们旅游、参观的兴趣。因此，旅游文体翻译的最终目的就是通过传递信息来吸引旅游者。翻译这类资料，译者要考虑到译语的可读性及读者的接受效果，所以，译者的自由度相对较大。

旅游文体的翻译不同于官方文件、文献、高级领导人讲话、经贸合同、法律文书等的翻译，后者属"信息型"文本，翻译时要求译语力求遣词用句严谨准确，最充分、最客观地体现源语的信息及语言风貌，译者的自由度相对较小。

在翻译过程遇到的众多问题之中，相当一部分是文化差异造成的交际困难。中西方文化差异相当之大，辐射的范围包括人们的生活方式、行为方式、思维方式、语言方式、历史习俗、等级观念、道德规范、审美情趣、政治法律等。而这些差异经常表现在语言文字这一文化的载体之中，更是无时无刻不表现在旅游资料的翻译当中。

要处理好旅游资料中大量的文化信息，译者必须要以偏向译语、侧重读者的方向为准则。译者既不能不顾及英语的表达习惯和读者的接受能力，让英语就范于汉语的概念和意象，追求语言文字和信息量的"对等"转换，也不能因两种文化的差异造成的"词汇空缺"而经常回避困难。

这里特别需要说明的是，汉语的旅游资料中富含中国传统文化的内涵的典故成语以及一些中国文化中特有的东西，而且嵌用古诗词多，这些内容无疑给旅游翻译增加了很大的难度，这就需要翻译工作者具有相当高的汉语言及中国传统文化素养，又要具备相当娴熟的英语语言表达能力，翻译起来才能得心应手。

6.2　旅游文本的文体特点

旅游文本，无论英语还是汉语，属应用文范畴，其形式灵活多样，内容无所不包，文体类别也是丰富多彩。如旅游指南属描写型，用词要生动形象，明白晓畅；旅游广告与其他广告语一样属呼唤型，用词短小精悍，富有创意，句式简洁活泼，具有极强的吸引力和号召力；旅游合同，属契约型，用词规范，表达准确，程式化明显；旅游行程，属信息型，用词简洁明了，具有提示性。本章节主要关注旅游景点介绍及菜肴名称的翻译。

中文的旅游资料各具特点，归纳起来有下列几方面：

6.2.1 词汇量丰富

这是由于旅游的综合性、全球性、文化性、经济性、政治性、商业性、教育性、专业性、休闲性、娱乐性、趣味性、宗教性、种族性、民族性、女权性、应用性和交叉性等因素所决定的。可以说上至天文下至地理，无所不包，无所不括。这一特点也决定了下一个特点。

6.2.2 知识面广

表现得尤为突出的知识是一个地区或一个景区的历史、典故、民间习俗、民间传说，以及与整个民族文化有关的方方面面的知识。

6.2.3 文化层面宽

最重要的是，旅游是一项跨文化的交际活动，它必须与景区的地区或国家的文化息息相关，诸如民族的、历史的、经济的、政治的、教育的、宗教的、艺术的、文学的、饮食的、服饰的、生活方式及风俗习惯等，在翻译实践中，译者常感到跨文化的难点较多。

6.2.4 措辞讲究

旅游资料为了达到某种宣传效果，常常在措辞上颇下工夫，尤其是中文资料，作者总是千方百计地用优美的文字，细腻的描写，运用风趣的写法，取得感人的效果。

6.2.5 风格活泼幽默

旅游资料大多是给游人阅读，或讲给游客听的，所以风格常常轻松幽默，清新明快，让读者于愉悦中接受知识。

6.2.6 多引用古诗词

在旅游资料中，特别是汉语资料中，因介绍景点景观的需要，常常引用古诗词的部分句子或整首诗词来增加资料的表达效果。这无疑给翻译增加了一定的难度。

6.3 旅游资料翻译方法

6.3.1 调整翻译手法

在翻译实践中，译者可根据实际需要，运用适当的手法，如常用的有释义、增补、类比、删减、再创造等对译文进行调整，尽量做到言之有物，言之有理，言之有情，言之有趣。

6.3.1.1 释义

释义是指对原文字面意义的解释。如：

西安古称长安。

译文：Xi'an was called Chang'an, or "everlasting peace" in ancient times.

天安门可译为：Tiananman, the Gate of Heavenly Peace

这样的译法将名称与其含义联系起来，便于英语读者记忆，加深他们的印象，增加他们的游兴。又如：

端午节那天，人们都要吃粽子。

译文：

During the Dragon Boat Festival (which falls on the fifth day of the fifth lunar month), it is a common practice to eat Zongzi, which is a rice pudding wrapped up with weed leaves.

译文对"粽子"的解释说明弥补了译入语的词汇空缺，很好地传递了文化信息。

6.3.1.2 增补

增补是为了易于读者的理解而添加的相关知识和背景资料。对有关中国历史文化的内容，通过增加字、词、句，对原文作进一步的解释。在译文中，对一些地名、人名、朝代名、佛名等，若根据字面意思再略加注释，则让人易于理解，并加深印象、增添乐趣。

- 秦始皇

译文：Qin Shihuang, the first emperor in Chinese history who unified China in 221 B. C.

在翻译中国的朝代名称时，需要补充该朝代的公元年份，以避免不谙中国历史的外国旅游者望字兴叹。

- 林则徐

译文：Lin Zexu, government official of the Qing Dynasty (1636-1911) and key figure in the Opium War

在译地名时，有时得为读者补充必要的相关知识及其地理方位。在有关丝绸之路的旅游资料中经常提到"西域"这个地理名称，如果不作任何增补而音译为"Xiyu"或再加释义"the Western Regions"，英文读者会误以为这是一地名。作过增补后，概念就清晰了：

- 西域

译文：the Western Regions (a Han Dynasty term for the area west of Yumenguan Pass, including what is now Xinjiang Uygur Autonomous Region and parts of Central Asia)

一是介绍崂山的资料中有这样一段：

- 三官殿里有一株茶花树，在寒冬腊月开出一树鲜花，璀璨如锦，因此又名"耐冬"。

译文：There is a camellia tree in the Sanguan Palace blooming fully in midwinter, so it is called *Naidong*, meaning it can stand bitterly cold winters.

译者根据原文的字面意思，在句末增加了一个非限定性定语从句，对"耐冬"作进一步的解释，加深了读者对茶花树的印象。又如：

- 路左有一巨石，石上原有苏东坡手书"云外流春"四个大字。

译文：To its left is a rock formerly engraved with four big Chinese characters Yun Wai Liu Chun (Beyond clouds flows spring) hand-written by SU Dongpo (1037-1101), the most versatile poet of the Northern Song Dynasty (960-1127).

译文增加了对苏东坡的说明，较好地表达了原文要想表达的意图："云外流春"四个

133

字具有较高的文物价值。

二是音译与意译相结合，用括号里的内容增加对原文的字面意思的解释。如：

- 天涯海角、鹿回头(海南岛两个著名的旅游景点)，分别译为：

Tianya-Haijiao（the end of the earth and the edge of the sea）

Luhuitou（Turn-Round Deer）scenic spot

上述意译可引起读者生动有趣的联想与美的享受。又如：

- 卦台山周围有龙马洞、分心石、洗脚石等景点。

译文：Around the Guatai Mountain are the *Longma*（Dragon-and-Horse）Cave，*Fenxin*（Distracting Attention）Rock，*Xijiao*（Washing Feet）Stone and other scenes.

6.3.1.3　类比或转译

为使旅游信息在英语读者中产生反响，我们用"以此比彼"的方法拉近读者与中国文化的距离，使他们产生亲近感，激发他们的游兴。译者可以把中文资料中有关的内容转化为外国游客熟悉的同类的内容。如：

- 将民间传说中的"梁山伯与祝英台"转作 Romeo and Juliet；

亦可把外国资料中的内容转译为中国游客所熟悉的东西，如：

- 美国亚洲旅行社的旅游资料中也把威尼斯比作中国的苏州；
- 北京的王府井可以比作美国纽约的第五大街(Fifth Avenue)；
- 郑州在其交通位置上可以比作美国的芝加哥(Chicago in America)，等。

这样可以简洁而较为准确地介绍人物或景点，使读者在自己的文化基础上理解异国文化，加深印象。又如：

- 西施(西子)

译文：Chinese Cleopatra(克利奥帕特拉)

美女西施在中国人心目中的地位与美女 Cleopatra 在西方人心目中的地位相当，容易被西方人接受。我们也将"西子"译为：Beauty Xi Zi（at her best）

- 清明节

译文：Chinese Easter 较能被西方人接受。

- 济公

译文：Chinese Robin Hood

- 鱼米之乡

译文：land of Milk and Honey（出自《圣经》）

- 苏堤

译文：Lover's Lane，现在，杭州西湖的苏堤晚上成了恋人幽会的地方。

- 故宫耗时 14 年，整个工程于 1420 年结束。

如果这份旅游资料针对北美市场发行，译者则可处理为：The construction of the Forbidden City took 14 years，and was finished in 1420，72 years before Christopher Columbus discovered the New World.

若这份资料的目标市场是欧洲，则可在"in 1420"后加上"14 years before Shakespeare was born"，采取这样的类比手法能使外国人将他们陌生的中国历史年代与他们熟悉的历史或人物所处的年代联系起来，给他们留下深刻的印象。

6.3.1.4 删减

删减即删去中文资料中对译文理解没有帮助的东西。中国人在写事状物时喜欢引用名人名言或古诗词加以验证，中国读者读了会加深印象，并从中得到艺术享受，而在外国人看来似乎是画蛇添足。译文中删去，反而干净利落，明白晓畅。如一本介绍青岛的旅游资料中有这样一段原文：

- 烟水苍茫月色迷，渔舟晚泊栈桥西。乘凉每至黄昏后，人依栏杆水拍堤。这是古人赞美青岛海滨的诗句。青岛是一座风光秀丽的海滨城市，夏无酷暑，冬无严寒。西起胶州湾入海处的团岛，东至崂山风景区的下清宫，绵延80多华里的海滨组成了一幅绚烂多彩的长轴画卷。

译文：*Qingdao* is a beautiful coastal city. It is not hot in summer and not cold in winter. The 40-km-long scenic line begins from *Tuan* Island at the west end to *Xiaqing Gong* of Mount Lao at the east end.

译者把古诗全部删减，但不影响译文读者对原文中其他部分的理解。

又如：

- 乐山水光山色独特，地理环境优越，素有"绿扬夹岸水平铺"之称，举行龙舟竞赛得天独厚。

译文：Famous for its "tranquil river fringed with rich vegetation", *Leshan* in Sichuan Province has the ideal setting for the Dragon Festival.

原文中"水光山色独特，地理环境优越"的具体表现就是"绿扬夹岸水平铺"，删去前两句，译文简练，更符合外国读者的习惯。

汉语旅游资料的撰写者们往往在描述一个景点时，喜欢旁征博引。例如下面一段对西安附近"八水"之一的"沣河"的描写：

- 在我国最早的典籍中，即有关于这条河的记载。《尚书·禹贡》："漆沮既从，沣水攸同"，《诗经·大雅》："沣水东注，维禹之绩"，说明沣水在远古就是一条著名的河流。

汉语撰写者引经据典的目的，无非是想证明沣河的悠久历史。但是，所引的汉语文字对大多数中国人来说都难以明白，更何况外国旅游者？纵然译者费九牛二虎之力将引文的来龙去脉及其意义在英语中交代清楚，效果又会如何？不如省些力气，作如下处理，求得功能上的对等：

Records about this river can be found even in the earliest Chinese classics, which proves that, the *Feng* River has been well-known since ancient times.

此外，关于华清池有这样一段文字描写：

- 华清池内有一贵妃池，相传是杨贵妃当年沐浴的地方。唐代名诗人白居易的《长恨歌》中有"春寒赐浴华清池，温泉水滑洗凝脂"的诗句。

译文：

Inside the *Huachingchih* Spring, there is a bathing pool called *Kueifeichih* which is said to have been the bathing place of Yang Kueifei. The famous poet Po Chu-i of the Tang Dynasty wrote

"The Ballad Endless Woe" which contains the following verses:

> "It was in the chilly springtime
> They bathed in *Huaching* lake.
> And in the tepid waters
> The crusted winter slack."

原文不过是想陈述华清池内有杨贵妃当年沐浴的贵妃池。如果说所引白居易《长恨歌》中的两句诗能使部分中国人联想起杨贵妃的"回头一笑百媚生，六宫粉黛无颜色"，"后宫佳丽三千人，三千宠爱在一身"这般的美丽与可爱，对英文读者来说，从这些诗句的译文中得到的仍不过是杨贵妃曾在此沐浴这个信息，如此说来，译它何用? 更何况诗句的译文并没有很好地传递原诗的信息。其中 they 的所指是不确切的，bathed in the *Huaching* Lake 错误地理解了原句，至于后一句的译文就离原意更远了，像这种翻译乃没有理解原文的瞎译，没能把原文的意境传达给读者，尤其是当你没有把握或力不从心的时候，这样费力不讨好的事情还是不做为好。

当然，省译古诗词也得考虑上下文，有时省译了就不能将原意表达出来，还是翻译出来为好。如西湖十景之一的"曲院风荷"是著名的西湖夏景：

每当农历六月，你在西湖边放眼展望，映入眼帘的是深深密密的荷叶，它们展绿叠翠，浑圆宽阔，形似小伞，覆盖了整个湖面，并将绿色引向无边的远方，绿叶丛中，一枝枝粉红色的荷花竞相开放，在灿烂的阳光下娇艳夺目。难怪当这迷人的景致闯入宋朝诗人杨万里的眼帘时，他一下子被征服了，禁不住脱口而出：

- 毕竟西湖六月中，
  风光不与四时同：
  接天莲叶无穷碧，
  映日荷花别样红。

  译文：

  After all it's the West Lake in summer hot,

  Displaying scenes no other seasons have got:

  Green lotus leaves stretch so far to the ruddy horizon,

  Bathed in sunshine are exceptionally pink lotus blossoms. （陈刚，2004，411）

这里译者以直译为主，仿佛诗人当时情不自禁，有感而发，脱口成诗，用词尽可能简练、口语化。

- 再如一首苏东坡描写西湖的脍炙人口的诗句：
  水光潋滟晴方好，
  山色空蒙雨亦奇。
  欲把西湖比西子，
  淡妆浓抹总相宜。

  译文：

  The shimmering ripples delight the eye on sunny days,

  The dimming hills present a rare view in rainy haze.

West Lake may be compared to Beauty Xi Zi at her best,

It becomes her to be richly adorned or plainly dressed. （陈刚，2004，406）

6.3.1.5 创造性翻译

创造性翻译指在不损害原文信息的前提下，不拘泥于原文，对原文不符合译语习惯的词句、语序进行必要的改造和调整，以期更好地服务于读者。何志范先生所译的"乐山龙舟会多姿多彩"堪称创造性翻译的范例。如描写龙舟赛前场面的第三段文字：

• 江岸上彩楼林立，彩灯高悬，旌旗飘摇，呈现出一派喜气洋洋的节日场面。千姿百态的各式彩龙在江面游弋，舒展着优美的身姿，有的摇头摆尾，风采奕奕；有的喷火吐水，威风八面。

译文：

High-rise buildings ornamented with colored lanterns and bright banners stand out along the river banks. On the river itself, gaily decorated dragon-shaped boats await their challenge, displaying their individual charms to their hearts' content. One boat wags its head and tail; another spits fire and sprays water.

译文中，译者多处灵活地处理了中英文行文上的习惯冲突，改变了原文中词藻堆砌的现象。如译文表面上虽没有与"呈现出一派喜气洋洋的节日场面"、"风采奕奕"、"威风八面"等对应的词句，但仍通过"gaily decorated"，"displaying their individual charms to their heart's content"将意义与气氛很好地表达出来。此外，正如译者自己认为的"译文打破了原文句子的排列，用 displaying their individual charms to their heart's content 来表示群龙在竞赛前各显其能、舒展各自身姿的风采和八面威风；await their challenge 又为龙舟夺标作了铺垫，起了承上启下的作用"。

• 满树金花、芳香四溢的金桂；花白如雪、香气扑鼻的银桂；红里透黄、花朵味浓的紫砂桂；花色似银、季季有花的四季桂；竞相开放，争妍媲美。进入桂林公园，阵阵桂香扑鼻而来。

译文： The Park of Sweet Osmanthus is noted for its profusion of osmanthus trees. Flowers from these trees in different colors are in full bloom which pervade the whole garden with the fragrance of their blossoms.

从译文中我们可以看到，译文打破原文的句子排列，改写原文的华丽辞藻和细节描写，整体概括，简洁明白。

6.4 敏感词的处理

旅游资料是一种对外宣传、推销的资料。它的读者由于生活在不同的文化及不同的社会制度之中，自然就形成了自己的政治信仰与思维方式。这就要求我们的翻译工作者在向世界介绍中国时，不但要了解本国的国情，还要了解他国国情及其他地区的情况，在翻译中注意到某些敏感词的历史背景及政治含义，掌握好译文的分寸。

如西安碑林艺术博物馆"昭陵六骏"展柜内的中文说明词中有这么一段：

• ……"昭陵六骏"是唐太宗李世民为纪念他征战时骑过的六匹骏马，在修建昭陵时诏令雕刻的……其中"飒露紫"和"拳毛䯄（guā）"两匹骏马 1914 年被美国人毕士博盗走，现存费城宾夕法尼亚大学博物馆。

如果查找更为详细的历史资料，就会发现其真实的经过：这位美国人与当地军阀勾结，购买了这两件唐代艺术珍品，将其运往美国。1918 年，他又返回陕西，将其余四个石刻每个打成四块，企图再次运往美国，但被当地群众发现后追回。而目前大多数中文旅游资料来源于博物馆的陈列说明，而译者也将这段话忠实地译为：

The six stone horses were sculpted when *Zhaoling* Maosoleum was built by the order of Emperor Li Shimin in memory of the six horses which served him in wars. Two of them, known as "*Saluzi*" and "*Quanmaogua*" were stolen by an American in 1914. They are now kept at the University of Pennsylvania in Philadelphia.

一位旅游者拿着他从宾夕法尼亚大学博物馆内复印的这位美国人当时在陕西从当地军阀手中购买的这两个石刻艺术品的收据，说明美国人不是"偷"的，而是"买"的。现在让我们来看一看世界著名的 Travel Guide 的创始人 Eugene Fodor 组织编写的 Fodor's People's Republic of China 是如何对这段文字加以处理的：

…These stone chargers are considered to be masterpieces of sculpture from the Tang period. Two of the original stone horses are on display in a museum in the United States, and the four that are on display in the museum here were damaged during an attempt by a private collector to have them shipped to the United States. This was during the period before 1949 when some great art treasures were stolen from China.

在这段说明中，作者没有指名道姓地说是谁"偷"了这两个石刻珍品，但他确费了些笔墨（画线部分），将这个历史事件和背景作了一些交代。经这位大师之笔处理后，这段文字就容易使外国读者信服，也使他们不易"对号入座"。

6.5　美学风格的等化

我们汉语的旅游资料中常用优美的词语、华丽的笔墨和高雅的格调来描述某一景点，以唤起游人美的享受。在译成英语时，我们应注意尽可能将这种美转化为等效的英语。例：

● 北京作为世界旅游名城，有着极为丰富的旅游资源：雄伟壮丽的天安门；金碧辉煌、气象万千的故宫；气势宏伟的万里长城；湖光山色、曲栏回廊的颐和园；建筑精巧、独具艺术风格的天坛；烟波浩渺、黛色风光的北海公园，以及建筑宏大的明代帝王陵寝——十三陵……这些举世无双、驰名中外的古代建筑，历来是旅游者的竞游之地。

从上文中我们可以看到，汉语四字结构工整对仗，读来朗朗上口，起伏跌宕，悦耳动听，首先满足了读者的视觉听觉上的享受，符合人们审美习惯与心理态势，同时又体现了作者扎实的文化功底，蕴含着丰富的语言符号意义。陈宏微（1998：132）认为，翻译时，译者"应力求达到译文与原文在内容和形式上的统一，向英语读者介绍中国的语言文化精华"。

译文：

Beijing, being one of the world's great cities, is full of tourist attractions. Among these are the magnificent Tiananmen Gate, the majestic Palace Museum, the imposing Great Wall, the scenic Summer Palace, the ingenious Temple of Heaven, the enchanting Beihai Park and the carefully laidout Ming Tombs. Unrivaled and of world renown, these ancient structures remain attractions to both domestic and foreign travellers.

这里，译者将多个装饰性的四字结构整合为极具特色的英语单词，充分表现了这些景点独具魅力之处。同样描写古建筑雄伟壮丽，译文则采用了 magnificent, majestic, imposing 构成几个短语排比，分别表现了天安门的雄伟、故宫的庄严、长城的壮丽；而对颐和园只用了一个 scenic 体现了其景色秀美如画，通过这些简单而不重复的词语再现了原文的美感功能。对烟波浩渺黛色风光的北海公园译者则认为它展现的是一幅妩媚迷人的画面，所以用 enchanting 更为细腻，贴切到位。

● 苏州位于沪宁线上，地处太湖之滨，建成于公元前 415 年，是我国江南著名的古老城市之一。

城内外遍布名胜古迹。寒山寺，诗韵钟声，脍炙人口；虎丘，千年古塔，巍然屹立；天平山，奇石嶙峋，枫林如锦；洞庭东山，湖光山色，花果连绵。

别具匠心的园林驰名中外。沧浪亭、狮子林、拙政园、留园、网师园、怡园等，亭台楼阁，池石林泉，疏密适度，相映生辉；廊榭曲折，沟壑幽深，移步换景，引人入胜；布局结构，各显特色，表现了宋、元、明、清各个时期园林艺术的不同风格，反映了我国历代劳动人民的高度智慧和卓越的创造才能。　　　　　　　　　　（朱葆琛，2002，284）

这段资料中同样大量使用了四字结构，浓缩了苏州园林的精华：亭台楼阁呈严谨均衡的几何图形空间布局的静态美与径缘池转、廊引人随、步移景换的立体动感美，将一幅美轮美奂的自然山水与人文景观在读者面前展露无遗。译文也应体现原文的动静之美，达到与原文形式美学上等化的效果。

译文：

Located on the Shanghai-Nanjing railway and off Lake *Taihu*, Suzhou is a city of historical fame south of the Yangtze, which claims its founding in 514 B. C.

The city abounds with fine scenery and historical interest. The popular haunt of *Hanshan* Temple, with its charming bell, has inspired many a poetic mind. On Tiger Hill, a thousand-year-old pagoda stands in majesty; and while luxuriant fruit-trees add to the natural beauty of East *Dongting* Hills and lake around, *Tianping* Hill is featured by grotesque rock formations and red maple woods.

The unique style of widely reputed Suzhou gardens is seen in Gentle Waves Pavilion, Lion Grove Garden, the Humble Administrator's Garden, Lingering Garden, the Master-of-Nets Garden and Joyous Garden. Their towers, gazeboes, terraces, winding corridors and water-side pavilions are so artistically laid out among ponds, rockeries, trees and grottoes that visitors are impressed by the depth they create, and find a different vista at every turn. All this makes a visit most enjoyable. The classical gardens of Suzhou bear the characteristics of the Chinese landscape architecture of the *Song*, *Yuan*, *Ming* and *Qing* Dynasties and stand as a monument to the wisdom and creativity of the working people of ancient China.

6.6　楹联的翻译

　　在我国的许多名胜景点有很多刻写在楹柱上的对联，我们称之为楹联。它是中国独特的文学艺术形式。对联是由韵律诗的对偶句发展而来的，它保留着韵律诗的某些特点。我国古人把吟诗作对相提并论，这在某种意义上说明了两者间的关系。对联是张贴的诗，但它与诗又不尽相同，因为它只有上联和下联，通常它比诗更为凝练，句式更加灵活，长短自如，在我国的建筑物中有长达数百字的长联。所以楹联的翻译是我们旅游翻译工作的一大难题。在翻译实践中，我们可以采用不同的方法来翻译不同的楹联俳语，如词汇的对应、句子结构的对应，必要时可改变句子结构等。如：

山海关有一副楹联为：

- 海水朝朝朝朝朝朝朝落
  浮云长长长长长长长消

采用字面对应（literal translation）可译为：

Sea waters tide, day to day tide, every day tide and every day ebb,

Floating clouds appear, often appear, often appear and often go.　　　　（金隄、奈达）

亦可改写或意译为：

Every day floating clouds come and go,

Very often sea waters ebb and flow.　　　　（吴伟雄）

上译中，ebb and flow 意为"潮的涨落，盛衰，消长"，还押尾韵，可称佳译。

苏州拙政园有一副明代书画家文徵明（1470 — 1559 A. D.）手书的唐代诗句组成的对联：

- 蝉噪林愈静
  鸟鸣山更幽

译文：

Cicadas, chirping, make the forest all the more peaceful,

Birds, singing, make the mountain all the more secluded

此译不但字面意义对应，而且句式对仗工整。

- 水水山山处处明明秀秀
  晴晴雨雨时时好好奇奇

按字面对应直译为：

Water Water Hill Hill Place Place Bright Bright Beautiful Beautiful;

Fine Fine Rain Rain Moment Moment Pleasant Pleasant Wonderful Wonderful.

如果意译则可译为：

With water and hill, every place looks bright and beautiful;

Rain or shine, every moment appears pleasant and wonderful.　　　　（陈刚，2004，421）

- 大肚能容容世上难容之事

开口便笑笑天下可笑之人

英译时可保持句子结构的对应：

His belly is big enough to contain all intolerable things on earth；

His mouth is ever ready to laugh at all snobbish persons under heaven.

（陈刚，2004，422）

- 峰峦或再有飞来坐山门老等

  泉水已渐生暖意放笑脸相迎

翻译时可改变句子结构：

Awaiting at the door another peak flying over；

Facing with a smile the cool spring warming up.

- 重重叠叠山，

  曲曲环环路，

  叮叮咚咚泉，

  高高下下树。

The hills — range after range；

The trails — winding and climbing；

The creeks — murmuring and gurgling；

The trees — high and lowly.

译文注意保持了词义层对应。又如：

- 疏影横斜水清浅，

  暗香浮动月黄昏。

译文：

Sparse shadows slant across the clear water shallow；

Subtle fragrance floats serenely in moonlight mellow.

6.7 中菜与主食的英译

民以食为天。饮食文化是中国传统文化的重要组成部分。源于历史的发展和地域的差别，我国形成了北有鲁菜（Shandong Cuisine），南有闽菜（Fujian Cuisine）、粤菜（Guangdong Cuisine），中西部有湘菜（Hunan Cuisine）、川菜（Sichuang Cuisine），东有徽菜（Anhui Cuisine）、江浙菜（Jiangsu Cuisine and Zhejiang Cuisine）等众多菜系（俗称"八大菜系"）及佳菜名肴，真可谓流派纷呈、丰富多彩。中国的菜肴命名方式特点显著，有的被赋予浪漫色彩，如"过桥米线"表达了妻子对丈夫的深切思念；有的用写实手法，如"冬菇菜心"见名即见菜；有的取自历史典故，如"鸿门宴"蟹黄和燕窝象征楚汉之争；也有取自民间传说，如"大救驾"说的是宋朝开国皇帝赵匡胤当年攻占寿县后，由于过度操劳，身心疲惫，食欲不好，厨师用猪油面粉果仁等做成饼，赵匡胤用后食欲大增，身体恢复，便赐此名。

6.7.1　中菜与主食英译的基本特点

在中菜与主食的英译中译者既要遵循翻译的原则，又要因地制宜，适时变通。如在宴会上或餐桌上口译时，译员就无法去咬文嚼字、反复推敲，只要"准确"、"忠实"于原文地英译。当然，还要兼顾"通顺"与"迅速"。笔译时，除了上述几点之外，还要注意"简洁"的要求。这是因为菜谱的印制、设计及装帧都是十分考究的，一般没有太多的空间位置去容纳冗长累赘的英译文。简言之，无论是口译还是笔译，都要"直入主题"，开门见山地点明菜肴的原料和烹调方法。口译时如时间允许，特别是在外国客人点菜时可抓住时机适当补充一些有关菜肴的营养价值、民俗风情的背景知识，额外撒点"文化佐料"，提起外国客人的食欲，达到活跃气氛和传播中国饮食文化的目的。

6.7.2　中菜与主食英译的若干方式

在明确了中菜与主食英译的基本特点之后，具体英译时应该如何下手呢？首先我们应当让外国读者或客人了解中国的饮食文化，包括某道菜的原料及烹调的方法，如果能介绍有关菜肴的营养价值、民俗风情或历史传说、民间故事等知识，可以让他们既品尝了美味佳肴，又了解了我们的饮食文化。归纳起来有以下几种方式供参考。

6.7.2.1　直译法　烹调法 + 原料

烹调法是指中国菜的做法，即煮、煎、炸、煸、炒、蒸等。英译时把对应的制作方法译出来，再以该菜的主要原料为中心词就可以了，比如：

煮花生仁	Boiled Peanuts/Groundnut Kernels
炒肉丝	Sautéed Shredded Pork
炖牛肉	Braised Beef
清蒸桂鱼	Steamed Mandarin Fish
煎鸡蛋	Fried Eggs
红烧鱼	Braised Fish with Brown Sauce
白灼海螺片	Scalded Sliced Conch
回锅肉	Sautéed Spicy Pork

6.7.2.2　直译 + 释义法

顾名思义，英译时直接按中文菜名译出其意，然后再补充说明其实际所指的含义。比如：

狮子头 Lion's Head — Stewed Pork Ball in Brown Sauce

全家福 Happy Family — Stewed Assorted Delicacies

龙凤配 Dragon & Phoenix — Two separate dishes characterize this distinctive plate. On one side, lobster meat in Sichuan chili sauce, which is inviting. On the other is house special chicken, which never fails in delighting.

左宗鸡 General Tso's chicken — A mouth watering dish made with large chunks of marinated chicken, sautéed with scorched red chili peppers in special, tangy sauce.

叫花鸡 Beggar's Chicken — There's a legendary story connected to it. Long long ago there was a beggar. One day he stole a chicken and was pursued by the owner. He was almost caught when he suddenly hit upon a good idea. He smeared the chicken all over with clay, which he found nearby and threw it into the fire he had built to cook it. After a long while the beggar removed the mud-coated from the fire. When he cracked open the clay he found, to his astonishment, that the clay together with the feather had formed a hard shell in which the chicken had been baked into a delicious dish with wonderful flavour. That night he had a very enjoyable meal. Hence the name of the dish.

6.7.2.3　意译法

6.7.2.3.1　原料 + with + 佐料

用原料为中心词,有时把烹调法也译出,再加上介词 with 或 in 与佐料构成的短语即可。如:

鱼香肉丝　Sautéed with Spicy Garlic Sauce

豆豉桂鱼　Mandarin Fish in Black Bean Sauce

黄焖大虾　Braised Prawns in Rice Wine

海米白菜　Chinese Cabbage with Dried Shrimps

椒盐排骨　Spare Ribs with Pepper and Salt

6.7.2.3.2　佐料 + 原料

此法是把佐料用作修饰语,放在中心词原料的前面,用英文译出。如:

咖喱鸡　Curry Chicken

咖喱牛肉　Curry Beef

麻辣豆腐　Spicy Bean Curd

怪味鸡　Multi-Flavored Chicken

古老肉/糖醋肉　Sweet & Sour Pork

6.7.2.3.3　以"实"对"虚"法

从严格的意义上说,该法也是意译法的一种。其方法是舍去中菜名里的喻义、夸张等说法而用平直、明白的英语译出。如:

白玉虾球　Crystal White Shrimp Balls

红烧狮子头　Stewed Pork Ball in Brown Sauce

发财好市　Black Moss Cooked with Oysters

龙虎凤大烩　Thick Soup of Snake, Cat and Chicken

6.7.2.4　移花接木法

用西方人熟悉并了解的欧洲菜名或主食名来译部分中菜名与少数主食,因为它们之间有许多相似处,故借彼之法为我所用。译文地道、通俗易懂,能收到事半功倍的效果。示例如下:

烤排骨　Barbecued Spare Ribs

鸡肉串　Teriyaki Chicken Stick

盖浇面　Chinese-Style Spaghetti

饺子　Chinese-Style Ravioli

　　锅贴　　Pot Stickers

　　这里的 teriyaki 一词是来自日语的借用词即"烤"的意思，该词用于此类英译在美国的中餐馆里十分流行。另外，spaghetti 和 ravioli 两词均源自意大利语，其含义与吃法恰巧分别与我们的"盖浇面"和"饺子"非常相似，外国人都异常熟悉。pot stickers 乃是一种通俗、诙谐的译法，较之呆板的译文 pan-fried dumplings 更显出其幽默而传神。另外，dumpling 一词似有滥用之嫌，例如，在译烧卖、馄饨、元宵、锅贴、粽子时，常用该词，往往容易引起误解。

6.7.2.5　音译 + 释义法

　　先按中文用拼音译出，然后再加以解释性的英译，使英译文保留点中国味儿。如：

包子	*Baozi*	Stuffed Bun
饺子	*Jiaozi*	Chinese-Style Ravioli
馒头	*Mantou*	Steamed Bread
锅贴	*Guotie*	Pot Stickers

6.7.2.6　"随机应变"法

6.7.2.6.1　原料 + 地名 + Style

　　应用此方法可以灵活地处理一些难以对付的地方风味特色菜名。英译出原料名后，再稍加"点拨"就可以大功告成。示例如下：

湖南肉	Pork Hunan Style
广东龙虾	Lobster Cantonese Style
家常豆腐	Fried Tofu, Home Style
麻婆豆腐	Mapo Tofu（Stir-Fried Tofu in Hot Sauce）
中式泡菜	Chinese-Style Pickles

　　关于主食的一些英译法较之于菜名来说就容易多了，这里就不赘述了，下面略举几个示例：

炒饭	Fried Rice
蛋炒饭	Egg Fried Rice
叉烧炒饭	Roast Pork Rice
汤面	Noodles in Soup
炒面	Stir-Fried Noodles

　　上文概括地归纳了中餐菜名与主食的六种常见而实用的英译方法。但这决不是说包罗了此类译法的方方面面。有些译法也非正式或固定译法，因为在口译或笔译时往往因人而异、因语境而异，常常会有不同的英译。如：

　　狮子头，可直译为 Lion's Head，也可意译为 Pork Balls；

　　羊肉串，也可译为 Mutton Skewer；

　　甚至还有一种幽默的译法，如：

　　豆腐，必要时，也可译为 Plant Meat（植物肉）；

　　啤酒，可译为 Liquid Bread（液体面包）。

　　总之，中菜英译以最佳效果为准绳。对于一些各地的风味小吃、有着浓郁地方特色的乡土菜，其英译除了上面介绍的几种方法外，许多名称仍需译者细心推敲定夺，建议译者参照北京市旅游局在 2008 北京奥运会前推出的官方版本中的译名。

6.7.3 常见中餐菜名的英译

中国菜的烹调方法至少有 50 多种，为翻译方便，可归纳为下列主要的种类：

煮 boiling，分为：即煮即食 instant boiling 和快煮 quick boiling 两种，北方的火锅以及广东的"打边炉"都属于前者，而将煮沸的汤加入盛有食物的器皿中，或把食物投进煮沸的水里，然后慢火煮熟则为后者，即快煮。

煸 stir-fry before stewing，把菜肴放在热油里炒到半熟以备再加佐料加水煮熟。

煨 simmering，是用低于沸点的热水慢慢加热，通常时间较长。

煲、焖 stewing，指把菜放在汤、汁中用文火慢慢加热，它与 simmering 类似，但 stewing 常把鱼、肉和蔬菜在肉汁或调料中混合在一起做出的食物或菜肴。如果将食物放在水中煲则译为 stewing in water，隔水炖是 stewing out of water，此法主要用于炖补品，如果放在调味汁里煮就是卤 stewing in gravy 了。

烧 braising，红烧 braising with soy sauce 是用酱油来烧。

炸(deep)frying：frying 是用热油炸，特别是在一专门的容器中用一定量的油炸。分为 dry deep-frying 干炸和 soft deep-frying 软炸以及 crisp deep-frying 酥炸。

煎 pan-frying

炒 stir-frying

爆 quick-frying

扒 frying and simmering

回锅 "twice-cooked" stir-frying

烘、烤 baking

铁烧 broiling/grilling

烧烤 roasting

浇油烧 basting

蒸 steaming

熏 smoking

白灼 scalding，此法多用于烹制河鲜海味。

在具体翻译时我们切忌望文生义，生搬硬套。比如煮鸡蛋为 boiled eggs，煮荷包蛋则译为 poached eggs；红烧肉、腐乳汁烧肉、干烧明虾三道菜中都含有"烧"字，但分别译为 braised pork with brown sauce, stewed pork with preserved bean curd, fried prawns with pepper sauce；炒蛋译为 scrambled egg，而不译为 fried egg，等。

所以，翻译时译者要先搞清英语不同的烹调法所表达的确切内涵，然后再选择最贴近的英语名称。

6.7.4 中国菜刀工的英译

切片 slicing　　　　　　切丝 shredding

切丁 dicing　　　　　　切柳 filleting

切碎 mincing　　　　　　　捣烂 mashing

酿入 stuffing

切之前有的要

去骨 boning　　　　　　　脱壳 shelling

剥皮 skinning　　　　　　刮鳞 scaling

腌制 pickling

6.7.5　中国菜常用料的英译

鱼片 sliced fish　　　　　　肉丝 shredded meat

薯泥 mashed potatoes　　　　鸡丁 diced chicken

酿豆腐 stuffed bean curd　　　炸鱼柳 fried fillet of fish

虾仁 shelled shrimp　　　　去鳞鱼 scaled fish

咸酸菜 pickled vegetables

6.7.6　常见的菜名英译

6.7.6.1　老北京传统小吃

北京传统小吃种类繁多，且名称具有强烈的地域色彩，如何让外国游客参照英文菜单便能感受京味文化，这个难题一直困扰着众多老字号。北京奥运会为这一难题的解决带来了契机。为了凸显北京特色，不少小吃的英文译名带上了儿化音，今后外国友人也会说"豆汁儿"。北京小吃的翻译标准按照音译附以英文解释的方式注明口味、原料及烹饪方法，例如此前备受争议的"豆汁"(Beijing Coke)已被否定，而音译为 DouZhir。

常见北京小吃英文译名

豆汁　*DouZhir*（fermented soybean drink）

艾窝窝 *AiWoWo*（steamed rice cakes with sweet stuffing）

焦圈 *JiaoQuanr*（deep-fried rolls）

糖火烧 *TangHuoShao*（sweet sesame paste cake）

桂花炸糕 *GuiHuaZhaGao*（fried cake with osmanthus）

菜窝头 Vegetarian（savoury）

炒肝 *Chaoganr*（stewed pork liver and intestine）

芥末墩 *JieMoTunr*（preserved Chinese cabbage with mustard）

炸咯吱 *ZhaGeZhi*（deep-fried shin of bean curd）

六家中华老字号英文译名

全聚德 *Quanjude* Peking Roast Duck — Since 1864

同仁堂 *Tongrentang* Chinese Medicine — Since 1669

吴裕泰 *Wuyutai* Tea Shop — Since 1887

瑞蚨祥 *Ruifuxiang* Silk — Since1862

荣宝斋 *Rongbaozhai* Art Gallery — Since 1672

王致和 *Wangzhihe* Gourmet Food — Since 1669

练习：

把下列段落译成英语。

1. 在十三陵区最先看到的建筑是一座五门六柱的高大汉白玉石牌坊，向前是陵城正门大红门。大红门内是一条通往长陵的神道，沿途依次有碑亭、华表、石象生（stone animal）、棂星门……

2. 中山陵，原名总理陵园，位于南京东郊钟山第一峰小茅山南麓，是伟大的革命先行者孙中山的陵墓。它坐北朝南，依山而筑，由半圆形广场、牌坊、墓道、陵门、碑亭、祭堂和墓室组成，均纵向排列在同一条南北轴线。墓室在海拔 165 米处，与起点平面距离 700 米，上下落差 73 米。整组建筑总平面取"自由钟"图案，表"使天下皆达道"之意。瞻仰者由下仰望，但见浩瀚林海衬映着碧瓦银墙，宛如伟人之浩然正气，与大地同存。恢宏的陵墓工程于 1926 年 3 月奠基，于 1929 年春竣工。同年 5 月 28 日，孙中山灵柩由北京运抵南京，6 月 1 日在中山陵举行奉安大典。中山陵的整体设计，除陵墓主体建筑外，还有一批纪念性或辅助建筑物，包括藏经楼、音乐台、光华亭、流徽榭、中山植物园等。这些建筑大多为奉安大典后，由各界人士和海外侨胞捐款修建。

3. 孙中山纪念馆位于中山陵与灵谷寺之间，原为藏经楼，1935 年由中国佛教协会募款兴建。这是一座仿清代喇嘛寺风格的宫殿式建筑，包括主楼、僧房和碑廊三部分，专门用来收藏孙中山经典著作和石刻。1989 年将其辟为孙中山纪念馆，主楼前有一尊孙中山全身铜像，为日本友人梅屋庄吉 1929 年捐赠。碑廊所陈 138 块石碑，刻《三民主义》全文，分别由十四位民国时期书法家书写。

4. 崂山，林木苍翠，繁花似锦，到处生机盎然。其中，更不乏古树名木。景区内，古树名木有近 300 株，50% 以上为国家一类保护植物，著名的有银杏、桧柏等。

5. （青岛鲁迅公园）园址是一片倾斜的海岸，没有刻意雕琢，也不震撼人心，似乎只是造物主的原作，幽静恬美。徜徉其间，但见白浪激礁，松林覆坡，红岩嶙峋，沙滩如银，景色如画如诗。

6. 宽广的湖泊，辽阔的草坪，花草树木一应俱全的上海最大的公园——世纪公园，如今又将成为忙碌的上班族的一个新去处。该公园是为那些住在高楼林立的大都市的居民设计、建造的。这是一个接近自然的所在，在这里你可以呼吸到新鲜的空气，享受绿草、花香、鸟语。

7. 位于杭州湾北岸海盐县境内的南北湖风景区，总面积 30 平方千米，由湖塘、鹰巢顶、谭仙岭、滨海四个景区组成，融山、海、湖自然景观于一体，兼有丰富的人文景观，是浙江省省级风景名胜区。

8. 山明水秀——无锡的绿色名片

江南山水中，无锡得天独厚，占一方精华。

太湖"包孕吴越"，揽三万六千顷的云水诗篇，描七十二峰丹青画卷，赐佳绝句、点睛笔留于无锡；

万里长江，浩荡东去，黄田岗前，波诡云谲，冲门凌浪，气象万千；

千年运河，流金淌银，裹着浓浓的历史文化异彩穿城而过，织就水乡的珍珠网衫；

一脉"天下第二泉"，滋润了梁溪之畔的山脉园林，使其飘逸出人文与灵秀。

第七章　公示语翻译

7.1　概　　述

"公示语"意思是给公众在公共场合看的文字语言，是人们生活中最常见的实用语言，是一种公开和面对公众的，以达到某种交际目的的特殊文体。

公示语在我们生活中应用广泛，几乎随处可见，例如路标、广告牌、商店招牌、公共场所的宣传语、旅游告示等。公示语是国际化都市、国际旅游目的地语言环境、人文环境的重要组成部分。

与公示语意义相近的语汇包括"标志语""标识语""标示语""标语"等。标志语与标志结合，广泛应用于交通、旅游、运输等公共领域；标示语在 IT 行业已经被广泛接纳，几乎成为这个行业的语言分支；标识语属于市场营销，广告促销中的推广语，经常和企业标识使用；标语则是人们比较熟悉的公益性、政治性、宣传性的文字语言。除了"公示语"能够包容下"标志语""标识语""标示语""标语"的内涵和外延，目前尚难以选择其他语汇广而括之。所以，公示语成了"标志语""标识语""标示语""标语"的集合名词，作为新的通用流行语汇。

由于公示语在公众和旅游者生活中的重要意义，对公示语的任何歧义、误解、滥用都会导致不良后果。错误的翻译会影响一个城市、一个地区的形象和对外交流，也给外国游客带来诸多不便。

常用公示语有交通标识语、商务标识语、公共场所标识语等。商务标识语因其特殊的作用，不同于其他标识语。在商务活动场所，如商场、酒店、机场等，其商用性质决定了这类公示语必须能吸引顾客或消费者的眼球，以利于提高企业的经济效益。

商务公示语信息具有静态和动态意义。静态公示语突出服务，具有指示功能，广泛用于旅游景点、商业、文体卫设施、街道名称、商品包装等诸多场合。

国际出发　International Departure
中国土特产　Chinese Products
加油站　Gas Station
物流中心　Logistics Center

而动态意义的公示语则突出提示、限制、强制功能。广泛用于公共交通、公共设施、紧急救援等场合。如：

握紧扶手　Hold the Hand Rail.
紧急时用　Emergency Use Only.

不使用信用卡　No Credit Card Please.

送货上门　Delivery to Your Door.

请将个人物品随身带走　Take Care. Not to Leave Things Behind.

静态公示语与动态公示语在特定语境中的交错排布，合理搭配，可以满足读者对信息的需求，有效提高生存与消费质量。动态公示语过密过频会使读者眼花缭乱、心神不安，也破坏了环境的整体效果。

在实际使用中，公共场合公示语具有规范、调节、制约、提示等信息功能，更多的公示语用来表示企业、地区、媒体、产品、服务、活动等的标语或告示。

7.2　公示语的语言特点

公示语的用语简单明晰，旨在让读者在最短的时间内获取最需要的信息。公示语通常呈现在一个范围有限的牌子上，受限于此，公示语自然形成了其独特的语言特点与风格。

7.2.1　语言简洁，醒目引人

公示语文体的特殊功能要求语言表达准确简洁，具体可体现在以下几个方面：

• 多用名词

在表示静态意义、服务、指示、说明性的公示语中大量使用名词来直接无误地提供特定的信息。如：

Disabled Toilet & Baby Changing 残疾人厕所及婴儿换巾处

Reception　接待室

Suggestion Box　意见箱

City Buses Only　市内公交车专用

Yard Sale 庭院旧货出售(又称 garage sale 车库售物，porch sale 或 moving sale，是美国一种独特的售物方式。主人把家中多余不用的物品放在庭院中、车库里或门廊下廉价出售，并在手写的广告中详细列出售卖的物品、时间和地点，而且用标签注明每件物品的价钱，没有标价的则可以还价。廉价处理的物品多种多样，多数属用过的东西，但也有全新的物品。为了吸引更多的买主，这种售货活动常在周末举行。)

• 动词和动名词

在表示动态意义的公示语中大量使用动词和动名词，把读者的注意力引向公示语所要求采取的行动上。

Keep clean. 保持清洁。

No crossing. 禁止横穿。

• 词组与短语

词组与短语结构简单，组合多样，大量用于公示语。

Out of Order　因故停用

Out of Service. Please Wait. 暂停使用，请稍候。

• 缩略语

在公众与游客经常接触到的公共设施与公共服务中（如道路、旅游点、医院等），人们经常使用缩略语。

P 停车场

VIP Lounge/Hall 贵宾厅

EVD（Enhanced Versatile Disc）Films，EVD 影片（Enhanced Versatile Disk 意为增强型多媒体盘片系统，俗称"新一代高密度数字激光视盘系统"，是 DVD 的升级产品。EVD 产品的解像度是 DVD 的五倍，在声音效果方面则于国际上首次同时实现高保真和环绕声，一张 EVD 影碟目前可存储约 110 分钟的影音节目。有关专家指出，EVD 将震撼音效和亮丽画质完美结合，在世界上首次基于光盘实现了高清晰度数字节目的存储和播放。）

ICU 重症监护室（Intensive Care Unit），是医院重症医学学科的临床基地，它对因各种原因导致一个或多个器官与系统功能障碍危及生命或具有潜在高危因素的患者，及时提供系统的、高质量的医学监护和救治技术，是医院集中监护和救治重症患者的专业科室。ICU 又分为综合性（General）重症监护病房（GICU）和 ICU 专科。综合性 ICU 主要包括外科（Surgery）重症监护病房（SICU）、内科（Medicine）重症监护病房（MICU）、急诊（Emergency）重症监护病房（EICU）等。

E. N. T.（Ear，Nose，Throat）Dept 耳鼻喉科

UCG（Ultrasonic Cardiogram）Room 超声心动室

CT（Computerized/Computed Tomography）Room CT 室

HIV（Human Immunodeficiency Virus）/Aids Counseling Clinic 艾滋病咨询门诊

MSRP（Manufacturer's Suggested Retail Price）厂家建议零售价

● 省略

公示语因为文体简洁需要，很多语法方面的成分可以省略，常见的有省略冠词、助动词、标点符号。如：

Turn off Engine Hand Broke on 关闭发动机 拉上手刹（the engine，冠词省略）

Stand behind red line until summoned by inspector. 红线后站立，等待检查员（the red line，the inspector 冠词省略，另有状语从句中的省略，until you are summoned by the inspector）

Fireworks prohibited 禁放烟火（are prohibited 助动词省略）

分行的公示语自然断句，标点全省略，不会引起歧义。

CAUTION
HAZARDOUS WASTE MATERIAL
STORAGE AREA
NO SMOKING, OPEN FLAMES OR
OPEN LIGHTS IN THIS AREA
EACH ITEM MUST HAVE A
DISPOSAL TAG ATTACHED

注意
危险废物存放区

禁止吸烟 禁止明火

每件物品须粘贴处置标签

有时"'"号亦可省略，如：MENS RESTROOM，WOMENS RESTROOM，CHILDRENS LIFE JACKETS，这里 MEN'S，WOMEN'S，CHILDREN'S 等的"'"号都省去，节省了空间，符合公示语简洁的原则。

7.2.2 大写字母，庄重规范

英语公示语中常使用大写字母，以显示庄重和规范的风格，请看下面一则美国的公示语：

警告

OSHA 条例规定

配电板前 42 吋保持畅通(不得堆放)

这里 OSHA 全称为：Occupational Safety and Health Act［Administration］（美国)职业安全与卫生条例[管理局]）。整个公示语全部大写，且 CAUTION 通过大字号突出显示，重要信息 ELECTRICAL PANEL MUST BE KEPT CLEAR 字号次大，其他内容字号更小，核心信息一目了然。

除了全部大写字母，也有用首字母大写的。

孩童们在玩耍，宠物不得在此拉便。

7.2.3 文图并用，增强视觉

公示语醒目的图文一起使用，相映生辉，增强视觉效果。

自行车礼让行人

禁止吸烟　禁用无罩灯火

未经许可　不得入内

警告 建筑工地

未经许可 不得入内
必须戴上安全头盔
必须穿上鲜亮衣服
必须穿上防滑鞋靴

7. 2. 4　词语倒序，同义解读

由于公示语文体的特定文本形式，很多公示语词语顺序颠倒仍可读解相同的意思。

Staff Only 闲人免进（cf：Only staff）

Wet Paint 油漆未干（cf：Paint（is）wet.）

Coin Only 只投硬币（cf：Only coin）

Drive Carefully 谨慎驾驶（cf：Carefully drive）

Keep Fire away 严禁火种（cf：Go away from fire）

7.3　公示语的应用示意功能

从公示语应用示意的功能来看，我们可以大致将公示语分为指示性公示语，管理性公示语和广告性公示语。

7.3.1 指示性公示语

指示性公示语提供给读者详尽周到的信息服务，没有限定强制的意义，不要求读者采取任何行动。

贵宾停车场　VIP Car Park

紧急出口　Emergency Exit

美食街　Food Street/Food Court

寄存处　Luggage Deposit

7.3.2 管理性公示语

管理性公示语常用于对公共场所的管理，向公众提出要求，对公众发出限制的信号或对某些行业发出强制性的命令。所以，管理性公示语又可分为提示性公示语、限制性公示语和强制性公示语。

● 提示性公示语

提示性公示语使用广泛，表示要求公众做什么或注意什么。

FASTEN YOUR SEATBELT　系上安全带

MIND YOUR HEAD　小心碰头

MIND YOUR STEP　小心跌倒

● 限制性公示语

限制性公示语对公众的行为提出限制、约束等要求。所用语言直截了当，又不使人感到生硬甚至粗暴无理。常用表示限制的词语有：unless, only, no...except (for), no...excepted 等。

20 MIN. PARKING ONLY　20 分钟停车处

TAXI PICK UP & DROP OFF ONLY　出租车上下乘客专用

KEEP RIGHT UNLESS OVERTAKING　靠右行驶 超车例外

PLEASE REFRAIN FROM EATING & DRINKING IN THIS SHOP　不要在店内饮食

NO PARKING EXCEPT FOR LOADING　装货车辆专用停车处

● 强制性公示语

强制性公示语要求公众必须采取或者不得不采取行动，语言直白、强制，没有商量的余地。常用的词语有：not permitted/allowed, do not, no, be strictly prohibited 等。如：

SMOKING IS NOT ALLOWED HERE　不许吸烟

NO FOOD AND DRINK PERMITTED IN THE STORE　店内禁止饮食

HEAVY PENALTIES APPLY　违者重罚

KEEP AWAY　请勿靠近

KEEP OFF THE GRASS　勿踏草坪

NO GRAFFITI　严禁涂画

LUGGAGE MUST NOT BE PUT IN THE GATEWAY　门口禁放行李

7.3.3 广告性功能

广告性公示语主要为城市公益广告和企业的服务进行承诺及商业推广，注意区别推销广告文本。

BETTER CITY　BETTER LIFE　城市，让生活更美好。（2010 年上海世博会主题）

7.4　商业公示语的特定应用功能

7.4.1　激发兴趣

这类公示语常用于吸引眼球，激发消费兴趣。多见于商家门面橱窗等。如：
装修前大甩卖 Closing down for modernization

7.4.2　提供信息

这类公示语常用于提供服务与消费信息，提示、告知消费者消费的类别或区域。如：
Duty free 免税柜/店

7.4.3　加深理解

此类公示语旨在使消费者对商家的经营有更深入的理解，为消费行动打下基础。如：
Accredited as a secure station 公认的安全车站

7.4.4　促进行动

此类公示语旨在让消费者采取行动，进行消费。如：
今日特价 Daily Special

7.4.5　巩固形象

一个商业机构不仅要促进消费，还要通过公示语来树立良好的企业形象。如：
谢谢您的光临！Thank you for visiting here.

7.5　警示性公示语的翻译

在此类公示语翻译实践中，译者需要注意的是，英语警示语中常把警示性词语置于句首，让读者直接警觉到危险的存在，而且根据危险程度的不同，使用不同的警示性词语。

7.5.1　小心 BEWARE, ATTENTION

Beware 表示警示的语气最弱，提示小心谨慎。
BEWARE CHILDREN AT PLAY 孩子们玩耍，小心！

7.5.2 当心、警告 CAUTION

Caution 表示的警示语气较弱。提醒引起读者的注意。

CAUTION MIND YOUR STEPS 小心跌倒（caution + mind）

CAUTION MAN WORKING OVERHEAD 注意高空作业（caution + 动作）

CAUTION DOOR OPENS OUTWARDS 当心车门外开（caution + 句子）

Caution 后接 please 开头的祈使句，让表达更委婉，更体贴：

CAUTION PLEASE MIND YOUR HEAD 请小心碰头

7.5.3 警告 WARNING

Warning 表示警告的语气较强，提示危险较大，必须引起重视。

WARNING DEEP WATER 水深危险！

WARNING DO NOT ATTEMPT A FORCED ENTRY TO THIS DOOR 警告：不得强行入室！

WARNING FRAGILE ROOF CRAWLING BOARDS OR LADDERS MUST BE USED 警告：屋顶易碎，必须使用防滑跳板或梯子。

7.5.4 紧急 EMERGENCY

Emergency 警示紧急情况出现，需要马上行动。

EMERGENCY EXIT 紧急出口

IN EMERGENCY, PULL HANDLE AND PUSH DOOR TO OPEN
紧急情况拉动把手，推开车门。

IN THE EVENT OF EMERGENCY KEEP CLEAR OF BUILDING
紧急情况撤离建筑物。

7.5.5 危险 DANGER

Danger 警示的是非常强烈的危险信号，必须采取立即有效的措施或行动，否则，后果不测，会造成生命或财产的损失。

DANGER Highly flammable material 高度易燃材料，危险！

DANGER THIN ICE 冰薄，危险！

7.6 常用公示语译例

禁止孩童在此玩耍

屋顶易碎，危险

脚手架未搭完，危险

上方吊车作业，危险

叉车作业，危险

施工安全
警告：危险作业中
所有来访人员须在工地办公室登记
必须戴上安全头盔
未经许可 严禁入内

水深，危险

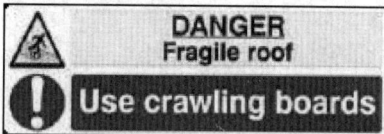

屋顶易碎，危险！请使用防滑跳板。

爆破拆除作业，危险

爆破拆除作业，危险！不得进入。

危险！易燃液体。禁止吸烟，禁用火柴，禁止明火。

危险！罐内装有易爆气体。轻搬轻放。

不得非法入侵，警犬看守。

禁止吸烟 禁止吃喝

路面湿滑，危险

警犬，危险

万伏高压，危险

一旦火灾，勿用电梯，请走楼梯

157

 消防通道，不得堆放！

 现场交通，注意！

 维修作业，请注意！

 警告：斜坡

 警告：小心跌倒

  小心碰头，危险

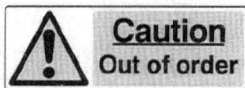 警告：故障

 警告：热水

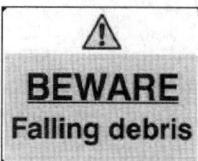 碎片掉落，小心

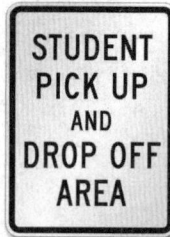 学生上车/下车区

 行人过街，停车

 警告 邻居犯罪监视 邻居保持监视，一旦发现可疑行为立即报告执法机构。

翻译公示语的最佳途径之一是借鉴国外的公示语，下面一组公示语是笔者在国外期间现场拍摄的图片，供学习翻译时思考、借用。

英国 Heathrow 机场登机通道

下面一组于 2017 年 4 月摄自苏格兰

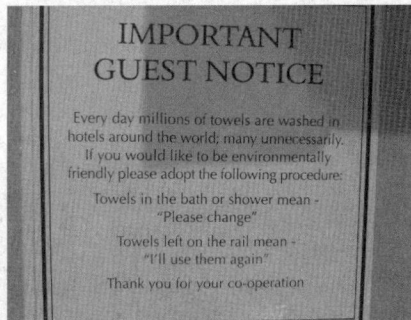

下面一组为 2018 年 4 月摄于英格兰。

以下为 2011 年 11 月摄于英国

7.7 公示语集锦

1）车道封闭 Lane Closed

2）请沿站台过往。Pass along the platform，please.

3）门票在检票处免费索取，如需帮助，请找工作人员。5：30 停止入园。Tickets are

160

FREE from the admissions desk. Please ask a member of staff if you require assistance. Last Admission：5：30.

4）接站人员请勿入内；旅客、乘客止步 Staff Only

5）先买票后上车。Please buy your ticket before you board the train.

6）先买票后乘车。违者罚款（至少 20 镑）。Please buy your ticket before you travel, otherwise you may have to pay a Penalty Fare(at least £20).

7）请清理狗便。Please clean up after your dog.

8）请随手关门，谢谢。Please close behind you. thank you.

9）出入时请关严大门。Please close this gate securely on entry or exit.

10）找寻自行车停车架，请参阅本站地图或询问工作人员。Please consult the station map or a member of staff for location of cycle racks.

11）此处请勿丢放废弃设备或垃圾。Please DO NOT leave equipment or rubbish within this area.

12）此处请勿停车。Please DO NOT park here.

13）请勿将其他塑料投入此箱。Please DO NOT put other types of plastics in the bin.

14）请勿搬动可疑装置。Please DO NOT remove any suspicious devices.

15）请从另端进入。Please enter at other end.

16）请按门票所示路线参观。Please follow the visitor route indicated on your guide ticket.

17）请准备好你的机票或登机牌接受检查。Please have your ticket or boarding card ready for inspection.

18）请勿将身体伸出扶梯外。WARNING Keep your body in escalator.

19）暂停售票/收款/服务/运营；临时关闭此口；临时停止进站；本柜台临时关闭 Temporarily Closed

20）当日使用，逾期作废。Only valid on day of issue.

21）此处可放童车。Please leave your buggy here.

22）每件行李取票一张，并将第 2 联粘贴在行李上。Please make sure that you collect a ticket for each piece of your luggage. Please stick the second copy of your ticket(s) on each piece of your luggage.

23）提请注意：行李存放风险自担，对于行李的丢失或被窃本店概不负责。Please note that all luggages are stored at the owner's risk. The hotel will not accept liability for any luggage lost or stolen.

24）请将此座留给老年人，残疾人及怀抱婴儿的乘客。Please offer this seat to elderly or disabled people or those carrying children.

25）请仅在紧急情况下使用。Please only use in an emergency.

26）请付费后返回车内。Please pay before returning to your car.

27）凭票入场 Ticket Holders Only 或 Admission by Ticket Only

28）此处请勿倒垃圾。Please refrain from dumping rubbish in this area.

29）切记：请将需清洗的毛巾放在地板上，继续使用的挂在毛巾架上。您的举手之劳有助于环境保护。谢谢！Please remember to put towels you want washed on the floor, leave towels you will use again on the towel racks. This simple gesture helps protect the environment. Thank you.

30）请慢速骑行，靠近行人，提前示意。Please ride slowly and warn pedestrians as you approach.

31）请为其他使用通道的人着想。Please show consideration for other path users.

32）请站右侧。Please stand on the right.

33）如电梯故障请呼叫 7363 9777 求助。为此给您带来任何不便我们深表歉意。If this lift is out of order, please call 7363 9777 for assistance. We apologize for any inconvenience caused.

34）停车场关闭，请使用宽便道。The car park is closed. Please use the Broadwalk.

35）请系好座椅安全带。Please wear the seatbelt provided.

36）购物车仅限超市购物使用，请勿推出商场停车场以外。Please don't take shopping carts out of the parking lot.

37）密码单妥善保管，请勿示人。Please do not lose your code slip or show it to others.

38）为了保证您的利益——为了给您提供一个安全的购物环境，商场内配备了 24 小时闭路电视监控录像系统。For your safety and interest, the store is under 24 hour live/recorded video surveillance.

第八章　商务文书文体翻译

商务文书涉及的内容较为广泛，有简单的书信及电报信文，稍复杂一点的报盘询盘，更正式的单证及提单，以及最为正式的合同和租约的草拟与翻译等。后两者属于法律文体的范畴，因为它们都又是文书的内容，故把它们放在本章讲述。纯法律文本的翻译将在下一章详述。

这类的文体大多具有正式书面文体的特点，翻译时更要注意兼及各类文体特点，做到表意准确，行文流畅。

8.1　电报的翻译

英文的电报分为明文电报和密码电报两大类，在通常的商务交往中前者使用相当广泛，所以本节主要介绍明文电报的翻译。

众所周知，英文电报按发报的类别、字数和发送的远近来计费。急电的收费是普通电报的两倍。而英文电报的字数是按英文电报的计费单位计算，即在英文的自然词、缩写词和合成词中，每 10 个字母计为一个"字"，超出 10 个少于 20 个字母的按两个"字"计费，依次类推。如 as soon as 按三个"字"计费，但 ASSOONAS 或 ASAP 只计一个字的费。所以，我们在翻译报文时，必须精练切题，言简意赅，利用约定俗成的简化规则。

8.1.1　省略(Ellipsis)

翻译报文时，我们通常可以省略助动词、系动词、冠词、代词、介词和连词，但特例除外。如：

代词"我"、"我们"通常可以省去不用。如要表达：

• We confirm having received your order No. 10 dated Nov. 4.

电文可译为：YOUR ORDER NO10 ACCEPTED

介词和助动词可以省略。如要表达：

• Referring to your cable of Jan. 10, we have opened L/C today.

电文可译为：RYC10TH L/C OPENED TODAY

但下列情况下介词不可省略，如：

• Please reduce your price by U. S. $889.

报文可译为：PLSREDUCE PRICE BY USD889

冠词、形容词及系动词的省略。如要表达：

• The quality of your goods is unsatisfactory.

电文可译为：GOODS QUALITY UNSATISFACTORY

再例：

- We are desirous to know further details.

电文可译为：DESIROUS TOKNOW DETAILS

动词带有双宾语时，第一人称、第二人称的间接宾语可省略。如：

- Please send me/us your B/L.

可译为：PLSSEND YRB/L

- 而 I'll remit you the money you requested.

可译为：REMITTING MONEY REQUESTED

连词可省略。如要表达：

- Referring to our cable of 9th September and your cable of 15th September, we wish to inform you that all prices include 4% commission.

报文可译为：ROC 9TH SEPTEMBER YC15TH INCLUDING 4PCT COMMISSION

8.1.2　转换(Transformation)

翻译报文时我们可以转换时态。通常地，完成时态、被动语态和定语从句转换成过去分词。如：

- The ship have/had completed discharging.

可译为：SHIP COMPLETED DISCHARGING

- We have airmailed the sample you required.

可译为：AIRMAILED SAMPLE REQUIRED

将来时态通常转换为现在分词。如：

- The ship will leave tomorrow.

译为：SHIP LEAVING TOMORROW

原句中的 do not, cannot, not be 等表示否定的形式通常转换成带有前缀 UN-, IN-, MIS-, DIS-, NON-的词。

- We cannot accept her offer.

可译为：HER/OFFER UNACCEPTABLE

- We are not interested in ordering such sewing machines.

可译为：SUCH SEWING MACHINES UNINTERESTED TO ORDER

原句中的 can, may…, be able to…, It is possible 转换成带有-ABLE 后缀的词来表示，如：

- If you can ship the goods, please cable us.

可译为：PLSADVISE IF SHIPABLE

- It is possible to do business on the basis of this price.

可译为：PRICE WORKABLE

我们还可将主动形式转换成被动形式，使电文符合英语表达。如：

- We have received your L/C and shipped the goods.

可译为：YRL/C RECEIVED GOODS SHIPPED

- We can accept your price and we'll place an order of 228 ton.

可译为：PRICE ACCEPTABLE ORDERING 228TON

8.1.3 词语合并(Combination)

为了减少字数，节约费用，我们经常根据句子的意群将一些词语合并。如：

at sight：ATSIGHT 见票即付

by airmail：BYAIRMAIL 航空邮件

per sample：PERSAMPLE 根据样品

out of stock：OUTOFSTOCK 无库存，脱销

ex factory：EXFACTORY 工厂交货

per metric ton：PERM/T 每公吨

owing to：OWINGTO 由于

in favor of：INFAVOROF 赞成

contract No：CONTRACTNO 合同号

import licence：IMPLICENCE 进口证

cable confirmation：CABLECFM 电报确认

time of shipment：TIMESHIP 装船时间

please rush L/C：PLSRUSHL/C 速开信用证

amend L/C：AMENDL/C 修改信用证

best offer：BESTOFFER 最优惠报价

please confirm：PLSCONFIRM 请确认

8.1.4 缩略语(Abbreviation)

为了使报文简短节省费用，我们通常在电报中大量使用缩略语，在翻译报文时，要注意正确地使用这些缩略语。翻译时可查阅相关的词典资料，并在翻译实践中不断积累，掌握词语缩略的规律及约定俗成的缩略语。缩略语使用最应注意的是不能产生歧义，以免误事。

词语缩略的几个常用方法：

- 略去元音，保留辅音

have→HV	received→RCVD	regards→RGDS	normal→NML
please→PLS	business→BSNS	sample→SPL	cash→CSH

- 首字母元音时，则保留

about→ABT	above→ABV	amount→AMT	again→AGN
agree→AGR	other→OTHR	obtain→OBTN	

- 保留为首的两个字母，或者三个四个字母

credit→CR	each→EA	require→REQ	immediate→IMM
subject→SUBJ	condition→COND		

- 只保留首尾字母

number→NR   check→CK   doctor→DR

- 保留首字母及词尾部分

otherwise→OWISE   Singapore→SPORE

meantime→MTIME   yesterday→YDY／YDAY

- 保留中间的字母

and→N

- 利用同音字母

you→U   are→R   your→UR   through→THRU

before→B4   excuse→XQS   would→WUD   see→C

low→LO   view→VU

- 词首为 ex-或 cr-时，缩略为 X

exhibit→XBT   expect→XPCT   extra→XTR

exchange→XCH   cross country→XCY

- th 缩略为 Z

this→ZS   this week→ZSWK

常用的后缀缩略

- -ed→D

sailed→SLD   loaded→LDD   acknowledged→ACKD

- -ing→G

loading→LDG   calling→CLG   reverting→RVTG

- -ment→MT 或 T

shipment→SHPT   government→GOVT   payment→PYMT

- -tion→TN

confirmation→CFMTN   application→APLCTN

- -able／-ible→BL

available→AVLBL   payable→PYBL

- 复数-s 及-ly 结尾的词尾缀不缩略

figures→FIGS   metric tons→MTS   directly→DRCTLY

immediately→IMMLY

词组或短句的缩略

- 取首字母

as soon as possible→ASAP   notice of readiness→NOR   准备就绪通知

suspend other servece→SOS 停止其他服务

- 首字母用斜线分开

not responsible→N/R   mate's receipt→M/R

instead of→I/O

- 各取前几个字母

cable address→CABADD

fresh water consumption→FWCON

telephone conversation→TELCON

- 结合 AND

profit and loss→PANDL

collected and delivered→CANDD

一些常用词的进一步缩略

telex→TLX→TX

dated→DTD→DD

vessel→VSL→V/L→VL

captain→CAPT→CPT

owners→OWRS→OWS

charterers→CHTRS→CHRS→CHS

before→BE4→B4

therefore→TFORE→TH4→T4

require→RQR/REQ→RQ

quotation→QTTN→QTN

transfer→TRNSFR/TFER→TFR

through→THRU→TRU

extention→EXTNTN→EXTN→XTN

8.1.5 电报翻译的步骤

汉语报文→将汉语译成英语信函→根据省略、转换、联合和缩写等规则把信函简化成电文。例：

- 我方意欲订购 DELL 计算机 980 台，请电报最低盘成本加保险、运费到南京价，含我方佣金 3%，并说明付款条件及装船日期。→

We are interested in ordering from you 980 DELL personal computers and shall be pleased if you will kindly cable us the lowest offer CIF Nanjing including our commission of 3%. When quoting, please state your terms of payment and time of shipment. →

(we are) INTERESTED (in ordering from you) 980 DELL PERSONAL COMPUTERS (and shall be pleased if you will) KINDLY CABLE (us the) LOWEST OFFER CIF NANJING INCLUDING (our) COMMISSIONS (of) 3PERCENT (when quoting, please state your) TERMS (of) PAYMENT (and) TIME (of) SHIPMENT→

INTERESTED 980 DELL COMPUTERS PLEASE CABLE LOWEST OFFER CIF NANJING INCLUDING COMMISSION 3PERCENT COMMA PLSADVISE TERMS PAYMENT TIME SHIPMENT→

使用外贸术语简化：INTERESTED 980 DELL COMPUTERS PLEASE CABLE LOWEST OFFER CIFC3 NANJING COMMA PLSADVISE TERMS PAYMENT TIME SHIPMENT→

进一步简化成：PLEASE CABLE LOWEST CIFC3 NANJING 980 DELL COMPUTERS ADVISING TERMS PAYMENT TIME SHIPMENT（13 个计费字）→

终稿：PLSCABLE LOWEST CIFC3 NANJING 980 DELL COMPUTERS ADVISING TERMS PAYMENT TIME SHIPMENT（12 个计费字）

8.2　信用证的翻译

信用证是由银行开具的证书，授权持证者可从开证行、其支行或其他有关银行或机构提取所述款项。（A Letter of Credit is a letter issued by a bank authorizing the bearer to draw a stated amount of money from the issuing bank, its branches, or other associated banks or agencies.）它是贸易上最重要的信用保证方法。代表买方的外汇银行，接受买方的委托，保证其货款的支付。万一买方付不出货款，根据契约规定，银行必须履行向卖方付款的责任。

信用证是保证卖方收到汇票后即可支取货款的信用文件。在卖方将货物装船后，外汇银行代替买方，开立汇票给卖方；卖方带着汇票和装船单证，到自己往来的外汇银行办理结算而取得货款。

信用证由开证行（Opening/Issuing Bank）经通知行（Informing Bank）交给卖方。装船后，由议付行（Negotiating Bank）结算后转回开证行。

信用证语言特点独特。从意义上来说，信用证是一项约定，它对双方均有约束力。它具有法律文书的语言特色，用词严谨、正规、专业性强，具体体现在以下几个方面，翻译时须谨慎为之。

8.2.1　格式化和规范化

信用证的句式虽然缺少一定的成分，但却独立成句，且这种句式主要出现在其对单证和装船的限定等部分。系动词或助动词 be 常省略。如：

- Latest shipment Mar. 10, 2019. 最近装船时间为 2019 年 3 月 10 日。
- Shipment from Dalian to Nagoya. 从大连运往名古屋的货物。
- Each document to show B/L number and date and to be dated not earlier than 7 days from B/L date. 显示提单编号和日期的每张信用证，其开具日期不得早于提单日期七天。
- All correspondence to be sent to Citibank import services department. 请将所有的信件送到花旗银行进口部。
- Transshipment prohibited. 禁止转运。
- Partial shipment allowed. 允许分批装运。

分词短语作定语，独立成句，如：

- Copy of beneficiaries' telex to buyer quoting L/C number mentioning details of shipment. 受益人的电传副本一份，显示信用证号码，注明装运细节。

8.2.2　多用书面语

这种现象主要体现在大量使用介词短语代替单个介词，常用的有：

in compliance with；

as per；

in view of；

in favor of，等。如：

- The bill is marked as per advice. 汇票上标明"按照通知"字样。

- This certificate of silk products is issued in compliance with the consignee's request.

丝绸产品证明书是根据收货人的要求开具的。

此外，很少使用口语词语，如表示"将来"一般用 be to do 结构或者 shall/will 结构，而不用 be going to do 或 be about to do，如：

- This credit (is) to be negotiated at sight basis. 本信用证以见票(即付)议付。

- We shall remit the proceeds to you in accordance with your instructions.

我行将根据贵方的指令汇去货款。

8.2.3 古体词的使用

高频率使用 therein, thereafter, thereinafter, thereby, thereof, hereby, hereto, hereof, hereunder 等。

- Usance bill drawn **hereunder** are to be negotiated at sight. 下面开具的远期汇票采取见票即付。

- The negotiating bank is **hereby** authorized to make advance to the beneficiary up to an aggregate amount of USD200,000 (20% of the amount of L/C). The advances, with the interest at the ruling rate of exchange at the time of payment of such advance, are to be deducted from the proceeds of the drafts drawn under this credit.

兹授权通知行给受益人预支信用证项下的款项，其金额不超过 200,000 美元(为本信用证金额的 20%)。本信用证项下的预支款，按付款当天公布的汇率折算并加付利息。预支款应从本信用证项下的汇票金额中扣除。

- We confirmed the credit and **thereby** undertake that all draft drawn and presented as above specified will be dully honored (及时支付) by us at our counter on or before.

我行保兑本信用证并承诺我们将于到期日之前及时在我行支付按以上说明开具并出示的所有汇票。

8.2.4 语气的变化

信用证英语中，情态动词 may, must, can, shall, should 的使用频率很高，且意义变化较大。所以我们在实际翻译中不但要着重理解其表层意义，而且要分析其内在的涵义，并弄清其语气的变化。

信用证属法律文书，开证行处于绝对的主导地位，其发号施令的强制性语气通常都是通过词语表达出来的。从下面这组信用证的属性和对单证要求语中，我们可以看出，信用证是一项约定，而在这个约定中开证行处在绝对的主导地位。受益人想要支取信用证项下的款项，必须满足信用证的条款，即必须满足开证行的要求。

- T. T. reimbursement (is) not acceptable.

不接受电汇付款。(TT：telegraphic transfer 电汇)

- This credit (is) not transferable. 本信用证不可转让。

这两句是开证行陈述事实，但传递的信息是强制性的，没有任何保留余地，不能更改。

- L/C No. should appear on all shipping documents.

信用证号码必须在所有的货运单证中标明。

- Marine insurance shall cover the risks until applicant's warehouse in Japan.

水渍险须包括运抵投保人日本仓库的所有风险。

- Packing list must show container Nos, and specify contents of each container.

装箱单必须写明箱号，并标明每箱的内容物。

上述三句为开证行的命令语，虽然语气比较委婉，但强硬的语气还是深含其中。

- Upon receipt of documents issued in strict conformity with credit terms and conditions, we shall cover you at your convenience. The present telex is the operative credit instrument and no written confirmation will follow.

一旦收到严格按照信用证条款开具的单证，我行将就贵方之便如数付款。本电传作为有效信用证，不再给书面保兑。

从上面这句我们不难看出，当谈到自己的责任时，语气明显变弱。

8.2.5　被动语态的使用

被动语态可以把所要论述的对象放在句子的主语位置，以引起读者的注意。而且被动语态的句法结构便于调节，利于采用修辞手法，增加句子的容量。另外，被动语态比主动语态更少主观色彩，符合严肃性和庄重性文体的需要。

- The advising bank is requested to notify the beneficiary without adding their confirmation.

我行(开证行)请求通知行通知受益人没有加具它们的保兑。

如果说将上面的句子改为主动结构：

The opening bank requests the advising bank to notify the beneficiary without adding their confirmation.

我们不难看出，主动结构平铺直叙，语气过于流露，显然没有被动结构严肃和庄重。

8.2.6　专业术语的使用

信用证常使用专业术语，因其具有国际通用性，且意义精确严谨，文体特色鲜明。为了描述进出口流程的各个环节和与此相关的各类单证，信用证使用大量表意清楚的专业术语。翻译时必须熟悉该专业知识和专业表达法，否则会贻笑大方。比如有关信用证类别的词汇：

documentary L/C	跟单信用证
clean L/C	光票信用证
reciprocal L/C	对开信用证
irrevocable L/C	不可撤销信用证

又如有关当事人的词汇：

party	当事人
applicant/principal	开证申请人

beneficiary	受益人
issuing bank	开证行

再如表示单证的词汇：

draft	汇票
invoice	发票
packing list	装箱单
bill of lading（B/L）	提单
inspection certificate	检验证书
fumigation certificate	熏舱证书

举例说明如下：

- back-to-back（letter of）credit 背对背信用证/转开信用证

英语亦说 countervailing（letter of）credit，secondary（letter of）credit，subsidiary（letter of）credit. 此术语指贸易商以客户开给他的信用证作担保，请求其往来银行另开以第三者为受益人的信用证。

- bona fida holder 善意持有人

议付行向受益人垫付资金、买入跟单汇票后，即成为汇票持有人，也就是善意持有人。

- neutral document 中性单证，指不表现出口商名称的单证。

- proforma invoice（拉丁语）形式发票，也称为"预开发票"或"估价发票"，是进出口商为了向其本国当局申请进口许可证或请求核批外汇，在未成交前要求出口商将拟出售成交的商品以名称、单价、规格等条件开立的一份参考性发票。

8.2.7 一词多义与一义多词

信用证里一词多义现象十分常见，有些词语在信用证里出现的频率很高，而且词义大相径庭，请注意下面句中的词义选择。

- The advising or confirming bank can refuse to accept the documents and return them to the beneficiary so that they can be corrected or replaced.

通知行或保兑行可拒绝接受单证并将这些单证退还受益人以便修改或替换新的单证。（accept 意为"接受"）

- We hereby engage with drawers and/or bona fida holders that drafts drawn in conformity with the terms of this credit will be duly accepted on presentation and duly honoured at maturity.

我行特此承诺出票人和/或善意持票人，只要提交根据本信用证条款开具的汇票我行就及时承兑，而且到期我行就及时支付。（accept 意为"承兑"；engage 意为"承诺"；honour 意为"支付"，其反义词为 dishonour"拒付"。）

- If the correspondent bank is instructed merely to advise the credit, it forwards the prescribed text to the beneficiary without engagement on its own part.

如果往来行只被批示通知信用证，它只需将规定的内容（指信用证）通知受益人，自身无须承担任何责任。（engagement 意为"承担"。）

- The confirmed letter of credit forced the paying bank to honour the transaction.

保兑信用证迫使付款行支付这笔交易的费用。(confirmed 意为"保兑的"。)

- We have added our confirmation on the credit and engage that documents presented to us in full compliance with the terms and conditions of the credit will be duly honoured.

我行已附加保兑本信用证并承诺提交给我方的单证只要是完全符合该信用证的条款我行将及时支付。(confirmation 保兑)

- The full set of shipping documents shall accompany the collection draft and only be released after full payment of the invoice value.

全部装运单证必须附于托收汇票,而且只有在发票面值全部付清后方可交单。(collection 托收)

再看下面三个例句,我们分别用 operative,valid,in full force and effect 来翻译汉语"有效的"含义:

- When an issuing bank instructs an advising bank by an authenticated tele-transmission to advise on credit or an amendment to credit, the tele-transmission will be deemed to be the operative instrument or the operative amendment, and no mail confirmation should be sent.

当开证行用经证实的电传指示通知行通知信用证或信用证的修改时,该电传将被认为是有效的信用证或有效的修改通知,无须再寄发证实信函。

- By irrevocable letter of credit it is to be available by sight draft and to remain valid for negotiation in China until the 15th day after the aforesaid time of shipment.

凭不可撤销的即期信用证付款,并与上述装运期后十五天内在中国议付有效。

- Unless sooner terminated as provided in Article 12 hereunder, this contract shall remain in full force and effect for one year from its date of execution.

除非由于下述第十二条规定导致提前终止,本合同自签署之日起,一年内保持有效。

所以我们要特别注意下列信用证高频使用词语的专业意义:confirm(ation), document,honour,collect(ion),accept(ance),instrument,operative 等。

另外,我们还要注意信用证中一义多词现象,"支付"的不同表达法就有下列多种: reimburse;honour;cover;levy;collect;charge;to be borne by;for account of;be payable;at one's expense, etc. 例如:

- This draft is payable on the 19th of November. 本汇票 11 月 19 日到期支付。
- Your expenses will be reimbursed in full. 贵方的开支将得到全部付还。
- This letter of credit will be honoured only if the seller submits a letter or telex from AAA Company certifying that all terms and requirements under L/C No. 83658 have been complied with.

本信用证将被承兑,只要卖方提交一份 AAA 公司发出的信函或电传,证明编号为 83658 信用证上所有的条款和要求已得到履行。

- The fee will always have to be borne by the beneficiary. 该费用总由受益人支付。

8.2.8　用简单介词来简化句子结构

下面一句中用了 5 个介词使句子言简意赅:

- This credit is valid until Feb. 26, 2019, in Vancouver for payment available against the presentation of the following documents.

本信用证有效期至 2019 年 2 月 26 日，到期地点为温哥华，(受益人)凭提交下列单证可以得到偿付。

介词 until 表示到期时间，in 表示到期地点，for 表示付款保证，against 表示付款条件。

8.2.9 数字和日期的翻译

8.2.9.1 份数的翻译

一式二份　in duplicate/2-fold

一式三份　in triplicate/3-fold

一式四份　in quadruplicate/4-fold

一式五份　in quintuplicate/5-fold

一式六份　in sextuplicate/6-fold

一式七份　in septuplicate/7-fold

一式八份　in octuplicate/8-fold

一式九份　in nonuplicate/9-fold

一式十份　in decuplicate/10-fold

如：

- 包装单一式三份：packing list in three fold
- 签署的商业发票一式四份：signed commercial invoice in quadruplicate

8.2.9.2 数字的翻译

在表示信用证中单证份数时，我们也可用分数，分母为所出单证的总数，而分子为所需单证的份数。如：

- 三份正本提单中的一份：1/3 original B/L
- 已装船三份正本清洁海运提单中的两份：2/3 of clean on board ocean original B/L
- 三份正本品质证书的三份，即全部证书：3/3 original certificate of quality

8.2.9.3 日期的翻译

•填写信用证时，如果想把装船时间定在 10 月 16 日与 26 日之间，则可译成：

Time of shipment：on or about 21 Oct.

信用证里 on or about 可理解为：包括该日前后各 5 天，读对方信用证时，也作同样理解。

•如果装船时间为：某月某日止，至某月某日，直至某月某日，从某月某日，我们可分别用 to, until, till, from 来翻译，此时应理解为包括所提到的日期。读对方信用证时，也作同样理解。如：

Time of shipment is from 18th to 28th this month 装船时间为本月 18 日到 28 日(即 18 日和 28 日包括在内)

•如果装船期为：在某月某日之后，可用 after，但理解为不包括所提到的日期。读对方信用证时，也作同样理解。如：

10 月 19 日后装船：Shipment will be effected after the 19th of Oct. 意指 20 日开始装船。

173

●如果装船时间为某月某日之前，可用 before，但目前尚无明确规定实际始装日期，通常参照 after 的用法来理解。

●如果装船日期为 1 到 15 日，即上半月，可译为 the first half；16 日至月底为下半月，可译为 the second half；1 日到 10 日即上旬，可译为 beginning of the month；11 日至 20 日即中旬，middle of the month；21 日至月底即下旬，end of the month。上述时间均包括起讫日。

●如果装船日期最晚不超过 10 月 31 日，可译为 within 31 October；如果装船日期为 10 月 1 日至 10 月 31 日期间均可，则译为 within/during October。

8.2.10　其他译例

● Within 30 days after the signing and coming into effect of this contract, the Buyer shall proceed to pay the price for the goods to the seller by opening an irrevocable L/C for the full amount of USD30,000 in favor of the Seller through a bank at export point so that the Seller may draw the sum in due time.

买方须于本合同签字并生效后 30 天内通过出口地银行开立以卖方为收益人的不可撤销信用证支付全部货款计 30,000 美元，以便卖方可以及时提取该款。

● We hasten to inform you that we have today been advised by the Bank of China of the establishment of an L/C in your favor to the amount of US $100,000 available on or before April 30, 2019.

We believe it will be in your hands within this week.

本公司急告贵方，我公司今天已接到中国银行通知，该行已开立一张信用证，以贵方为受益人，金额 100,000 美元，有效期至 2019 年 4 月 30 日。

本公司相信本周内贵方就可以收到该信用证。

● The goods of your order are being manufactured in time for the shipping date requested.

You inform us that you will open an irrevocable L/C, valid until August 31 and we ask you to send it promptly.

Immediately on arrival of the L/C we will pack and ship the goods urgently as requested.

贵方所订货物正在赶制中，以便赶上贵方所要求的装船日期。

贵方通知本公司，将开立一张不可撤销信用证，有效期到 8 月 31 日止，本公司要求贵方尽快寄出。

本公司一收到信用证，即按照贵方的要求包装并装运这批货物。

● We have just received your advice that you cannot carry out the complete shipment covering our order at one sailing.

Therefore we have instructed our bankers to amend the L/C so that partial shipments may be allowed.

本公司刚收到贵方通知，贵方无法将本公司所订货物一次装运完毕。

因此，本公司已指示本公司的往来银行修正信用证，以许可分批装运。

● In spite of our effort, we find it impossible to secure space for the shipment owing to the unusual shortage of shipping space.

Please allow us to request that you extend your L/C to Dec. 20.

尽管本公司百般努力，但由于船位极度紧张，故本公司无法确保一定能取得货运船位。
请允许本公司的请求，将信用证延期至 12 月 20 日。

• As requested in your letter of Oct. 6, we have instructed our bankers to extend the L/C No. 1069 up to and including Dec. 20.

Therefore you will receive the extension advice by this weekend.

按贵方 10 月 6 日来函要求，我行已指示本公司的往来银行，将编号为 1069 的信用证延期至 12 月 20 日，包括当天。

因此，贵方于本周末之前将收到延期通知。

• All bank charges outside U. K. are for our principals' account, but must be claimed at the time of presentation of documents.

在英国境外发生的所有银行费用，应由开证人负担，但必须在提交单证时索取。

• Upon receipt of compliant documents, we undertake to remit proceeds by telegraphic transfer in terms of your instructions.

收到该项下相符的单证时，我(开证行)保证在两个工作日内按贵行指令付款。

• Drawee bank's charges and acceptance commission are for buyer's account.

付款行的费用和承兑费用由卖方负担。

• Full set of 3/3 clean on board bills of lading or multimodal transport document and two nonnegotiable copies made out to order of Bangkok Bank Company Limited, Bangkok marked freight prepaid and notify applicant.

全套(一式三份)正本已装船清洁提单或联运单证加上两份非流通副本，以 Bangkok Bank Company Limited, Bangkok 为抬头做成，注明运费预付，通知开证申请人。

• Insurance policy or certificate or declaration in two negotiable forms indicating "Original" and "Duplicate" plus one non-negotiable copy endorsed in bank for full invoice value plus 10 percent with claim payable in Bangkok in the same currency as the draft, covering institute cargo clauses (all risks) and institute war clauses (cargo).

保险单两份分别注明 ORIGINAL 和 DUPLICATE 加上一份非流通副本，空白背书；投保金额为 110%发票金额，表明索赔地为曼谷，索赔币种为汇票币种；投保险别包括伦敦协会一切险条款和战争险条款。

8.2.11 关于 offer, quote/quotation, bid

这些词有各自的含义和用法，请注意区别。

Offer 译为报/发盘，通常指卖方向对方提出贸易成交条件，如货名、数量、规格、价格、船期、有效期等。它可作名词，也可作动词。名词又可分为实盘 firm offer 和虚盘 non-firm offer，前者附有效期，如：Firm for 5 days.

虚盘须附有条件，如：

subject to our final confirmation 以我方最后确认为准

subject to prior sale 货未售出为有效

所有报盘如果规定了有效期而未附加任何条件，即使无 firm 字样，也默认为实盘。

此外，还有搭配报盘，即 combined offer，也称联盘，指两种以上的商品，还有买方的还盘，即 counter-offer.

This is a combined offer, which must be accepted in its entirety.

这是搭配报盘，必须一起接受。

offer 常与下列动词搭配，以表示报盘的各个方面。

to make/forward an offer 发盘

Please make us an offer C. I. F. London for 20 metric tons peanut.

请报 20 公吨花生伦敦到岸价实盘。

to accept an offer	接受报盘
to decline an offer	谢绝报盘
to entertain an offer	考虑是否接受报盘
to extend an offer	延长报盘
to renew an offer	恢复报盘

We renew our offer for reply here Wednesday our time.

兹恢复报盘，以我方时间星期三复到为有效。

to withdraw an offer	撤回报盘

Quote 为动词，后可接双宾语。作"报价"解时，其直接宾语只能是 price 或与 price 相关的价格术语，如 FOB、C&F、CIF 等，或者两者同时出现。如：

Please quote (us) your lowest price CIF London for walnut.

请报我方胡桃最低伦敦到岸价。

Quotation 为 quote 的名词形式。它与 offer 不同，主要指"提出价格"，一般可译为"报价""行市""行情""时价"等。如：

Please send us your lowest quotation CIF London for walnut.

请报我方胡桃最低伦敦到岸价。

These quotations are said to be nominal. 这些价格据说是有行无市。

These are the latest quotations from the Stock Exchange. 这些是证交所的最新行情。

Bid 译作"递盘/价"，与 offer 相对，系指买方的主动出价，买方还价时说 counter bid/counter offer. Bid 既可用作动词也可用作名词。作动词用时其句式与 quote 相似。Bid 为不规则动词，过去式与过去分词词形不变。

We will try to get a bid from the buyers. 我们要设法从买主那里获得一个递盘。

As your prices were too high, we made a counter bid at RMB ￥4,000 per ton.

由于你方价格太高，现还价每吨人民币 4,000 元。

Last week we bid RMB ￥4,000 per ton for green tea. Now we can do a little better.

上周我方绿茶递价每吨人民币 4,000 元，现在我方可以递价稍高些。

8.2.12 不可撤销信用证的格式

IRREVOCABLE LETTER OF CREDIT　不可撤销信用证

Irrevocable Credit No. _____ Date：_____　不可撤销信用证编号：____日期：____

All drafts drawn must be　全部汇票必须注明：

marked："Drawn under　"根据信用证_____号开出"

Credit No. _____"

Messrs. _____（Beneficiary）　受益人：_____

Gentlemen：

You are authorized to value on _____ Bank（Bank on which to draw）for the account of _____（client）up to the aggregate amount of（currency）by drawing your draft within _____ days for _____%（percentage）invoice cost of Consular Invoice, accompanied by Bills of Lading and Commercial Invoice（evidencing shipment of the commodity）. Bills of Lading must be dated no later than _____（date）.

敬启者：

兹授权贵方向_____银行（议付行）开出付款人为_____（委托人），金额限于_____（货币），有效期为_____天，按领事发票面值的_____%（百分比）为票额的汇票。并凭下列单证议付：提货单、商业发票（证明货物已装船）。提货单日期不迟于_____（日期）。

A copy of the Consular Invoice, Commercial Invoice, and Bill of Lading must be mailed to _____（Issuing Bank or Paying Bank）, and a statement to that effect must be attached to the draft.

领事发票、商业发票副本及提货单须邮寄至_____（开证行或付款行），并将交单说明附于汇票后。

We hereby agree with the drawers, endorsers, and bona fide holders of drafts drawn in compliance with the terms of credit that such drafts shall be dully honoured on presentation and paid at maturity.

Yours very truly,

Signature _____

本行向出票人、背书人及正当汇票持有人表示同意，凡符合本信用证所列条件的汇票，本行将见票按期支付。

顺致谢意。

签字：_____

8.3 提单及租船合约的翻译

8.3.1 提单及租约的概念

提单，英语为 bill of lading，常用缩略形式 B/L，是证明海上运输合同和承运人（carrier）接管或装载货物以及承运人保证据以交付货物的单证。当承运人或实际承运人接受货物时或货物装船以后，必须按照托运人的要求，签发给托运人一式数份的提单。提单条款规定了承运人、托运人之间相应的责任、义务、权利和豁免。按货物是否已装船，提单分为已装船提单（shipped bill of lading）和收讫待运提单（received for shipment bill of lading）；按收货人抬头分，有指示提单（order bill of lading）、记名提单（straight bill of lading）和不记名提单（bearer bill of lading, blank bill of lading, open bill of lading, 中文又称"空白提单"）；按货物外表状况批注与否分，有清洁提单（clean bill of lading）和不洁提单（foul bill of lading）；按运输过程分，有直达提单（direct bill of lading）、联运提单（through bill of lading）和转船提单（transshipment bill of lading）。我国外贸运输中，一般采用的提单格式为中国远洋运输总公司的提单范本（COSCO B/L）。

国际上租船合约比较通用的为"金康"格式（GENCON）以及"土产格式"（NYPE Form）。前者的全称是 Uniform General Charter，即"统一杂货租船合同"，它是适用范围较广的航次租船合同的标准格式；而后者的全称为 Time Charter, PRODUCE FORM，即定期租船合同土产格式，为纽约土产交易所采纳（approved by the New York Produce Exchange），也是国际贸易运输经常采用的标准格式。

8.3.2 提单及租约的句法特点（Syntactic features）

8.3.2.1 多用条件句

通常引导这类条件句用 if，但还有 when(ever), where(ever), provided that, unless, 甚至用 in (the) case of, in the event of/that，有时，if 省略，将 should 放到句首；在句中情态动词 shall 通常表示"义务"，即"应当""必须"的意义，其语气比使用 will, should, may, must 要强。如中远提单对"赔偿金额"（AMOUNT OF COMPENSATION）规定：

- When the Carrier is liable for compensation in respect of loss of or damage to the goods, such compensation shall be calculated by reference to the invoice value of the goods plus freight charges and insurance if paid.

当承运人应对货失货损予以赔偿时，此种赔偿应根据该项货物的发票价格加运费及保险费（如已支付）计算。

- If there is no invoice value of the goods, such compensation shall be calculated by reference to the value of such goods at the place and time they are delivered to the Merchant in accordance with the contract or should have been so delivered. The value of the goods shall be fixed according to the commodity exchange price or, if there be no such price, according to the current market price or, if there be no commodity exchange price or current market price, by reference to the normal value of goods of the same kind and quality.

如无货物发票价值，则此项赔偿额应根据该项货物在依照合同交付货方的地点和当时的价值，或本应如此交付时的价值计算。货物价值应根据商品交易价格计算，如无此种价格时，则按现时市价计算；如无商品交易价或现时市价，则应根据相同品种及质量的货物的正常价值计算。

- If the goods are unclaimed during a reasonable time, or wherever the goods will become deteriorated, decayed or worthless, the Carrier may, at his discretion and subject to his lien, and without any responsibility attaching to him, sell, abandon or otherwise dispose of such goods solely at the risk and expense of the Merchant.

如货物在一个合理的时间内无人认领，或者货物即将变质、腐烂或丧失价值，承运人可以自行决定并根据其留置权对该货物进行变卖、抛弃或作其他处置而不承担任何责任，风险和费用全部由货方承担。

- Should ice prevent the Vessel from reaching port of discharge, the Charterers shall have the option of keeping the Vessel waiting until the reopening of navigation and paying demurrage or of ordering the Vessel to a safe and immediately accessible port where she can safely discharge without risk of detention by ice.

如果结冰而导致船舶不能驶入卸货港，租船人应当有权在支付滞期费的前提下使船舶等候至航行重新开放，也有权指示船舶驶至一个安全的、可立即进入的港口，船舶在该港可安全卸货而无结冰滞留的风险。（金康格式）

- Unless otherwise agreed, the Charterers shall have the liberty to sublet the Vessel for all or any part of the time covered by this Charter Party, but the Charterers remain responsible for the fulfillment of this Charter Party.

除非另有约定，租船人应有权在本租船合同的整个期间或部分期间将船舶转租，但租船人仍应对本租船合同的履行负责。（土产格式）

- In the event the demurrage is not paid in accordance with the above, the Owners shall give the Charterers 96 running hours written notice to rectify the failure.

如果未能按上述约定支付滞期费，出租人应当书面通知承运人在 96 小时内支付。（金康格式）

8.3.2.2 多用名词短语

名词短语可以使句子结构简洁、正式，翻译时注意将名词还原成动词或动词短语。

- On the receipt by one party of the nomination in writing of the other party's arbitrator, that party shall appoint their arbitrator within fourteen days, failing which the decision of the single arbitrator appointed shall be final.

在收到另一方仲裁员的书面通知后，接通知需指定仲裁员的一方应当在 14 天之内指定自己一方的仲裁员，否则，另一方指定的仲裁员所作出的裁决应当是终局的裁决。

- Cargo claims as between the Owners and the Charterers shall be settled in accordance with the Inter-Club New York Produce Exchange Agreement of February 1970, as amended May, 1984, or any subsequent modification or replacement thereof.

发生于出租人和承租人之间的货物索赔应<u>按照</u>经 1984 年 5 月修订的纽约土产交易所 1970 年 2 月协会协议或其以后的任何修订或更换的文本加以解决。(土产格式)

8.3.2.3　多用非谓语形式作定语

非谓语形式作定语大部分后置，使文体更庄重、更准确。

- Should the Vessel deviate or put back during a voyage, contrary to the orders or directions of the Charterers, for any reason other than accident to the cargo or where permitted in lines 257 to 258 hereunder, the hire is to be suspended from the time of her <u>deviating or putting back</u> until she is again in the same or equidistant position from the destination and the voyage resumed therefrom.

如果船舶在航次中违反租船人的指令，由于除货物事故或本租船合同第 257 至 258 行准许的情况外的任何原因而<u>绕航或返航</u>，租金应自船舶<u>绕航或返航</u>之时至船舶回到其开始绕航或返航的位置或与终点港等距离的位置并于该位置恢复航行这一段时间停付。(土产格式)

- Fumigation ordered because of cargoes <u>carried</u> or ports <u>visited</u> while the Vessel is employed under this Charter Party shall be for the Charterers' account. 船舶在本租船合同期间因<u>所载</u>货物或<u>所停靠</u>港口而需要熏舱，费用由租船人负担。(土产格式)

8.3.2.4　长句的使用

一般而言，在正式文体中，因表达严谨的需要，常使用各种修饰成分使得句子变得冗长，结构也复杂起来，翻译中我们要注意理清各句子成分之间的逻辑关系，抓住句子的主干结构，避免误译。

- It is agreed between the party mentioned in Box 3 as the Owners of the Vessel named in Box 5, of the GT/NT indicated in Box 6 and carrying about the number of metric tons of deadweight capacity all told on summer loadline stated in Box 7, now in position as stated in Box 8 and expected ready to load under this Charter Party about the date indicated in Box 9, and the party mentioned as the Charterers in Box 4 that:

The said Vessel shall, as soon as her prior commitments have been completed, proceed to the loading port(s) or place(s) stated in Box 10 or so near thereto as she may safely get and lie always afloat, and there load a full and complete cargo (if shipment of deck cargo agree same to be at the Charterers' risk and responsibility) as stated in Box 12, which the charterers bind themselves to ship, and being so loaded the Vessel shall proceed to the discharging port(s) or place(s) stated in Box 11 as ordered on signing Bills of Lading or so near thereto as she may safely get and lie always afloat, and there deliver the cargo.

兹有与主要条款第 5 条规定之船名、第 6 条规定之船舶的总吨及净吨、第 7 条规定之夏季载重线具有的载货吨位、第 8 条规定之现在船位及第 9 条规定之预计抵港日期相符合的及第 3 条规定的一方即船舶所有人和第 4 条规定的一方即船舶租用人达成如下协议：

上述船舶在完成其上一航次任务后，即应驶往主要条款第 10 条规定的装货港或装货地或其附近的、船舶能安全抵达的并能始终处于漂浮状态的装货港或装货地，按 12 条之规定在该地装载满载货物(如果双方同意装甲板货，则应由租船人承担风险与责任)。船舶按租船合同装货完毕并签发提单后，将驶向主要条款第 11 条规定之卸货港或卸货地或其附近的、船舶能安全抵达的并能始终处于漂浮状态的装货港或装货地，并在该地交货。（金康格式）

上句虽长，但其主干结构为 It is agreed between the party…and the party…that…，其他部分都是修饰语。

8.3.3 提单翻译节选

- DANGEROUS GOODS (1) The Carrier undertakes to carry the goods of an explosive, inflammable, radioactive, corrosive, damaging, noxious, hazardous, poisonous injurious or dangerous nature only upon the Carrier's acceptance of a prior written application by the Merchant for the carriage of such goods. Such application must accurately state the nature, name, label and classification of the goods as well as the method of rendering them innocuous, with the full names and addresses of the shipper and the consignee.

危险货 对具有爆炸性、易燃性、放射性、腐蚀性、破坏性、有害性、剧险性、有毒性、伤害性或危险性货物，只有在承运人事先接受货方为运输此种货物而提出的书面申请时，承运人才负责承运。此种申请必须准确地说明货物的性质、品名、标签及分类，以及使之变为无害的办法，并载明托运人及收货人的全名及地址。

(2) The merchant shall undertake that the nature of the goods referred to in the preceding paragraph is distinctly and permanently marked and manifested on the outside of the package(s) and container(s) and shall also undertake to submit the documents or certificates required by any applicable statutes or regulations or by the Carrier.

货方应保证，前款所述货物性质已清晰、永久性地在货物包件及集装箱外表上进行标注，并应保证提供为任何所适用的法律、规章或承运人所要求的单证或证书。

(3) Whenever the goods are discovered to have been received by the Carrier without complying with paragraph (1) or (2) above or the goods are found to be contraband or prohibited by any laws or regulations of the port of loading, discharge or call or any place or waters during the transport, the Carrier shall be entitled to have such goods rendered innocuous, thrown overboard or discharged or otherwise disposed of at the Carrier's discretion without compensation and the Merchant shall be liable for and indemnify the Carrier against any kind of loss, damage or liability including loss of freight and any expenses directly or indirectly arising out of or resulting therefrom.

无论何时，一旦发现承运人接受的货物未遵守上述第(1)款或第(2)款的规定，或者发现货物系违禁品或为装货港、卸货港、中途港或在运输途中的任何地点或水域的任何法规、规章所禁止时，承运人有权使此种货物变为无害、将其抛弃入海、卸下或由承运人决定以其他方式加以处置而不予赔偿，而货方则应就承运人所受任何损失、损坏或所负责任，包括运费损失以及直接或间接由此而产生的任何费用，给予承运人赔偿。

(4) The Carrier may exercise or enjoy the right or benefit conferred upon the Carrier under the preceding paragraph whenever it is apprehended that the goods received in compliance with

paragraphs（1）and（2）above become dangerous to the Carrier vessel, cargo, persons and/or other property.

无论何时，一当发现根据上述第（1）款及第（2）款规定所接受的货物对承运人、船舶、货物、人员和/或其他财产构成危险时，承运人可行使或享有其根据前款规定所赋予的权利或利益。

（5）The Carrier has the right to inspect the contents of the package（s）or container（s）at any time and anywhere without the Merchant's agreement but only at the risk and expense of the Merchant.

承运人有权在任何时候、任何地点检查包件或集装箱所装货物，而无需征得货方同意，且仅由货方承担风险及费用。

● NOTIFICATION AND DELIVERY（1）Any mention in this Bill of Lading of parties to be notified of the arrival of the goods is solely for information of the Carrier and failure to give such notification shall not involve the Carrier in any liability nor relieve the Merchant of any obligation hereunder.

通知及交货　（1）本提单关于将货物到达事项通知有关方的任何规定，只是为承运人提供的情况，因而未能发出此种通知书，不得使承运人承担任何赔偿责任，亦不解除货方根据本提单应承担的任何义务。

（2）The Merchant shall take delivery of the goods within the time provided for in the Carrier's applicable tariff.

货方应在所适用的承运人的运价本中规定的期限内提取货物。

（3）If the Merchant fails to take delivery of the goods or part of it, than in accordance with this Bill of Lading, the Carrier may without notice unstow the goods or that part thereof and/or store the goods or that part thereof ashore, afloat in the open or under cover. Such storage shall constitute due delivery hereunder and thereupon all liability whatsoever of the Carrier in respect of the goods or that part thereof shall cease.

如货方不能按提单提取全部或部分货物、承运人可不经通知把货物或部分货物卸载或存储在岸上或水面，加以遮盖或在露天存放。此种存储应构成按本提单交付货物，承运人对全部或部分货物的任何赔偿责任应终止。

（4）The Merchant's attention is drawn to the stipulations concerning free storage time and demurrage contained in the Carrier's applicable tariff which is incorporated in this Bill of Lading.

请货方注意已并入本提单的所适用的承运人运价本中关于免费存放的期限及滞期费的规定。

（5）Goods will only be delivered in the container to the Merchant if all Bills of Lading in respect of the contents of the container have been surrendered authorising delivery to a single Merchant at a single place of delivery. In the event this requirement is not fulfilled, the Carrier may unstow the container and deliver the goods without the container to the Merchant. Such delivery shall constitute due delivery hereunder but will only be effected against payment by the Merchant of L. C. L. service charges and any charges appropriate to L. C. L. cargo（as laid down in the tariff) together with the actual costs incurred for any additional services rendered.

如集装箱内货物的所有提单授权在单一收货地交与单一货方时，则货物可连同集装箱一起交与货方。如不能达到此种要求，承运人可拆箱交货，而不连同集装箱一并交与货方。此种交货应构成按本提单适当交货，货方应支付拼箱服务费和任何与拼箱货有关的费用（按费率本中的规定）以及进行任何额外服务所实际发生的费用。（L. C. L. 为 less than container load 或 less than carload lots 的缩写形式。）

- GENERAL AVERAGE   General Average, if any is to be adjusted in the People's Republic of China according to China Council for the Promotion of International Trade Provisional Rules for General Average Adjustment dated January 1st 1975.

共同海损   如发生共同海损，应在中华人民共和国根据 1975 年 1 月 1 日中国国际贸易促进委员会共同海损理算暂行规则进行理算。

- BOTH-TO-BLAME COLLISION   If the vessel comes into collision with another vessel as a result of the negligence of the other vessel and any act, neglect or default of the master, mariner, pilot or of the servants of the Carrier in the navigation or in the management of the vessel, the owners of the goods carried hereunder will indemnify the Carrier against all loss or liability to the other or non-carrying vessel or her owners as part of their claim against the carrying ship or Carrier. The foregoing provisions shall also apply where the Owners, operators or those in charge of any vessel or vessels or objects other than or in addition to the colliding vessels or objects are at fault in respect of a collision, contact stranding or other accident.

双方有责碰撞条款   如本船由于他船疏忽以及本船船长、船员、引航员或承运人的雇佣人员在驾驶或管理船舶中的行为、疏忽或不履行职责而与他船碰撞，则根据本提单承运的货物的所有人应补偿承运人的一切损失或对他船亦即非载货船舶或其所有人的赔偿责任，但此种补偿应以上述损失或赔偿责任所体现的已由或应由他船亦即非载货船舶或其所有人付与上述货物所有人其货物所受灭失或损坏或其提出的任何索赔数额为限，且这种损失或赔偿责任已由他船即非载货船舶作为其向载货船的或承运人提出的索赔的一部分，将其冲抵、扣除或收回。在非属相碰船舶或物体的、或在相碰船舶之外的任何船舶或物体的所有人、经营人或主管人，在碰撞、触碰、搁浅或其他事故中犯有过失时，上述规定亦应适用。

8.3.4   租船合同翻译节选

- Owners' Responsibility Clause

Owners are to be responsible for loss of or damage to the goods of for delay in delivery of the goods only in case the loss, damage or delay has been caused by the improper or negligent stowage of the goods (unless stowage performed by Shippers/Charterers or their stevedores or servants) or by personal want of due diligence on the part of the Owners or their Manager to make the vessel in all respects seaworthy and to secure that she is properly manned, equipped and supplied or by the personal act or default of the Owners or their Manager.

And the Owners are responsible for no loss or damage or delay arising from any other cause whatsoever, even from the neglect or default of the Captain or crew or some other person employed by the Owners on board or ashore for whose acts they would, but for this clause, be responsible, or from unseaworthiness of the vessel on loading or commencement of the voyage or at any time whatsoever. Damage caused by contact with or leakage, smell or evaporation from other goods or by the inflammable or explosive nature or insufficient package of other goods not to be considered as caused by improper or negligent stowage, even if in fact so caused.

船舶所有人责任条款

船舶所有人对货物的灭失、损坏或延迟交付的责任限于造成灭失、损坏或延迟的原因是由于货物积载不当或疏忽(积载由托运人/承租人或其装卸工人或受雇人完成者除外),或者是由于船舶所有人或其经理人本身没有恪尽职守使船舶各方面适航,并保证适当配备船员、装备船舶和配备供应品,或由于船舶所有人或其经理人本身的行为或不履行职责。

船舶所有人对由于其他任何原因造成的货物灭失、损坏或延迟,即使是由于船长或船员或其他船舶所有人雇佣的船上或岸上的人员的疏忽或不履行职责(如无本条规定,船舶所有人应对他们的行为负责)、或是由于船舶在装货或开航当时或其他任何时候不适航所造成,亦概不负责。由于其他货物的接触或泄漏、气味或挥发,或由于其他货物的易燃或易爆性质或包装不充分而造成的损坏,即使事实上是由于积载不当或疏忽所致亦不应视为由此而造成。

("GENCON" CHARTER "金康"租船合同)

- In the event of accident, danger, damage, or disaster, before or after commencement of the voyage resulting from any cause whatsoever, whether due to negligence or not, for which, or for the consequence of which, the carrier is not responsible, by statute, contract, or otherwise, the goods, the shipper and the consignee, jointly and severally, shall contribute with the carrier in general average to the payment of any sacrifices, losses, or expenses of a general average nature that may be made or incurred, and shall pay salvage and special charges incurred in respect of the goods. If a salving ship is owned or operated by the carrier, salvage shall be paid for as fully and in the same manner as if such salving ship or ships belonged to strangers.

Provisions as to General Average in accordance with the above are to be included in all bills of lading issued hereunder.

船舶在开航之前或开航之后,由于任何原因,不论是否因疏忽所致,发生事故、危险、损害或灾难,而承运人依据法规、合同或其他规定对此或其后果不负责任,则货物、托运人和收货人应连带地同承运人在共同海损中分摊因此所产生或引起的具有共同海损性质的任何牺牲、灭失或费用,并应支付有关货物的救助报酬和特别费用。如救助船为承运人所拥有或经营,救助报酬应如同此救助船属于他人一样,以同样的方式全额支付。

上述有关共同海损的规定应订入根据本租船合同签发的所有提单。

(Time Charter, PRODUCE FORM 定期租船合同"土产格式")

8.4 商务合同的翻译

8.4.1 合同文体概述

A contract shall be an agreement whereby the parties establish, change or terminate their civil relationship.《中华人民共和国民法通则》之 85 条：合同是当事人之间设立、变更、终止民事关系的协议。

Contracts referred to in this Law are agreements between equal natural persons, legal persons and other organizations for the purpose of establishing, altering and terminating mutual civil rights and obligations.《中华人民共和国合同法》之第 2 条：合同是平等主体的自然人、法人、其他组织之间设立、变更、终止民事权利义务关系的协议。

合同的文体特征主要体现在合同使用的词汇和句法结构上。

从用词范围来看，英语合同的用词属普通词汇及文学词汇，即标准英语的范畴。在文学词汇中，最具特色的是由 where，there 与 in，by，with，after 等构成的复合词汇，它们仅用于合同及法律文体中。这类词汇的特点是明晰古朴。尽管 thereinafter 的意义与 in that part which follows 相等，但前者简洁明了，后者却累赘冗长。

常用古体词的意义及用法举例：

Hereby：by means of；by reason of this 特此，因此，兹等意，常用于法律文件、合同、协议书等正式文件的开头语；在条款中需要强调时也可用。

- This Contract is hereby made and concluded by and between _____ Co. (hereinafter referred to as Party A) and _____ Co. (hereinafter referred to as Party B) on _____ (Date), in _____ (Place), China, on the principle of equality and mutual benefit and through amicable consultation.

本合同双方，_____公司(以下称甲方)与_____公司(以下称乙方)，在平等互利基础上，通过友好协商，于_____年_____月_____日在中国_____ (地点)，特签订本合同。

- The Parties to this Contract, in the spirit of friendly cooperation, hereby signed and concluded this Contract in accordance with the following terms and conditions：

双方本着友好合作的精神，特签订本合同，其条款如下：

Hereof：of this 关于此点，在本文件中。

- Foreign trade dealers as mentioned in this Law shall, in accordance with the provisions hereof, cover such legal entities and other organizations as are engaged in foreign trade dealings. 本法所称对外贸易经营者，是指依照本法规定从事对外贸易经营活动的法人和其他组织。

- If, as a result of withdrawal or any other reasons, an arbitrator fails to perform his duties as an arbitrator, another arbitrator shall, in accordance with the provisions hereof, be selected or appointed. 仲裁员因回避或者其他原因不能履行职责的，应当依照本法规定重新选定或指定仲裁员。

- The Attachments to this Contract shall be deemed a part hereof and shall be effective as any other provision hereof. 本合同的附件应被视为本合同的一部分，与其他条款有同样效力。

Hereto：to this 至此，对此。

- This Contract shall be in duplicate, to be held by each of the Parties hereto and shall have two copies kept by each of the Parties hereto for the record.

本合同一式两份，合同双方各执一份，并各保留两份复印件，供双方存档。

- The scope of Works of this Contract shall be specified in such Drawings and bills of Quantities as are attached hereto. 本合同工程范围应按所附的图纸及工程量表中规定的范围。

- In the event that there shall be newly increased items of Work, the Parties hereto shall enter into an agreement for the unit price of such items.

如果需新增加工程，双方应另行协定该项新增工程的单价。

Herein：in this 此中，于此。

- The term "company" mentioned herein refers to a limited liability company or a company limited by shares established within the territory of China in accordance with this Law.

本法所称公司是指依照本法在中国境内设立的有限责任公司和股份有限公司。

- The terms "FOB", "CFR" or "CIF" shall be subject to the "International Rules for the Interpretation of Trade Terms" (INCOTERMS, 2010) provided by International Chamber of Commerce (ICC) unless otherwise specified herein (in this Contract).

除非本合同另有规定，"FOB"、"CFR"和"CIF"均应依照国际商会制定的《国际贸易术语解释通则(INCOTERMS) 2010》办理。

- The procedures contained herein shall be followed by the concerned agencies of the People's Republic of China (PRC), responsible for the implementation of the Bank-supported projects.

执行世界银行贷款项目的中华人民共和国各有关机构，均遵循本文所规定的程序。

Hereinafter：later in the same Contract 以下，在下文。一般与 to be referred to as, referred to as, called 等词组连用，以避免重复。

- In accordance with the Law of the People's Republic of China on Chinese-Foreign Equity Joint Ventures and the Contract signed by and between _____ Co. (hereinafter referred to as Party A) and _____ Co. (hereinafter referred to as Party B), the articles of association hereby is formulated and prepared.

根据《中华人民共和国中外合资经营企业法》以及由_____公司(以下称甲方)与_____公司(以下称乙方)所订的合资经营的合同，特制订本公司章程。

- When existing Chinese-foreign equity joint ventures, Chinese-foreign cooperative joint ventures and wholly foreign-owned enterprises (hereinafter referred to as "enterprises with foreign investment") apply to reorganize themselves into a company, the enterprises with foreign investment shall have a record of making profits for the recent three consecutive years.

已设立的中外合资经营企业、中外合作经营企业、外资企业(以下简称外商投资企业），如申请转变为公司，应有最近连续 3 年的盈利记录。

• The following words and expressions in the Contract (as hereinafter defined) shall have the meanings hereby assigned to them, except where the Contract otherwise requires.

以下合同（如下文定义）中的用语和用词，除根据合同另有要求者外，应具有下述所赋予它们的涵义。

Therein：in that；in that particular context；in that respect. 在那里；在那点上，在那方面。

• "Temporary Works" means all temporary works of every kind (other than the Contractor's Equipment) required in or about the execution and completion of the Works and the remedying of any defects therein.

"临时工程"是指在工程施工、竣工和修补工程中任何缺陷时需要或与上述工程阶段有关的所有各种临时工程，但承包人的设备除外。

• A certificate of the Borrower shall, substantially, comply with the form set forth in Appendix 4, and the attachments specified therein.

借款人证明书，其格式基本上应遵照附录 4 规定的格式及其规定的附件。

• The Contractor shall, with due care and diligence, design (to the extent provided for by the Contract), execute and complete the Works and remedy any defects therein under the provisions of the Contract.

承包人应根据合同的各项规定，细心谨慎，恪尽职守，设计（在合同规定的范围内）、施工和完成工程，并修补工程中缺陷。

Thereof：of that, of it 它的，其。

• The headings and marginal notes in these conditions shall not be deemed part thereof or be taken into consideration in the interpretation or construction thereof of the Contract.

合同条款中的标题及旁注不应视为条款的一部分，在合同条款或合同本身的解释中也不应加以考虑。

• Arbitration：All disputes in connection with the Contract or arising in the execution thereof shall first be settled amicably by negotiation. In case no settlement can be reached, the case under dispute may then be submitted for arbitration.

凡有关该合同或因执行该合同而发生的一切争执，双方应以友好的方式协商解决，如协商不能解决，可提交仲裁。

• "Time for Completion" means the time for completing the execution of and passing the Test on Completion of the Works or any section or part thereof as stated in the Contract (or as extended under Clause 44) calculated from the Commencement Date.

"竣工时间"指合同规定从工程开工日期算起（或按第 44 条延长工期）到工程或其任何部分或区段施工结束并且通过竣工检验的时间。

Thereafter：after that 此后。

• The Contractor shall, during the execution of the Works and thereafter, provide all necessary superintendence as long as the Engineer may consider necessary for the proper fulfilling of the Contractor's obligations under the Contract.

只要工程师认为是为正确履行合同规定的承包人义务所必需时，承包人应在工程施工期间及其后，提供一切必要的监督。

Thereto：to that 向那里。

• "Contract Products" means the products specified in Appendix 2 to this Contract, together with all improvement and modifications thereof or developments with respect thereto.

"合同产品"，系指本合同附件 2 中规定的产品及其改进开发的产品。

Therewith：with that 以此；此外。

• The Contractor shall be deemed to have inspected and examined the Site and its surroundings and information available in connection therewith and to have satisfied himself.

承包人应被视为对现场、其周围环境及其相关已有资料已进行了检查和考察。

合同词汇的另一个特征是同义词或近义词叠用。这种叠用，确保了合同所用词语的意思不被曲解，并使原文意思高度完整、准确，更好地体现合同作为法律文书的严肃性。如：

• It is the intent of the parties that all documents and annexes forming part hereof shall be read and taken together and that each and every provision or stipulation hereof be given full force, effect and applicability. However, in the event that one or more provisions or stipulations herein be declared null and void by the courts, or otherwise rendered ineffective, the remaining provisions and stipulations shall not be affected thereby.

在这两个句子中，近义词并用多达七处之多，的确是英语合同文体的语言特征之一。然而，这种现象在中文合同中并不多见，不仅是因为中英文的语言表达习惯不同，而且还与中国和英语国家之间的法律文化传统的差异有关。因此，在翻译英语近义词叠用的时候应谨慎为之。

再以下列叠用为例：

• able and willing 能够与愿意

• accord and satisfaction 协议与补偿；和解与清偿协议（允许合同一方支付一笔款项，以获得免除合同中规定的责任）

• agent or representative 代表

• alteration，modification or substitution 变更，修改或替代

• any part or parts of it 其中任何部分

• arising or resulting from 引起

• arrest or restraint 拘捕/留

• be null and void and of no effect 作废并无效

• claim or allegation 主张

• covenants or agreements 契约或协议

• express or imply 明指或暗示

• insufficiency or inadequacy 不足

• loss，injury or damage 失踪，受伤或伤害

- loss or damage 灭失或损坏
- negligence，fault，or failure in the duties and obligations 未履行责任和义务
- purchase or sell 买卖
- stipulations and provisions 条款
- survey or inspection 勘验或检查
- terms or conditions 条款
- use，misuse or abuse 使用，误用或滥用
- void and voidable 无效的和可以撤销的
- voidable and void 可以撤销的甚至无效的
- approve and accept 认可并接受

上述这种词语叠用并非可有可无，在合同中它们可使合同语言更加精确严谨。根据词性分类，这种词语叠用包括：

名词叠用，如：
- power and authority 权力与威信
- kind and nature 种类

动词叠用，如：
- alter and change 变更
- bind and obligate 承担

形容词叠用，如：
- sole and exclusive 唯一的
- final and conclusive 确定的

连词叠用，如：
- when and as 当……时候

介词叠用，如：
- before and on 在……以前
- from and above 上述

从词语叠用的功能来考察，在合同中只有少数近义词并列使用是为了追求它们之间的意义相同，以不被曲解，翻译时，我们只要取其相同含义即可，例如：
- null and void 无效
- terms and conditions 条款
- provisions and stipulations 规定

而多数近义词叠用是为了强调它们之间的意义差别，使表达更加完整准确。难点是识别近义词之间的细微的差别，找出汉语中对应的词语，并符合中文的措辞习惯。此外，我们还要弄清近义词叠用的意图，以免误译。下面举两例说明。

- All permits，taxes and other fees arising from the <u>prosecution and execution</u> of the project shall be solely shouldered by the Contractor.

原译：项目<u>施工过程</u>中所产生的许可证费、税费及其他费用全部由承包方负担。

改译：项目<u>执行、施工过程</u>中所产生的许可证费、税费及其他费用均由承包方承担。

句中，prosecution and execution 为近义词，分别译为"执行"和"施工"。由于该句中有 permits"许可证费"一词，而许可证手续通常应在工程施工前办理，否则就算违规操作。因此，这里叠用是为了强调词语的差别意义。而原译中的"施工"仅指工程动工、建设进行之中，没有包括"工程动工前办理必要的手续等准备工作"这一含义，与原文的含义不吻合。

● Any supplement, <u>modification or alternation</u> agreed by both parties shall be taken as an integral part of the contract, and has the equal legal force as the contract itself.

原译：经双方同意对本合同的任何补充、<u>修改</u>应作为合同不可分割的组成部分，并具有与合同同等的法律效力。

改译：经双方同意对本合同所作的任何补充、<u>修改或变更</u>应作为合同不可分割的组成部分，并具有与合同同等的法律效力。

原译也只追求 modification or alteration 两词之间的相同意义，而忽视了合同当事人还可对合同做出实质性变动，使原合同在法律上无效这一层含义。所以原文中 modification or alteration 叠用是为了强调它们之间的差别，可译为"修改或变更"。

从句法结构上说，合同文体多用陈述句和祈使句，而平行结构在合同中用得较多，这种结构利于扩充句子的含量。平行的部分一般表示名称及目的。平行结构采取具体地逐一列举的形式而不采用概括形式，既有条理又能准确无误地表达思想。

8.4.2　合同翻译须遵循的原则

根据合同的文体特征，合同翻译必须遵循八字基本原则：准确严谨，规范通顺。译文既要准确无误地表达原文的内容，这种表达是要符合法律语言的要求与规律，又要符合合同文体的规范标准，读起来通顺流畅。通顺不能简单地理解为易解和流畅，翻译时不能拘泥于原文的词句结构的束缚，通顺的合同翻译应体现在条理清晰上，因为涉外合同的条款一般相当繁复，翻译时译者首先要弄清全文的条理，仔细揣摩各条款间的制约关系，吃透其实质内涵。合同条款表现方式独特，英汉语言有时出入很大，所以在理解原文的基础上，应尽量使译文明确清晰，符合法律文件的语言特点，切不可望文生义或按原文逐字逐句死翻硬译。当准确严谨与规范通顺不能兼顾时，一定要选择准确严谨。

由于国际商务合同的专业性和兼容性越来越强，因此，合同的内容也就越来越精确。译者在翻译合同文件时应把准确严谨作为首要标准，要特别重视合同中法律术语、关键词语的翻译，仅做到忠实原文，是很难体现出合同语言的准确严谨的。以 offer 和 accept 两词为例，将前者译为"提供、提议"，而将后者译为"接受、认可、同意"，从字面上来说是对的，译出了该词的本义，做到了"信"。然而在商务合同中，offer 应译为"要约"，相应地，"要约人"为 offerer，offeree 为"受要约人"；accept 应译为"承诺"，相应地，"承诺人"是 acceptor，acceptee 则为"接受承诺人"，其他译法皆属不当。

合同文本的翻译不同于文学作品的翻译，它要求的是把"准确严谨"置于首位，避免产生歧义。在翻译专业术语和关键词语时，译者必须透彻地理解原语的所指，对原文的内容既不歪曲，也不随意增减。"独占区域"exclusive territory，表示许可方不得再把同样内容的技术许可协议授予该地域内的任何第三方，就连许可人本身也不得在该地域使用该技术；但是，exclusive contract 则为"专销合同"，表示 An agreement between manufacturer and retailer that prohibits the retailer from carrying the product lines of firms to firms that are the rivals of the manufacturer，术语必须准确。

翻译国际商务合同的第二个标准是"规范通顺"（Expressiveness and Smoothness）。译者要把理解了的原文，用规范通顺的、合乎合同语言要求的目的语表达出来。例：

● By irrevocable Letter of Credit available by Sellers documentary bill at sight to be valid for negotiation in China until 15 days after date of shipment，the Letter of Credit must reach the Sellers 30 days before the contracted month of shipment.

原译文：以不可取消的信用证，凭卖方即期付有单据的票据协商，有效期应为装运期15 天后在中国到期，该信用证必须于合同规定的装运月份前 30 天到达卖方。

原译文下列几处翻译不妥。（1）Irrevocable Letter of Credit 是指 a Letter of Credit which cannot be altered or cancelled once it has been negotiated between the buyer and his bank，原译文用"不可取消的信用证"也能表达原文，但其行话应该是"不可撤销的信用证"。（2）documentary bill at sight 译为"即期付有单据的票据"，概念不清，因为"票据"是指出票人签名于票上，约定自己或委托他人，以无条件支付一定金额为目的的有价证券。其本身的含义是广义的，按照《中华人民共和国票据法》的规定，票据包括汇票、本票和支票。那么，在涉外合同支付中的票据主要指"汇票"。因此，该条约中的 bill 应理解为"汇票"。至于 documentary bill 是指 a bill to which documents are attached，应译为"跟单汇票"。（3）negotiation 在涉外票据结算中是指 the giving of value for bills（drafts）or documents by the bank authorized to negotiate，其行话应该译成"议付"。（4）until 15 days after date of shipment，应该是"装运期后的 15 天"。

改译：以不可撤销信用证，凭卖方即期跟单汇票议付，有效期应为装运期后 15 天在中国到期。该信用证必须于合同规定的装运月份前 30 天到达卖方。

● 乙方保证是本合同规定提供的一切专有技术和技术资料的合法所有者，并有权向甲方转让。如果发生第三方指控侵权，由乙方负责与第三方交涉，并承担法律上和经济上的全部责任。

原译文：Party B guarantees that he is the legitimate owner of the know-how and technical documentation supplied to Party A in accordance with the contract and that he has the right to transfer them to Party A. If the third party accuses Party B of infringement，Party B shall take up the matter with the third party and bear all legal and economic responsibilities arising therefrom.

对上面的译文分析如下：

1. Party B guarantees that he…，该句的宾语从句中的主语用 he 不符合本文体限用代词的要求；

2. supplied to Party A 应加上 supplied 动作的发出者 by Party B，使全句意思完整表达清晰；

3. in accordance with the Contract，这句原文的含义是指"按合同中规定的条款"，所以应改成 in accordance with the stipulations of the Contract 才能体现出与原文的一致性；

4. Party B has the right to transfer 应改译为 Party B is lawfully in a position to transfer，这

样更能强调乙方对技术和资料的绝对合法性；

5. if the third party accuses Party B of infringement 有两处明显错误：（1）the third party 给人一种印象：甲乙双方似乎都已知道"第三方"是谁。而实际并非如此，所以应改为 any/a third party；（2）to accuse sb. of sth. 一般是"控诉某人触犯刑律"，而这句中的"指控"仅指一般的民事侵权，故应改译成 to bring a charge of infringement；

6. Party B shall take up the matter with the third party，此译文中的 take up sth with sb 是指"口头或书面向某人提出某事"，没有能确切地译出原文中"由乙方负责与第三方交涉"的本意，故应改译成 Party B shall be responsible for dealing with the third party. 最后，bear all the legal and economic responsibilities arising therefrom，"全部责任"指的是"由于上述"原因而发生的乙方应承担的责任，所以"全部"应选用 full 而不用 all。另外，"承担由此引起的法律和经济责任"应译为 bear the legal and financial responsibilities which may arise。

改译：Party B guarantees that Party B, is the legitimate owner of the know-how and technical documentation supplied by Party B to Party A in accordance with the stipulations of the Contract, and that Party B is lawfully in a position to transfer the above-mentioned know-how and technical documentation to Party A. If any/a third party brings a charge of infringement, Party B shall be responsible for dealing with the third party and bear the full legal and financial responsibilities which may arise therefrom.

• During the period from the date of effectiveness to the termination of the Contract, the two Parties shall hold a meeting every year to discuss problems in the execution of the Contract, to exchange views on technical development and improvement and lay a foundation for further technical cooperation. The aforesaid meeting shall be held in the two countries in turn. The contents and conclusion of such discussions shall be written in memorandum. The number of attendants of each party shall be no more than five persons. Each party shall bear its own expenses.

原译：在合同生效之日起到合同终止之日的期间内，双方每年举行一次会议，讨论合同履行中出现的问题，以及就技术发展与改善问题进行交换意见，这样可以为进一步的技术合作打下一个基础。前面提及的会议，轮流在两国举行，讨论的内容和结论将载入备忘录中，各方参加人员不超过5人，各方承担自己的费用。

原文没有难以理解的内容，原译文也基本上符合原文的意思，但是译文只是逐字逐句地照译，读起来感觉像读大白话，译文没有体现合同文献的语言特点。

改译：本合同有效期间，双方应每年正式会晤一次，以便讨论本合同履行期间存在的问题，以及就技术改进与创新问题进行交流，为加强双方的技术合作奠定基础。双方的会晤应轮流在两国举行。讨论的内容和结论应记入备忘录，各方参加人员仅限5人，费用自理。

上述的翻译原则要求译者具备相当广博的国际商务及贸易知识，精通相关的术语及行话。这些知识包括：我国的涉外法律、法规，WTO 规则，国际贸易惯例，以及相关的业务知识如商品、市场、商检、保险、国际金融、仲裁、汇率乃至投资、税法、外汇管理、技术服务、知识产权等。

同样的一个词，在不同的上下文里有其不一样的意义。即使在同一商务文体中也是这样。以英语 market 一词为例，在不同的上下文中，该词具有不同的释义。

- The retail list price of party A's products represents the fair market value（公平市价）to the consumer. 甲方产品的零售定价对于顾客来讲是一种公平市价。

- We shall write to you again once our end-users are in the market（要买货）for your product. 一旦我方用户对贵方产品有需要时，我们会另函告知你。

- We are glad to say that just now the market（行情）is in a very strong position.
我们高兴地告知贵方现在行情上涨。

此外，译者还须具备踏实严谨的译风，具有高度的责任心，因为商务合同的翻译涉及各方的经济利益，甚至某国的主权原则。译者在翻译合同时不应仅考虑翻译本身，还要考虑到法律、经济、社会等诸方面的因素。对于合同中的条款细节逐一看清弄明，尤其是名称、符号、数据等，一旦误译，损失不可估量。如果合同内容与我国现行的法律、政策等相悖，译者就应及时指出，不可含糊照译，不计后果。

译者除了具备翻译理论外，还必须进行大量的翻译实践，才能不断提高翻译水平。

- 买方应在货到目的港 30 天内向卖方提交索赔通知，在此期间如卖方未接到买方索赔通知及公证行开立的公证报告，则认为买方无索赔要求。

译文：Buyer must give Seller notice of any claim within 30 days after arrival of goods at port of destination. Unless such notice, accompanied by proof certified by an authorized surveyor, arrives at the Seller's office during such 30 days period, Buyer shall be deemed to have no claim.

初看，上述译文似乎没什么大问题，但仔细推敲我们还会发现一些不尽如人意的地方。在 notice of any claim 前应加上 written 一词，表示索赔须以书面形式提出；"无索赔要求"译为 to have no claim 欠妥。原文的内涵应被理解为：买方在规定的索赔期内提出索赔的要求，这是买方的权利，但是如果有效期届满而买方没有提出索赔要求，应该认为买方放弃了这种权利。所以，最好改译为：to have waived any claim。

- Licensee will furnish to Party A copies of insurance policies and/or the endorsements.

原译：领有许可证者将给甲方提供几份保险政策和背书。

上述译文行家一看便知有问题。一是 policies，二是 endorsements。insurance policy 保险业中指 an agreement between an insurance company and person insured，即"保险单"；endorsement 这里的含义是 a signature on the reverse of a negotiable instrument made primarily for the purpose of transferring the holder's rights to another person，这是票据业务中的概念"保险单上的变更条款"。

改译：受让方（受证人）将给甲方提供几份保险单和/或保险单上所加的变更保险范围的条款。

- Three full sets of negotiable, clean on board, original ocean Bill of Lading made out to the order of shipper and blank endorsed, notifying China National Foreign Trade Transportation Corporation at the port of destination.

原译：全套清洁海运提单正本三份，可议付的，以发运人为命令的，空白背书通知目的港的中国对外贸易运输公司。

Negotiable 有"可议付的"意思，当它用来修饰 bill of lading 时，则理解为"可转让的"，negotiable bill of lading 指"可凭借背书将提单所列货物的所有权转让给他人的提单"，通常译为"可转让提单"。to the order of…在票据和提单业务中意为"以……为抬头，凭……指示"，如：Clean shipped on board Ocean Bills of Lading in full set made out to the order of shipper and endorsed to the order of Bank of China，Tianjin Branch. 全套清洁的已装船海运提单，以发运人为抬头，背书凭中国银行天津分行指示。

改译：全套清洁海运提单正本三份，可转让，以发运人为抬头，空白背书，通知目的港的中国外贸运输公司。

8.4.3　合同中一些常见词语的用法及翻译

8.4.3.1　shall 的正确使用

从英语单词在合同中的使用频率来说，shall 为频率最高的词汇之一。它是一个极为严谨的法律文件的专用词。在国际商务合同中，shall 主要表示应当履行的义务、债务和应承担的法律责任。如果未履行 shall 表明的合同上的义务（obligation），则视为违约（breach of contract）而构成违约责任。因此，在使用 shall 一词时，一定要说明一种合同上的义务，如果与权利、义务无关，则应避免使用。Shall 一词不受主语的人称影响。至于 shall 一词的译法，应根据合同的具体内容采用灵活的译法，一般可译为"应当""必须"，也可处理为"将""可以"或不译出来。如：

• Any dispute, controversy or claim arising out of or relating to this Contract, or the breach, termination or invalidity thereof, shall be settled through amicable negotiation, in case no settlement can be reached through negotiation, the case shall then be submitted for arbitration. The location of arbitration shall be in the Country of the domicile of the defendant.

由于违反本合同，终止本合同或者本合同无效而发生的、或与此有关的任何争端、争议或索赔，双方应通过友好协商解决；如果协商不能解决，应当提交仲裁。仲裁应当在被诉方所在国进行。

表示责任、义务和行文禁令的 shall

shall 在合同条款中最常见的用法有两种：一是主语为合同的签约方，谓语动词用 shall + 动词原形，表示该签约方必须履行的义务或责任，shall 也可接否定形式；二是句子主语是表示义务或责任的名词，shall 后接被动形式，表示必须被履行的义务或责任，或不得发生的行为。如：

• All technical documents shall be handed over in accordance with the requirements of the recipient's schedule for the project.

技术文件的交付时间应当符合受方工程计划的进度要求。

• The recipient shall undertake the obligation to keep confidential in accordance with the scope and duration agreed on in the Contract, the proprietary technology and related technology information provided or imparted by the supplier.

对供方提供或者传授的专有技术和有关技术资料，受方应当按照合同约定的范围和期

194

限承担保密义务。

- Party A <u>shall not</u> supply the contracted commodity to other buyers in the above mentioned territory. Direct enquires, if any, <u>shall</u> be referred to party B.

甲方<u>不得</u>向上述地区其他买主供应本合同项下商品。如有直接询价者，<u>应</u>让他们向乙方询价。

在合同中，当我们要平铺直叙地阐明签约的意图和内容，不是规定某合约方必须履行或不得采取的某种行为时，就不能滥用 shall，如：

- The organization form of the JVC is a limited liability company. The parties <u>shall</u> have no liability whatsoever for the debts or obligations of the JVC. The liability of each party in connection with the JVC <u>shall</u> be limited to its contribution to the equity capital of the JVC.

合资公司的组织形式为有限责任公司。双方对所合营公司的债务和义务不负任何责任。各方对合营公司的责任只限于其对合营公司的出资额。

上文中的两个 shall 均使用不当，因为所述均为理所当然的事，不是规定的义务或责任。

- This agreement <u>shall</u> (will) come into effect on its execution by the parties hereto, and the effective period of the agreement <u>shall</u> (will) cover 5 years. In case both parties find it desirable to carry on the cooperation between them upon the expiration of the agreement, an application to the effect **shall** be submitted to the department concerned under the Chinese Government for an extension thereof. The agreement <u>shall</u> (may) then be extended for another 5 years, or a new similar agreement <u>shall</u> (may) be executed by the two parties.

协议自签字之日起生效，有效期为五年。期满后，若双方有意继续合作，经向中国政府有关部门申请并获得批准后，可延期五年或重新签订相同的协议。

上句中只有第三个 shall 的使用是正确的，其余四个均为滥用，用括弧中所给的 will 或 may 是合适的。

shall 与 should

如前所述，"应""须""应当"在合同文本中出现频率很高，在合同及其他法律文书中，这些词实属法律词汇，译为"**shall**"表明其内容为"<u>强制性规范</u>"，即当事人必须遵守，否则就违约。而在实务中，把"应""须""应当"译为 should 的事例屡见不鲜。从法律角度而言，**should** 所表明的内容为"提倡性规范"，即当事人最好如此，如果不能，也就算了，最多受到道义上的谴责，并不构成违约。由此可见，将"应""须""应当"译为 should 实际上已将"强制性规范"变成了"提倡性规范"，两者间的含义有了本质的区别。例：

- 卖方应将下列单证递交银行议付。

原译：The seller <u>should</u> present the following documents to the bank for negotiation.

改译：The seller **shall** present the following documents to the bank for negotiation.

原译和改译仅一字之差，但其法律含义相差甚远。按原译，即使在缺少几份单证或单证不符的情况下，卖方亦可要求银行付款，而且银行不得以单证的不完整性为由而强行拒付。而 should 改为 shall 明确表示卖方必须向银行递交所有要求的单证，缺一不可，而单证应相符，否则银行可拒付。显然原译没有体现合同的严肃性。

8.4.3.2　be subject to

合同英语中，subject to 的基本含义为 depending on… as a condition，例如：

- The Contract is subject to government approval. 本合同须经政府批准方可生效。

其意相当于 The Contract shall be valid only if it is approved by the government；

它还可以表示 under the authority of or be obliged to obey，例：

- Subject to the terms to this Agreement, the Producer agrees to be bound by the terms to the following marketing agreement.

在本协议条件下，制造商同意接受下列销售协议各条款的约束。

- Subject to Clause 17, no variation in or modification of the terms to the Contract shall be made except by written amendment signed by the parties.

根据第 17 条规定，合同的任何变更或修改，必须以双方签定的修改文本为准。（这里 subject to 意为 in conformity with，同时，no…except 译成肯定的结构"必须"。）

- Subject to the above stipulations, the profits, losses and risks of the Joint Venture Company shall be borne by the Parties in proportion to their respective contributions to the registered capital of the Joint Venture Company.

在上述规定范围内，各方按各自对合资企业的注册资本出资比例分享合资企业的利润额，并承担合资企业遭受的亏损额和风险额。

- If any change is required regarding the terms and conditions of this Agreement, then both parties shall negotiate in order to find a suitable solution, provided that any change of this Agreement shall be subject to the approval by the Canadian Government.

如需对本协议条款进行修改，双方应协商解决，但对协议的任何修改内容必须经加拿大政府批准方为有效。

- The Contract is subject to approval of the Government of Import Country.

本合同须经进口国政府的批准。

- We make you the following offer, subject to the goods being unsold.

我方做出的如下报盘以货物未售出为有效。

8.4.3.3　provided that

例句：

- No salary shall be paid and charged against the operating expenses, provided that the commission or brokerage of the Second Party shall be paid and charged as a part of the operating expenses.

若应将支付第二方的佣金或回扣作为营业费用的一部分，则不应在营业费中支付和计算薪金。

使用 provided (that) 引导从句表示条件时，常表示当事人所希望的条件，它与 if 引导的条件从句不一样，试比较下例句子：

a) We can sell a lot of garments provided that your price is highly competitive.

如果贵方价格很有竞争性，我方就可大量出售服装。

b）If the technical documentation supplied by Party B is not in conformity with Clause 9. 1 to the Contract，Party B shall，within 30 days after the receipt of Party A's notification，airmail free of charge to Party A the correct，complete and legible version.

如果乙方提供技术资料不符合第 9 条第 1 款之规定，乙方应收到甲方的通知之日起 30 天内，免费将正确的、完整的、清晰易读的技术资料航空邮寄给甲方。

以上两例句中，第一例的条件是当事人所希望的条件，故用 provided that 引导；而第二例中的条件显然不是当事人所希望的或者应该出现的，只能用 if 引导。

• The Seller，provided that Buyer so agrees，may retain the whole or part of the said incomplete equipment，fabricated or unfabricated parts，work in process，and other material referred to in paragraph （D） of this Article in which the amount to be paid by the Buyer shall be reduced by a sum equal to the value of the property so retained.

如果买方同意，卖方可以全部或部分地保留上述未完成的设备、已加工或未加工的零件以及正在进行的工作和本条(D)款所述其他材料，这样就减去了买方支付这部分货物的费用。

• Provided that Party B desires to continue leasing the flat，Party B shall notify Party A in writing two months in advance of the expiry of the leased and a new lease contract shall be signed.

乙方若续租该套房，必须于合同期满前两个月书面通知甲方并另订租赁合同。

• Either party may at anytime replace the chairman，deputy chairman or director(s) it has appointed，provided that it gives written notice to the Joint Venture Company and the other party.

任何一方可随时更换自己委派的董事长、副董事长或董事，但必须书面通知合资公司和合资的另一方。

本句中的 provided that 译为"但是"，可使译文的过渡显得自然，符合汉语的表达习惯。如果译成"假如"则达不到此效果。

Provided that 是在商务合同中常见的表达法，此外我们还可用：

on condition that；

where；

suppose/supposing 等。如：

• Should the Seller fail to make delivery on time as stipulated in the Contract with the exception of *Force Majeure* specified in Clause 18 to this contract，the Buyers shall agree to postpone the delivery on condition that the Seller （should） agree to pay a penalty which shall be deducted by the paying bank from the payment under negotiation.

如果卖方并非因本合同第 18 条规定的不可抗力而未按合同规定的期限交货，那么，只要卖方同意支付罚金，并由付款行从议付款中扣除，买方便同意卖方延期交货。

8.4.3.4 "根据，依照，凭……，据……，按照"的几种不同译法

As per 按照，根据。例：

• Quality to be strictly as per the sample submitted by the Seller.

质量严格按照卖方提供的样品为准。

197

● We will soon send you our quotations by airmail <u>as per</u> your letter of Feb. 8, 2019.

根据贵方 2019 年 2 月 8 日函，我方尽快将报价航邮贵方。

In accordance with 根据，依据。这是一个书面语表达，语气较重，常含有"遵循"的意思。例：

● All disputes arising from the execution of, or in connection with this contract shall be settled amicably through friendly negotiation. In case no settlement can be reached through negotiation, the case shall then be submitted for arbitration. The location of arbitration shall be in the country of the domicile of the Defendant. If in China, the arbitration shall be conducted by the Foreign Trade Arbitration Commission of the China Council for the Promotion of International Trade, Beijing, <u>in accordance with</u> its Provisional Rules of Procedure.

凡因执行本合同所发生的或与本合同有关的一切争议，双方应通过友好协商来解决；如果协商不能解决，应提交仲裁。仲裁在被诉人所在国进行。在中国，由中国国际贸易促进委员会对外贸易仲裁委员会<u>根据</u>该会仲裁程序暂行规则进行仲裁。

According to 按照，根据，依照。本词语较之 IN ACCORDANCE WITH 更口语化，或者不那么正式。如：

● The undersigned Seller and Buyer have agreed to close the following transactions <u>according to</u> the terms and conditions stipulated below.

签约的买卖双方同意<u>按照</u>以下规定的条款达成下面的交易。

● <u>According to</u> our investigation, the goods were delivered as early as in February.

据我方所查，该货早在 2 月就交付了。

On the basis of 以……为根据，以……为依据。此词语本意为"在……基础上"，在合同文本中引申为"以……为根据/依据"。在实际应用中，此词语可用 **based on** 代替。例：

● We set the price of our crude oil <u>on the basis of</u> the price of the market.

我们<u>根据</u>市面价格给自己的原油定价。

● In the event that Party B fails to complete the work in time owing to such reasons as Party B shall be liable for, Party B shall pay a penalty for the default <u>based on</u> 1‰ of the total price for work per day, i. e., Party B shall pay one thousand one hundred and twenty nine (1, 129) U. S. Dollars only for each day of such default.

如果乙方因自身的原因而未及时完工，乙方应付违约罚金，每天<u>按</u>总价的千分之一计，即 1129 美元整。

In accord with 符合，与……一致。合同文本中，本词语着重强调"与……一致"的意思。例：

● Quality shall be <u>in accord with</u> the national standard. 产品必须<u>符合</u>国家标准。

Pursuant to 根据，按照。这是一个典型的契约书面语，一般文体很少用。例：

● Except as otherwise expressly provided herein, all notice <u>pursuant to</u> this Agreement shall be given by telex or cable or by notice in writing hand-delivered, sent by facsimile transmission or sent by airmail, postage prepaid.

除非另有规定，<u>按照</u>本协议，所有通知应以电传或电报方式送交，或专人递送的书面通知，也可由传真发送或邮资已付航邮寄达。

Under 根据，按照。如：

• All disputes arising in connection with the present contract shall be finally settled <u>under</u> the Rules of Conciliation and Arbitration of the International Chamber of Commerce by one or more arbitrators approved in accordance with the Rules.

与本合同有关的争议应<u>按照</u>国际商会的调解及仲裁规则由根据该规则核准认可的一名或多名仲裁员最终裁决。

• <u>Under</u> instruction from our head office, we are quoting our rates as follows.

<u>按</u>我方总部的指令，我们向贵方报价如下。

By 凭，依据。本词常用于合同的支付条款中，表示"以……为依据"。如：

• Payment <u>by</u> draft payable 90 days after sight, documents against acceptance.

<u>凭</u>见票后 90 天付款的汇票付款，承兑交单。

• Sales <u>by</u> specification, grade or standard.

<u>按照</u>规格、等级或标准销售。（by 相当于 as per）

Under and by 根据，按照。此两词叠用体现合同语的正式和准确无误。如：

• The trade terms shall be governed and construed <u>under and by</u> the latest Incoterms 2010.

贸易条款<u>根据</u>《2010 年国际贸易术语解释通则》的规定和解释为准。

Against 凭，依据，以……为条件。此词语也常用在支付条款中，相当于 subject to 的意思。

• Upon first presentation the buyers shall pay <u>against</u> documentary draft drawn by the sellers at sight, the shipping documents are to be delivered <u>against</u> payment only.

买方应<u>凭</u>卖方开具的即期跟单汇票见票即付，付款后即交装运单证。

上述条款中两个 against 的意思相当于 subject to，即"以……为条件"，前一个说明以卖方开具的即期跟单汇票为付款条件，而后一个意为先付款后交装运单证。又如：

• Documents <u>against</u> payment D/P 付款交单，指出口方在委托银行收款时，指示银行只有在付款人（进口方）付清货款时，才能向其交出货运单证，即交单以付款为条件，称为付款交单。

• Document <u>against</u> acceptance D/A 承兑交单，意为：Documents tendered to importer subject to his acceptance of the draft. 以进口人承兑汇票为条件而交货运单证。

In the light of 根据，依据。此词语通常后接 Condition，Principle，Theory，Spirit 等词。如：

<u>In the light of</u> the principle of equality, mutual benefits and supplying each other's needed goods, a trade protocol was signed between the two countries.

<u>根据</u>平等、互利、互通有无的原则两国签署了贸易协定书。

• Both Party A and Party B shall exccute the works <u>in the light of</u> the conditions of the said contract. 甲乙双方须<u>根据</u>所述合同条款进行施工。

In line with 依据/照。此语与 in accordance 可以互换。如：

• We don't think that your explanations are <u>in line with</u> the contractual stipulations.

我方认为，贵方未按合同规定进行解释。(贵方解释与合同规定不符。)

At 按、按照。此词常接 price 表示"按……价格"。如：

- Where the seller delivers to the buyer a quantity less than he has contracted to sell, the buyer may reject them, but if the buyer accepts the goods so dilivered he must pay for them <u>at</u> the contract price.

如果卖方交付给买方的货物少于合同所规定的数量，买方可以拒收此货。如果买方接受所交货物，则<u>应</u>按合同所定价格支付货款。

- Seller shall have the option of delivering 5% more or less on the contract quantity. Such surplus or deficiency shall be settled <u>at</u> the market price on the day of the vessel's arrival, the value shall be fixed by arbitration unless mutually agreed.

卖方有权按合同规定数量的 5% 溢短交货，溢短部分的价格<u>依</u>船抵之日的市价来定。如双方不能达成协议，该价格须通过仲裁确定。

In conformity with 遵照，按照。如：

- In consideration of the payments to be made by the Employer to the Contractor as hereinafter mentioned the contractor hereby covenants with the Employer to execute, complete and maintain the Works <u>in conformity</u> in all respects <u>with</u> the provisions of the Contract.

考虑到下文所述雇主将支付给承包人的各种款项，承包人特立此约向雇主保证全面<u>遵照</u>合同规定负责本工程的施工、交付和维修。

By virtue of 按照，根据。如：

- "Provisional Sum" means a sum included in the Contract and so designated in the Bill of Quantities for the execution of work or the supply of goods, materials, or services, or for contingencies, which sum may be used, in whole or in part, or not at all, at the direction and discretion of the Engineer. The contract price shall include only such amounts in respect of the work, supply or service to which such Provisional Sums relates as the Engineer shall approve or determine <u>by virtue of</u> this Clause.

"备用款"是指合同所含并在工程清单中指定的款项。它可用于施工、供货、供料、服务，或其他备用，按工程师的指令或由他决定全部或部分使用或完全不用。合同价须包括<u>根据</u>本条款由工程师批准或决定的与此备用款相关的工程、供应、或服务费用。

Subject to 根据，依据。此词主要指"依据……"，其意相当于 on the basis of/be based on. 例：

- "Contract Price" means the sum named in the Letter of Acceptance, <u>subject to</u> such additions thereto or deductions therefrom as may be made under the provisions hereinafter contained.

"合同价格"(亦说"发包价")是指中标通知书所述总额，该总额可<u>根据</u>下列各条规定增加或减少。

- The Contractor shall, <u>subject to</u> the provisions of the Contract, and with due care and diligence, execute and maintain the Works and provide all labor, including the supervision thereof, materials, constructional plant and all other things, whether of a temporary or permanent nature, required in and for such execution and maintenance.

承包人须根据本合同的各项规定，小心谨慎，恪尽职守地进行施工和维修，并提供所有劳务，包括工程监理、材料、施工设备以及施工和维修临时或永久需要的其他全部材料。

Hereby 根据，以此，据此。如：

- In the contract, as hereinafter defined, the following words and expressions shall have the meanings hereby assigned to them, except where the context otherwise requires.

本合同中，正如下文定义的，除非语境另有要求，下列词语及表达须具有本条款所确定的涵义。(hereby 这里相当于 by means of this clause.)

Whereby 据此。

- The terms shall include a provision whereby, in the event of any claim in respect of which, the Contractor would be entitled to receive indemnity under the policy being brought or made against the Employer, the insurer will indemnify the Employer against such claims and any costs, charges and expenses in respect thereof.

条款中须包括这一规定，根据此规定，如果承包人根据不利于雇主的保险单而有资格向雇主提出任何索赔，保险人应保障雇主不承担与此相关的赔偿金、诉讼费，及与此有关的费用。

As 按，按照。例：

- The Contractor shall ensure completion of the Works within the time for completion as defined in Clause 43 hereof.

承包人须确保该工程按本合同第43条之规定工期内竣工。

- As set forth in Clauses 2, 3, and 4 above.

按上述2, 3, 和4条规定。

8.4.4 常见的合同开头套用格式

- 由_____与_____于_____(时间)订立。

to be made by _____ and _____ on (date) _____.

- 由_____与_____同意按下列条款，签订本合同。

to be made by and between _____ and _____ according to the terms and conditions below.

- 合同由_____为一方和_____为另一方于_____(时间)在_____(地点)签订。

This Contract is signed in _____ (place) on _____ (day, month, year), by and between _____ on one hand and _____ on the other hand.

- 根据_____，本着_____，经过_____，双方同意_____。兹订立本合同。

In accordance with _____, adhering to _____ and through _____, both parties agree _____. The Contract is worked out thereunder.

201

• _____和_____经过_____，以_____和_____为基础签订本合同，并同意以下所述条款。

_____ and _____, through _____, have executed this contract on a basis of _____ and _____, agreed to the terms and conditions stipulated below:

8.4.5　合同翻译举例（靳涵身，2002）

8.4.5.1　开头语 Beginning

本合同由_____（以下称"卖方"）为一方和_____（以下称"买方"）为另一方于_____年_____月_____日在签订。

This Contract signed in _____（month）on _____（date），_____（year），by and between _____（hereinafter referred to as the "Seller"）and _____（hereinafter referred to as the "Buyer"）on the other hand.

8.4.5.2　买卖协议 Agreement

卖方将出售并交付给买方_____件产品，每件装_____千克。据此协议提供的产品符合_____贸易协会所规定的标准规格。

The Seller shall sell and deliver to the Buyer _____ units of products each unit to contain _____ kilograms of product. The product delivered under this Agreement shall conform to the standard specifications for the product adopted by the _____ Trade Association.

8.4.5.3　价格 Price

• _____（地名）离岸价格为每件_____美元。

The price shall be _____ dollars per unit, F. O. B. _____（place）.

• 卖方有权随时提高本合同所规定货物的价格。如果买方拒绝接受卖方的提价，买方可撤销合同。否则，此后发运的所有货物均按提高的价格计算。

The Seller shall have the right to increase the price of the goods specified in this contract at any time. If the Buyer refuses to accept the price increase specified by the Seller, the Buyer may cancel this Agreement. Unless this contract is so canceled, the increased price shall be charged for all goods shipped thereafter.

• 上述价格根据卖方工厂至买方仓库间的运费确定，如果运费增加或减少，规定价格须作相应的调整。

The price specified above is based on freight rates on the goods between the warehouse of the Buyer and the factory of the Seller. If such freight rates increase or decrease, the price specified shall be adjusted accordingly.

8.4.5.4　支付条款 Payment Terms

• 凭即期汇票和所附表明货物发运的提单通过_____银行以现金支付。汇票未付清之前，提单不交给买主。

Payment shall be made by net cash against sight draft with bill of lading attached showing the shipment of the goods. Such payment shall be made through the _____（bank）of _____（place）. The bill of lading shall not be delivered to the Buyer until such draft is paid.

● 从合同达成之日起在_____天内，买方根据本协议规定的条款，由一级银行开具不可撤销的信用证。

Within _____ days from the date of this Agreement, the Buyer shall establish an irrevocable letter of credit with a first class bank in compliance with the terms and conditions set forth in this contract.

● 对合同规定的货物付款不等于买方已接受货物的质量，所有货物须经买方检验后接受。

Payment for the goods specified herein shall not mean an acceptance there of by the Buyer with regard to its quality. All goods shall be accepted only after the Buyer's inspection.

● 在人民币基础上，合同价_____%用_____支付，_____% 用_____元支付。甲方将向乙方_____银行总行账号_____电汇上述以人民币为基础的_____元数额。人民币与_____元之间的汇率按收单当天银行公布的电传交易买价确定。

_____ percent of contract price shall be paid in _____ on the basis of RMB. _____ percent of contract price shall be paid in _____ dollar on the basis of RMB. Party A shall remit by cable the amount which is paid in _____ dollar on the basis of RMB as mentioned above to Party B Account No. _____ in the Bank of _____. The exchange rate between RMB and _____ dollar shall be computed according to _____ dollar telegraphic transfer buying rate quoted by the Bank of _____ on the date of the bill.

● 总额_____元以下列方式支付：

The total of ＄_____ should be disbursed in the following manner.

a)签约时付总额的40%，此款用于筹建动员。

40% of the total should be made during the signing of the Agreement. This payment should be used for mobilization.

b)工程完成75%时，第二期分期付款30%。

A second installment payment of 30% should be made upon completion of 75% of the works to be executed.

c)工程全部完成时，第三次分期付款完毕。

A third installment payment should be made upon 100% completion.

● 凭即期汇票和所附装运货物的提单以净现金支付。

Payment shall be made by net cash against sight draft with bill of lading attached showing the shipment of the goods.

8.4.5.5　数量 Quantity

● 如果无法售出所订购数量的货物，买方有权在卖方发货之前向卖方发出减货通知。如果卖方不同意减货，卖方可以撤销本合同。

If the Buyer is unable to sell out the amount of goods which he has agreed to purchase from the Seller, the Buyer may reduce the quantity of goods to be delivered to him by giving notice thereof to the Seller before the shipment is made. If the Seller refuses to agree to the reduction of the amount of goods to be delivered, the Seller may cancel this Agreement.

● 卖方有权减少发货量。若买方因减少发货而拒绝收货，此协议随即解除。

The Seller shall have the right to reduce the amount of the goods to be delivered to the Buyer. If the Buyer refuses to accept delivery of goods because of such reduction, this Agreement shall then be terminated.

● 合同允许_____%的溢短差额。

It is agreed that a margin of _____ percent shall be allowed for over or short count.

8.4.5.6　装运 Shipping

● 买方必须在指定的装船日期_____天以前提供装运通知，未提供上述装运通知应视为授权卖方无需另行通知就可以取消待发运的订货或在指定的装船日期_____天内的适当时候按原定价格装运。

The Buyer must get the shipping informed of at least _____ days before the designated date of shipment. Failure to furnish above mentioned shipping information will entitle the Seller, without further notice, to cancel order or to ship at its convenience within _____ days from the designated date of shipment at the agreed price.

● 合同达成后，由于意外情况而发生运费、保险费及装船时发生的其他额外费用，所增加的费用应由买方承担。

Should the freight, insurance premium and other extra expenses at the time of shipment be raised owing to unexpected circumstances after this contract is made, such additional expenses shall be borne by the Buyer.

● 买方必须及时提供装船通知和必需的舱位，否则，卖方没有按规定时间装船的义务。

The Buyer shall give shipping instructions in time and provide necessary shipping space, otherwise, the Seller shall not be under the obligation to make the shipment within the stipulated time.

● 买方未在_____（日期）或在_____（日期）之前向卖方提供装船通知时，卖方可撤销本合同，并要求买方赔偿由于其未提供装船通知给卖方所造成的损失。

In the event the Buyer does not furnish the Seller with shipping information on or before _____（date）, the Seller may at his option cancel this contract and demand the Buyer to pay any damages he has sustained on account of such failure on the part of the Buyer to give such information.

8.4.5.7　包装 PACKING

● 包装本合同所售货物所用的一次性容器费已包括在规定的价格之内。

The cost of the non-returnable containers of the goods sold under this Agreement is included in the price herein specified.

● 包装必须标有买方的订货单号，标明毛重、皮重和净重或数量。

The package must bear the Buyer's order number showing the gross, tare, and net weight or quantity.

8.4.5.8　货物交付 DELIVERY

● 买方可不仅限于前段所规定的条件而指定在任何地方交货，但买方应首先在规定的装船日期前至少_____天向卖方提供完整的书面装船通知，而且，买方要承担因变更交货地点所增加的额外运输费。

The Buyer shall have the right to order the goods delivered at any place in addition to that specified in the preceding paragraph, provided that he shall first furnish the Seller with full written shipping information at least _____ days prior to the day on which the shipment is to be made; and, the Buyer shall bear the additional transportation expense caused by the said change of delivery place.

• 卖方应按本合同规定的种类和数量，在指定的装运港口把货交到船边起重机吊钩能够达到的地方。

The Seller shall deliver the goods in the kind and quantity specified herein alongside the Buyer's vessel, within the reach of its loading tackle, at the appointed port of shipment.

• 交货必须在购货订单规定的时间内进行，否则，买方可取消订货而不承担任何损失，并要求卖方赔偿由于不交货所导致的一切损失。若延迟交货或不交货是由火灾、罢工、瘟疫、封港禁运、政府命令等卖方所不能控制的原因所引起，卖方则不负责任。

Delivery must be effected within the time stated on the purchase order, otherwise the Buyer may at its option cancel the order without cost to him, and charge the Seller for any loss incurred as a result of the latter's failure to make such delivery. The Seller shall not be held responsible for delay or failure of delivery when it is caused by fire, strike, epidemic, embargo, or instruction from the government or any other circumstances which, by their nature, the Seller is not in a position to control.

• 每票由卖方装运的货物将在_____港以离岸价格的方式交货。每票货只在一个港口交货。一旦所运货物越过买方所指定船只的船舷，便认定这些货物已由卖方转交给买方。

Each lot of EQUIPMTNE AND MATERIALS to be shipped by the SELLER shall be F. O. B. delivery at _____ port (place). Each lot is at one port only. The title and risk of the EQUIPMENT and MATERIALS shall be transferred from the Seller to the Buyer immediately after the same have passed the ship's rail of the carrying vessel designated by BUYER.

8.4.5.9 质量与检验 QUALITY AND SURVEY

• 买方有权在目的地接受货物之前对货物进行检验。卖方保证货物达到质量标准，没有瑕疵。卖方应付买方拒收瑕疵货物的检验费和运输费，并自检验之日起_____天内自费更换有瑕疵的货物。

The Buyer shall have the right to inspect the goods at the destination before accepting it. The Seller hereby is to warrant that the goods is up to the quality standard and is free from all defects. The Seller shall pay the cost of inspection and all transportation charges with regard to the rejected goods. The Seller shall replace at his expense all the goods, which are found to be defective with those up to standard within _____ days from the date of inspection.

• 双方同意制造厂（或_____商检人员）出具的质量、数量或重量检验证明书，并作为有关信用证项下的付款单证之一。对货物的质量、数量或重量的检验应按下列规定办理：货到目的港后_____天内由_____商品检验局复验，如发现质量、数量或重量与本合同规定不符，除属保险公司和船运公司负责者外，买方凭商品检验局出具的检验证明书，向卖方提出退货或索赔。退货或索赔引起的一切费用（包括保险费）及损失由卖方负担。在此情况下，如抽样可行的话，买方可应卖方的要求，将有关货物的样品寄给卖方。

It is mutually agreed that the Certificate of Quality and Quantity or Weight issued by the Manufacturer (or _____ Surveyor) shall be part of the document for payment with the adopted L/C. However, the inspection of quality and quantity or weight shall be made in accordance with the following:

In case the quality, quantity or weight of the goods is found not in conformity to those stipulated in this Contract after re-inspection by _____ within _____ days after the arrival of the goods at the port of destination, the Buyers shall return the goods to, or lodge claim against, the Seller for compensation of losses upon the strength of Inspection Certificate issued by the said Bureau, with the exception of those claims for which the insurers or the carriers are liable. All expenses (including insurance fees) and losses arising from the return of the goods or claims should be borne by the Sellers. In such cases, the Buyers may, if so requested, send some samples of the goods in question to the Sellers, so far as sampling is practicable.

8.4.5.10　保险 INSURANCE

● 在到岸价格基础上订立的合同，将由卖方按发票金额110%投保综合险、战争险、SRCC(即罢工、暴乱和民变)险。

In case the contract is concluded on CIF basis, the insurance shall be effected by the Seller for 110% of invoice value covering all risks, war risk, S. R. C. C. risks (i. e. Strike, Riot, and Civil Commotion).

● 如果合同签订以离岸价格或离岸加运费价格为基础，则由买方负责保险。货物装船完毕后，卖方应立即用电报或电传通知买方和收货人合同号码、商品名称、数量、毛重、发票金额和提单号、船名(或卡车号)和启运日期。如果因卖方未按时通知而造成货物不能及时投保，由此引起的一切损失由卖方承担。

The Buyer should effect the insurance if the contract is concluded on FOB or C&F basis. However, the Seller shall, immediately after the goods are completely loaded, cable or telex to notify the Buyer and the consignee of the contract number, name of the commodity, quantity, gross weight, invoice value and its number of B/L, name of the vessel (or truck No.), the date of shipment and ETS. In case the goods are not insured in time, owing to the Seller having failed to effect timely advice, any and all consequent losses shall be borne by the Seller.

8.4.5.11　不可抗力 FORCE MAJEURE/ACT OF GOD

● 不可抗力(免责风险)指当事人不能控制和没有过错或过失的偶发事件，包括但不仅仅限于战争、敌对行动(无论是否宣战)、侵略、外敌行为、叛乱、革命、暴动、军事或篡权行为、内战、罢工、暴乱、骚乱或混乱、地震或类似的自然力量引起的事件。这些事件是当事人不能控制、或虽通过正当途径但无法防止或抵御的。

Force Majeure ("Excepted Risks") shall mean an occurrence beyond the control and without the fault or negligence of the party affected including, but not limited to war, hostilities (whether war to be declared or not), invasion, act of foreign enemies, rebellion, revolution, insurrection or military or usurped power, civil war, strikes, riots, commotion or disorder, earthquakes, or any similar operation of forces of nature as are not within the control of the party affected and which, by the exercise of reasonable diligence, the said party is unable to prevent or provide against.

8.4.5.12　索赔 CLAIM

- 对本合同所售货物各种性质的索赔应在货物运抵提货单所指定的目的地后_____天内通知卖方。索赔的详细情况和合法鉴定人的书面报告在上述索赔通知卖方后_____天内空寄给卖方。

Any claims of whatever nature regarding the goods sold hereunder shall be notified to the Seller within _____ days after the arrival of the goods at the destination specified in the Bills of Lading. Full particulars of such claim, together with sworn surveyor's written report, shall be made and forwarded by airmail within _____ days after the said notification to the Seller.

- 货物运抵交付地点后，买方应立即检验货物，并在货到_____天内向卖方提出书面索赔通知。除非有铁路运输代理人对货运单的认可证明，否则，卖方将不对货物短失或损坏理赔。如未提出索赔通知，则表示买方无争议地接受了货物并应据本合同条款支付货款。

Upon the arrival of the goods at place of delivery, the Buyer shall immediately inspect the goods and shall give written notice of any claim to the Seller within _____ days after their arrival. Claims for loss or damage will not be considered unless supported by railroad agent's acknowledgement on freight bill. The failure to file such notice shall constitute irrevocable acceptance of the goods by the Buyer, who shall be bound to pay the price of the goods in accordance with the terms of the Agreement.

- 货物运抵目的港后_____天内，除应由保险公司和船主负责的索赔外，如果发现货物的质量、规格和数量与本合同规定不符，买方可凭由_____出具的检验证书，要求更换新货，或要求补偿。所有的费用(如检验费、退回不合格货物和运送替换物的运费、保险费、仓储费和装卸费等)由卖方负担。

Within _____ days after arrival of the goods at destination, should the quality, specification, or quantity be found not in conformity with the stipulations of the Contract except those claims for which the insurance company or the owners of the vessels are liable, the Buyer shall, on the strength of the Inspection Certificate issued by _____, have the right to claim for replacement with new goods, or for compensation, and all the expenses (such as inspection charges, freight for returning the goods and for sending the replacement, insurance premium, storage and loading and unloading charges, etc.) shall be borne by the Seller.

8.4.5.13　仲裁 ARBITRATION

- 凡因执行本合同所发生的或与本合同有关的一切争议，双方应通过友好协商解决。协商不能解决的应提交仲裁。仲裁地点为被告驻地所在国。在中国，由中国国际经济贸易仲裁委员会根据该会仲裁程序规则进行仲裁。在_____国(对方所在国国名)，则由_____(对方所在国仲裁机构的名称)根据该组织的仲裁程序和规则进行仲裁。仲裁裁决是终局的，对双方都有约束力。

All disputes arising from the execution of, or in connection with, this contract shall be settled amicably through friendly negotiation. In case no settlement can be reached through negotiation, the case shall then be submitted for arbitration. The location of arbitration shall be in the country where the defendant has his domicile. If in China, the arbitration shall be conducted by China International Economic and Trade Arbitration Commission, in accordance with its Rules of Procedure. If in _____ (country) the arbitration shall be conducted by _____ in accordance with its arbitrate rules of procedure. The arbitration award is final and binding upon both parties.

8.4.5.14　终止合同 TERMINATION

● 如果任何一方未能履行本协议对其规定的义务，另一方在向有过错的一方提出书面要求后有取消本协议的权利。如果有过错的一方未能满足其要求，协议将立即终止。

In case any party fails to perform any of its obligations under this Agreement, the other party reserves the right to cancel the Agreement after the demand in writing addressed to the defaulting party. If the defaulting party has not complied with the demand, the Agreement shall immediately terminate.

● 如果一方违背本合同的任何条款，并且未能在接到另一方的书面通知后_____日内予以补救，未违约方可向违约方书面通知终止本协议。

If any terms and conditions of this Agreement are breached and the breach is not corrected by any party within _____ days after a written notice thereof is given by the other party, the non-breaching party shall have the option to terminate this Agreement by giving written notice thereof to the breaching party.

练习

一、英译汉下列信用证常用句子。

1. We are pleased to inform you that we have opened an irrevocable and confirmed L/C.

2. As your L/C was negotiated through one of our bankers, please open a general L/C.

3. As this L/C is an open L/C, the negotiating bank is at your option.

4. We are glad to inform you that we have opened an L/C of US $88,000.
(We are pleased to let you know our opening of L/C for a sum of US $88,000.)

5. As you have not executed the order within the validity of L/C, we will make cancellation of L/C.

6. As the balance of L/C is US $80,000, please make shipment within the amount.

7. We think the details of L/C will be found on your close checking of the L/C.

8. We think the credit opened by us will be with you through the informing bank at the latest by the end of this week.

二、汉译英下列信用证常用句子。

1. 本信用证于 11 月 29 日到期。

2. 请让本公司了解信用证状况以便本公司安排装运。

3. 一旦贵方确认订单，本公司将立即申请开立信用证。

4. 本公司应贵方的要求允许将信用证延期至 10 月 19 日。

5. 由于接近装船时间，本公司要求贵方用传真开立信用证。

6. 贵方所述货物名称有误，请立即修正信用证。

7. 本公司信用证的有效期至 8 月 19 日。

8. 我方对外贸易时使用跟单信用证。

三、翻译下列信用证。

1. According to your request for opening L/C, we are pleased to inform you that we have airmailed today through the Bank of China an irrevocable L/C for US $1, 256,000 in favor of the New York Trading Co., Inc. on the following terms and conditions.

2. We have instructed the Bank of China to open an irrevocable letter of credit for US $188,000. This will be advised by the bankers' correspondents, Beijing City Commercial Bank. They will accept your draft on them at 30 days after sight for the amount of your invoice.

The credit is valid until January 20.

3. The letter of credit covering your order No. 89 has not yet reached us in spite of our repeated requests.

We have been working on the manufacturers to execute your order at higher prices.

Therefore we request you open an L/C urgently so that we can make the shipment stipulated.

4. Your order has been accepted on FOB basis.

Your L/C is described as C&F basis and some differences will be made between the invoice amount and the amount you require.

Therefore please amend the price of your L/C to FOB basis.

5. We pleased to confirm your order for PCs amounting to US $238,000.

As requested, we are preparing to make shipment by the end of June and would request you open an irrevocable L/C in our favor as soon as possible, valid until July 18.

四、翻译下列合同条款。

1. TRANSFER   Neither Party hereto shall assign this Agreement or any of its rights and interests hereunder without the other Party's prior written consent, which shall not be unreasonably withheld. Notwithstanding the above provision of this Clause, (a) Party A shall have the right to assign its rights to any subsidiary, affiliate or successor entity as long as Party A remains liable to perform all of its obligations under this Agreement as applicable, and (b) Party B may, without the consent of Party A, assign in whole, but not in part, its rights hereunder to any subsidiary, affiliate or successor entity of Party B or its ultimate parent company (provided that any such assignment to any such subsidiary shall not be deemed as a release of Party B's obligations hereunder unless Party A shall have given prior written consent to any such release and

Party B shall remain liable to Party A in respect of any breach of this Clause). Any attempted assignment in contravention of this Clause shall be void.

2. BREACH　If Party A materially breaches this Contract, Party B or its successor in interest is entitled to terminate this Contract or claim damages for the breach of contract. If Party B materially breaches this Contract, Party A is entitled to request Party B, by issuing a written notice, to redress the breach within fifteen (15) days upon receiving such notice. If Party B fails to redress the breach within the fifteen (15)-day period, Party A is entitled to rescind the Contract and claim damages for the breach of contract.

3. INFRINGEMENT AND LEGAL PROCEEDINGS

(a) The Licensee shall give the Licensor in writing full particulars of any use or proposed use by any other person, firm or company of a trade name, trademark or get-up of goods or means of promotion or advertising which amounts to or is likely to amount to infringement of the rights of the Licensor in relation to the Licensed Trademarks or contravention of the Anti-unfair Competition Law as soon as it becomes aware of such use or proposed use.

(b) If the Licensee becomes aware that any other person, firm or company alleges that any of the Licensed Trademarks is invalid or that use of the Licensed Trademarks infringes any rights of another party, the Licensee shall immediately give the Licensor in writing full particulars thereof and may make no disclosure of information or admission to any third party in respect thereof.

(c) The Licensor shall conduct all legal proceedings in respect of any infringement or alleged infringement of the Licensed Trademarks and any claim or counterclaim brought or threatened to be brought in connection with the use or registration of the Licensed Trademarks and shall in its absolute discretion decide what to do. The Licensor shall not be obliged to bring or defend any proceedings in relation to the Licensed Trademarks if the Licensee decides in its sole discretion to do so.

(d) The Licensee will, at the request of the Licensor and at the Licensor's expense, give full cooperation to the Licensor in any action or claim brought or threatened to be brought in respect of the Licensed Trademarks, including joining in as a party to any proceedings.

4. CONFIDENTIALITY

During the term of this Agreement, all the oral and written information, including but not limited to manufacturing technologies, procedures, methods, formulas, data, techniques, experiences, know-how, and business information ("Confidential Information") to be provided by Party A to Party B shall be treated as strictly confidential and shall be used only for the purpose set forth herein. Title to such information and the interest related thereto shall remain with Party A at all time.

Party B agrees to take all necessary steps to prevent Confidential Information from being disclosed to third parties and shall require its personnel to abide by the same confidentiality regulation. Party B shall not disclose Confidential Information to anyone other than to such persons who require access thereto for the exclusive purpose provided hereunder and who are aware of their obligations of confidentiality hereunder.

5. DEFINITIONS AND INTERPRETATIONS

"Affiliate" means any person or company that directly or indirectly controls a Party or is directly or indirectly controlled by a Party, including a Party's parent or subsidiary, or is under direct or indirect common control with such Party. For the purpose of this Agreement, "control" shall mean either the ownership of fifty per cent (50%) or more of the ordinary share capital of the company carrying the right to vote at general meetings or the power to nominate a majority of the board of directors of the Company.

"Proprietary Know-how" shall mean processes, methods and manufacturing techniques, experience and other information and materials including but not limited to the Technical Information and Technical Assistance supplied or rendered by the Licensor to the Licensee hereunder which have been developed by and are known to the Licensor on the date hereof and/or which may be further developed by the Licensor or become known to it during the continuance of this Agreement excepting, however, any secret know-how acquired by the Licensor from third party which the Licensor is precluded from disclosing to the Licensee.

6. ENTIRE AGREEMENT

This Agreement, including any Statement of Work entered into pursuant hereto, constitutes the entire agreement of the parties hereto with respect to its subject matter and supersedes all prior and contemporaneous representations, proposals, discussions, and communications, whether oral or in writing. In the event of a conflict between the provisions of this Agreement and the specific provisions set forth in a Statement of Work, the provisions of the Agreement shall control, except to the extent the provisions in a Statement of Work expressly provide otherwise.

7. AMENDMENT

Amendments to this Contract may be made only by a written instrument signed by a duly authorised representative of each of the Parties and, unless prior approval from the Examination and Approval Authority/the appropriate government department is statutorily required, such amendments shall become effective upon the signing by the duly authorised representatives of both Parties.

8. LANGUAGES

This Agreement shall be signed in four (4) counterparts and all such counterparts taken together shall be deemed to constitute one and the same instrument. The Parties shall sign a Chinese language version of this Agreement as soon as reasonably possible. Should there be any discrepancy between the two language versions, the English version of this Agreement shall prevail.

9. FORCE MAJEURE

Should any Party be directly prevented from executing this Agreement or be delayed in performing this Agreement by any event of force majeure, such as earthquake, typhoon, flood, fire and war and other unforeseen events, the happening and consequences of which are unpreventable and unavoidable, the affected Party shall notify the other Parties without delay and, within fifteen (15) days thereafter, provide detailed information regarding the events of force majeure and sufficient proof thereof, explaining the reason for its inability to perform or the delay in the execution of all or part of this Agreement. A certificate issued by the Chamber of Commerce or other appropriate authority where such circumstances occur shall be sufficient proof of the existence of such circumstances and their duration. The Parties shall, through consultations, decide whether to alter the Agreement to reflect the effects of the event of force majeure on the performance of this Agreement or to terminate the Agreement in the event that such force majeure persists for a period of six (6) months or more.

10. ARBITRATION　Any dispute arising from, out of, or in connection with, this Agreement shall be settled by the Parties through friendly consultation. Such consultation shall begin immediately after one Party has delivered to the other party a written request for such consultation. If the dispute cannot be settled through consultation within thirty (30) days after such notice is given, the Parties shall submit the dispute to China International Trade Arbitration Committee, Shanghai Branch ("Arbitration Institute") to be arbitrated according to its rules and regulations.

There shall be three (3) arbitrators. Party A and Party B shall appoint one (1) arbitrator each. The two arbitrators shall be selected within thirty (30) days after giving or receiving of the request for arbitration. The chairman of the Arbitration Institute shall select the third arbitrator. If a Party fails to appoint an arbitrator within thirty (30) days after the other Party has appointed an arbitrator, the chairman of the Arbitration Institute shall make the appointment.

The arbitration proceedings shall be conducted in Chinese language. The arbitration tribunal shall apply the arbitration rules of the Arbitration Institute in effect on the date of the signing of this Agreement. However, if such rules are in conflict with the provisions of the previous paragraph of this Article, including the provisions for appointing arbitrators, the provisions of this Article shall prevail.

The arbitration award shall be final and binding on both parties. No party shall appeal in connection with the matters in relation to the arbitration award.

Each Party may request any court having jurisdiction to make a judgement for enforcing the arbitration award, or apply with such court for judicial recognition of the award or any order of enforcement thereof.

During the process of arbitration, the Parties shall continue to implement this Agreement without interruption, except for the matters in dispute.

11. TERM/TERMINATION　This Contract shall terminate upon expiration of the Joint Venture Term. In addition, any Party may terminate this Contract prior to the expiration of the Joint Venture Term by delivery to the other Parties of a written notice of its intention to terminate under any of the following circumstances, or as otherwise provided in this Contract or under law:

(a) if any other Party materially breaches this Contract and such breach is not cured within sixty (60) days of a written notice to the breaching Party;

(b) if the JVC becomes bankrupt or is the subject of proceedings for liquidation or dissolution by reason of insolvency or ceases to carry on business or becomes unable to pay its debts as they become due;

(c)if any other Party purports to transfer or takes any steps for the transfer of its equity participation in the JVC in violation of the provisions of this Contract;

(d)if all or any part of the assets of the JVC are temporarily or permanently expropriated by any government authority;

(e)if any government department having authority over any Party requires any provision of this Contract to be revised or imposes conditions or restrictions upon the implementation of this Contract in a such a way as to cause significant adverse consequences to the JVC or any Party.

12. 买方应从装运之日起_____日内，在卖方_____（地名）营业处以_____（地名）兑换率用现金净额支付。装运前任何时候，如果卖方感到买方偿付能力减弱或令人不满意，卖方可在装运前要求买方支付现金或给予满意的担保。

13. 买方同意按现金价格向卖方支付货款，卖方同意接受。

14. 应支付的_____（国名）货币数目应依官方汇率确定。

15. 合同价格要根据承包人提出的_____（货币名），在议定的银行以不可撤销的信用证方式支付。

16. 遗留未支付的全部款额到期立即支付。

17. 如买方未按照本合同付款，卖方可以延迟装货或中止运送货物，直至买方付清货款并提前付清装运费用。

18. 若装船未能按本购货订单中规定的时间进行，除非造成装船延期是由于无法控制、无法预见等非卖方过错的原因所致，买方可到其他地方购买，并要求卖方承担由此造成的损失。

19. 在不迟于每公历季度末_____日内，卖方在_____（地名）向买方交付成品，其费用和风险由卖方承担，并在装船后_____日内电传通知买方有关数量、船名、装运港、装船日期、预计到达目的港的日期及有关装运的其他情况。

20. 卖方将根据向买方提供的"最终月交货计划表"交货。

21. 如果由于战争、火灾、洪水、禁运、爆炸、材料短缺、禁止进口或出口、司法或政府限制、罢工或其他劳工问题，或其他当事人不能控制的原因不能执行本合同时，双方均不负责。

22. 货物运抵目的港后，买方发现质量不符合要求时，可在_____天内持权威货检人员开具的检验证明向卖方提出索赔。卖方应根据实际情况考虑索赔要求。但对船主或保险商责任范围内由自然原因造成的损失，卖方将不予赔偿。

23. 凡因执行本合同所发生的或与本合同有关的争议，双方应通过友好协商解决。经协商不能解决的，应提交_____（第三国名称）仲裁机构根据该仲裁组织的仲裁程序规则进行仲裁。仲裁裁决是终局的，对双方都有约束力。

24. 所有与本协议有关的争议都可由任何一方提交仲裁，任何提交仲裁的争议依_____（仲裁协会名）的仲裁规则由指定的3名仲裁员作终局裁定。仲裁在_____（地名）举行，仲裁员的裁定是终局的，对双方都有约束力。有管辖权的法院可对仲裁决定做出评价，申请人可向法院申请强制执行。

第九章 商务法律文体翻译

商务法律文体主要包括两大类，一类是法律法规文献，如合同法、公司法、仲裁法等行政法规，还包括国际公约、公司章程等；另一类是当事方缔结的合同契约以及外贸运输中的一些法律文件，如提单、租船合同及其他运输文件等。第二大类中的有关内容已在上一章商务文书文体中详述。

本章主要讲述第一大类的法律文体的翻译。要做好这类文件的翻译，首先要研究法律文件的文体特征。法律文件的行文逻辑和论证方式已逐步形成特定模式，主要包括两方面的内容：一是对义务的规定；二是对权利的确认。其次，要分析英汉两种语言在法律文件中的特点。法律语言准确、规范、鲜明，专业术语独特，语言结构自成一家。词语、词义、专业用语和表达方式有别于普通英语。同时，英汉法律文体可能涉及不同法律体系，即大陆法系和英美法系，这两大法系中的法律行为规范和术语使用规范不尽相同。因此，我们要掌握不同法系中法律语言的特点，这是译好法律文件的根本。

孙万彪(2003：1)认为，"语言学界把这种文体归为'庄重的'（solemn）、'刻板的'（rigid）文体，是因为法律英语语句正规，有一定的程式，专用于严肃客观地表述所涉事项。也有人认为这种文体是'神秘的'（mystical），甚至是'矫揉造作的'（assiduously stilted），理由是法律英语文词艰涩难懂，语句冗长复杂"。

9.1 法律英语的文体特点

Martin Joos 按照正式程度提出了五种语言变体，它们是（1）庄重文体（the frozen style）；（2）正式文体（the formal style）；（3）商议文体（the consultative style）；（4）随便文体（the casual style）；（5）亲密文体（the intimate style）。法律英语是各种英语文体中正式程度最高的，即"庄重文体"。法律英语的正式性主要体现在专业性词汇和用语的使用上。法律文件中包含大量法律行业特有的词汇，其内涵不同于它们在其他语体中的含义。从语义的角度来看，法律英语具有以下几个明显的文体特点。

9.1.1 专业术语

法律文体区别于其他文体的首要特点就在于法律事务的特殊性，在这一特殊的法律情境之中，法律用语应避免意义含混而造成歧义，语体色彩应庄重。

在文体特征中，频率特征是最重要的特征之一。法律专业术语在普通英语中也可能出现，但在法律英语中出现的频率要高得多，且语义精炼，表意准确，规范严谨。这正符合法律英语正规、严肃的文体特征，例如，下列词语的含义，a)为一般文体，b)为法律用语：

action	a）行动	b）诉讼	
alienation	a）疏远	b）转让	
avoidance	a）逃避	b）宣告无效	
consideration	a）考虑	b）对价	
counterpart	a）极相似的人或物，对方，对手	b）有同等效力的副本	
execution	a）执行	b）签订，签署	
hand	a）手	b）签名	
instrument	a）工具，手段	b）法律文件	
limitation	a）限制	b）时效	
negligence	a）疏忽	b）过失	
prejudice	a）偏见	b）损害	
presents	a）呈现，礼物	b）本法律文件	
satisfaction	a）满意	b）清偿，补偿	
save	a）节省，救	b）除了	
serve	a）服务	b）送达	
subject/matter	a）主题	b）标的物	

同时，法律英语常采用大量正式词语，替代普通英语词汇。如：

用 prior 替代 before；用 subsequent 替代 after；用 provided that 替代 but 等。

其他常见正式用语还包括：

construe 解释，分析；deem 认为；subject to 以……为条件，以……依据，从属于；without prejudice 无偏袒，等。

此外，行话套话也是法律文件中的常用表达方式。如：

and for no other purposes 不得擅自挪作他用

shall not operate as a waiver 不得作为弃权

shall not be deemed as consent 不得视为同意

including but not limited to 包括但不限于

or other similar or dissimilar causes 或其他类似或不同的原因

9.1.2 古体词的沿用

作为一种高度正规的书面语，法律英语的另一个标志是古体词语的使用，尤其是那些由 here，there 和 where 加上一个或几个介词构成的复合副词。这些词在口头语和一般书面语中已罕见，但在法律英语中十分普遍。例如，法律文件常用 herein，hereafter，hereto，hereunder，therein，thereunder，whereby，wherein 等词。here = this 指本文件（法律，合同，条约等），there = that 指另外的文件，where = which 指那个文件并引出定语从句。例如：

hereat	因此
hereby	借此

herein	本文件中，如此，鉴于
hereinafter	以下，此后，在下文中
hereof	于此
hereon	于是，关于这个
hereto	至此
heretofore	在此以前
hereunder	根据本文件
herewith	同此，附此
thereafter	据此
therefore	因此
therein	那样，在其中
therefrom	由此
whereas	鉴于
whereof	关于那个
whereby	因此，由是，靠那个
wherein	在那方面

古体词的使用有利于法律文书行文的确切性。同时，这也反映了法律英语正式、严肃、古板的文体特征。例如，come here 是个意思明确的简单短语，但在法律文件中却常以 approach the bench 来表达；caught in the act（当场被抓）用 arrested in flagrante delicto 来表示；

dead 被 deceased 替代等。

常见古体词还有：

aforesaid	前述的
forthwith	即刻
thenceforth	从那以后
deem	认为

9.1.3 外来词语的使用

从英语词源角度来看，英语法律语言中法语、拉丁语借词数量最多，这种现象在其他语体中并不多见。这些借词进入英语法律语体之后，在形式上不受归化（naturalized），而且意义明确，成了英语法律词汇中具有区别性的核心部分。

借自法语的法律词汇中，很大一部分是十一世纪诺曼底人征服英国后逐渐从法语的法律词汇中吸收而来。例如：

amerce	罚款
assurance	担保
bar	禁止
complaint	起诉
culpable	重大过失，有罪

demurrer	抗诉
easement	地役权
fee simple	无条件继承的地产
hue and cry	大声抗议，大声报警
indictment	控告
intestate	无遗嘱的
jury	陪审团/员
loi-cadre	纲要法
non-lieu	不予起诉
plaintiff	原告
proposal	提案
ransom	敲诈，勒索；赎金
reconduction	押解出境
schedule	时间表，进度表
suit	诉讼
summons	传票，传唤到庭
tort	侵权行为
verdict	判决，裁决

基督教于公元 597 年传入英国后，拉丁语法律词汇也渗入英语中，如：

ab	自，从
ad hoc	特别的，专门的
alias	别名，化名
apprehensio	拘押
basis	基础/本
bona fide	真诚地（的），真实地（的）
corpus delicti	罪体
declaration	宣布，申报，报单
de facto	事实上，根据事实
ejusdem generic	同类性质的
in flagrante delicto	在犯罪现场
inguria	不法行为
in personam	对人诉讼
in re	关于，案由(= in the matter of)
lex lociactus	行为地法
locus standi	出庭资格
mutatis mutandis	在细节上作适当修正以后
nolle prosequi	撤回诉讼
pari passu	按相同一比例

per se	本身，自身，本质上
pro bono publico	为公众利益（= for the public good）
pro rata	按比例
quasi	准，类似
res gestae	真事实
register	登记，注册
res judicata	定案
suijuris	主权人
testificandum	立证
tulela	监护人
vis major	不可抗力

许多法语和拉丁语进入英语后，在语音上和词形上被英语同化，成为英语词汇的组成部分，但还有一些法律词汇未被同化，保留至今，如源自法语的 estoppel（禁止翻供）和 fee，lash，quash（取消/废除）；来自拉丁语的有：

alias 别/假/化名；

amicus curiae 直译为"法院之友"，指（对案件中涉及公共利益事项陈述自己看法的）法院临时法律顾问，字面意义为 friend of the court；

nolle prosequi 原告（或检察官）撤回诉讼；中止起诉（字面意义为 do not pursue/prosecute）；

res judicata（当事人不得就此再提起诉讼的）已决事件（字面意义 thing decided），等。

9.1.4　词语的叠用

法律英语的古体性和正式性还表现在词汇的并列使用上，即，同义词或近义词往往由 or 或 and 连接并列使用，这种词汇并列的现象表明法律语言对词义正确性、语意确凿性的刻意追求，从而形成了法律语言的复杂性和保守性。这类短语的作用通常是关涉语义的全面性和互补性。6.4.1 已列出此类词语，又如：

breaking and entering	闯入
goods and chattels	私人财产
have and hold	持有
made and signed	签名的
will and testament	遗嘱
terms or provisons	条款
vary and modify	修改和变更
reputation or goodwill	名誉或商誉

9.1.5　shall 的使用

根据 *The Oxford Dictionary of Current English*，shall 一词的解释是 command or duty，但在非正式文体或口语中，常常为 must，should，或 have to 取代。张道真认为 shall 的这种

用法现在不太普遍。Michael Swan 称 shall 的这种用法是"较古老的英语"。

Shall 在法律文件中有其特殊的含义,表示"应当承担的责任和义务",不履行特定法律义务则产生违反法律的后果。Shall 通常表述各项具体的规定与要求,带有指令性和强制性,充分体现了法律文件的权威性和约束性。Shall 可以用于各种时态,既可起助动词的作用表示时间,也可用作情态动词表示语气。所以,shall 通常译为"应"。should 所蕴含的法律力度不如 shall 那样重,它不强调法律性质的义务,只表示一般的义务或道义上的义务。所以,法律文件中的 should 一般译为"应当"或"应该",以示与"应"(shall)有区别。

9.1.6 惯用"大词"

这里说的"大词",既包括又长又艰涩的书卷词语,也包括那些虚张声势的"浮夸词语"(pompous words)。下面是一位律师在法庭上陈述的一段话,尽管是口头语,却仍保持着法律语体的用词特点:

In accordance with C146 of the Ordinance the appellant submitted a development application and a building application for the land in question. The Council, as to the responsible authority, granted consent to the development application subject to a number of conditions which were stated to be imposed "in order to safeguard the present and future amenity of the neighbourhood". The relevant condition reads as follows "The hours of work being limited to between 7:00 a. m. to 5:00 p. m. Mondays to Fridays and 7:00 a. m. to 1:00 p. m. on Saturdays with no work on Sundays.

这一段话语中采用了较多的"长词"和正式的说法,如: in accordance with, submit, application, in question, authority grant consent to, subject to, impose, amenity, relevant, read as follows 等。

另外, the people in their wisdom, in the discharge of that important duty, trifles with justices, the result will be to weaken or subvert what it conceives to be a principle of the fundamental law of the land 等表述也常出现在法律语体中。正因为如此,有时法律语体会显得有些累赘。

9.1.7 对代词严格限制

在法律英语中,指代人或物的词项往往被郑重地一再重复。代词之所以少用,是因为我们在起草法律条文,尤其是签订合同、契约时,要避免代词指代不明确而引起不同的理解与解释。所以,法律文件允许这种限制代词而重复词项的现象,以保证准确性。下面是一份合同的片段:

The Author should bear the cost of any necessary fees for textual and illustrative permissions but the Publishers agree to pay such fees on **the Author's** behalf up to an agreed maximum amount and may deduct the same from my sums that may become due to **the Author** under this Agreement.

句中每次提到作者,都是用 the Author,而不是用 he 或 him。

9.1.8　词语的对义性

buyer（买方）	——	seller（卖方）
consigner（发货人）	——	consignee（收货人）
creditor（债权人）	——	debtor（债务人）
Party A（甲方）	——	Party B（乙方）
right（权利）	——	obligation（义务）
subject（主体）	——	object（客体）
principal criminal（主犯）	——	accessorial criminal（从犯）
plaintiff（原告）	——	（the）defendant（被告）

9.2　英译技巧

　　法律文件通常是由法律专业人员按照固定程式写成的条文。条文讲究用词准确，结构严谨，采取一切手段防止误解和歧义现象的产生。法律文件往往援引成规范例，这就构成了法律文体特有的稳定性和保守性。

　　下面从句型的角度来探讨以下几种主要的英译技巧：

9.2.1　陈述句

- 对投标的邀请通常被认为是要约邀请。

A request for tenders is normally an invitation to treat.（张素华，2004：11）

- 不实陈述导致合同无效。

Misrepresentation renders a contract voidable.（张素华，2004：155）

- 条款(20)规定的保密义务，在本协议期满或终止二(2)年后终止。

The confidentiality obligations imposed by Provision（20）shall terminate two（2）years after the expiration or termination of this agreement.（孙万彪，2003：74）

- 消费者享有公平交易的权利。

Consumers shall enjoy the right of fair deal.（《经济法》，2005：165）

- 货物未能在明确约定的时间内在约定的卸货港交付的，为迟延交付。

Delay in delivery occurs when the goods have not been delivered at the designated port of discharge within the time expressly agreed upon.（《海商法》，2003：20）

- 汇票分为银行汇票和商业汇票。

Bills of exchange include banker's bills and commercial bills.（《商法》，2004：102）

　　法律关系的确认及法律条令的贯彻是人们社会生活的重要方面。法律语言是执行这种社会职能的一种文体，其特殊性决定了此类文体中动词词义的范围比较狭窄。谓语动词中较多的是"申述""承诺"一类意思的动词。谓语动词往往以与 shall 相结合的方式出现。如上面第一个例句：Consumers shall enjoy the right of fair deal.

　　根据 J. Austin，这些动词可分成四类：

1）判断语，根据价值或事实所作出判断。如：acquit, calculate, describe, analyze, estimate, assess, characterize 等。

2）裁定语，表示赞成或反对某事或某过程。如：order, command, direct, recommend, appoint, dismiss, nominate, declare, announce, warn, proclaim 等。

3）承诺语，表示说话人的承诺。如：promise, vow, pledge, covenant, guarantee, contract, commit, ensure, agree, acknowledge 等。

4）阐述语，阐明观点、论据。如：affirm, deny, emphasize, illustrate, concede, identify, accept, object to, report, answer 等。

9.2.2 条件句

- 合营者注册资本的转让必须经合营各方同意。

If any of the joint venturers wishes to assign its registered capital, it must obtain the consent of the other parties to the venture. (《经济法》，2005：103)

- 因产品存在缺陷造成人身、缺陷产品以外的其他财产损害的，生产者应当承担赔偿责任。

If a producer's defective product causes physical injury to a person or damage to property other than the defective product itself, he shall be liable for compensation. (《经济法》，2005：199)

- 产品标识不符合本法第二十七条规定的，责令改正。

Where the marks of a product do not conform to the provisions of Article 27 of this Law, the producer or seller concerned shall be ordered to make rectification. (《经济法》，2005：204)

- 见票后定期付款的汇票，应当在承兑时记载付款日期。

In the case of a bill of exchange payable at a fixed period after sight, the date of payment shall be recorded at the time of acceptance. (《商法》，2004：107)

- 未按照前款规定期限通知的，持票人仍可以行使追索权。

In case of failure to do what is stipulated in the preceding paragraph, the holder may still exercise the right of recourse. (《商法》，2004：112)

- 支票未记载付款地的，付款人的营业场所为付款地。

In case the place of payment is missing in a cheque, the business premises of the drawee is the place of payment. (《商法》，2004：117)

- 在国家对证券发行、交易活动实行集中统一监督管理的前提下，依法设立证券业协会，实行自律性管理。

On condition that the State regulates the issuing and trading of securities on a centralized and unified basis, a Securities Industry Association shall, in accordance with law, be established for self-regulation. (《商法》，2004：126)

- 在下述情况下，A 公司将保护买方不受损失。

Subject to the conditions hereinafter set forth, company A will indemnify and protect the Purchaser against any losses or damages.

- 除了第三方应负责的索赔，买方应对卖方发出索赔通知，并有权对卖方提出索赔。

Except those claims for which a third party is liable, the Buyer shall give a notice of claims to the Seller and shall have the right to lodge claims against the Seller.

- 鉴于甲方愿意采用乙方的专用技术设计，生产上述液压件……

Whereas Party A desires to design and manufacture the above-mentioned hydraulic components by using Party B's know-how...

- 除非合同中另有说明，本合同的条款将……

Unless otherwise stipulated in this Contract, the terms and conditions of this Contract shall...

- 如果这些机构的中央主管机关可以采取步骤……

Provided that the central administration of such agency may take steps...

- 如果合资公司无法继续经营或未达到合同中规定的经营目的……

Should the joint venture company be unable to continue its operations or achieve the business purpose stipulated in the Contract...

法律文件要求思维缜密，逻辑性强，既要考虑到各种不同情况，又要排除各种例外情形。法律条文除了规定双方应履行的义务外，还设想了各种可能发生的情况和处理的办法，所以，法律条款中有较多的条件句。

有时，为了考虑到各种情况，在一个句子中使用多个条件句，这是普通英语少见的，条件句一般由连词引导，但在实际应用中，为了充分显示所述客体在表达上的细微差异，还可使用其他几种表达方法，但在内涵上是有所不同的。例如：

- 由 whereas 引导的条件句常称为"鉴于句"，即鉴于存在某种情形，故主语应采取某种措施，以期达到一定的目的；
- should 为虚拟语气的省略形式，表示一种不太可能发生的情况；
- unless 在意义上是一个否定词，表示"除非"出现某种情况，否则其条件将不能满足，因此，它的主语部分通常为否定形式；
- subject to 后引出的宾语为满足某项要求的必要条件；
- 由 case 组成的词组，如 in case of, in case, in case that, 所表示的含义为，要求采取某种预防措施，以防止某种情况发生；
- 由 event 组成的词组，如 in the event of, in event that, 强调事情发生的事实；
- provided 或 providing 表示"在……前提下"，"在……条件下"；
- except 意为"排除某种情形"。

9.2.3　词类的转换

在英汉法律文本翻译中，词类转换包含两种情况，一是将常见的英语名词化结构转换为汉语动词的译法，另一种是将英语形容词转换为汉语副词的译法。汉英法律翻译亦可采取类似方法。

- Prior to the commencement of the insurance liability, the insured may demand the **termination** of the insurance contract but shall pay the handling fees to the insurer, and the insurer shall refund the premium.

保险责任开始前，被保险人可以要求解除合同，但是应当向保险人支付手续费，保险人应当退还保险费。（名词→动词的转换）（《海商法》，2003：94）

- If anyone, in **violation** of the statutory procedures for the takeover of listed companies, gains illegitimate profits by taking advantage of the takeover of a listed company, the offender shall be ordered to make **rectification**, the illegal gains shall be confiscated and a fine of not less than the amount of but not more than five times the illegal gains shall be imposed.

违反上市公司收购的法定程序，利用上市公司收购谋取不正当收益的，责令**改正**，没收违法所得，并处以违法所得一倍以上五倍以下的罚款。（名词→动词的转换）（《商法》，2004：180）

- Unless otherwise provided for herein, <u>failure</u> or <u>delay</u> on the part of any party to exercise any right, power or privilege under this Agreement shall not operate as a <u>waiver</u> thereof, nor shall any single or partial <u>exercise</u> of any right, power or privilege preclude further <u>exercise</u> thereof or <u>exercise</u> of any other right, power or privilege.

除非本协议另有规定，任何一方**未能或延迟**行使其在本协议项下的任何权利、权力或特权，不应视为其**放弃**该权利、权力或特权；单项或部分**行使**任何权利、权力或特权，亦不妨碍其进一步**行使**该权利、权力或特权或**行使**其他权利、权力或特权。（名词→动词的转换）

- Party A represents and warrants that there are no conditions at, on, under, or related to, the real property constituting all or any portion of the Land which presently or potentially pose a hazard to human health or the environment, and there has been no <u>manufacture, use, treatment, storage, transportation, or disposal</u> of any hazardous or toxic substance, pollutant, or contaminant on the Land nor any <u>release</u> of any hazardous or toxic substance, pollutant, or contaminant into or upon or over the Land.

甲方陈述和保证，构成土地全部或任何部分的房地产，其内部、上面、下面或其相关部位现在不存在，也不可能存在危害人身健康或环境的情况，且土地上从未**生产、使用、处理、储存、运输或处置**任何危险的或有毒的物质、污染物或致污物，土地内部、上面或上空亦未曾**释放**任何危险的或有毒的物质、污染物或致污物。（名词→动词的转换）

- Unless otherwise provided for herein, failure or delay on the part of any party to exercise any right, power or privilege under this Agreement shall not operate as a waiver thereof, nor shall any <u>single or partial</u> exercise of any right, power or privilege preclude <u>further</u> exercise thereof or exercise of any other right, power or privilege.

除非本协议另有规定，任何一方未能或延迟行使其在本协议项下的任何权利、权力或特权，不应视为其放弃该权利、权力或特权；**单项或部分**行使任何权利、权力或特权，亦不妨碍其**进一步**行使该权利、权力或特权或行使其他权利、权力或特权。（形容词→副词的转换）

- If one Party hereto shall commit any <u>material</u> breach of this Agreement or its representations and warranties hereunder and fail to remedy the breach within thirty (30) days of notice from the other Party requesting it to remedy such breach (if capable of remedy), or offer adequate compensation therefore （adv.）, the other Party may terminate this Agreement immediately by notice to the Party in breach.

如果本协议一方实质性违反本协议或其在本协议项下的陈述和保证, 且在另一方向其发出要求其纠正违约行为(若可以纠正)的通知后三十(30)日内未予以纠正, 或为违约行为给予足够赔偿, 则另一方可向违约方发出通知立即终止本协议。(形容词→副词的转换)

- If, due to special reasons unexpected at the time the trust is created, the methods for administrating the trust property are not favorable to the realization of trust purposes or do not conform to the interests or the beneficiary, the settler shall have the right to ask the trustee to modify such methods.

因设立信托时未能预见的特别事由, 致使信托财产的管理办法不利于实现信托目的或者不符合受益人的利益时, 委托人有权要求受托人调整该信托财产的管理办法。(《商法》, 2004: 328)(名词→动词, 形容词→副词的转换)

9.2.4　结构复杂的长句

英语法律文体主题严肃, 意蕴深刻, 结构严谨, 所述法律关系相当复杂, 因此往往采用长句句式, 尤以复合句居多, 一般由诸多从句和其他修饰成分组成, 如形容词、副词、现在分词和过去分词, 且结构上叠床架屋, 前后编插。有时一个条款相当长, 远远超出英语句子的平均长度(17个单词), 往往一个句子就是一个段落, 中间还插入了表示时间或条件的状语, 将句子主语、助动词和谓语部分隔开。从形式上看, 这些句子似乎是松散的、零乱的, 但在逻辑上是严谨的。如:

- If, after the signing of this Agreement, the Chinese government either at the State, provincial, municipal or local level adopts any new law, regulation, decree or rule, amends or repeals any provision of any law, regulation, decree or rule, or adopts any different interpretation or method of implementation of any law, regulation, decree or rule, which contravenes this Agreement or which materially and adversely affects a Party's economic benefit under this Agreement, then upon written notice thereof from the affected party to the other Party, the Parties shall promptly consult and decide whether （i） to continue to implement this Agreement in accordance with the original provisions thereof as per the relevant provisions of the Contract Law of the People's Republic of China; or （ii） to effectuate necessary adjustments in order to preserve each Party's economic benefit under this Agreement on a basis no less favourable than the economic benefit it would have received if such law, regulation, decree or rule had not been adopted, amended, repealed or so interpreted or implemented.

上面的句子中, 主句的前面有一个很长的条件状语从句和时间状语, 主句本身也有多个状语, 而且状语从句中又有表示时间的状语和定语从句, 修饰语套修饰语, 一个接一个叠加, 一环扣一环相连, 构成了复杂的修饰和被修饰关系。要理解并翻译这个长句的完整意思, 必须首先弄清楚句子里各个成分的相互关系。

译文: 如果本协议签署之后, 中国国家、省、市或地方政府通过任何新的法律、法规、法令或条例，修改或废除任何法律、法规、法令或条例的任何条款，或对任何法律、法规、法令或条例给予不同的解释或采取不同的实施办法，导致与本协议相冲突，或对一方在本协议项下的经济利益造成实质性的不利影响，受到影响的一方经书面通知另一方后，双方应立即协商并决定是否（1）根据《中华人民共和国合同法》的有关规定继续按照本协议的原条款执行本协议，或（2）做出必要的调整，以保持各方在本协议项下的经济利益，使之不逊于各方在该等法律、法规、法令或条例未通过、未修改、未废除、未做出不同的解释或未采取不同的实施方法之前所能获得的经济利益。　　（孙万彪，2003：113）

- ①With respect to customs duties and charges of any kind imposed on or in connection with importation or exportation or imposed on the international transfer of payments for imports or exports，and ②with respect to the method of levying such duties and charges，and ③with respect to all rules and formalities in connection with importation and exportation，and ④with respect to all matters referred to in paragraphs 2 and 4 of Article Ⅲ，⑤any advantage，favour，product originating in or destined for any other country ⑥granted by any contracting party to any product originating in or destined for any other country ⑦shall be accorded immediately and unconditionally to ⑧the like product originating in or destined for the territories of all other contracting parties.

上面的这个长句中①②③④为方式状语(Aspect Adverbial)，均为 with respect to 引导；⑤为被动语态的并列主语；⑥由过去分词 granted 引导的后置定语，修饰主语；⑦由 shall be accorded to 构成被动语态谓语部分；⑧为被动语态的宾语部分。这样的分析仅是一个大致的框架，实际上，在每个分句中还带有若干由现在分词、过去分词或介词短语组成的修饰成分。

译文：在对输出或输入、有关输出或输入及输出入货物的国际支付转账所征收的关税和费用方面，在征收上述关税和费用的方法方面，在输出和输入的规章手续方面，以及本协定第三条第 2 款及第 4 款所述事项方面，一缔约国对来自或运往任一其他国家的产品给予的利益、优待、特权或豁免，应当立即无条件地给予来自或运往所有其他缔约国的相同产品。

9.3　近义词和同义词的翻译

用词准确是法律文件的特点之一，可突出并加强法律文件的权威性。所以，我们要保证译文准确无误地表达出原文的真正含义。选词时要考虑到近义和同义词的区分，单复数的不同含义，还要注意到中英词汇广义、狭义、具体意义和抽象意义的不同之处。下面我们借助法律文件英译的一些译例，探讨见诸法律文件中这类英语近义和同义词的正确用法，以确保译入语的准确性。

9.3.1　request 和 require

- 人民法院有权要求当事人提供或者补充证据。

原译：A people's court shall have the authority to request the parties to provide or supplement evidence.

改译：

A peoples' court shall have the authority to require the parties to provide or supplement evidence.

英语中表示"要求"这个含义的词大致有 3 个，即 ask，request，require。ask 为泛指，request 和 require 为特指。request 表示 make a request，所以 request（sb. to do sth.）是"请求（某人做某事）"，是下对上的要求；而 require 表示 order，demand，是"命令，要求"之意，指上对下的要求，比如法律条款对当事人的要求，业主对雇员的要求。此句中人民法院对当事人的要求，当然是 require。译文使用 request 不准确。

9.3.2　legal，lawful 和 legitimate

● 公司职工依法组织工会，开展工会活动，维护职工的合法权益。

原译： The staff and workers of a company organize a trade union in accordance with the law to carry out union activities and protect the lawful rights and interests of the staff and workers.

原文的"维护职工的合法权益"意为"维护职工的合法正当权益"，因此译文用 lawful 欠准确，应译为"legitimate"。

关于"合法的"，英文中有 legal，lawful 和 legitimate 三个词，它们意思相近，但内涵存在差别。

按照《牛津现代高级辞典》，legal 意为 connected with，in accordance with，authorized or required by the law（法律上的，合法的，法律承认的，法律要求的，法定的），它强调"合乎国家正式颁布的法律的"，或"经法律许可的"。例如"诉讼过程"应译为 the course of legal proceedings，即法定程序，所谓"法定"是指"合乎国家正式颁布的"，所以下面这些词语应翻译为：

法律行为 legal act

法定地址 legal address

法定代理人 legal agent

司法协助 legal assistance

法人 legal entity

法律事务 legal business

法律效力 legal effect

法律效用 legal effectiveness

法定财产 legal estate，等。

lawful 意为 allowed by law；according to law（合法的，法定的），是强调"合理合法的"，意为"合乎或不违反国家的法律、教会的戒律或道德的标准"，与 legal，legitimate 有差别。例如：

合法行为 lawful action

合法政党 lawful party

合法财产 lawful property

合法席位 lawful seat

合法婚姻 lawful wedlock，等。

legitimate 意为 lawful，regular，reasonable(合法的，正规的，合理的，可说明为正当的)，是强调既是合法的，又是正当的，指根据法律、公认权威与准则为正当的。例如：

合法防卫，正当防卫 legitimate defence

合法的自由，正当的自由 legitimate freedom

合法收入，正当收入 legitimate income

合法的宗教活动 legitimate religious activities，等。

因此，原文的"职工的合法权益"应理解为"合法正当权益"，译文中 lawful rights and interests of the staff and workers 应改为 legitimate rights and interests of the staff and workers. 而且原译系叙事，而原文是法律规定，含义大有出入。

改译：The staff and workers of a company may, in accordance with the law, organize a trade union to carry out union activities and protect the legitimate rights and interests of the staff and workers.

9.3.3　formulate 和 enact

• 为了发展对外贸易，维护对外贸易秩序，促进社会主义市场经济的健康发展，制定本法。

原译：This Law is formulated with a view to developing the foreign trade, maintaining the foreign trade order and promoting a healthy development of the socialist market economy.

"制定"译为 formulated 不十分准确。目前国内法律文件中，凡提及"制定法律"一般用此词，各文件相互参照，似乎 formulate 已成为惯用法。

根据《牛津现代高级英文辞典》定义，formulate 意为 express clearly and exactly，即明确表达，比如 formulate one's thoughts/a doctrine(明确表达思想或宗旨)。法律英语中表示"制定法律"，应用动词 enact。按上述辞典定义，enact 意为 make (a law)；decree, ordain (制定(法律)，颁令，规定)。比如：

制定法律 enact a law

制定条文 enact clauses

名词 enactment 也有"制定，规定，颁布，通过，法令，法规"等意。比如：

enactment of law 制定法律，法的制定。

为顾及习惯用法并按照英文法律文件的语言特点，采用同义词连用。

改译：　This Law is formulated and enacted in order to develop the foreign trade, maintain the foreign trade order and promote a healthy development of the socialist market economy.

9.3.4　terms 和 clause；in reasonable ways 和 in a reasonable manner

• 采用格式条款订立合同的，提供格式条款的一方应当遵循公平原则确定当事人之间的权利和义务，并采取合理的方式请对方注意免除或者限制其责任的条款，按照对方的要求，对该条款予以说明。

原译：Where standard terms are adopted in concluding a contract, the party which supplies the standard terms shall define the rights and obligations between the parties abiding by the principle of fairness, request the other party to note the exclusion or restriction of its liabilities in reasonable ways, and explain the standard terms according to the requirement of the other party.

改译：Where standard clauses are adopted in concluding and entering into a contract, the party supplying the standard clauses shall, under the principle of fairness, define the rights and obligations between the parties thereto, ask the other party, in a reasonable manner, to note the clause on the exclusion or restriction of its liabilities, and explain the standard clauses in accordance with the requirement of the other party.

原文的"格式条款"，不能直接按字面译出。中文的"条款"一词有两种含义，一是表示"条件、条款"，意为"规定"，二是表示合同法律文件中某一具体条款，例如第几条款，这里的"格式条款"应该属于后一种，因为合同有"格式条款"与"非格式条款"两种，而不是"规定"。因此，"格式条款"不能译成 standard terms，本条文里的"格式条款"应译成 standard clauses。clause 意为（legal）complete paragraph in an agreement，or legal document（法律），即"合同协议，法律文件的条款"。所以"合同第 10 条款"应译成 Clause 10 of the contract。

原文中的"合理的方式"译成 in reasonable ways 不妥。way 一般表示 method（方法），有时也表示 condition，state，degree（情形，状态及程度），比如"大规模地"可译成 in a big way。"合理的方式"应译成 in a reasonable manner。manner 表示"方式"（可数，通常作单数），比如：

以这种方式 in this manner

9.3.5 revoke 和 rescind

● 合同无效或者被撤销后，因该合同取得的财产，应当予以返还。

原译：The property acquired as a result of a contract shall be returned after the contract is confirmed to be null and void or has been revoked.

改译：The property acquired by either party as a result of a contract shall be returned to the other party after the contract is confirmed to be null and void or has been rescinded.

原文的"被撤销"译为 has been revoked，欠准确，应为 rescind。

《牛津现代高级双解辞典》释义，revoke 为 repeal，cancel，withdraw（a decree, consent, permission, etc.），即"废止，撤销，取消；宣告（命令，同意，允许等）无效"，例如：

取消决定 revoke a decision

撤销委托 revoke commission

吊销执照 revoke a licence，等。

rescind 意为 legally repeal，annual，cancel（a law, contract, etc）即"（法律）废止，撤销（法规，合约等）"，例如：

取消合约 rescind an agreement

废除法律 rescind a law

废除不合理的规章 rescind the unreasonable rules

取消判决 rescind a judgment

9.3.6 reject 和 refuse

● 合同生效后，当事人不得因姓名、名称的变更或者法定代表人、负责人、承办人的变更而不履行合同义务。

原译：After a contract becomes effective, the parties may not reject to perform the obligations of the contract because of modification of the title or name of the parties, or change of the statutory representative, the responsible person or the executive person of the parties.

改译：After a contract becomes effective, the parties thereto shall not refuse to perform the obligations of the contract due to the modification of the title or name of the parties thereto, or the change of the statutory representative, the person in a responsible position of the executive person of the parties thereto.

原文中的"不得……而不履行合同义务"不应译为 may not reject to perform the obligations of the contract。应将 reject 改为 refuse。

按《牛津现代高级英文辞典》，reject 法律上意为 refuse to accept，即"拒绝，不接受，驳回"。比如：

不受理申诉 reject a complaint

驳回证据 reject (a) proof

驳回上诉 reject an appeal

refuse 意为 show unwillingness to accept (something offered)，"拒绝，拒受，拒给，不愿"等意。例如：

不准保释；拒绝保释 refuse bail

拒绝履行 refuse to perform

拒绝查账 refuse inspection of books

抗税 refuse to pay tax

原文中的"负责人"译成 responsible person 不妥。Responsible 指"负有职责""有责任感""可靠"，与"负责人"不是一回事。例如：

● Isn't he too young for such a responsible job?

让他负责如此重要的职责，他是否太年轻了？

● Alice is a very responsible baby-sitter. 艾莉丝看小孩很负责任。

● Give the job to a responsible man. 把工作交给负责任的人。

● Betty is a responsible young lady. 贝蒂是个有责任感的姑娘。

position 作可数名词(多作单数)，表示"处境，境地"之意。例如：

● A man in his position might have done the same thing.

一个处于他位置的人也会做出同样的事。

● Madame Michel found herself in an embarrassing position.

米歇尔夫人发现她处境很尴尬。

"负责人"应译为 the person in a responsible position，即"处于负责岗位上的人"。

9.3.7　enlarge 和 increase

• 当事人一方违约后，对方应当采取适当措施防止损失的扩大，没有采取适当措施致使损失扩大的，不得就扩大的损失要求赔偿。

原译：After one party violates a contract, the other party shall take proper measures to prevent from the enlargement of losses; if the other party fails to take proper measures so that the losses are enlarged, it may not claim any compensation as to the enlarged losses.

改译：After either party violates a contract, the other party shall take proper measures to prevent the increase of the loss. Provided that if the other party fails to take proper measures so that the losses are increased, the party in question shall not claim any compensation in relation to the increased losses.

原文中的"防止损失的扩大"应理解为"防止损失的增加"，因此译成 enlarge 不妥，应改为 increase。

根据《牛津现代高级英文辞典》的定义，enlarge 意为 make or become larger(扩大，增大)，比如：

放大相片 enlarge a photograph

扩建房屋 enlarge one's house

increase 意为 make or become greater in size, number, degree, etc.，即在尺寸、大小、数量、程度方面的增加、增大、增多。"损失的扩大"意为"损失程度的增加"，故应为 increase。另外，原译中 from 和 as to 均为误译。

9.3.8　package 和 packing

• 买卖合同的内容除依照本法第十二条的规定以外，还可以包括包装方式、检验标准和方法、结算方式、合同使用的文字及其效力等条款。

原译：Other than those as stipulated in Article l2 of this Law, a sales contract may also contain such clauses as package manner, inspection standards and method, method of settlement and clearance, language adopted in the contract and its authenticity.

改译：Besides those specified in Article 12 of this Law, a sales Contract may also contain such clauses as manner of packing, inspection standards and method of settlement and clearance, and the language adopted in the contract and its authenticity.

原文中的"包装方式"，不能译成 package manner，而应译为 manner of packing。这两个词看似相近，实际含义并不相同，中译英时应特别注意。

package 意为 parcel of things, packed together，即"包、包裹"。比如：

一捆信件 a package of letters

二十支装的一包香烟 a package of 20 cigarettes

packing（不可数名词）意为 process of packing（goods），"包装货物的过程，打包，打

包行李"等意。此句中的"包装方式"自然是指"包装的方式""打包的方式"，而不是"包裹的式样"，因此应译成 packing。

9.3.9 above，over 和 beyond

● 租赁期限六个月以上的，应当采用书面形式。当事人不采用书面形式的，视为不定期租赁。

原译：Where the lease term is above 6 months, the lease contract shall be in written form. If the parties do not conclude it in written form, it shall be deemed an unfixed lease.

改译：Where the lease term is beyond 6 months, the lease contract shall be made and concluded in a written form. If the parties thereto fall to conclude the lease contract in written form, the lease in question shall be deemed an unfixed lease.

英语中有三个词表示"超过"或"高于"，即 above，over，beyond，但这三个词的用法不同。

"六个月以上"译成 above 6 months，不如 beyond 6 months 好。介词 above 表示 greater in number，price，weight，etc.，即"（数目）大于，（价格）高于，（重量）超过"，但 above 有"在……之上"的意思，指位置高低，引申为"超出""多余"或"与……无关"之意，因此通常在表示位置、温度等高低时才用 above。比如：

● The temperature is three degrees above zero. 现在的温度是 3 度。

表示数量与长度时，over 较为常用，意为 more than。比如：

● You have to be over l8 to see this film. 18 岁以上的人才能看这部电影。

● There were over 100,000 people at the pop art festival. 参加流行艺术节的人数超过 10 万。

● beyond 意为（of time）later than，指超过某段时间。比如：

● Don't stay out beyond 10 o'clock. 10 点以后不要待在外面。

● He never sees beyond the present. 他眼光只看到现在。

9.3.10 urge 和 remind

● 承租人应当按照约定支付租金，承租人经催告在合理期限内仍不支付租金的，出租人可以要求支付全部租金，也可以解除合同，收回租赁物。

原译：The lessee shall pay the rent according to the terms of the contract. If the lessee still does not pay the rent within a reasonable time limit after being urged, the lessor may request it to pay all the rent, or rescind the contract and take back the leased property.

原文中的"催告"译成 urged，欠准确，应用 remind。根据《牛津现代高级英文辞典》，urge 表示 request earnestly，try to persuade；strongly recommend，"力请，力劝，推荐"之意。比如：

● The salesman urged me to buy a new car. 售货员力劝我买一辆新车。

而 remind somebody to do something，表示 cause（somebody）to remember to do

231

something，提醒（某人）做某事。比如：

Please remind me to answer that letter. 请提醒我回信。

因此，原文中的"承租人经催告"应理解为"承租人经提醒"，才有利于译文的准确。原译文中尚有其他不妥之处，一并改译为：

The lessee shall, under the requirements and provisions of the contract, pay rent. If within a reasonable time limit after being reminded to do so, the lessee still fails to pay the rent, the lessor may request the lessee to pay all the rent, or may rescind the contract and take back the leased property.

9.3.11　at risk 和 in danger "处于危险之中"与"处境危险"

● 承运人在运输过程中，应当尽力援助患有急病、分娩、遇险的旅客。

原译：A carrier shall, during the period of carriage, render whatever help assistance as it can to passenger who is seriously ill, or who is giving birth to a child or whose life is at risk.

改译：A carrier shall, during the period of carriage, render whatever help and assistance as it can to passenger who is seriously ill, or who is giving birth or whose life is in danger.

原文中的"遇险的旅客"译成 whose life is at risk 是误译。

遇险的旅客，即"旅客生命遇到危险"，应该译成 whose life is in danger。

at risk 意为 threatened by uncertainties（such as failure, loss, etc.）指"可能遭到失败，损失"等意。比如：

● Is the government's income tax policy seriously at risk?

政府的税收政策有可能招来大损失吗？

in danger 意为"处境危险""遇险"，例如：

● He was in danger of losing his life. 他那时生命危在旦夕。

● We were in danger of being hit by a stone. 我们有随时被石头砸伤的危险。

9.3.12　untrue 和 false

● 因托运人申报不实或者遗漏重要情况，造成承运人损失的，托运人应当承担损害赔偿责任。

原译：Where a carrier suffers from damage due to untrue declaration or omission of important information by the shipper, the shipper shall be liable for damages.

改译：Where, due to the false declaration or omission of important information by the shipper, a carrier suffers from damage, the shipper shall be liable for the compensation for the damages.

"申报不实"直译为 untrue declaration 欠准确。其实，"申报不实"即为"虚报"，对应的英语术语应是 false declaration。False 有 not right/true/real "错误，不对，不真实"之意，也有 deceiving, lying "欺骗，不诚实"之意，比如：

假账 false account

诬告 false accusation

欺骗性广告 false advertisement

假报告 false report，等。

9.3.13 warehousing 和 warehoused

• 保管人根据存货人或者仓单持有人的要求，应同意其检查仓储物或者提取样品。

原译：At the request of the storing party or the person who holds the warehouse voucher, the safekeeping party shall permit the person to check the warehousing goods or take samples.

改译：Upon the requirement of the storing party or the person who holds the warehouse warrant, the safekeeping party shall permit the person in question to inspect the warehoused goods or take samples.

与"仓储物"对应的术语为 warehousing goods，而非 warehoused goods。warehouse 是及物动词，意为 to deposit, store, or store in or as if in a warehouse(在仓库存放)；warehousing 一般作名词，意为"仓储""仓储费"。因此，原文中的"仓储物"应理解为"储放在仓库里的货物"，译为 warehoused goods。

9.3.14 goods carriage 和 the carriage of goods

• 货物运输需要办理审批、检验等手续的，托运人应当将办理完有关手续的文件提交承运人。

原译：Where such formalities as examination and approval or inspection are required for goods carriage, the Shipper shall submit the documents of fulfillment of the relevant formalities to the carrier.

改译：Where such formalities as examination and approval or/and inspection are required for the carriage of goods, the shipper shall submit the documents of fulfillment of the relevant formalities to the carrier.

原文中的"货物运输"应译为 the carriage of goods，意为 carrying of goods from place to place，比如：

旅客运输 carriage of passengers

货物空运 carriage of goods by air

陆地货物运输 carriage of goods by land

海上货物运输 carriage of goods by sea

Carriage of Goods by Sea Act 英国《海洋货物运输法》(1924 年)

Goods carriage 指 goods that are carried 运载的货物。

法律文件用词严谨，近义词和同义词表达的法律含义有时不互等或不互用，一字之差就有可能引起预想不到的后果。因此，我们对原文的含义要把握确切，这样在语言转换时，译语与源语才能具有法律上对等的意义和功能。

9.4　文本翻译范例

UNITED NATIONS CONVENTION ON THE CARRIAGE OF GOODS BY SEA，1978（extracted）

1978 联合国海上运输公约(节选)

Preamble 序言

THE STATES PARTIES TO THIS CONVENTION,

本公约各缔约国

HAVING RECOGNIZED the desirability of determining by agreement certain rules relating to the carriage of goods by sea,

认识到通过协议确定一些关于海上货物运输的规则的需要，

HAVING DECIDED to conclude a Convention for this purpose and have thereto agreed as follows：

决定为此目的而缔结一项公约，并已协议如下：

PART I　GENERAL PROVISIONS
第一章　总　则

Article 1. Definitions
第一条　定　义

In this Convention：

在本公约中：

1. "Carrier" means any person by whom or in whose name a contract of carriage of goods by sea has been concluded with a shipper.

1. "承运人"，是指由其本人或以其名义与托运人订立海上货物运输契约的任何人。

2. "Actual carrier" means any person to whom the performance of the carriage of the goods, or of part of the carriage, has been entrusted by the carrier, and includes any other person to whom such performance has been entrusted.

2. "实际承运人"是指受承运人委托从事货物运输或部分货物运输的任何人，包括受托从事此项工作的任何其他人。

3. "Shipper" means any person by whom or in whose name or on whose behalf a contract of carriage of goods by sea has been concluded with a carrier, or any person by whom or in whose

name or on whose behalf the goods are actually delivered to the carrier in relation to the contract of carriage by sea.

3. "托运人"是指由其本人或以其名义或代其与承运人订立海上货物运输契约的任何人，或是由其本人或以其名义或代其将海上货物运输契约所载货物实际提交承运人的任何人。

4. "Consignee" means the person entitled to take delivery of the goods.

4. "收货人"是指有权提取货物的人。

5. "Goods" includes live animals; where the goods are consolidated in a container, pallet or similar article of transport or where they are packed, "goods" includes such article of transport or packaging if supplied by the shipper.

5. "货物"包括活动物；如果货物是用集装箱、货盘或类似装运工具集装，或者货物带有包装，而此种装运工具或包装系由托运人提供，则"货物"应包括这些装运工具或包装。

6. "Contract of carriage by sea" means any contract whereby the carrier undertakes against payment of freight to carry goods by sea from one port to another; however, a contract which involves carriage by sea and also carriage by some other means is deemed to be a contract of carriage by sea for the purposes of this Convention only in so far as it relates to the carriage by sea.

6. "海上运输契约"是指承运人收取运费据以将货物从一个港口运往另一港口的契约；但是，对于既包括海上运输又包括某些其他运输方式的契约而言，只有在其涉及海上运输时，才应视为本公约所指的海上运输契约。

7. "Bill of lading" means a document which evidences a contract of carriage by sea and the taking over or loading of the goods by the carrier, and by which the carrier undertakes to deliver the goods against surrender of the document. A provision in the document that the goods are to be delivered to the order of a named person, or to order of an unnamed person, or to bearer, constitutes such an undertaking.

7. "提单"是指用以证明海上运输契约和由承运人接管或装载货物，以及承运人保证据以交付货物的单证。单证中关于货物应按记名人的指示或者不记名人的指示交付，或者交付给提单持有人的规定，便是这一保证。

8. "Writing" includes, inter alia, telegram and telex.

8. "书面"，除其他方式外，包括电报和电传。

Article 2. Scope of application
第二条　适用范围

1. The provisions of this Convention are applicable to all contracts of carriage by sea between two different States, if:

1. 本公约各项规定，适用于在两个不同国家之间的所有海上运输契约，如果：

235

（a）the port of loading as provided for in the contract of carriage by sea is located in a Contracting State，or

（1）海上运输契约规定的装货港位于一个缔约国之内；或者

（b）the port of discharge as provided for in the contract of carriage by sea is located in a Contracting State，or

（2）海上运输契约规定的卸货港位于一个缔约国之内；或者

（c）one of the optional ports of discharge provided for in the contract of carriage by sea is the actual port of discharge and such port is located in a Contracting State，or

（3）海上运输契约规定的备选卸货港之一是实际卸货港，并位于一个缔约国之内；或者

（d）the bill of lading or other document evidencing the contract of carriage by sea is issued in a Contracting State，or

（4）提单或作为海上运输契约证明的其他单证，是在一个缔约国之内签发；或者

（e）the bill of lading or other document evidencing the contract of carriage by sea provides that the provisions of this Convention or the legislation of any State giving effect to them are to govern the contract.

（5）提单或作为海上运输契约证明的其他单证规定，本公约各项规定或者使其生效的任何国家立法，应对该契约加以管辖。

2. The provisions of this Convention are applicable Without regard to the nationality of the ship，the carrier，the actual carrier，the shipper，the consignee or any other interested person.

2. 本公约各项规定，对船舶、承运人，实际承运人、托运人、收货人或任何其他有关的人，不论其国籍如何，一律适用。

3. The provisions of this Convention are not applicable to charter-parties. However，where a bill of lading is issued pursuant to a charter-party，the provisions of the Convention apply to such a bill of lading if it governs the relation between the carrier and the holder of the bill of lading not being the charterer.

3. 本公约各项规定不适用于租船契约，但是，如果提单是根据租船契约签发，并对承运人和非属承租人的提单持有人之间的关系加以制约，则本公约各项规定应适用于此种提单。

4. If a contract provides for future carriage of goods in a series of shipments during an agreed period，the provisions of this Convention apply to each shipment. However，where a shipment is made under a charter-party，the provisions of paragraph 3 of this article apply.

4. 如果契约规定，今后的货载将在一个议定期间内分批运输，则本公约的规定应适用于每一批货载。但如运输系根据租船契约进行，则应适用本条第3款规定。

Article 3. Interpretation of the Convention
第三条　对本约的解释

In the interpretation and application of the provisions of this Convention regard shall be had to its international character and to the need to promote uniformity.

在解释或适用本公约各项规定时，应注意本公约的国际性质和促进统一的需要。

PART Ⅱ　LIABILITY OF THE CARRIER
第二章　承运人的赔偿责任

Article 4. Period of responsibility
第四条　责任期限

1. The responsibility of the carrier for the goods under this Convention covers the period during which the carrier is in charge of the goods at the port of loading, during the carriage and at the port of discharge.

1. 按照本公约，承运人对货物的责任期限，包括货物在装货港、运输途中和卸货港处于承运人掌握管理之下的期间。

2. For the purpose of paragraph 1 of this article, the carrier is deemed to be in charge of the goods:

2. 就本条第 1 款而言，在下述期间，承运人应被视为已经掌管货物：

(a) from the time he has taken over the goods from:

(1) 自承运人从下述各方接管货物时起：

(i) the shipper, or a person acting on his behalf; or

① 从托运人或代其行事的人；或者

(ii) an authority or other third party to whom, pursuant to law or regulations applicable at the port of loading, the goods must be handed over for shipment.

② 根据装货港适用的法律或规章，从须将货物交其发运的当局或其他第三方接管时起。

(b) until the time he bas delivered the goods:

(2) 直至他按下列方式交付货物之时为止：

(i) by handing over the goods to the consignee or

① 将货物交付收货人；或者

(ii) in cases where the consignee does not receive the goods from the carrier, by placing them at the disposal of the consignee in accordance with the contract or with the law or with the usage of the particular trade, applicable at the port of discharge; or

② 如果收货人不向承运人提货，则依照契约或在卸货港适用的法律或特定商业习惯，将货物置于收货人支配之下；或者

(iii) by handing over the goods to an authority or other third party to whom, pursuant to law or regulation applicable at the port of discharge, the goods must be handed over.

③ 根据卸货港适用的法律或规章，将货物交付所需交付的当局或其他第三方。

3. In paragraphs 1 and 2 of this article, reference to the carrier or to the consignee means, in addition to the carrier or the consignee, the servants or the agents, respectively of the carrier or the consignee.

3. 本条第 1、2 款所述承运人或收货人，除他们本人之外，还包括承运人或收货人的雇佣人或代理人。

Article 5. Basis of liability
第五条　赔偿责任的基础

1. The carrier is liable for loss resulting from loss of or damage to the goods, as well as from delay in delivery, if the occurrence which caused the loss, damage or delay took place while the goods were in his charge as defined in article 4, unless the carrier proves that he, his servants and agents took all measures that could reasonably be required to avoid the occurrence and its consequences.

1. 除非承运人证明，其本人及其雇佣人和代理人已为避免事故的发生及其后果而采取一切所能合理要求的措施，承运人对由于货物的灭失、损坏以及延迟交付所造成的损失，便应负赔偿责任，如果引起该项灭失、损坏或延迟交付的事故，如第四条所述，是在他掌管货物期间发生。

2. Delay in delivery occurs when the goods have not been delivered at the port of discharge provided for in the contract of carriage by sea within the time expressly agreed upon or, in the absence of such agreement, within the time which it would be reasonable to require of a diligent carrier, having regard to the circumstances of the case.

2. 如果货物未在明确约定的时间内，或者在没有这种约定时，未在按照具体情况对一个勤勉的承运人所能合理要求的时间内，在海上运输契约规定的卸货港交付，便是延迟交货。

3. The person entitled to make a claim for the loss of goods may treat the goods as lost when they have not been delivered as required by article 4 within 60 consecutive days following the expiry of the time for delivery according to paragraph 2 of this article.

3. 如果在本条第二款规定的交付时间届满之后连续六十天之内，尚未根据第四条要求交付货物，则有权对货物的灭失提出索赔的人，可以视为货物已经灭失。

4. (a) The carrier is liable

4. (1) 承运人应对下列事项负赔偿责任：

(i) for loss of or damage to the goods or delay in delivery caused by fire, if the claimant proves that the fire arose from fault or neglect on the part of the Carrier, his servants or agents;

① 由火灾所引起的货物灭失、损坏或延迟交付，如果索赔人证明，火灾是由于承运人、其雇佣人或代理人的过失或疏忽所造成；

(ii) for such loss, damage or delay in delivery which is proved by the claimant to have resulted from the fault or neglect of the carrier, his servants or agents, in taking all measures that could reasonably be required to put out the fire and avoid or mitigate its consequences.

②经索赔人证明，由于承运人、其雇佣人或代理人在可能合理的要求他采取灭火以及避免或减轻其后果的一切措施方面的过失或疏忽所造成的货物的灭失、损坏或延迟交付。

(b) In case of fire on board the ship affecting the goods, if the claimant or the carrier so desires, a survey in accordance with shipping practices must be held into the cause and circumstances of the fire, and a copy of the surveyor's report shall be made available on demand to the carrier and the claimant.

（2）凡在船上发生火灾影响货物时，如果索赔人或承运人要求，便应根据航运惯例，对火灾的起因和情况进行检验，并根据要求，向索赔人和承运人提交检验人报告。

5. With respect to live animals, the carrier is not liable for loss, damage or delay in delivery resulting from any special risks inherent in that kind of carriage. If the carrier proves that he has complied with any special instructions given him by the shipper respecting the animals and that, in the circumstances of the case, the loss, damage or delay in delivery could be attributed to such risks, it is presumed that the loss, damage or delay in delivery was so caused unless there is proof that all or a part of the loss, damage or delay in delivery resulted from fault or neglect on the part of the carrier, his servants or agents.

5. 关于活动物，如果其灭失、损害或延迟交付起因于这类运输所固有的任何特殊风险，承运人便不负赔偿责任。如果承运人证明，他是按照托运人对有关该项动物所作的专门指示行事，并且证明，根据具体情况，灭失、损害或延迟交付可以归之于这种风险，便应推定灭失、损害或延迟交付乃是如此产生，除非提出证明，该项灭失、损害或延迟交付的全部或一部，是由于承运人、其雇佣人或代理人的过失或疏忽所引起。

6. The carrier is not liable, except in general average, where loss, damage or delay in delivery resulted from measures to save life or from reasonable measures to save property at sea.

6. 除共同海损外，承运人对于海上救助人命的措施或救助财产的合理措施所引起的货物灭失、损坏或延迟交付，不负赔偿责任。

7. Where fault or neglect on the part of the carrier, his servants or agents combines with another cause to produce loss, damage or delay in delivery the carrier is liable only to the extent that the loss, damage or delay in delivery is attributable to such fault or neglect, provided that the carrier proves the amount of the loss, damage or delay in delivery not attributable thereto.

7. 如果货物的灭失、损坏或延迟交付是由于承运人，其雇佣人或代理人的过失或疏忽连同另一原因所引起，承运人只在能归之于这种过失或疏忽所引起的灭失、损坏或延迟交付的范围内负责。但是，承运人应对不属于这种灭失、损坏或延迟交付的数额，提出证明。

Article 6. Limits of liability
第六条 责任范围

1. (a) The liability of the carrier for loss resulting from loss of or damage to goods according

to the provisions of article 5 is limited to an amount equivalent to 835 units of account per package or other shipping unit or 2. 5 units of account per kilogramme of gross weight of the goods lost or damaged, whichever is the higher.

1. (1) 按照第五条规定，承运人对于货物的灭失或损坏的赔偿责任，以每件或每一其他装运单位的灭失或损坏货物赔偿相当于 835 结算单位或毛重每公斤相当于 2. 5 结算单位的金额为限，二者之中以较高者为准。

(b) The liability of the carrier for delay in delivery according to the provisions of article 5 is limited to an amount equivalent to two and a half times the freight payable for the goods delayed, but not exceeding the total freight payable under the contract of carriage of goods by sea.

(2) 按照第五条规定，承运人对延迟交付的赔偿责任，以相当于该项延迟交付货物应付运费的 2. 5 倍金额为限，但不超过海上运输契约中规定的应付运费总额。

(c) In no case shall the aggregate liability of the carrier under both subparagraphs (a) and (b) of this paragraph, exceed the limitation which would be established under subparagraph (a) of this paragraph for total loss of the goods with respect to which such liability was incurred.

(3) 承运人根据本款(1)(2)两项所应承担的总赔偿责任，在任何情况下，都不得超过根据本款第(1)项对引起货物全部灭失的这种赔偿责任所确定的限度。

2. For the purpose of calculating which amount is the higher in accordance with paragraph 1 (a) of this article, the following rules apply:

2. 按照本条第 1 款规定，计算其中较高的金额时，适用下列规则：

(a) where a container, pallet or similar article of transport is used to consolidate goods, the package or other shipping units enumerated in the bill of lading, if issued, or otherwise in any other document evidencing the contract of carriage by sea, as packed in such article of transport are deemed packages or shipping units. Except as aforesaid the goods in such article of transport are deemed one shipping unit.

(1) 当以集装箱、货盘或类似的装运工具集装货物时，如已签发提单，则在提单中所载的，否则，在作为海上运输契约证明的其他单证中所载的，装在这种工具中的件数或其他装运单位数，即视为货物的件数或其他装运单位数。除上述情况之外，装在此种装运工具中的货物，即视为一个装运单位。

(b) In cases where the article of transport itself has been lost or damaged, that article of transport shall, when not owned or otherwise supplied by the carrier, be considered one separate shipping unit.

(2) 如果装运工具本身遭到灭失或损坏，而该项装运工具非为承运人所有，或非由他以其他方式提供，便应将其视为一个单独的装运单位。

3. Unit of account means the unit of account mentioned in article 26.

3. 结算单位是指第二十六条所述结算单位。

4. By agreement between the carrier and the shipper, limits of liability exceeding those provided for in paragraph 1 may be fixed.

4. 根据承运人和托运人之间的协议，可以确定高于第 1 款规定的赔偿责任限度。

Article 7. Application to non-contractual claims
第七条　对非契约索赔的适用

1. The defences and limits of liability provided for in this Convention apply in any action against the carrier in respect of loss or damage to the goods covered by the contract of carriage by sea, as well as of delay in delivery, whether the action be founded in contract, in tort or otherwise.

1. 本公约所规定的抗辩和责任限度，适用于就海上运输契约所涉及的货物灭失或损坏以及延迟交付而对承运人提起的任何诉讼，不论其为根据契约还是根据侵权行为或其他原因所提起。

2. If such an action is brought against a servant or agent of the carrier, such servant or agent, if he proves that he acted within the scope of his employment, is entitled to avail himself of the defences and limits of liability which the carrier is entitled to invoke under this Convention.

2. 如果这种诉讼是对承运人的雇佣人或代理人提起，而且该雇佣人或代理人证明，他是在其受雇的职务范围内行事，他便有权援用承运人根据本公约有权提出的抗辩和责任限度。

3. Except as provided in article 8, the aggregate of the amounts recoverable from the carrier and from any persons referred to in paragraph 2 of this article shall not exceed the limits of liability provided for in this Convention.

3. 除第八条规定者外，从承运人和本条第 2 款所指任何人取得的赔偿金额总数，不得超过本公约所规定的责任限度。

Article 8. Loss of right to limit responsibility
第八条　限制责任的权利的丧失

1. The carrier is not entitled to the benefit of the limitation of liability provided for in article 6 if it is proved that the loss, damage or delay in delivery resulted from an act or omission of the carrier done with the intent to cause such loss, damage or delay, or recklessly and with knowledge that such loss, damage or delay would probably result.

1. 如经证明，货物的灭失、损坏或延迟交付是由于承运人为蓄意造成这一灭失、损坏或延期交付，或是明知可能造成这一灭失、损坏或延迟交付，但却轻率地采取的行为或不为所引起，承运人便无权享受第六条规定的责任限度的利益。

2. Notwithstanding the provisions of paragraph 2 of article 7, a servant or agent of the carrier is not entitled to the benefit of the limitation of liability provided for in article 6 if it is proved that the loss, damage or delay in delivery resulted from an act or omission of such servant or agent, done with the intent to cause such loss, damage or delay or recklessly and with knowledge that

such loss, damage or delay would probably result.

2. 虽有第七条第 2 款规定，如经证明，货物的灭失、损坏或延迟交付是由于承运人的雇佣人或代理人为蓄意造成这一灭失、损坏或延迟交付，或是明知可能造成这一灭失、损坏或延迟交付，但却轻率地采取的行为或不为所引起，该承运人的雇佣人或代理人便无权享受第六条规定的责任限度的利益。

Article 9. Deck cargo
第九条　舱面货

1. The carrier is entitled to carry the goods on deck only if such carriage is in accordance with an agreement with the shipper or with the usage of the particular trade or is required by statutory rules or regulations.

1. 承运人只有在依据和托运人签订的协议或该特定贸易的习惯，或为法规或条款所要求时，才有权在舱面载运货物。

2. If the carrier and the shipper have agreed that the goods shall or may be carried on deck, the carrier must insert in the bill of lading or other document evidencing the contract of carriage by sea a statement to that effect. In the absence of such a statement the carrier has the burden of proving that an agreement for carriage on deck has been entered into; however, the carrier is not entitled to invoke such an agreement against a third party, including a consignee, who has acquired the bill of lading in good faith.

2. 如果承运人和托运人已经商定，应当或者可以舱面载运货物，承运人便须在提单或其他作为海上运输契约证明的单证上作如是说明。如无此种说明，承运人便须证明，已就在舱面载运货物达成协议。但承运人无权援用此种协议以对抗正当取得提单的包括收货人在内的第三方。

3. Where the goods have been carried on deck contrary to the provisions of paragraph 1 of this article or where the carrier may not under paragraph 2 of this article invoke an agreement for carriage on deck, the carrier, notwithstanding the provisions of paragraph 1 of article 5, is liable for loss of or damage to the goods, as well as for delay in delivery, resulting solely from the carriage on deck, and the extent of his liability is to be determined in accordance with the provisions of article 6 or article 8 of this Convention, as the case may be.

3. 如果违反本条第 1 款的规定而在舱面载运货物，或者承运人不能按照本条第 2 款规定援用在舱面载货的协议，则虽有第五条第 I 款的规定，承运人对完全是由于舱面载货而造成的货物灭失或损坏以及延迟交付，应负赔偿责任。他所负责的程度，应分别按照本公约第六条或第八条的规定加以确定。

4. Carriage of goods on deck contrary to express agreement for carriage under deck is deemed to be an act or omission of the carrier within the meaning of article 8.

4. 违反在舱内载运的明文协议而在舱面载运货物者，视为第八条所述承运人的一种行为或不为。

Article 10. Liability of the carrier and actual carrier
第十条 承运人和实际承运人的赔偿责任

1. Where the performance of the carriage or part thereof has been entrusted to an actual carrier, whether or not in pursuance of a liberty under the contract of carriage by sea to do so, the carrier nevertheless remains responsible for the entire carriage according to the provisions of this Convention. The carrier is responsible, in relation to the carriage performed by the actual carrier, for the acts and omissions of the actual carrier and of his servants and agents acting within the scope of their employment.

1. 如已将运输工作或部分运输工作委托实际承运人执行，则不论是否根据海上运输契约而有权如此，承运人仍应按照本公约规定对全程运输负责。就实际承运人从事的运输工作而言，承运人应对实际承运人及其在受雇的职务范围内行事的雇佣人和代理人的行为或不为负责。

2. All the provisions of this Convention governing the responsibility of the carrier also apply to the responsibility of the actual carrier for the carriage performed by him. The provisions of paragraphs 2 and 3 of article 8 apply if an action is brought against a servant or agent of the actual carrier.

2. 本公约关于承运人责任的所有规定，也适用于实际承运人对他所从事的运输的责任。如果对实际承运人的雇佣人或代理人提起诉讼，便适用第七条第2款、第3款和第八条第2款的规定。

3. Any special agreement under which the carrier assumes obligations not imposed by this Convention or waives rights conferred by this Convention affects the actual carrier only if agreed to by him expressly and in writing whether or not the actual carrier has so agreed, the carrier nevertheless remains bound by the obligations or waivers resulting from such special agreement.

3. 承运人据以承担非由本公约所规定的义务，或放弃本公约所赋予的权利的任何特别协议，只有在实际承运人以书面明确同意时，才能对实际承运人发生影响。不论实际承运人已经同意与否，承运人仍受这种特别协议所规定的义务或弃权的约束。

4. Where and to the extent that both the carrier and the actual carrier are liable, their liability is joint and several.

4. 如果承运人和实际承运人均须负责，则在其应负责的范围内，他们负有连带责任。

5. The aggregate of the amounts recoverable from the carrier, the actual carrier and their servants and agents shall not exceed the limits of liability provided for in this Convention.

5. 从承运人、实际承运人及其雇佣人和代理人取得的赔偿金额总数，不得超过本公约所规定的责任限度。

6. Nothing in this article shall prejudice any right of recourse as between the carrier and the actual carrier.

6. 本条规定毫不妨碍承运人和实际承运人之间的追偿权利。

Article 11. Through carriage
第十一条　联运

1. Notwithstanding the provisions of paragraph 1 of article 10, where a contract of carriage by sea provides explicitly that a specified part of the carriage covered by the said contract is to be performed by a named person other than the carrier, the contract may also provide that the carrier is not liable for loss, damage or delay in delivery caused by an occurrence which takes place while the goods are in the charge of the actual carrier during such part of the carriage. Nevertheless, any stipulation limiting or excluding such liability is without effect if no judicial proceedings can be instituted against the actual carrier in a court competent under paragraph 1 or 2 of article 21. The burden of proving that any loss, damage or delay in delivery has been caused by such an occurrence rests upon the carrier.

1. 虽有第十条第 1 款各项规定，如果海上运输契约明确规定，该契约所载某一特定阶段的运输工作应由承运人以外的指定人员执行，则该契约亦可规定，就这一特定运输阶段而言，承运人对由于货物在实际承运人掌管之下发生的事故所引起的灭失，损坏或延期交付，不负赔偿责任。但是，如果不能在按照第二十一条第 1 款、第 2 款规定有权管辖的法院提起；法律诉讼，则任何限定或免除这种赔偿责任的条款，均属无效。关于货物的灭失、损坏或延迟交付系由上述事故所引起一事，应由承运人负责举证。

2. The actual carrier is responsible in accordance with the provisions of paragraph 2 of article 10 for loss, damage or delay in delivery caused by an occurrence which takes place while the goods are in his charge.

2. 按照第十条第 2 款规定，实际承运人应对货物在他掌管期间所发生的事故而引起的灭失、损坏或延迟交付负责。

PART Ⅲ　LIABILITY OF THE SHIPPER
第三章　托运人的责任

Article 12. General rule
第十二条　一般规则

The shipper is not liable for loss sustained by the carrier or the actual carrier, or for damage sustained by the ship, unless such loss or damage was caused by the fault or neglect of the shipper, his servants or agents. Nor is any servant or agent of the shipper liable for such loss or damage unless the loss or damage was caused by fault or neglect on his part.

托运人对承运人或实际承运人所受损失或船舶所受损坏，不负赔偿责任，除非这种损失或损坏是由于托运人、托运人的雇佣人或代理人的过失或疏忽所造成。托运人的任何雇用人或代理人对此项损失或损坏亦不负赔偿责任。除非该项损失或损坏是由他的过失或疏忽所造成。托运人的任何雇用人或代理人对此项损失或损坏亦不负赔偿责任，除非该项损失或损坏是由于他的过失或疏忽所造成。

Article 13. Special rules on dangerous goods
第十三条　关于危险货物的特殊规则

1. The shipper must mark or label in a suitable manner dangerous goods as dangerous.

1. 托运人必须以适宜的方式，在危险货物上制备危险标志或标签。

2. Where the shipper hands over dangerous goods to the carrier or an actual carrier as the case may be, the shipper must inform him of the dangerous character of the goods and, if necessary, of the precautions to be taken. If the shipper fails to do so and such carrier or actual carrier does not otherwise have knowledge of their dangerous character.

2. 当托运人将危险货物交与承运人或实际承运人时，托运人须将货物的危险性质和必要时所应采取的预防措施通知承运人和实际承运人。如果托运人未能通知，而承运人或实际承运人也未从别处得知其危险性质，则：

(a) the shipper is liable to the carrier or actual carrier for the loss resulting from the shipment of such goods, and

(1) 托运人应对承运人或实际承运人因载运这类货物而造成的损失负赔偿责任；并且

(b) the goods may at any time be unloaded, destroyed or rendered innocuous, as the circumstances may require, without payment of compensation.

(2) 可以根据情况随时将该货卸下，销毁，或使之无害，而无须给予赔偿。

3. The provisions of paragraph 2 of this article may not be invoked by any person if during the carriage he has taken the goods in his charge with knowledge of their dangerous character.

3. 如果在运输期间是在了解其危险性质的情况下接管货物的，任何人都不得援用本条第2款的规定。

4. If, in cases where the provisions of paragraph 2, subparagraph (b), of this article do not apply or may not be invoked, dangerous goods become an actual danger to life or property, they may be unloaded, destroyed or rendered innocuous as the circumstances may require without payment of compensation except where there is an obligation to contribute in general average or where the carrier is liable in accordance with the provisions of article 5.

4. 如果不适用或者不得援用本条第2款(2)项的规定，而危险货物对生命或财产造成实际危险时，可以根据情况需要，将其卸下、销毁，或使之无害；除有分摊共同海损义务或按第五条规定承运人负有赔偿责任外，无需给予赔偿。

PART Ⅳ   TRANSPORT DOCUMENTS
第四章   运输单证

Article 14. Issue of bill of lading
第十四条   提单的签发

1. When the carrier or the actual carrier takes the goods in his charge, the carrier must, on demand of the shipper, issue to the shipper a bill of lading.

1. 当承运人或实际承运人接管货物时，他必须按照托运人的要求，为托运人签发提单。

2. The bill of lading may be signed by a person having authority from the carrier. A bill of lading signed by the master of the ship carrying the goods is deemed to have been signed on behalf of the carrier.

2. 提单可由承运人授权的人签字。经承运船船长签字的提单，视为代表承运人所签。

3. The signature on the bill of lading may be in handwriting, printed in facsimile, perforated, stamped, in symbols, or made by any other mechanical or electronic means, if not inconsistent with the law of the country where the bill of lading is issued.

3. 提单上的签字，如不违反签发提单所在国法律，可以是手写、签字复印，打透花字，盖章、使用符号或任何其他机械或电子工具。

Article 15. Contents of bill of lading
第十五条   提单的内容

1. The bill of lading must include, inter alia the following particulars:

1. 提单中必须载有下列事项：

(a) the general nature of the goods, the leading marks necessary for identification of the goods, an express statement, if applicable, as to the dangerous character of the goods, the number of packages or pieces and the weight of the goods or their quantity otherwise expressed: all such particulars as furnished by the shippers;

（1）货物的品类，识别货物所需的主要标志，对货物的危险性质的明确说明（如属适用），包数或件数，货物重量或以其他方式表示的数量。上述全部资料均由托运人提供。

(b) the apparent condition of the goods;

（2）货物的外表状况；

(c) the name and principal place of business of the carriers;

（3）承运人姓名及其主要营业所；

(d) the name of the shipper;

（4）托运人姓名；

(e) the consignee if named by the shippers;

（5）在由托运人指定收货人时的收货人姓名；

(f) the port of loading under the contract of carriage by sea and the date on which the goods were taken over by the carrier at the port of loading;

（6）海上运输契约规定的装货港以及货物由承运人在装货港接管的日期；

(g) the port of discharge under the contract of carriage by sea;

（7）海上运输契约规定的卸货港；

(h) the number of originals of the bill of lading, if more than one;

（8）提单正本超过一份时的提单正本份数；

(i) the place of issuance of the bill of lading;

（9）签发提单地点；

(j) the signature of the carrier or a person acting on his behalf;

（10）承运人或其代表的签字；

(k) the freight to the extent payable by the consignee or other indication that freight is payable by him;

（11）收货人应付运费金额，或者应由收货人支付运费的其他说明；

(l) the statement referred to in paragraph 3 of article 23;

（12）第二十三条第 3 款所指声明；

(m) the statement, if applicable, that the goods shall or may be carried on deck;

（13）在适用时，货物应在或可在舱面载运的声明；

(n) the date or the period of delivery of the goods at the port of discharge if expressly agreed upon between the parties and

（14）经双方明确协议的货物在卸货港的交付日期或期限，以及

(o) any increased limit or limits of liability where agreed in accordance with paragraph 4 of article 6.

（15）依照第六条第 4 款规定而商定的赔偿责任限度的提高。

2. After the goods have been loaded on board, if the shipper so demands, the carrier must issue to the shipper a "shipped" bill of lading which in addition to the particulars required under paragraph 1 of this article, must state that the goods are on board a named ship or ships, and the date or dates of loading. If the carrier has previously issued to the shipper a bill of lading or other document of title with respect to any of such goods, on request of the carrier, the shipper must surrender such document in exchange for a "shipped" bill of lading. The carrier may amend any previously issued document in order to meet the shipper's demand for a "shipped" bill of lading if, as amended, such document includes all the information required to be contained in a "shipped" bill of lading.

2. 货物装船后，如果托运人作此要求，承运人须为托运人签发"已装船"提单。"已装船"提单除载明本条第 I 款所规定的事项外，还须载明货物已经装上指定船舶和装船日

期。如果承运人已在先前就某些货物签发提单或其他物权凭证，则经承运人要求，托运人须交还此项单证，换取"已装船"提单。承运人为了满足托运人对"已装船"提单的要求，可以修改任何先前签发的单证，如果修改后的单证载有"已装船"提单所需载有的全部情况。

3. The absence in the bill of lading of one or more particulars referred to in this article does not affect the legal character of the document as a bill of lading provided that it nevertheless meets the requirements set out in paragraph 7 of article 1.

3. 提单中缺少本条规定的一项或几项内容，并不影响其作为提单的法律性质；但该提单须符合第一条第 7 款所规定的要求。

Article 16. Bills of lading: reservations and evidentiary effect
第十六条 提单：保留和证据效力

1. If the bill of lading contains particulars concerning the general nature, leading marks number of packages or pieces, weight or quantity of the goods which the carrier or other person issuing the bill of lading on his behalf knows or has reasonable grounds to suspect do not accurately represent the goods actually taken over or, where a "shipped" bill of lading is issued, loaded, or if he had no reasonable means of checking such particulars, the carrier or such other person must insert in the bill of lading a reservation specifying these inaccuracies, grounds of suspicion or the absence of reasonable means of checking.

1. 如果承运人或代其签发提单的其他人，得知或有合理根据怀疑提单中所载有关货物的品类、主要标志、包数或件数、重量或数量等项，并不能准确地代表其实际接管的货物，或者在签发"已装船"提单时，上述各项并不能准确地代表已经装船的货物，或者没有核对这些事项的适当手段，则承运人或上述其他人必须在提单中作出保留，说明这些不符之处、怀疑的根据或无适当核对手段等。

2. If the carrier or other person issuing the bill of lading on his behalf fails to note on the bill of lading the apparent condition of the goods, he is deemed to have noted on the bill of lading that the goods were in apparent good condition.

2. 如果承运人或代其签发提单的其他人，未在提单中对货物的外表状况加以批注，便应视为已在提单中注明货物的外表状况良好。

3. Except for particulars in respect of which and to the extent to which a reservation permitted under paragraph 1 of this article has been entered.

3. 除已就本条第 1 款所允许的事项在允许的范围内作出保留外：

（a）the bill of lading is prima facie evidence of the taking over or, where a "shipped" bill of lading is issued, loading by the carrier of the goods as described in the bill of lading; and

（1）该提单是其中所载货物由承运人接管，而如签发"已装船"提单时，则是由承运人装船的表面证据；而且，

（b）proof to the contrary by the carrier is not admissible if the bill of lading has been transferred to a third party, including a consignee, who in good faith has acted in reliance on the description of the goods therein.

（2）如果提单已经转让给正当地按照提单中所载货物情况行事的、包括收货人在内的第三方，则对承运人提出的与此相反的证据，便不予接受。

4. A bill of lading which does not, as provided in paragraph 1, subparagraph (k) or article 15, set forth the freight or otherwise indicate that freight is payable by the consignee or does not set forth demurrage incurred at the port of loading payable by the consignee, is prima facie evidence that no freight or such demurrage is payable by him. However, proof to the contrary by the carrier is not admissible when the bill of lading has been transferred to a third party, including a consignee, who in good faith has acted in reliance on the absence in the bill of lading of any such indication.

4. 如果提单未按第十五条第 1 款第(11)项规定载明运费，或者未以其他方式表明运费由收货人支付，或未载明由收货人支付在装货港的滞期费，则该提单便是运费或此种滞期费不是由收货人支付的表面证据。然而，当提单已被转让给正当地依据提单中未作此种记载而行事的、包括收货人在内的第三方时，对承运人提出的与此相反的证据，便不予接受。

Article 17. Guarantees by the shipper
第十七条　托运人的保证

1. The shipper is deemed to have guaranteed to the carrier the accuracy of particulars relating to the general nature of the goods, their marks, number, weight and quantity as furnished by him for insertion in the bill of lading. The shipper must indemnify the carrier against the loss resulting from inaccuracies in such particulars. The shipper remains liable even if the bill of lading has been transferred by him. The right of the carrier to such indemnity in no way limits his liability under the contract of carriage by sea to any person other than the shipper.

1. 托运人应被视为已就其为列入提单而向承运人提供的有关货物的品类、标志、件数、重量及数量的正确性，向承运人提出保证。托运人须就由于此种事项之不正确而造成的损失，给予承运人赔偿。即使托运人已将提单转让，托运人仍应负赔偿责任。承运人取得此种赔偿的权利，毫不足以限制其根据海上运输契约对托运人以外的任何人所负的赔偿责任。

2. Any letter of guarantee or agreement by which the shipper undertakes to indemnify the carrier against loss resulting from the issuance of the bill of lading by the carrier, or by a person acting on his behalf without entering a reservation relating to particulars furnished by the shipper for insertion in the bill of lading, or to the apparent condition of the goods, is void and of no effect as against any third party, including a consignee, to whom the bill of lading has been transferred.

2. 托运人为就承运人或代其行事的人，未对由托运人提供作为载入提单之用的事项或货物的外表状况注有保留而签发提单所引起的损失，而据以向承运人提出赔偿的任何保函或协议，对包括受让提单的收货人在内的第三方，一概无效。

3. Such letter of guarantee or agreement is valid as against the shipper unless the carrier or the person acting on his behalf by omitting the reservation referred to in paragraph 2 of this article, intends to defraud a third party, including a consignee, who acts in reliance on the description of the goods in the bill of lading. In the latter case, if the reservation omitted relates to particulars furnished by the shipper for insertion in the bill of lading the carrier has no right of indemnity from the shipper pursuant to paragraph 1 of this article.

3. 除非承运人或代其行事的人出于对信赖提单中所载货物情况的，包括收货人在内的第三方进行欺诈，而不将本条第 2 款所述保留载入，此种保函或协议，针对托运人而言，便属有效。在发生欺诈的情况下，如果未予列入的保留，乃是关于由托运人提供以备载入提单的事项，承运人便无权根据本条第 1 款自托运人取得赔偿。

4. In the case of intended fraud referred to in paragraph 3 of this article the carrier is liable, without the benefit of the limitation of liability provided for in this Convention, for the loss incurred by a third party, including a consignee, because he has acted in reliance on the description of the goods in the bill of lading.

4. 在本条第 3 款所述意欲欺诈的情况下，承运人应对信赖其所发提单中所载货物情况的、包括收货人在内的第三方所受任何损失，负赔偿责任，而不能享受本公约中规定的责任限度的利益。

Article 18. Documents other than bills of lading
第十八条　提单以外的单证

Where a carrier issues a document other than a bill of lading to evidence the receipt of the goods to be carried, such a document is prima facie evidence of the conclusion of the contract of carriage by sea and the taking over by the carrier of the goods as therein described.

如果承运人签发提单以外的单证用以证明收到交运的货物，这种单证就是订立海上运输契约和由承运人接管该单证中所载货物的表面证据。

PART V　CLAIMS AND ACTIONS
第五章　索赔和诉讼

Article 19. Notice of loss, damage or delay
第十九条　灭失，损坏或延迟交付的通知

1. Unless notice of loss or damage, specifying the general nature of such loss or damage, is given in writing by the consignee to the carrier not later than the working day after the day when the goods were handed over to the consignee, such handing over is prima facie evidence of the

delivery by the carrier of the goods as described in the document of transport or, if no such document has been issued, in good condition.

1. 除非收货人已在不迟于其接受货物的下一工作日，将写明灭失或损坏的一般性质的灭失或损坏通知书送交承运人，这种交接便是承运人已按运输单证所载交付货物，而在未签发此种单证时，则是以良好状态交付货物的表面证据。

2. Where the loss or damage is not apparent, the provisions of paragraph 1 of this article apply correspondingly if notice in writing is not given within 15 consecutive days after the day when the goods were handed over to the consignee.

2. 如果灭失或损坏不是显而易见，且在货物交付收货人之日以后连续十五日内未曾提出书面通知，则应据以适用本条第 1 款的规定。

3. If the state of the goods at the time they were handed over to the consignee has been the subject of a joint survey or inspection by the parties, notice in writing need not be given of loss or damage ascertained during such survey or inspection.

3. 如果货物的状况在其被交付收货人之时已经当事各方联合检查或检验，便无需就调查或检验时查明的灭失或损坏，送交书面通知。

4. In the case of any actual or apprehended loss or damage the carrier and the consignee must give all reasonable facilities to each other for inspecting and tallying the goods.

4. 遇有任何实际的或预料可能发生的灭失或损坏时，承运人和收货人须为检验和清点货物而相互提供一切合理的便利。

5. No compensation shall be payable for loss resulting from delay in delivery unless a notice has been given in writing to the carrier within 60 consecutive days after the day when the goods were handed over to the consignee.

5. 除非在将货物交付收货人之日以后连续六十天之内，已将书面通知送交承运人，对因延迟交付所造成的损失，便不应予以赔偿。

6. If the goods have been delivered by an actual carrier, any notice given under this article to him shall have the same effect as if it had been given to the carrier and any notice given to the carrier shall have effect as if given to such actual carrier.

6. 如果货物已由实际承运人交付，则根据本条规定送交的任何通知具有犹如送交承运人的通知的同等效力；而送交承运人的任何通知，则具有犹如送交实际承运人的通知的同等效力。

7. Unless notice of loss or damage, specifying the general nature of the loss or damage, is given in writing by the carrier or actual carrier to the shipper not later than 90 consecutive days after the occurrence of such loss or damage or after the delivery of the goods in accordance with paragraph 2 of article 4, whichever is later, the failure to give such notice is prima facie evidence that the carrier or the actual carrier has sustained no loss or damage due to the fault or neglect of the shipper, his servants or agents.

7. 除承运人或实际承运人已在不迟于灭失或损坏发生之后，或依照第四条第 2 款在货物交付之后(以较迟发生者为准)，连续九十天之内，将载明灭失或损坏一般性质的灭失或损坏通知，以书面送交托运人外，凡是未能提交此种通知时，便是承运人或实际承运人并未由于托运人、其雇佣人或代理人的过失或疏忽而遭受灭失或损坏的表面证据。

8. For the purpose of this article, notice given to a person acting on the carrier's or the actual carrier's behalf, including the master or the officer in charge of the ship, or to a person acting on the shipper's behalf is deemed to have been given to the carrier, to the actual carrier or to the shipper, respectively.

8. 就本条而言，凡是已将通知送交代表承运人或实际承运人行事的人，包括船长或该船主管人员，或已送交代表托运人行事的人，便视为已经分别送交承运人、实际承运人或托运人。

Article 20. Limitation of actions
第二十条　诉讼时效

1. Any action relating to carriage of goods under this Convention is time-barred if judicial or arbitral proceedings have not been instituted within a period of two years.

1. 根据本公约而提出的关于货物运输的任何诉讼，如果在两年之内尚未提出或未提付仲裁，即失去时效。

2. The limitation period commences on the day on which the carrier has delivered the goods or part thereof or, in cases where no goods have been delivered, on the last day on which the goods should have been delivered.

2. 时效期限自承运人交付货物或交付部分货物之日起算，而在未交付货物时，则自应交付货物的最后一日起算。

3. The day on which the limitation period commences is not included in the period.

3. 时效期限起算的当日，不包括在期限之内。

4. The person against whom a claim is made may at any time during the running of the limitation period extend that period by a declaration in writing to the claimant. This period may be further extended by another declaration or declarations.

4. 被要求赔偿的人，可在时效期限之内的任何时间向索赔人提出书面声明，延长时效期限。该期限可以通过再次声明而进一步延长。

5. An action for indemnity by a person held liable may be instituted even after the expiration of the limitation period provided for in the preceding paragraphs if instituted within the time allowed by the law of the State where proceedings are instituted. However, the time allowed shall not be less than 90 days commencing from the day when the person instituting such action for indemnity has settled the claim or has been served with process in the action against himself.

5. 由负有赔偿的人提起的要求清偿的诉讼，如果是在提起诉讼所在国法律所许可的时间之内提出，即使是在上述各款规定的时效期限届满之后，亦可进行。但是，所许可的时间，自提起此种诉讼之人已经处理其索赔案件，或已接到向其本人送交的起诉传票之日起算，不得少于九十天。

Article 21. Jurisdiction
第二十一条 管辖权

1. In judicial proceedings relating to carriage of goods under this Convention the plaintiff, at his option, may institute an action in a court which according to the law of the State where the court is situated, is competent and within the jurisdiction of which is situated one of the following places:

1. 对于与根据本公约载运货物有关的法律诉讼，原告可以自行选定在此种法院提出，即根据该法院所在国家的法律有权进行管辖，而且下列地点之一，是在其管辖范围之内：

（a）the principal place of business or, in the absence thereof, the habitual residence of the defendant, or

（1）被告的主要营业所，而在无主要营业所时，则为其通常住所；或者

（b）the place where the contract was made provided that the defendant has there a place of business, branch or agency through which the contract was made, or

（2）契约订立地，而契约是通过被告在该地的营业所、分支或代理机构订立；或者

（c）the port of loading or the port of discharge, or

（3）装货港或卸货港；或者

（d）any additional place designated for that purpose in the contract of carriage by sea.

（4）海上运输契约中为此目的而指定的任何其他地点。

2. （a）Notwithstanding the preceding provisions of this article, an action may be instituted in the courts of any port or place in a Contracting State at which the carrying vessel or any other vessel of the same ownership may have been arrested in accordance with applicable rules of the law of that State and of international law. However, in such a case at the petition of the defendant, the claimant must remove the action, at his choice, to one of the jurisdictions referred to in paragraph 1 of this article for the determination of the claim, but before such removal the defendant must furnish security sufficient to ensure payment of any judgement that may subsequently be awarded to the claimant in the action.

2. （1）虽有本规前述规定，如果载货船舶或属于该同一船舶所有人的任何其他船舶，在一个缔约国的任何港口或地点依照适用于该国的法律或国际法的规则而被扣，便可向该港口或地点所在法院提起诉讼。但是，在这种情况下，经被告请求，原告须将诉讼转移到他所选定的本条第 1 款所述管辖法院之一，以作出对索赔的决定。而在诉讼转移之前，被告必须提供足够的保证，以偿付日后可能判归原告的赔偿金额。

（b）All questions relating to the sufficiency or otherwise of the security shall be determined by the court of the port or place of the arrest.

（2）一切有关担保是否足够等问题，应由扣留港口或地点的法院裁定。

3. No judicial proceedings relating to carriage of goods under this Convention may be instituted in a place not specified in paragraph 1 or 2 of this article. The provisions of this paragraph do not constitute an obstacle to the jurisdiction of the Contracting States for provisional

or protective measures.

3. 根据本公约而提起的有关货物运输的任何法律诉讼，不得在本条第 2 款所未规定的地点提出。本款上述规定并不妨碍缔约国采取临时性或保护性措施的管辖权。

4. (a) Where an action has been instituted in a court competent under paragraph 1 or 2 of this article or where judgement has been delivered by such a court, no new action may be started between the same parties on the same grounds unless the judgement of the court before which the first action was instituted is not enforceable in the country in which the new proceedings are instituted;

4. (1) 如已向根据本条第 1 款或第 2 款而有管辖权的法院提起诉讼，或已由此种法院作出判决，则除非受理第一次诉讼的法院的判决不能在提起新的诉讼的国家执行，相同当事人之间不得就同一案情提起新的诉讼。

(b) for the purpose of this article the institution of measures with a view to obtaining enforcement of a judgement is not to be considered as the starting of a new action;

(2) 就本条而言，为了求得判决的执行而采取的措施，不应视为提起新的诉讼。

(c) for the purpose of this article, the removal of an action to a different court within the same country, or to a court in another country, in accordance with paragraph 2 (a) of this article, is not to be considered as the starting of a new action.

(3) 就本条而言，诉讼转移到同一国家的另一法院，或者依照本条第 2 款第(1)项转移到另一国家的法院时，不应视为提起新的诉讼。

5. Notwithstanding the provisions of the preceding paragraphs, an agreement made by the parties, after a claim under the contract of carriage by sea has arisen, which designates the place where the claimant may institute an action, is effective.

5. 虽有上述各款规定，在根据海上运输契约提出索赔之后，当事各方达成的关于索赔人可以提起诉讼地点的协议，仍属有效。

Article 22. Arbitration
第二十二条 仲裁

1. Subject to the provisions of this article, parties may provide by agreement evidenced in writing that any dispute that may arise relating to carriage of goods under this Convention shall be referred to arbitration.

1. 根据本条规定，当事各方可用以书面证明的协议规定，凡是关于按本公约运输货物所发生的争议，都应提付仲裁。

2. Where a charter-party contains a provision that disputes arising thereunder shall be referred to arbitration and a bill of lading issued pursuant to the charter-party does not contain a special annotation providing that such provision shall be binding upon the holder of the bill of lading, the carrier may not invoke such provision as against a holder having acquired the bill of lading in good faith.

2. 如果租船契约中载有应将该租约所引起的争议提付仲裁的条款，而根据租船契约签发的提单并未载有一项特别注解，规定该条款对提单持有人具有约束力，则承运人不得援用该条款以对抗正当地取得提单的人。

3. The arbitration proceedings shall, at the option of the claimant, be instituted at one of the following places:

3. 仲裁案件可由索赔人决定，在下列地点之一提起：

(a) a place in a State within whose territory is situated:

(1) 一个国家的某一地方，而在该国境内设有：

(i) the principal place of business of the defendant or, in the absence thereof the habitual residence of the defendant; or

① 被告的主要营业所，而如无主要营业所，则为其通常住所；或者

(ii) the place where the contract was made, provided that the defendant has there a place of business, branch or agency through which the contract was made;

② 契约订立地，而契约是通过被告在该地的营业所、分支或代理机构订立；或者

(iii) the port of loading or the port of discharge; or

③装货港或卸货港；或者

(b) any place designated for that purpose in the arbitration clause or agreement.

(2) 仲裁条款或协议中为此目的而指定的任何地点。

4. The arbitrator or arbitration tribunal shall apply the rules of this Convention.

4. 仲裁员或仲裁庭应当适用本公约各项规则。

5. The provisions of paragraphs 3 and 4 of this article are deemed to be part of every arbitration clause or agreement, and any term of such clause or agreement which is inconsistent therewith is null and void.

5. 本条第3款、第4款的规定，视为每一仲裁条款或协议的一部分，仲裁条款或协议中凡是与此相抵触的任何规定，概属无效。

6. Nothing in this article affects the validity of an agreement relating to arbitration made by the parties after the claim under the contract of Carriage by sea has arisen.

6. 本条规定，不影响当事各方在根据海上运输契约提出索赔之后订立的有关仲裁协议的效力，

PART VI　SUPPLEMENTARY PROVISIONS
第六章　补充规定

Article 23　Contractual stipulations
第二十三条　契约条款

1. Any stipulation in a contract of carriage by sea, in a bill of lading or in any other

document evidencing the contract of carriage by sea is null and void to the extent that it derogates, directly or indirectly, from the provisions of this Convention. The nullity of such a stipulation does not affect the validity of the other provisions of the contract or document of which it forms a part. A clause assigning benefit of insurance of the goods in favour of the carrier, or any similar clause, is null and void.

1. 海上运输契约中或作为海上运输契约证明的提单或任何其他单证中的任何条款，在其直接或间接背离本公约规定的范围内，概属无效。此种条款之无效，并不影响以其作为部分内容的该契约或单证的其他规定的效力。将货物的保险利益转让与承运人的条款，或任何类似条款，概属无效。

2. Notwithstanding the provisions of paragraph of this article, a carrier may increase his responsibilities and obligations under this Convention.

2. 虽有本条第 1 款的规定，承运人仍可增加其根据本公约所承担的责任和义务。

3. Where a bill of lading or any other document evidencing the contract of carriage by sea is issued, it must contain a statement that the carriage is subject to the provisions of this Convention which nullify any stipulation derogating therefrom to the detriment of the shipper or the consignee.

3. 在签发提单或作为海上运输契约证明的任何其他单证时，其中必须载有一项声明，说明该项运输应当遵守本公约各项规定；凡是与此相背离的有损于托运人或收货人的条款，概属无效。

4. Where the claimant in respect of the goods has incurred loss as a result of a stipulation which is null and void by virtue of the present article, or as a result of the omission of the statement referred to in paragraph 3 of this article, the carrier must pay compensation to the extent required in order to give the claimant compensation in accordance with the provisions of this Convention for any loss of or damage to the goods as well as for delay in delivery. The carrier must, in addition, pay compensation for costs incurred by the claimant for the purpose of exercising his right, provided that costs incurred in the action where the fore going provision is invoked are to be determined in accordance with the law of the State where proceedings are instituted.

4. 如果有关货物的索赔人由于根据本条而无效的条款，或由于未载有本条第 3 款所述声明而遭受损失，则承运人必须按照本公约规定，就货物的灭失或损坏以及延迟交付等项，在赔偿索赔人所需限度之内，支付赔偿金。此外，承运人还须赔偿索赔人为行使其权利而发生的费用。但援用上述规定的起诉费用，应根据诉讼所在国法律办理。

Article 24. General average
第二十四条　共同海损

1. Nothing in this Convention shall prevent the application of provisions in the contract of carriage by sea or national law regarding the adjustment of general average.

1. 本公约中的任何规定，都不得妨碍海上运输契约或国内法中关于共同海损理算的规则。

2. With the exception of article 20, the provisions of this Convention relating to the liability of the carrier for loss of or damage to the goods also determine whether the consignee may refuse contribution in general average and the liability of the carrier to indemnify the consignee in respect of any such contribution made or any salvage paid.

2. 除第二十条外，本公约关于承运人对于货物的灭失或损坏的赔偿责任的规定，也适用于确定收货人可否拒绝在共同海损中的分摊，以及承运人就收货人所作此项分摊所付救助费用而给予收货人赔偿的责任。

练习

翻译下列短文。

1. A corporation is a legal entity — an artificial legal "person" — created on the approval of the appropriate governmental authority. To form a corporation, the incorporators (often at least three are required) must apply for a charter. The incorporators prepare and file the articles of incorporation, which delineate the basic structure of the corporation, including the purposes for which it is formed, the amount of capital stock to be authorized, and the number of shares into which the stock is to be divided. If the incorporators meet the requirements of the law, the government issues a charter of certificate of incorporation. After the charter has been granted, the incorporators hold an organization meeting to elect the first board of directors and adopt the corporation's bylaws.

Because assets are essential to corporate operations, the corporation issues capital stock certificates (股票，股权证) to obtain the necessary funds. Owners of the corporation, stockholders, or shareholders, are entitled to a voice in the control and management of the company. Stockholders with voting stock may vote at the annual meeting and participate in the election of the board of directors. The board of directors is responsible for the overall management of the corporation. Normally, the board selects such corporate officers as a president, one or more vice presidents, a controller, a treasurer, and a secretary. The officers implement the policies of the board of directors and actively manage the day-to-day affairs of the corporation.

2. CONTRACT LAW A document or instrument containing the terms of an enforceable obligation between the parties is called a "contract". Why do we need contract? The obvious answer is because promises should be binding, but in fact the law only enforces certain types of promise, essentially those which involve some form of exchange. Why do we need laws specifically designed to enforce promises involving an exchange? The major reason appears to be the kind of society we live in, which is called a market commodity society. In such a society, we make contracts when we buy goods at the supermarket, when we get on a bus or train, and when we put money into a machine to buy chocolate or drinks. It would be impossible to run a society if promises were not binding. In fact contract law rarely forces a party to fulfill contractual promises, but what it does do is to try to compensate innocent parties financially, usually by attempting to

put them in the position they would have been in if the contract had been performed as agreed. This has the double function of helping parties to know what they can expect if the contract is not performed, and encouraging performance by ensuring that those who fail to perform cannot simply get away with their breach.

For a contract to exist, usually one party must have made an offer, and the other must have accepted it. Once acceptance takes effect, a contract will usually be binding on both parties. Offer and acceptance are essential elements to form a contract, and we discuss them in a detailed description now.

An offer is a statement by one party of a willingness to enter into a contract on stated terms, provided that these terms are, in turn, accepted by the party or parties to whom the offer is addressed. The person making an offer is called the offeror, and the person to whom the offer is made is called the offeree. A communication will be treated as an offer if it indicates the terms on which the offeror is prepared to make a contract, and gives a clear indication that the offeror intends to be bound by those terms if they are accepted by the offeree.

Care must be taken, however, in distinguishing between an offer and an invitation to treat. Some kinds of transaction involve preliminary stage in which one party invites the other to make an offer. This stage is called an invitation to treat. In other words, an invitation to treat is simply an expression of willingness to enter into negotiations which, it is hoped, will lead to the conclusion of a contract at a later date. The distinction between the two is said to be primarily the intention, that is, did the maker of the statement intend to be bound by an acceptance of his terms without further negotiation or did he only intend his statement to be part of the continuing negotiating process?

Then how long does an offer last? In general, an offer may cease to exist under any of the following circumstances.

(a) **Specified time**　Where an offeror states that an offeror will remain open for a specific length of time, it lapses when that time is up.

(b) **Reasonable length of time**　Where the offeror has not specified how long the offer will remain open, it will lapse after a reasonable length of time has passed. How much time will depend upon whether the means of communication of the offer was fast or slow and on its subject matter — for example, offers to buy perishable goods, or a commodity whose price fluctuates daily, will lapse quite quickly. Offerors to buy shares on the stock market may last only seconds.

(c) **Rejection**　An offer lapses when the offeree rejects it. For example, if A offers to sell B his computer on Saturday, and B, says no, B cannot come back on Sunday and insist on accepting the offer.

(d) **Counter offer**　A purported acceptance, which does not accept all the terms and conditions proposed by the offeror, but which in fact introduces new terms, is not an acceptance but a counter-offer which is then treated as a new offer which is capable of acceptance or rejection. The effect of a counter-offer is to "kill off" the original offer so that it cannot subsequently be accepted by the offeree. A counter offer terminates the original offer. For example, A offered to sell his car for $10,000, and B responded by offering to buy it at $9,500 — this is called making a counter offer. The car owner refused to sell at that price, and when B tried to accept the offer to buy at $10,000, it was no longer available, as it had been terminated by the counter offer.

(e) **Death of the offeror** The position is not entirely clear, but it appears that if the offeree knows that the offeror has died, the offer will lapse; if the offeree is unaware of the offeror's death, it probably will not. However, where an offer requires personal performance by the offeror (such as painting a picture, or appearing in a film) it will usually lapse on the offeror's death.

(f) **Death of the offeree** There is no English case on this point, but it seems probably that the offer lapses and cannot be accepted after the afferee's death by the offeree's representatives.

(g) **Revocation by the offeror** An offer may be revoked at any time up until it is accepted. It is not enough for an offeror simply to change his mind about an offer; he must notify the offeree that it is being revoked. There are two main exceptions to the rule that the withdrawal must be communicated to the offeree. First, if an offeree moves to a new address without notifying the offeror, a withdrawal which was delivered to the offeree's last known address will be effective on delivery there. In the same way, where a withdrawal reaches the offeree, but the offeree simply fails to read it, it probably still takes effect on reaching them. Secondly, where a unilateral offeror is made to the world at large, to be accepted by conduct, it can probably be revoked without the need for communication if the revocation takes place before performance has begun.

3. OCEAN MARINE CARGO INSURANCE CLAUSE

I. Scope of Cover

This insurance is classified into the following three Conditions: Free From Particular Average (F. P. A.), With Average (W. A.) and All Risks. Where the goods insured hereunder sustain loss or damage, the Company shall undertake to indemnify therefore according to the Insured Condition specified in the Policy and Provisions of these Clauses:

(a) Free From Particular Average (F. P. A)

This insurance covers:.

(1) Total or Constructive Total Loss of the whole consignment hereby insured caused in the course of transit by natural calamities — heavy weather, lightning, tsunami, earthquake and flood. In case a constructive total loss is claimed for, the insured shall abandon to the Company the damaged goods and all his rights and title pertaining thereto. The goods on each lighter to or from seagoing vessel shall be deemed a separate risk.

"Constructive Total Loss" refers to the loss where an actual total loss appears to be unavoidable or the cost to be incurred in recovering or reconditioning the goods together with the forwarding cost to the destination named in the Policy would exceed their value on arrival.

(2) Total or Partial Loss caused by accidents — the carrying conveyance being grounded, stranded, sunk or in collision with floating ice or other objects as fire or explosion.

(3) Partial loss of the insured goods attributable to heavy weather, lightning and/or tsunami, where the conveyance has been grounded, stranded, sunk or burnt, irrespective of whether the event or events took place before or after such accidents.

(4) Partial or total loss consequent on falling of entire package or packages into sea during loading, transshipment or discharge.

(5) Reasonable cost incurred by the insured in salvaging the goods or averting or minimizing a loss recoverable under the Policy, provided that such cost shall not exceed the sum insured of the consignment so saved.

(6) Losses attributable to discharge of the insured goods at a port or distress following a sea peril as well as special charges arising from loading, warehousing and forwarding of the goods at an intermediate port of call or refuge.

(7) Sacrifice in and Contribution to General Average and Salvage Charges.

(8) Such proportion of losses sustained by the ship-owners as is to be reimbursed by the Cargo Owner under the Contract of Affreightment "Both to Blame Collision" clause.

(b) With Average (W. A.)

Aside from the risks covered under F. P. A. condition as above, this insurance also covers partial losses of the insured goods caused by heavy weather, lightning, tsunami, earthquake and/or flood.

(c) All Risks

Aside from the risks covered under the F. P. A. and W. A. conditions as above, this insurance also covers all risks of loss of/or damage to the insured goods whether partial or total, arising from external causes in the course of transit.

Ⅱ. Exclusion

This insurance does not cover:

(a) Loss or damage caused by the intentional act or fault of the Insured.

(b) Loss or damage falling under the liability of the consignor.

(c) Loss or damage arising from the inferior quality or shortage of the insured goods prior to the attachment of this insurance.

(d) Loss or damage arising from normal loss, inherent vice or nature of the insured goods, loss of market and/or delay in transit and any expenses arising therefrom.

(e) Risks and liabilities covered and excluded by the Ocean Marine Cargo War Risks Clauses and Strike, Riot and Civil Commotion Clauses of this Company.

Ⅲ. Commencement and Termination of Cover

(a) Warehouse to Warehouse Clause:

This insurance attaches from the time the goods hereby insured leave the warehouse or place of storage named in the Policy for the commencement of the transit and continues in force in the ordinary course of transit including sea, land and inland waterway transits and transit in lighter until the insured goods are delivered to the consignee's final warehouse or place of storage at the destination named in the Policy or to any other place used by the insured for allocation or distribution of the goods or for storage other than in the ordinary course of transit. This insurance shall, however, be limited to sixty (60) days after completion of discharge of the insured goods from the seagoing vessel at the final port of discharge before they reach the above mentioned warehouse or place of storage. If prior to the expiry of the above mentioned sixty (60) days, the insured goods are to be forwarded to a destination other than that named in the Policy, this insurance shall terminate at the commencement of such transit.

(b) If, owing to delay, deviation, forced discharge, reshipment or transshipment beyond the control of the insured or any change or termination of the voyage arising from the exercise of a liberty granted to the ship-owners under the contract of affreightment, the insured goods arrive at a port or place other than that named in the Policy, subject to immediate notice being given to the Company by the insured and an additional premium being paid, if required, this insurance shall remain in force and shall terminate as hereunder:

(1) If the insured goods are sold at port or place not named in the Policy, this insurance shall terminate on delivery of the goods sold, but in no event shall this insurance extend beyond sixty (60) days after completion of discharge of the insured goods from the carrying vessel at such port or place.

(2) If the insured goods are to be forwarded to the final destination named in the Policy or any other destination, this insurance shall terminate in accordance with Section I above.

Ⅳ. Duty of the Insured

It is the duty of the insured to attend to all matters as specified hereunder, failing which the Company reserves the right to reject his claim for any loss if and when such failure prejudice the rights of the Company:

(a) The insured shall take delivery of the insured goods in good time upon their arrival at the port of destination named in Policy. In the event of any damage to the goods, the insured shall immediately apply for survey to the surveyor and/or settling agent stipulated in the Policy. If the insured goods are found short in entire package or packages or to show apparent traces of damage, the insured shall obtain from the carrier, bailee or other relevant authorities (Customs and Port Authorities etc.) certificate of loss or damage and/or shortlanded memo. Should the carrier, bailee or the other relevant authorities be responsible for such shortage or damage, the Insured shall lodge a claim with them in writing and, if necessary, obtain their confirmation of an extension of the time limit of validity of such claim.

(b) The Insured shall, and the Company may also, take reasonable measures immediately in salvaging the goods or prevention or minimizing a loss or damage thereto. The measures so taken by the Insured or by the Company shall not be considered respectively, as a waiver of

261

abandonment hereunder, or as an acceptance thereof.

(c) In case of a change of voyage or any omission or error in the description of the interest, the name of the vessel or voyage, this insurance shall remain in force only upon prompt notice to this Company when the Insured becomes aware of the same and makes payment of an additional premium if required.

(d) The following documents shall accompany any claim hereunder made against this Company:

Original Policy, Bill of Lading, Invoice, Packing List, Tally Sheet, Weight Memo, Certificate of Loss or Damage and/or Shortland Memo, Survey Report, Statement of Claim.

If any third party is involved, documents relative to pursuing of recovery from such party shall also be included.

(e) Immediate notice should be given to the Company when the Cargo Owner's actual responsibility under the contract of affreightment "Both to Blame Collision" clause becomes known.

Ⅴ. The Time of Validity of a Claim

The time of validity of a claim under this insurance shall not exceed a period of two years counting from the time of completion of discharge of the insured goods from the seagoing vessel at the final port of discharge.

2018. 11. 29. 于南京聚福园

练习参考答案

第四章 广告文体

一、翻译下列广告语，说出所用的修辞手法。

1. 看上去像跳舞鞋，穿起来似运动鞋。Simile
2. 《新闻周刊》——明天的高科技办公室。Metaphor
3. 来与我小坐片刻。（旅游景点）Personification
4. 摩尔牌烟令我更满意！Pun
5. 举世无双的加拿大精神尽在"加拿大"酒中。spirit of Canada，Pun
6. 滋味无穷，热量正好。Repetition
7. 没有它(蜡笔)，童年就不像童年。Repetition
8. "天时"表到万家，万家好时光。Chiasmus 交错排列：交错排列是重复修辞法的一种，它通过交叉重复特定的词或短语达到强调商品的优良性能之目的。读起来朗朗上口，抑扬顿挫，流畅回环。
9. 美味便捷，美味之极。（快餐）Chiasmus
10. 并非所有的移动电话都出类拔萃。Parody 仿拟。这里作者仿拟林肯《葛底斯堡演说》中的名言 All men are created equal. 反意而用之，以说明所有的移动电话功能平平，唯有我们的产品才出类拔萃。
11. 实践的确创造完美。Parody，仿拟 Practice makes perfect. 谚语，加上强势助动词 does 和表强调的赞美性副词 really 进一步增强了 perfect 的语意，让读者感到这款手表从设计的式样到功能确实是完美无缺、无可挑剔。
12. 事半功倍(苹果电脑)。Contrast
13. 昔日帝王宫殿，今日豪华宾馆。Contrast
14. 尽情品尝杯中酒。（酒家）Metonymy 借代，以酒杯借代杯中酒，劝你开怀畅饮。
15. 精心选择您的酒杯。（酒）Metonymy 用酒杯借代酒，劝读者买酒时要谨慎挑选，不要上当。意含买我们的酒您尽可放心。
16. 万贯生意，分毫薄利。（商业）Parallelism 排比——用一连串结构相似、内容密切相关、语气一致的句子或句子成分来表示意思，用以增强语势，使内容得到强调的修辞手法。也称"并列结构"parataxis，即把分句、从句或短语依次排列而不用连词或从属连词。
17. 名片世界，复印天地。Parataxis

18. 在您意想不到的一个地方，我们珍藏了满园的蔬菜——在一个小馅饼里。Hyperbole 夸张。

19. 难怪他们不像以前那样制造汽车了，制造一支钢笔就已经够难的了。Hyperbole 夸张

20. 如果有人苦口婆心地劝你戒烟，不要理睬——他们大概是想骗你活得长久些。Irony. 此广告妙不可言，在其庄重严肃的语气中不乏诙谐幽默，使读者在不知不觉中感悟吸烟有害健康。

二、将下列英语广告语译成中文。参考译文

1. 阿迪达斯运动鞋

28 年前（译注：阿迪达斯公司创建于 1948 年），阿迪达斯为运动鞋带来了全新的概念。从那之后，脚穿阿迪达斯的人们健步如飞，频频夺标。事实上，阿迪达斯仅在田径场上就帮助人们创造了 400 多项世界纪录。

这或许就是越来越多的足球、篮球、网球、棒球和橄榄球运动员求助于阿迪达斯的原因。他们知道，无论从事哪项运动，他们都可以信赖阿迪达斯精湛的工艺和优秀的质量。

因此，不管是沿马拉松赛道飞奔，还是在社区周围小跑，你都可以穿上阿迪达斯。

（曹明伦，《中国翻译》2006 年第 6 期）

2. 天鹅，浪漫一生的象征

有关天鹅的传说说道，当两只天鹅恋爱时，它们会游到一个鲜为人知的地方，互相接触以培养感情，最后结为终身伴侣。它们如痴如幻般滑过梦想中的池塘，翅尖挂着的水珠在光的折射下熠熠生辉，这些翅尖用 14 颗小钻石点饰而成。

作为浪漫一生的象征，十字型天鹅胸针是一件动人的礼物，它传递着那种关爱的心灵感应的精髓。眼睛为纯正的红宝石，鹅身为用 14K 黄金打制的一对组合胸针。这对组合胸针别在一张小卡片上，放在包装精美的天鹅绒礼盒中，表达着一片深情。

3. 独特的设计，独特的品位。

如今的"苗条"牌香烟，连价格也很"苗条"。

4. 早在 1822 年，当国王乔治四世驾临本地时，他只喝 Glenlivet，那年，苏格兰荣幸地接待了四世陛下的国事访问。同时他也带来了对 Glenlivet 淡味麦芽威士忌的浓厚兴趣。

伊丽莎白·格朗特，当年乔治四世下榻的旅店老板的女儿，在她的回忆录中写道，"Coryingham 勋爵，国王的内阁大臣，当时正四处寻找纯正的 Glenlivet 威士忌，因为国王只喝这个。"马上有人从我们的酒窖中取出一瓶呈送到国王手中。"可惜当时没有记录，"Sandy Milne 说，"不知陛下是否舍得让别人也闻一下。"

Glenlivet，苏格兰威士忌的鼻祖。

5. 夏日的太阳镜，

定配的太阳镜 59.99 英镑起价。

配一副款式新颖的太阳镜，准备度夏，我们是独一无二的眼镜大集成！起价仅 59.99 英镑，另有老光和近视镜片供选，加上特殊的涂层，可保护你的眼睛免受太阳紫外线的

侵害。

当然，所有的太阳镜上，都加贴了我们独有的金色质量保证印记。

欲知详情或要看看全部系列产品，只要垂访一下你那里的分店便可悉数知晓。

6. 美国

如果你静下来稍稍想想，你就会发现这个国家的好东西比世界上其他任何地方都多。

想想这片国土吧，从大瑟尔（译注：大瑟尔，加利福尼亚州蒙特雷县（Monterey County）境内濒临太平洋的一处度假胜地。）的海浪到佛罗里达的日出。再想想这东西两岸之间的所有地方。

亚利桑那的大峡谷，堪萨斯州的小麦地，新罕布什尔的秋天……

你可以永远想下去。可美国不仅仅是个美不胜收的国度，它还是一个度良辰春宵的地方。

它是你轻松愉快的周末夜晚。

它是你开着破车在泥路上颠簸的旅程。

它是你的球队获胜的时刻。

它是你百看不厌的夜场电影。

啊，对啦，当你口渴的时候，它就是冰镇可口可乐的滋味。那可是一种实实在在的滋味。

当然，这个国家的所有好东西都很实在。它们就在你身边，随处可见。我们在广告里说了不少，可你还能够发现许多，甚至不看我们的广告你能发现更多。

那就先来上一瓶可乐，再开始去发现。

——可口可乐公司

（曹明伦，《中国翻译》2006 年第 6 期）

7. "来纽约，看世界"。如果你想寻找包罗万象之地，只有一处可以造访——那就是纽约。一座城市，一个世界。

（陈刚，2004）

8. 树上长不出钱来，但存入我们各家支行它就好像花朵在树枝上绽放。

在这则广告里的 branch 是一词两义：字面意义，即树枝，而另一深层含义指银行的各个分行。这样我们就能领会该广告的真正含义是：只要顾客把钱存到劳埃德银行，他们的钱就会不断地增加。

9. （这是一则直述式广告，注意译文语气也应当是摆事实、讲道理，直接、精练地将内容表达出来。）

请君感受世界首创涡轮式复印机的力量

隆重推出有史以来第一台涡轮启动式复印机——新型 Toshiba 2230 Turbo.

在精秀的机壳下，是一套业经授予专利的先进复印系统。

拥有它，你一分钟能复印 22 份材料。如果按下涡轮键，则一分钟可复印 30 份。现在你可以提高工作效率 40%，同时节约 33% 的增色剂。更具创新精神的是，我们并没有因为增加涡轮启动而提高价格。

如需要安排免费的示范表演，只需拨打 1-800 转 Toshiba.

10. （这是一则描写式广告，注意译文应表现出细腻、生动的描写特色，否则，枯燥乏味的表达方法无法给人留下深刻、鲜明的印象。）

沐浴在菲律宾群岛的阳光里

美丽的白色沙滩上，沐浴在金色的阳光里，恣情嬉戏，尽情享受……美妙的风景，激动人心的奇观……世界一流的设施，高效的服务。

不仅这些，最令人神往的是，你可以享受到菲律宾群岛带给你的独有的温暖、热情与舒适。

三、将下列汉语广告语译成英语。参考译文

1. The well-known Hunan TV forces undertook successfully with all its strength and creations the past two Golden Eagle TV Art Festivals, presenting with an amazing effect a series of fantastic programs boasting of its spectacularity, high investment, and high standard, which has created a fresh TV art style and offered the audience a grand artistic feast. Due to its special operation and high audience rating, it has now become a nation's audience focus and served as a super media platform in the media industry across China. (贾文波，2004：168)

2. Affiliated with BB Group Corp., AA Industrial Development Corporation has, based on its industrial operation in China, developed its business with its sales net not only in mainland China but also in the United States, Europe, the Philippines, Brazil, Hong Kong, Macao, etc. (贾文波，2004：170)

3. CC Railway Rolling Stock (Group) Co., Ltd. is now striving hard in confidence and well on the way towards a global-market-oriented enterprise group to be well developed in management, marketing and product series. Focusing on our clients, we will continue with our credit to provide our customers with high quality and advanced products as well as our cover-all services. (贾文波，2004：173)

4. "Snow Mountain" Cashmere Sweaters are lustrous in colour, and supple, light, warm and comfortable to wear. Owing to their fine quality, excellent workmanship, novel designs and style, and complete size range, they have gained popularity from consumers at home and abroad. (邵志洪，2005，322)

5. Quanxing Daqu Liquor, one of the famous spirits of China, is made from first-class sorghum and wheat. Produced on the bank of the Jinjiang River in Chengdu City, Sichuang Province, its history can be traced back to the days of Daoguang, the emperor of the Qing Dynasty (A.D. 1824). It is fermented in aged cellars and brewed in a meticulous way with traditional method. Being mildly mellow and crisply refreshing, the liquor boasts its own unique style with a harmonious nature and delicate bouquet. (邵志洪，2005，323)

6. Xifeng Liquor, one of the most famous spirits in China, has long been enjoying a resounding reputation. Early in the Tang Dynasty, it was already ranked among treasures of the time. At the end of the Song Dynasty, Su Dongpo, a great master of ancient poetry, ardently loved the liquor during his tenure of office in Fengxiang County and thus made it even more well-known. At a brewing competition held in 1910 in Southeast Asia, the liquor was awarded a high prize and has become world-famous since then.

Being clear and transparent, mild and mellow, the aromatic Xifeng presents a **lingering** taste of a unique style. After drinking it, one would be agreeably refreshed all over. The liquor has long been cherished by many people for its function of being able to **whet** appetite and relieve fatigue. (邵志洪，2005，324)

第六章　旅游资料翻译　参考译文

一、把下列各段落译成英语。

1. In the Ming Tombs area, visitors first pass by a quite impressive marble Memorial Gateway with five arches and six pillars. A little further down the way stands Dahong Gate that marks the beginning of the Way of the Spirit leading to the entrance of the Changling Tomb. Continuing on, one comes to the Tablet House, the Ornamental Pillars, and 24 stone animals in various poses as well as Lingxing Gate guiding the way…

2. With a former name of the Cemetery of the Prime Minister, The Mausoleum of Dr. Sun Yat-sen lies at the foot of Xiaomao Hill, in the east of Nanjing, the second top peak of Zhongshan Hill. It is the tomb of Dr. Sun Yat-sen, a great pioneer of revolutionists. The Mausoleum is composed of the square, the memorial archway, the tomb passage, the door of the tomb, the pavilion housing a tablet, the memorial hall and the coffin chamber, which all lie in a straight line from the north to the south. The coffin is 165 meters in altitude, 700 meters from the entrance and has a drop of 73 meters. The planimetric map (平面图，地物图) of the whole Mausoleum likes a picture of "a free clock", which expressing the meaning of "to obtain the peace and success of the world". The works that started from 1926 was accomplished in 1929. The coffin of Dr. Sun Yat-sen was carried here from Beijing on May 28th, 1929, and on Jun 1st of the same year the grand respect ceremony was held here.

There are many memorial or auxiliary buildings that were constructed by the donation of various circles and countrymen residing abroad after the grand respect ceremony, such as inscription-collecting tower. Music platform, Guanghua Pavilion and Zhongshan botanical garden.

3. As the former Tower for Keeping Buddhist Scriptures built in 1935 with funds raised by the Buddhist Association of China, Dr. Sun Yat-sen's Memorial Hall lies between Dr. Sun Yat-sen's Mausoleum and Linggu Temple. It is a palace-like building fashioned after a lamasery of the Qing Dynasty, including the main tower, Buddhist rooms and the stone-tablet corridor specially for the collection of Dr. Sun Yat-sen's classic works and stone carvings concerned. The year 1989 saw the establishment of Dr. Sun Yat-sen's Memorial Hall. In front of the main tower stands a full-size bronze sculpture of Dr. Sun Yat-sen donated by a Japanese friend named Umeya Shokichi in 1929. Along the stone-tablet corridor, 138 stone tablets are carved with the full text of "Three People's Principles" (Nationalism, Democracy and People's Livelihood), respectively written by 14 calligraphers during the period under the Republic of China. (曹建新，2004)

4. Laoshan Scenic Area is thickly covered with trees of many species, which add credit for its scenery. Among them over 300 are considered rare and precious, half of which are plants under state-top-level protection. The most famous species include ginkgo and cypress.

5. Sitting on the rocky, sloping side of the coast, the park shows little signs of man's refinement, appearing as an original work of nature. Strolling in the park, you can enjoy a scene full of poetic and artistic conception: waves, rocks, white sands and pines-covered slopes.

6. With a large lake, extensive grasslands, flowers, trees and shrub beds, the Century Park — the largest public park in Shanghai — is now ready to provide a new escape from bustling urban life. The park is designed to offer local residents, who live in a vast concrete forest like Shanghai, a site close to nature, where they can breathe fresh air, enjoy green land and hear birds twitter.

7. Located in Haiyan county north of the Hangzhou Bay, the Nanbei Lake is one of the scenic resorts in Zhejiang Province characterized by its divergent scenic, cultural and historical highlights. With an area of 30 sqkms, the resort comprises four sections: the Lake Area, Yingchaoding (eagle-nest top), Tanxian Hill and the Seashore.

8. Green Hills and Crystal Waters

— Wuxi's Natural Name Card

Of all picturesque hills and rivers endowed by Nature in the southern lower reaches of Yangtze River, Wuxi is exceptionall favored and gifted.

The Taihu Lake, harboring and cradling ancient Kingdoms Wu and Yue, covers an area of 36,000 *qing* of crystal waters dotted with 72 exquisite peaks, which adds a finishing touch of Wuxi fascinating scenery.

The Yantze River rolls ceaselessly thousands of miles eastward, and it takes on a grand and treacherous look with its bizarre waves when reaching Huang-ting Cliffs.

The Great Canal, with a long history and brilliant culture, flows its golden watercourse across the city, waving a peal-like tatery web.

The Second Spring in the empire at the Hui Hill, well-known in history, streams its sweet and transparent water to breed all green hills, fairy land-like gardens and lots of excellences.

第八章　商务文书翻译　参考译文

一、英译汉下列信用证常用句子。

1. 本公司很高兴通知贵方，本公司已开立了一张不可撤销保兑信用证。

2. 由于贵方的信用证是经由我方的银行之一所让购，因此请开立一张无指定议付银行的一般信用证。

3. 因本信用证未指定议付行，所以贵方可自行选择议付行。

4. 本公司很高兴通知贵方本公司已开立了一张金额为 88000 美元的信用证。

5. 由于贵方未在信用证有效期内履行订单，本公司将取消信用证。

6. 由于信用证余额为 80000 美元，请将装运费用控制在此数额以内。

7. 本公司认为如果贵方审读信用证是可以发现信用证细节的。

8. 本公司相信本公司所开立的信用证最迟将在本周末之前经由通知行到达贵处。

二、汉译英下列信用证常用句子。

1. This L/C expires on Nov. 29. 或：

   The expiration of this L/C is Nov. 29. 或：

   The expiry date of this L/C is Nov. 29.

2. Please let us know the situation of L/C so that we can arrange for shipment.

3. We will make an application of L/C immediately on your confirmation of order.

4. We will grant an extension of L/C to Oct. 19 in response to your request.

5. As the shipping time comes near, we ask you to open your L/C by fax.

6. As the name of commodity is wrong, please make amendment of L/C at once.

7. Our credit is valid until Aug. 19. 或：

   Our L/C is good until Aug. 19. 或：

   Our letter of credit is good up to Aug. 19.

8. We use a documentary credit for foreign trade.

三、翻译下列信用证。参考译文

1. 本公司很高兴通知贵方，按贵公司开立信用证的要求，今天已航空邮寄出一张由中国银行开立的不可撤销信用证，金额为 1256000 美元，根据下列条款以纽约贸易公司为受益人。

2. 本公司已指示中国银行开立一张金额为 188000 美元的不可撤销信用证。此信用证将由中国银行的往来银行(correspondent)北京市商业银行来通知。该银行将按照贵方收据金额在见票后 30 天内承兑贵方汇票。

   此信用证有效期至 1 月 20 日。

3. 虽然本公司一再要求，但本公司仍未收到贵方保兑编号 89 订单的信用证。

   本公司一直在设法使厂商以高成本执行贵方的订货。

   因此，本公司要求贵方尽速开立信用证，以便本公司按约装运。

4. 贵方的订单以离岸价为准。

   然而贵方的信用证是以成本加运费为准的，这样发票金额总数和贵方所要求的总数会有些出入。

   因此，请将贵方信用证的金额改为以离岸价为准。

5. 本公司很乐意确认贵方金额为 238000 美元的 PC 机订单。

   按照要求，本公司准备于六月底前装运这批货。同时本公司要求贵方尽快开立一张不可撤销信用证，以本公司为受益人，有效期至七月十八日。

四、翻译下列合同条款。

参考译文（下列译文均引自孙万彪编著《英汉法律翻译教程》，有个别改动。）

1. 转让　本协议任何一方未经另一方事先书面同意（该另一方不得无理拒绝同意），不得转让本协议或其在本协议项下的任何权利和权益。尽管本条有上述规定，但（1）甲方有权将其权利让与任何子公司、关联公司或继承实体，只要在适用情况下，甲方仍有责任履行其在本协议项下的全部义务，（2）乙方可以无须经甲方同意，将其在本协议项下的全部（而不是部分）权利让与乙方的任何子公司、关联公司或继承实体或其最终的母公司（但是向任何该等子公司进行转让，不应被视为解除乙方在本协议项下的义务，除非甲方已事先书面同意予以解除，且乙方若违反本条规定仍须对甲方负有责任）。任何试图违反本条规定进行的转让均为无效。

2. 违约　如果甲方实质性违反本合同，乙方或其权益承继人有权终止本合同或要求得到损害赔偿。如果乙方实质性违反本合同，甲方经发出书面通知，有权要求乙方在收到书面通知后十五（15）天内改正违约行为。如果乙方在十五（15）天期限内未予改正，甲方则有权解除合同并要求得到违约赔偿。

3. 侵权和法律诉讼

（1）被许可方一旦获悉任何其他人、商行或公司使用或拟使用的商品名称、商标、商品装饰、促销或广告手段相当于或可能相当于侵犯许可方对于受许可商标的权利或违反反不正当竞争法，应立即以书面形式将详细情况告知许可方。

（2）如果被许可方获悉任何其他人、商行或公司宣称受许可商标是无效的或受许可商标的使用侵犯了他方权利，应立即以书面形式将详细情况告知许可方，并不得向任何第三方披露有关此方面的信息或对此做出承认。

（3）对于受许可商标所受到的侵权或侵权指控，以及就受许可商标的使用或注册提出或拟将提出的索赔或反索赔，许可方应进行一切法律诉讼，并完全由其自行决定采取何种行动。如果被许可方自行决定就受许可商标提起诉讼或进行抗辩，许可方无义务就此提起诉讼或进行抗辩。

（4）对于就受许可商标提起或拟将提起的诉讼或索赔，应许可方要求并由许可方支付费用，被许可方将给予许可方充分合作，包括作为当事人参与任何诉讼。

4. 保密　在本协议期限内，甲方向乙方提供的一切口头和书面信息，包括但不限于制造工艺、程序、方法、配方、数据、技术、经验、诀窍和商业信息（"机密信息"），均以绝密对待，且只用于本协议规定的目的。该等信息的所有权及相关权益始终属于甲方。

乙方同意采取一切必要步骤，以防止机密信息披露给第三方，并且应要求其人员遵守同样的保密规定。乙方除了向为了本协议规定的目的而需要接触机密信息、且了解本协议规定的保密义务的人员披露机密信息外，不得向其他任何人披露。

5. 定义与解释　"关联公司"指直接或间接控制一方（包括其母公司或子公司）或受一方直接或间接控制，或与该方共同受直接或间接控制的任何人或公司。在本协议中，"控制"系指拥有在股东大会上有投票权的百分之五十（50%）或50%以上的公司普通股股本，或拥有任命公司董事会中多数董事的权力。

"专有技术"指本协议签订之日，已由许可方开发和为许可方所知，和/或在本协议持续期间可能由许可方进一步开发和为许可方获知的工序、方法、生产技术、经验及其他信息和资料，包括但不限于许可方根据本协议向被许可方提供的技术信息和技术协助，但许可方从第三方获得的不允许向被许可人披露的任何秘密技术除外。

6. 完整协议　本协议，包括根据本协议订立的工作一览表，构成本协议双方关于本协议标的的完整协议，并取代双方先前的或现在的所有陈述、建议、讨论和通讯，无论是口头的还是书面的。若本协议的规定与工作一览表的具体规定发生冲突，以本协议的规定为准，但工作一览表另有明示规定的除外。

7. 修改　对本合同的修改，只能通过各方的正式授权代表签署书面协议进行。除法律要求须经审批机构/政府有关部门事先批准外，该等修改经双方授权代表签字后立即生效。

8. 语言　本协议签署本一式四(4)份，四份文本视为共同构成同一份协议。双方应尽快签署本协议的中文文本。协议的英文文本和中文文本如有不一致之处，以英文文本为准。

9. 不可抗力　如果任何一方因不可抗力事件，如地震、台风、水灾、火灾、战争、其发生和后果不可预防和不可避免的其他意外事件的直接影响，而不能履行或延迟履行本协议，受影响的一方应立即通知另一方，并在此后十五(15)日内提供有关不可抗力事件的详情和足够的证明材料，解释其不能履行或延迟履行本协议的全部或部分条款的理由。不可抗力事件发生地的商会或其他有关部门出具的证明，应足以证明不可抗力事件的存在及其延续的时间。如果不可抗力事件持续时间超过六(6)个月，双方应通过协商决定变更协议以反映不可抗力事件对履行本合同的影响，抑或终止本协议。

10. 仲裁　因本协议引起、产生于本协议或与本协议有关的任何争议，应由双方通过友好协商解决。协商在一方向另一方交付进行协商的书面要求后立即开始。倘若在该通知发出后三十(30)天内，争议未能通过协商解决，双方应将争议提交中国国际经济贸易仲裁委员会上海分会("仲裁机构")进行仲裁。

仲裁员为三(3)名。甲方和乙方各委派一(1)名仲裁员，两名仲裁员应在发出或收到仲裁要求后三十(30)天内选定。仲裁机构主席选出第三名仲裁员。如果一方委派仲裁员后三十(30)天内，另一方未委派仲裁员，则该名仲裁员应由仲裁机构主席委派。

仲裁程序以中文进行，仲裁庭应实行本协议签署日有效的仲裁机构的仲裁规则。但是，若该等规则与本条前款规定相抵触，包括与关于委派仲裁员的规定相抵触，则以本条规定为准。

仲裁裁决为终局裁决，对双方都具有约束力。任何一方不得就仲裁裁决所涉及的事项上诉。

各方均可要求具有管辖权的法院做出强制执行仲裁裁决的判决，或向该等法院申请对仲裁裁决给予司法承认或发布强制执行令。

在仲裁进行过程中，除争议事项外，双方应继续不停地履行本协议。

11. 期限/终止　本协议在合营期限届满时终止。此外，在下列情况下，或本合同或法律另有规定，任何一方均可以经向另一方提交其意欲终止合同的书面通知，在合营期限届满前终止本合同：

（1）如果另一方实质性违反本合同，且在收到书面通知后六十（60）日内未纠正其违约行为；

（2）如果合营公司破产，或因资不抵债而进入清算程序或解散，或终止其业务，或无力偿付到期债务；

（3）如果另一方违反本合同规定意欲转让或采取步骤转让其在合营公司中的股权；

（4）如果合营公司的全部或部分资产被任何政府部门暂时或永久没收；

（5）如果对任何一方有管辖权的任何政府部门要求对本合同的任何条款进行修改或对本合同的履行规定条件或限制，从而对合营公司或任何一方造成重大的不利后果。

12. Terms of payment shall be net cash in _____（place）exchange，due at the Seller's _____（place）office in _____ days from date of shipment. If, at any time before shipment, the financial responsibility of the Buyer becomes impaired or unsatisfactory to the Seller, in the Seller's judgement, cash payment or satisfactory security may be required by the Seller before shipment.

13. The Purchaser agrees to pay to the Seller, and the Seller agrees to receive as payment the cash price of _____.

14. The _____（country）currency amount of any sum payable shall be determined on the basis of the official exchange rate.

15. The part of the contract price shall be paid in _____（currency）by way of an irrevocable letter of credit against presentation by Contractor to the negotiating bank.

16. The entire sum remaining unpaid shall become immediately due and payable.

17. If the Buyer should fail to make payment pursuant to this Agreement, the Seller may, at its option, defer any further shipment or stop any shipments in transit until the Buyer has made such overdue payment and has paid in advance for such shipment.

18. In the event that the shipment should not be made within the time stated in the purchase order, the Buyer may make the purchase elsewhere and charge the Seller for any loss incurred, unless the delay in shipment is due to unforeseeable causes beyond one's control, for which the Seller is not responsible.

19. SELLER shall deliver the finished products to BUYER at _____（place）at his own expense and risk not later than _____ days after the end of each calendar quarter, and shall advise BUYER by telex, within _____ days after loading, of the quantity, vessel's name, port of shipment, date, estimated date of arrival to the destination and other information regarding the shipment.

20. The Seller shall deliver the equipment in accordance with "Final Monthly Delivery Schedule" to be provided by the Seller to the Buyer.

21. Neither party hereto shall be responsible for the failure of the performance hereunder if caused by war, fire, flood, embargo, explosion, shortage of materials, prohibition of import or export, judicial or governmental restrictions, strike or other labor troubles, or any other causes

beyond the control of the party.

22. In case discrepancy on the quality of the goods is found by the Buyers after arrival of the goods at the port of destination, claim may be lodged against the Sellers within _____ days after arrival of the goods at the port of destination being supported by Inspection Certificate issued by a reputable public surveyor. The Sellers shall then consider the claim in light of actual circumstances. For the loss or losses due to natural causes within the responsibilities of the Ship-owners or the Underwriters, the Sellers shall not consider any claim for compensation.

23. All disputes arising from the execution of, or in connection with, this contract shall be settled amicably through friendly negotiation. In case no settlement can be reached through negotiation, the case shall them be submitted to _____ (a third country), in accordance with its arbitrate rules of procedure. The decision shall be accepted as final and binding upon both parties.

24. All disputes arising in connection with this Agreement shall be submitted to arbitration by any party and any dispute so submitted to arbitration shall be finally settled under the rules of the _____ (name of arbitration association) by three arbitrators appointed in accordance with such rules. Arbitration shall be held in _____ (place). The award of the arbitration shall be final and binding on the parties. Judgment upon the award rendered in the arbitration may be entered in any court having jurisdiction, or application may be made to such court for an order of enforcement.

第九章　商务法律文体翻译　参考译文

1. 股份有限公司即"法人"是经过政府专门机构批准之后而成立的合法实体。要成立一个股份有限公司，公司创办人（通常至少要求三人）必须申请公司特许证，还要准备和整理公司章程。章程介绍公司的基本结构，包括组建公司的目的、额定股本金额和所要发行股票的数量。如果公司创办人按照法律的要求办事，政府就发给公司特许证。得到公司特许证之后，公司创办人要召集组建大会，选举第一届董事会并制定公司细则。

资产对公司的经营很重要，所以，公司要发行股票（股权证）以筹集所需资金。公司的所有者，即股东或叫股权人，对公司的管理都有发言权。有投票权的股东有权在年度股东大会上投票并参与董事会的选举。董事会负责公司的全面管理。在正常情况下，董事会任命公司高级管理人员，如总裁一人、副总裁一人或数人、会计主管一人、财务主管一人和秘书一人。这些高级职员负责执行董事会制定的政策，并积极地管理公司的日常事务。

2. 合同法　所谓合同，是指当事人订立的包含可执行义务条款的文书。我们为什么需要合同呢？显然，答案是允诺应该具有约束力。但事实上，法律仅强制执行一定种类的允诺，尤其是那些包含某种交换形式的允诺。那么，为什么我们又要专门制定法律强制执行与交换有关的允诺呢？最主要的原因取决于我们所生活的社会，即市场经济社会。在这样的一个社会里，当我们在超市购物的时候要订立合同，当我们乘坐公共汽车或火车的时候要订立合同，当我们把钱投入自动售货机购买巧克力或饮料的时候也是在订立合同。所以，如果允诺不具有约束力，一个社会是难以正常运转的。但是事实上，合同法很少强制一方当事人履行合同允诺，合同法所做的主要是在经济上补偿无过错的当事人，通常的做法是将其置于如果合同如约履行他们所能达到的境遇。这种做法具有双重功能：首先，它使当事人知晓如果合同不履行他们可以期待什么；其次，它通过确保不履行合同的当事人不能轻易地逃脱对违约责任的承担来鼓励合同的履行。

一个合同的有效成立，通常先由一方当事人发出要约，然后由另一方当事人进行承诺。一旦承诺发生法律效力，合同就会对双方当事人具有法律约束力。要约和承诺是合同成立的实质性要素，我们将对其内容进行详细的探讨。

要约是一方当事人向对方当事人表明愿意按照一定的条款订立合同，并希望对方当事人接受的表示。发出要约的人称为要约人，要约所指向的人被称为受要约人。如果一个意思表明要约人愿意按照一定的条款订立合同，并且一旦这些条款被受要约人接受即将受其约束，那么该意思表示的就是要约。

然而，我们必须注意区分要约和要约邀请。一些交易过程包含一个准备阶段，在该阶段一方当事人邀请对方向自己发出要约。我们称这一阶段为要约邀请。换句话说，要约邀请仅仅是表明愿意进行谈判，并且希望谈判能够在将来产生订立合同的结果。要约和要约邀请的区别主要在于意思表示的内容，即意思表示者是愿意不经过进一步的磋商，其条款一旦被接受即受其约束，还是他只想将自己的意思表示作为连续的谈判过程的一部分。

那么，要约存续的时间有多久呢？通常以下几种情况将导致要约失效。

1. 规定时间　如果要约人明确表明要约仅在规定的时间内有效，该规定时间一到期，要约便失效。

2. 合理时间段　如果要约人没有明确指明要约的有效期间，那么合理时间段一到要约即失效。合理时间段的长短取决于要约送达方式的快慢以及要约标的物的性质。例如：要约购买的标的物为易腐烂的货物或价格日常波动很大的商品，那么，要约的有效存续期间将非常短；股市上购买股票的要约可能只存续几秒钟。

3. 拒绝　要约因受要约人的拒绝而失效。例如：甲向乙发出于星期六将其计算机卖与乙的要约，乙拒绝购买。那么，乙在星期日的时候就不可能再主张接受该要约。

4. 反要约　一个所谓的"承诺"没有接受要约的全部条款和条件，而是在事实上提出新的条款，那么，它不是承诺而是反要约。反要约被认为是一个新的要约，可以被接受或拒绝，反要约的作用在于终止最初的要约以使受要约人不能再接受最初的要约。反要约使最初的要约失效。例如：甲发出以 10000 美元的价格出售其汽车的要约，而乙表示愿意以 9500 美元的价格购买，那么，乙的意思表示即为反要约。汽车所有者拒绝以 9500 美元的价格出售，那么乙就不能再接受最初的要约并以 10000 美元的价格购买该汽车，因为该要约已经因反要约而失效。

5. 要约人的死亡　该情形不甚明了，但是可以确定的是：如果受要约人知道要约人已经死亡，则要约失效；如果受要约人不知道要约人已经死亡，那么该要约可能有效。然而，在要约需要由要约人亲自履行的情况下，例如绘画、出演电影角色等，要约通常会因要约人的死亡而失效。

6. 受要约人的死亡　关于受要约人的死亡是否会导致要约的失效还没有相关的判例，

但是在理论上通常认为要约可能因受要约人的死亡而失效。受要约人死后，该要约不能由受要约人的继承人承诺。

7. 要约人撤销要约　要约人可以在要约被承诺前的任一时间撤销要约。要约人仅仅改变有关要约的意思表示是不够的，他必须通知受要约人要约已经被撤销。但是撤销要约的通知必须到达受要约人这一原则有两个例外。第一，受要约人移居新址并且没有告知要约人，被送达至受要约人原址的撤销要约的通知为有效。同样，撤销要约的通知已经到达受要约人，即使受要约人并不知晓，仍然发生撤销要约的法律效力。第二，对全世界不特定的人发出单方要约并以行为作为承诺方式时，如果在履行行为开始前撤销要约，撤销要约的通知无需到达受要约人。　　　　　　　　　　　（李朝，李蛟，2004：138～140）

3. 海运货物保险合同

一、责任范围

本保险分为平安险、水渍险及一切险三种。被保险货物遭受损失时，本保险按照保险单上订明承保险别的条款规定负赔偿责任。

（一）平安险

本保险负责赔偿：

1. 被保险货物在运输途中由于恶劣气候、雷电、海啸、地震、洪水自然灾害造成整批货物的全部损失或推定全损。当被保险人要求赔付推定全损时，须将受损货物及其权利委付给保险公司。被保险货物用驳船运往或运离海轮的，每一驳船所装的货物可视作一个整批。

推定全损是指被保险货物的实际全损已经不可避免，或者恢复、修复受损货物以及运送货物到原定目的地的费用超过运抵该目的地的货物价值。

2. 由于运输工具遭受搁浅、触礁、沉没、互撞、与流冰或其他物体碰撞以及失火、爆炸意外事故造成货物的全部或部分损失。

3. 在运输工具发生搁浅、触礁、沉没、焚毁意外事故的情况下，货物在此前或此后又在海上遭受恶劣气候、雷电、海啸等自然灾害所造成的部分损失。

4. 在装卸或转运时由于一件或数件整件货物落海造成的全部或部分损失。

5. 被保险人对遭受承保责任内危险的货物采取抢救、防止或减少货损的措施而支付的合理费用，但以不超过该批被救货物的保险金额为限。

6. 运输工具遭遇海难后，在避难港由于卸货所引起的损失以及在中途港、避难港由于卸货、存仓以及运送货物所产生的特别费用。

7. 共同海损的牺牲、分摊和救助费用。

8. 运输契约订有"双方有责碰撞"条款，根据该条款规定应由贷方偿还船方的损失。

（二）水渍险

除包括上列平安险的各项责任外，本保险还负责被保险货物由于恶劣气候、雷电、海啸、地震、洪水自然灾害所造成的部分损失。

（三）一切险

除包括上列平安险和水渍险的各项责任外，本保险还负责被保险货物在运输途中由于外来原因所致的全部或部分损失。

二、除外责任

本保险对下列损失，不负赔偿责任：

（一）被保险人的故意行为或过失所造成的损失。

（二）属于发货人责任所引起的损失。

（三）在保险责任开始前，被保险货物已存在的品质不良或数量短差所造成的损失。

（四）被保险货物的自然损耗、潜在缺陷、特性以及市价跌落、运输延迟所引起的损失或费用。

（五）本公司海洋运输货物战争险条款和货物运输罢工暴动和内乱险条款规定的责任范围和除外责任。

三、责任起讫

（一）仓到仓条款

本条款自被保险货物运离保险单所载明的起运地仓库或储存处所开始运输时生效，包括正常运输过程中的海运、陆运、内河运输、驳船运输直至运抵目的地收货人的最后仓库或储存处所或被保险人用作调拨、分销货物或非正常运输的其他储存处所为止。如未抵达上述仓库或储存处所，则以被保险货物在最后卸载港全部卸离海轮后满六十天为止。如在上述六十天内被保险货物需转运到非保险单所载明的目的地时，则以该项货物开始转运时终止。

（二）由于被保险人无法控制的运输延迟、绕航、被迫卸货、重行装载、转运或承运人运用运输契约赋予的权限所作的任何航程的变更或终止，致使被保险货物运到非保险单所载明目的地时，在被保险人及时将获知的情况通知保险人，并在必要时加缴保险费的情况下，本保险仍继续有效。保险责任按下列规定终止：

1. 被保险货物如在非保险单所载明的目的地出售，保险责任至交货时为止，但不论任何情况，均以被保险货物在卸货港全部卸离船舶后满六十天为止。

2. 被保险货物如果继续运往保险单所载原目的地或其他目的地时，保险责任仍按上述第(一)款的规定终止。

四、被保险人的义务

被保险人应按照以下规定的应尽义务办理有关事项，如因未履行规定的义务而影响保险人利益时，本公司对有关损失有权拒绝赔偿。

（一）当被保险货物运抵保险单所载明的目的港（地）以后，被保险人应及时提货，当发现被保险货物遭受任何损失时，应即向保险单上所载明的海损鉴定员、理赔代理人申请检验，如发现被保险货物整件短少或有明显残损痕迹应即向承运人、受托人或有关当局（海关、港务当局等）索取货损货差证明。如果货损货差是由于承运人、受托人或其他有关方面的责任所造成，应以书面方式向他们提出索赔，必要时还须取得延长时效的认证。

（二）对承保责任内遭受危险的货物，被保险人和本公司都可迅速采取合理的抢救措施，以防止货损或将货损减小到最低限度。被保险人采取此项措施，不应视为放弃委付的表示，本公司采取此项措施，也不得视为接受委付的表示。

（三）如遇航程变更或发现保险单所载明的货物、船名或航程有遗漏或错误时，被保险人应在获悉后立即通知保险人并在必要时加缴保险费，本保险才继续有效。

（四）在向保险人索赔时，必须提供下列单证：

保险单正本、提单、发票、装箱单、理货单、磅码单、货损货差证明、检验报告及索赔清单。如涉及第三者责任，还须提供向责任方追偿的有关函电及其他必要单证或文件。

（五）在获悉有关运输契约中"双方有责碰撞"条款的实际责任后，应及时通知保险人。

五、索赔期限

本保险索赔时效，从被保险货物在最后卸载港全部卸离海轮后起算，最多不超过两年。

《国际商务英语通典》228—234

主要参考文献

BEIJING REVIEW[J]. BEIJING. . 2010-2012.

EDITED BY LEO HICKEY. *THE PRAGMATICS OF TRANSLATION*[M]. 上海：上海外语教育出版社，2001.

HINKELMAN, EDWARD G., 李月菊导读. *INTERNATIONAL TRADE DOCUMENTATION*[M]. 上海：上海外语教育出版社，2009.

NEWMARK, PETER. *APPROACHES TO TRANSLATION*[M]. 上海：上海外语教育出版社，2001.

NEWMARK, PETER. *A TEXTBOOK OF TRANSLATION*[M]. 上海：上海外语教育出版社，2001.

NIDA, EUGENE A. *LANGUAGE, CULTURE, AND TRANSLATING*[M]. 上海：上海外语教育出版社，1993.

NIDA, EUGENE A. *LANGUAGE, CULTURE—CONTEXTS IN TRANSLATING*[M]. 上海：上海外语教育出版社，2001.

NIDA, EUGENE A. *TOWARD A SCIENCE OF TRANSLATING：WITH SPECIAL REFERENCE TO PRICIPLES AND PROCEDURES INVOLVED IN BIBLE TRANSLATING*[M]. Leiden：E. J. Brill, 1964.

NIDA, EUGENE A & C. R. TABER. *THE THEORY AND PRACTICE OF TRANSLATION*[M]. Leiden：E. J. Brill, 1969.

NORD, CHRISTIANE. *TRANSLATING AS A PURPOSEFUL ACTIVITY, FUNCTIONALIST APPROACHES EXPLAINED* [M]. 上海：上海外语教育出版社，2001.

WOLFRAM WILSS. *THE SCIENCE OF TRANSLATION*[M]. 上海：上海外语教育出版社，2001.

包惠南. 文化语境与语言翻译[M]. 北京：中国对外翻译出版公司，2001.

常玉田. 经贸汉译英教程[M]. 北京：对外经济贸易大学出版社，2002.

曹建新 译. 孙中山纪念馆[N]. 现代快报，B21，2004-08-18.

曹明伦. 广告语言的基本特点及其翻译[J]. 中国翻译，2006(6).

陈福康. 中国译学理论史稿[M]. 上海：上海外语教育出版社，1992.

陈浩然. 外贸英语翻译[M]. 北京：知识产权出版社，2005.

陈宏微. 汉英翻译基础[M]. 上海：上海外语教育出版社，1998.

陈忠诚. 法窗译话[M]. 北京：中国对外翻译出版公司，1992.

陈忠诚. 英语汉法律用语正误辨析[M]. 北京：法律出版社，1998.

《辞海》编辑委员会. 辞海 1999 年版缩印本[Z]. 上海：上海辞书出版社，2000.

丁衡祁. 翻译广告文字的立体思维[J]. 中国翻译，2004(1).

杜承南、文军. 中国当代翻译百论[M]. 重庆：重庆大学出版社，1994.

范仲英. 实用翻译教程[M]. 北京：外语教学与研究出版社，1994.

方梦之. 中国译学大辞典[Z]. 上海：上海外语教育出版社，2011.

冯庆华. 实用翻译教程[M]. 上海：上海外语教育出版社，2002.

傅伟良. 法律文件中的近义词和同义词翻译[J]. 中国翻译，2003(4).

傅勇林，唐跃勤. 科技翻译[M]. 北京：外语教学与研究出版社，2012.

傅仲选. 实用翻译美学[M]. 上海：上海外语教育出版社，1993.

葛正明. 荷兰专家谈饭店和菜单的译名[J]. 中国翻译，1995(6).

顾维勇. 揣摩语境，选取语义[J]. 南京晓庄学院学报，2004(3).

顾维勇. 析几种商务英语翻译教材及其译例[J]，上海翻译，2007(1).

顾维勇. 商务英语词典原语语用信息的读取与翻译[J]，上海翻译，2008(1).

顾维勇. 新编国际金融英语教程[M]. 北京：清华大学出版社，北京交通大学出版社，2010.

顾维勇. 实用文体翻译[M]. 北京：国防工业出版社，2012.

顾维勇. 商务英语复数形式词语的翻译[J]. 中国翻译，2007(5).

顾维勇. 翻译——找到原语的所指 对规划教材《商务英语翻译》误译译例的批判研究[J]. 中国翻译，2014(1).

顾维勇. 商务英语无专不译[J]. 商务翻译，2018(1)(创刊号).

顾维勇. 国际金融英语[M]. 南京：东南大学出版社，2015.

韩宁. 商务英语翻译中语境制约语义[J]. 福建教育学院学报，2010(1).

胡庚申等. 国际商务合同起草与翻译[M]. 北京：外文出版社，2003.

黄海翔. 中餐菜单音译浅谈[J]. 中国科技翻译，1999(1).

贾文波. 应用翻译功能论[M]. 北京：中国对外翻译出版公司，2004.

金隄. 等效翻译探索[M]. 北京：中国对外翻译出版公司，1998.

金惠康. 跨文化交际翻译[M]. 北京：中国对外翻译出版公司，2003.

金惠康. 跨文化交际翻译续编[M]. 北京：中国对外翻译出版公司，2004.

靳涵身. 商贸文书实用手册[M]. 广州：广东教育出版社，2002.

郭尚兴. 论商标的确立与翻译[J]. 中国科技翻译，1995(4).

李朝. 实用商务英语翻译教程[M]. 上海：复旦大学出版社，2003.

李朝，李蛟. 实用商务英语基础教程[M]. 上海：复旦大学出版社，2004.

李长栓. 非文学翻译理论与实践[M]. 北京：中国对外翻译出版公司，2004.

李长栓. 非文学翻译[M]. 北京：外语教学与研究出版社，2009.

李景端. 听季羡林先生谈翻译[N]. 光明日报，2005-02-17(第 9 版).

李景端. 翻译可有"快餐"但不可"快餐化"[N]. 光明日报，2011-12-13(第 13 版).

林戊荪，刘习良，黄友义. 中国翻译. 中国翻译工作者协会会刊，1996 — 2012.

刘法公. 商贸汉英翻译的原则探索[J]. 中国翻译，2002(1).

刘季春. 实用翻译教程[M]. 广州：中山大学出版社，1996.

刘宓庆. 当代翻译理论[M]. 北京：中国对外翻译出版公司，1999.

刘宓庆. 翻译教学：实务与理论[M]. 北京：中国对外翻译出版公司，2003.

刘宓庆. 文体与翻译[M]. 北京：中国对外翻译出版公司，1998.

刘延玫. 论述商务英语的文体特征及翻译[J]. 长春理工大学学报，2011(1).

陆谷孙. 我与译文[J]. 中国翻译，1998(1).

陆谷孙. 英语大词典[Z]. 上海：上海译文出版社，1993.

马会娟. 论商务文本翻译标准的多元化[J]. 中国翻译，2005(3).

彭萍. 商务文本翻译尺度的探讨[J]. 上海科技翻译，2004(1).

邵志洪. 翻译理论、实践与评析[M]. 上海：华东理工大学出版社，2003.

邵志洪. 汉英对比翻译导论[M]. 上海：华东理工大学出版社，2005.

申雨平，戴宁. 实用英汉翻译教程[M]. 北京：外语教学与研究出版社，2002.

孙利. 汉语新词英译与文化内涵的传递，中国科技翻译，2012(2).

孙万彪. 英汉法律翻译教程[M]. 上海：上海外语教育出版社，2003.

孙致礼，周晔. 高级英汉翻译[M]. 北京：外语教学与研究出版社，2010.

汪璧辉，顾维勇. 从认知角度看商务英语翻译偏差[J]. 上海翻译，2011(3).

王善武 译注. 密西西比河的汽船年代[J]. 英语世界，1996(5).

王学文，张富林. 国际商务英语通典[M]. 北京：中国社会科学出版社，2001.

王佐良. 新时期的翻译观[A]. 翻译：思考与试笔[C]. 北京：外语教学与研究出版社，1989.

魏志成. 英汉比较翻译教程[M]. 北京：清华大学出版社，2004.

翁凤翔. 实用翻译[M]. 杭州：浙江大学出版社，2002.

伍小龙，王东风. 破解译学七大难题[J]. 中国翻译，2004(4).

肖曼君. 英语商务文书的语体特征及汉译的规范性[J]. 中国科技翻译，1998(8).

许钧. 翻译论[M]. 武汉：湖北教育出版社，2003.

许钧. 关键在于为翻译正确定位[N]. 光明日报，2005-03-21(第7版).

许钧. 翻译概论[M]. 北京：外语教学与研究出版社，2009.

徐有志. 英语文体学教程[M]. 北京：高等教育出版社，2005.

杨大亮. 大学商务英语翻译教程[M]. 北京：北京大学出版社，2003.

杨一秋. 合同英语文体特点及翻译要点[J]. 中国科技翻译，2003(4).

杨佑方. 外贸经济英语用法词典[Z]. 成都：四川人民出版社，2002.

叶玉龙等. 商务英语汉译教程[M]. 天津：南开大学出版社，1998.

《英语》教参编写组. 教师参考书[M]. 广州：广东高等教育出版社，1989.

于岚译. 黄河夜泊[J]. 英语世界，1995(1).

张丽. 谈商务英语翻译中的词语选择[J]. 时代文学，2010(3).

张美芳. 从语境分析看动态对等论的局限性[J]. 上海科技翻译，1999(4).

张培基等. 英汉翻译教程[M]. 上海：上海外语教育出版社，1980.

张素华 译. 合同法[M]. 武汉：武汉大学出版社，2004.

张新红，李明. 商务英语翻译(英译汉)[M]. 北京：高等教育出版社，2003.

张逸. 商务英语精读1[M]. 北京：高等教育出版社，2000.

中华人民共和国海商法[M]. 北京：中国法制出版社，2003.

中英文对照法规系列. 经济法[M]. 北京：中国法制出版社，2005.

赵军峰. 商务英语口译[M]. 北京：高等教育出版社，2004.

赵琏 译注. 马可·波罗[J]. 英语世界，1982(1).

赵琏 译注. "女巫号"帆船[J]. 英语世界，1986(1).

周陵生 译. 困在沉船中[J]. 英语世界，1986(5).

周燕，廖瑛. 英文商务合同长句的语用分析及其翻译[J]. 中国科技翻译，2004(4).

宗奕扬 译. 我们迷人的神奇航行[J]. 英语世界，1996(10).

庄绎传. 英汉翻译教程[M]. 北京：外语教学与研究出版社，1999.

庄绎传. 英汉翻译简明教程[M]. 北京：外语教学与研究出版社，2002.